AN IMAGE OF WAR

By the same author:

Memoirs of a Junior Officer (Blackwood)
Red Shadow Over Malaya (Blackwood)

AN IMAGE
OF WAR

Mark Henniker

LEO COOPER
LONDON

First published 1987 by Leo Cooper

Leo Cooper
is an independent imprint of
the Heinemann Group of Publishers,
10 Upper Grosvenor Street, London W1X 9PA
LONDON   MELBOURNE   JOHANNESBURG   AUCKLAND

ISBN 0–85052–2811

Filmset by Deltatype, Ellesmere Port, South Wirral
Printed by Mackays of Chatham Ltd, Kent

Contents

1. Marching to the Sound of the Guns   1
2. From Phoney to Real War   13
3. The Retreat Continues   31
4. A Worm's-Eye View of a Miracle   50
5. Home Defence   62
6. Two Operations   84
7. North Africa   101
8. The Invasion of Sicily   123
9. The Invasion of Italy   144
10. The Last Months with First Airborne Division   162
11. Operation Market Garden   173
12. The Close Bridge Garrison   194
13. The Battle for the Rhineland   202
14. Battles of the Rhineland   211
15. The Rhineland Cleared of the Enemy   229
16. The Last Lap   248
Bibliography   259
Index   260

Maps

		Page
1.	The German Blitzkrieg 1940 and the Allied Response.	2
2.	The Retreat to Dunkirk and Evacuation by Sea.	41
3.	North Africa: A Staging Post for 1 Airborne Division.	106
4.	The Invasion of Sicily and Mainland Italy.	124
5.	Operation Market Garden: the Outline Plan.	174
6.	The Island.	181
7.	A Difference of Strategies.	184
8.	Battle Area, 43 Division, Winter 1944–45.	204
9.	German Surprise Offensive: 'The Bulge'.	220
10.	The Rhineland Battlefield.	230
11.	The Last Lap.	250

Acknowledgements

I am much indebted to many helpers to whom I give my thanks. They were all most generous.

Dr Ian Beckett, F.R.Hist.S read the first draft and made many suggestions and corrections. He also gave a lot of wise advice about the length to aim at and the general format. Several officers with whom I served during the Second World War have been kind enough to read various drafts of the manuscript to correct errors of all sorts in historical parts. I am particularly indebted to Major (now Brigadier, retired) M. L. Crosthwaite, who at one time commanded a Field Company of 43 Infantry Division, mentioned in the book, and to Mr Gordon Lilley, a wartime warrior, who was my Adjutant for some time in 1944. Both these gentlemen kept me on the "straight and narrow" as much in peacetime as in war. Their help was tremendous.

The maps caused some trouble. So many of the proper names seemed to have changed since 1939–40, particularly in Belgium, Holland and North Africa. I was eventually persuaded to follow the spelling adopted by *The Times Atlas* when dealing with controversial place-names, except for a few place-names immortalized by the British Army, such as Ypres. The bulk of the spadework in all this has been done by military personnel of the Survey Department of the Army Apprentices College, Chepstow, in their spare time. QMS I Jones, RE, L/Corporal Winship and Apprentice L/Corporal Hudson have all "had a go" and helped in the task. Captain C. Anderson, RE, while an Instructor at Chepstow, took a paternal interest in the work and his wife very kindly prepared the Index. For all these kind people I am extremely grateful.

Several ladies have taken a hand in typing my bad notes. All of them must have despaired of my spelling. Particularly I must thank two neighbours – Mrs Scott-Bell and Mrs S. Urquhart.

Preface

Thirty or forty years ago the author was one among many who might have told a tale like this, or a better one. But since those days a marching column has answered *Adsum* to another call, leaving its tales untold. Nonetheless, "of making many books there is no end" and the library shelves are loaded with books about the Second World War; and this tale will take its place in the ranks as one among many books.

The reader is asked to take a lenient view of any inaccuracies he sees in the names of places or people, or in the dates. "Old men forget", declaimed Henry V before the Battle of Agincourt; and I too have forgotten many things, though I have tried to verify what I can from credible sources. One of these sources I take to be the contemporary letters I wrote to my parents, addressed to my mother, who thought fit to preserve them. Some of these letters seem sufficiently quaint, after all these years, to warrant a place in the tale, and are included without much alteration – except for correcting the spelling mistakes and the insertion of a few place-names that were prohibited at the time of writing.

Though Henry V may say that "Old men forget" – and he is quite right – there is one thing I shall never forget, and that is the kindness and friendship shown me by the officers and men with whom I had the honour to serve. I gratefully salute them. It was they who make the tale I tell.

27 Western Road,
Abergavenny,
Gwent

M.C.A.H.
1981/6

1

Marching to the Sound
of the Guns

10 May, 1940: The rising sun streamed through my bedroom window; I was at home with my parents, on leave from the British Expeditionary Force in France. The night before, I had dined in the Officers' Mess of a Territorial Highland Regiment billeted in Woodbridge, Suffolk. We had of course discussed the War, and as a regular officer and Adjutant of 2 Divisional Engineers in France, it was supposed by my hosts – wrongly – that I must know something and be a bit of an expert. In fact our discussions were hopeless for a number of reasons.

In the first place the only War that I had seen was what has come to be known as the "phoney war". The British Expeditionary Force was a numerically insignificant addition to the French Army, and we were lined up along the Franco–Belgian frontier in the vicinity of Lille. We were not even facing the Germans, but facing the Belgians who were neutral. The French provided the Supreme Command, and for reasons best known to themselves they elected to rely upon a defensive attitude behind the Maginot Line – where it existed – and to eschew all forms of offensive action for the time being. Meanwhile the Germans were many miles away digesting Poland which they had overrun in the Autumn of 1939.

The main task of the BEF was to try and fortify its sector of the Franco–Belgian frontier against the day when the Germans turned upon the Belgians and tore them to bits, which the Belgians seemed to think inconceivable.

In general terms the French plan was to hold with fortress troops their frontier behind the Maginot Line from Switzerland, running northwards towards the Ardennes. The Ardennes were, for some obscure reason,

1

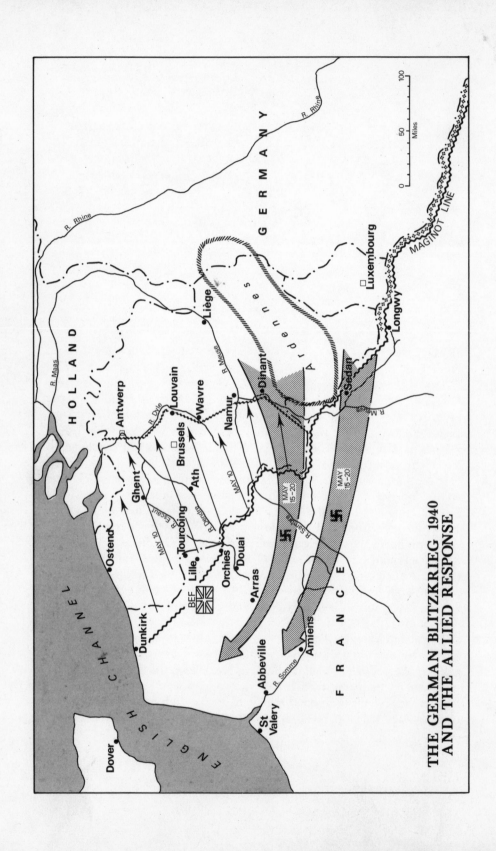

THE GERMAN BLITZKRIEG 1940
AND THE ALLIED RESPONSE

supposed to be impenetrable by armoured forces and were barely held at all.

North of the Ardennes they had prepared no defences and our business in the BEF was to build fortification along this stretch of the frontier. The French idea was that the existence of the Maginot Line would make it possible to defend the fortified part of the frontier – which was certainly more than half its length – with a minimum number of fortress troops; so that there would be a *masse de manoeuvre*, or mobile reserve, held ready in rear for whatever the Germans might do. The hitch to the arrangement was that they had nothing like enough troops to form any sort of mass for manoeuvre; and those they had were not correctly positioned for moving quickly to wherever they were needed.

It is very easy to be critical of the French in the after-light, but we were no better ourselves. Our contribution in troops was insignificant numerically, and we had practically no tanks in the BEF. As far as I know, the only anti-tank guns we had were a few borrowed from the French, which were of too small a calibre to be very effective; and, on our own account, we only had a few curious weapons known as Boyes Anti-Tank Rifles. They were a type of elephant rifle that you fired from the shoulder, with a terrific recoil unless you did it properly. It was subsequently demonstrated that its bullets would not penetrate a German tank.

The part of the frontier allotted to 2 Division was near Orchies and was very difficult to defend. It was partly industrial, like the Midlands of England, and covered with coal mines and factories; and partly it was flat, low-lying farmland, where the water table was only two feet below the surface and digging was impossible. Moreover, the French were very averse to letting us do what defensive work seemed necessary. To get permission to build defences on the Maginot principle in our sector of the front was as unthinkable to a Frenchman then as it would be to a Londoner today to build a motorway through Kew Gardens or Hampton Court. All was a matter of planning permission, and planning permission was hard to achieve.

My job, therefore, as Adjutant of the Second Divisional Engineers, was entirely a bureaucratic one. I worked long hours in my office, organizing supplies of building material, maintaining records of what we had done, and grappling with the bureaucratic difficulties of getting planning permission from French civilians to undertake such work as seemed to us necessary for their defence. All this had to be done in French at which I was more persevering than proficient. There were also innumerable secret French plans concerning what would be done if the Germans attacked. The latest plan for such an eventuality was known as Plan D. This comprised a vast pile of paper locked up in my safe in the Headquarters, and everything was marked "Secret". (The expression "Top Secret" had not yet come from America.)

Any knowledge or experience I had gained during the winter and early

3

spring thus consisted either of maddening details of the administrative processes that I had to follow, or of paper plans that were much too secret to talk about at the dinner table. During the past six months we had frequently been warned to refrain from what was generally termed "indiscreet conversation in public places" and I found it quite impossible to tell these Highlanders anything either interesting or useful. They had, however, been very hospitable and now, early on the morning of 10 May, the hammers of Hell were clanging in my skull and the burble of the BBC 7 o'clock news was vaguely audible in my parents' room across the landing.

Presently my mother entered my bedroom with a cup of tea.

"The Germans," she announced, "have invaded Belgium and Holland. Rotterdam has been bombed, and the Dutch are flooding the dykes. The BEF have advanced into Belgium and I suppose we shall have to endure a second retreat from Mons."

My mother, who was a most heroic person, was not unnaturally disturbed, to say the least of it. Well she might be. She had seen my father continually wracked by malaria and blackwater fever in Assam for the first fifteen years of her married life; and she had seen him donning khaki when he happened to be at home on leave in 1914. Now she would have to go through it all again, with an only surviving son in the thick of another World War. But she never faltered, nor said a word to distract me from any intention I might feel about cutting short my leave and getting back to France as soon as possible. She had marvellous fortitude and even smiled wanly when I jumped from my bed exclaiming rather melodramatically, "Hoorah, now we will show them! These Germans have not been up against the real thing. They could beat up the Poles, the Danes and the Norwegians, but by Golly we will give them hell now."

"What will you do then?" she asked.

"I shall put away the sails of the boat after breakfast," I replied, "and I must then catch the first train to London."

"Yes", she said. "You must march to the sound of the guns."

My mother had a wonderful gift for the right phrase.

"Meanwhile", she said, "your father and I will repaper the staircase to keep our minds occupied."

After breakfast, having put away the oars and the sails, the three of us set off for the railway station with such baggage as I had. My parents believed that there was something immoral in using the car in wartime, so we set off on foot with my kitbag in the wheelbarrow and my father and I pushed it in turns the half-mile to the station. They dutifully bought platform tickets for themselves and we walked over the bridge to the up platform. My mother gave me a pound note, as she always had done before seeing me off to school, saying at the same time, "Now you will be able to take a taxi in London won't you?"

4

My mother and I kissed each other goodbye and my father raised his cap gravely as I saluted.

"Good luck," he said gruffly, and laid his hand on my shoulder.

The engine whistled, the door slammed, and I waved from my window to the two grief-stricken figures who waved their handkerchiefs in reply till the smoke blotted them out from view. I have seldom felt more miserable.

Years later the vicar told me that he had seen a wheelbarrow in the church porch and my mother and father emerging from within to wheel it home. He had guessed why they had gone to the church and he hoped that I had also remembered to pray for them. I wish I could now write "yes"; but I only learnt that lesson later. Looking back on it, I am thankful I was not then married. What it can have been like for young men and young wives with children, I cannot imagine.

I suppose that it was about five o'clock by the time I got to Victoria Station, from which, in those days, the leave trains departed for France. The station was thronged with soldiers of all ranks, cluttered up with equipment, tin hats, gas masks and kit-bags, but, I think, no rifles. On most evenings I suppose there would have been enough soldiers on the platform to fill one train only; but on this particular evening there must have been sufficient to fill half-a-dozen trains, because of the hundreds of men, who (like me) had cut short their leave to get back to their units. But there were no trains in sight, not one.

No one seemed to know why there were no trains; and I could only suppose that Folkestone or Dover or both had been bombed. However, the Royal Engineers play a prominent part in the control of military movements, so I thought I might be able to find some brother officer who could tell me about trains. I accordingly tried my luck at the office of the Railway Transport Officer. The office was full of officers of every rank jostling to get to the counter, behind which sat an enigmatical Sapper Corporal. He blandly regretted that he could answer no questions, and, as if to amplify this proposition, he pointed at a poster warning all and sundry that "Careless talk in public places is a court-martial offence." It sounded heroic to march to the sound of the guns, but they were evidently not audible in Victoria Station.

Against the babel of voices in the RTO's office, I suddenly heard a call for silence. The speaker was a tall, thin Brigadier with a commanding presence. I knew him by sight and I knew he was the Commander of an Infantry Brigade in the same division that I was in in France. He seemed to exude authority, and the voices gave way before his.

"Pay attention, will you," he said, when he had got the silence he had called for.

Writing it now, over forty years later, it sounds rather rude not to have said "please" after the command for silence, but in those days, and perhaps today

5

too, the expression "if you please" was as rare in the Army as on board HMS *Pinafore*. This is what he said:

"It is unbecoming for officers to bully this unfortunate Corporal. He is only trying to do his duty. It is now about 6 o'clock and everyone must report here in the morning. Meanwhile I shall find some way of ensuring an evening meal for the troops. Officers, of course, must fend for themselves."

I set off on foot for my Club. It was a fine evening and I walked past Buckingham Palace with its Royal Standard hanging limply at its staff. Inside the Palace, had I known it, Winston Churchill was at that very moment receiving the King's command to form a National Government. I walked down the Mall, up the Duke of York's Steps to the now defunct United Services Club. The Club was crowded but subdued. A group of members, all in uniform, clustered round the ticker tape and the evening papers carried headlines of an avalanche of fire and sword pouring into the Low Countries. There was a notice to say that at 9 pm Mr Chamberlain, the Prime Minister, would broadcast.

"It will be Churchill," I heard someone remark. I knew the speaker slightly and I knew he had some junior post on the slopes of Mount Olympus.

"Will Churchill be any good?" I asked him.

"God knows," came the reply. "At least there will always be some sort of decision before it's too late."

I walked into the Coffee Room, overlooking Waterloo Place, and ordered a drink. There were one or two waitresses working in the Club even in those more spacious days, and a plump, jolly waitress called Margaret, who seemed to know all the members by name, took my order. Seeing a vacant chair I walked across to it and sat down. I thought I was bound to see someone whom I knew well enough to enquire discreetly how to get back to France. I knew nothing about the customs of Whitehall, but I was determined not to risk indulging in "indiscreet talk in a public place". All seemed to hinge about meeting someone whom I knew really well and whom I could talk to confidentially.

It was then that I noticed, sitting almost alongside me, a large, robust and formidable-looking senior officer. He was wearing half-moon glasses and reading a book as though he had not a care in the world. I recognized him as General Ironside, under whom I had served in India about ten years before. Now he was none other than Chief of the Imperial General Staff.

What a day he must have had, I thought. Never a signal from anywhere or anyone but telling a tale of disaster. And he knowing that if we lost the war he would be one of the first for the gallows at Tyburn. Surely to God, I thought, he must know about getting the troops back to France? But dare I ask him? He might easily take a dim view of a junior officer asking questions about military secrets in a public place. Might he not send for the Provost Marshal, who was

6

probably in the room too, and command him to put this tiresome young officer under arrest at once? I looked at the great man wondering what to do, when, as if reading my thoughts, he lowered his book and our eyes met.

"Hello," he said. "Haven't we met before?"

"Yes, Sir," I replied, and told him where.

"And what are you supposed to be doing now?" he asked.

"I am trying to get back to my unit in France, Sir," I said, "but I have not been very lucky so far."

"Why?" he boomed, and I told him in as few words as possible about my troubles at Victoria.

General Ironside was evidently a man of few words. He thought for a moment and boomed again:

"Try Waterloo," he said, resuming his book. The interview was ended.

I had dinner in the Club, but I did not stop the night there. I went straight to Waterloo. There were a few others camped on the platform, and quite a number began to collect early next morning, among whom I recognised the Brigadier of the night before. He seemed to recognize me, for he said:

"Come along with me. I expect you will come in useful."

I felt much flattered but very unworthy as I had never been on the Staff and never wanted to be. About then a Major with a white armband came on to the platform and started talking to the Brigadier. I noticed that the Sergeant who accompanied him was a man I had known as a Corporal in the Training Battalion at Chatham before the war. We had rowed together in a pulling race on the Medway. Rowing together, like galley slaves in a whaler, welds a strong bond among its devotees, and we were soon in conversation. He told me that the Major and he were part of a liaison team between the railway management and the General Staff, and that a train would be arriving in about an hour. He told me that trolley-loads of food for the troops would be arriving on the platform in a few minutes.

"But if I were you Sir," he concluded, "I would see if it were possible to arrange something similar for the officers from the buffet."

I consulted the Brigadier on this proposition.

"Good idea," he said. "Try and fix up something or other as quick as you can."

My Sergeant friend showed me where to go and a still sleepy manager in the buffet, with two or three minions from the nether regions, soon had tables with white cloths on the platform, loaded with tea, coffee, porridge and boiled eggs. A similar sort of arrangement for the troops had meanwhile been organized by the Staff and the Brigadier sent an Infantry Captain, whom he had enrolled on to his staff, to find out whether the troops had all had enough to eat. There were apparently no complaints. The buffet manager had done a good trade in breakfast for us too and everyone seemed to be happy.

A train soon pulled in to the station, and a Lieutenant-Colonel, whom the Brigadier had appointed OC Troops, began to do whatever was necessary. I was not quite sure whether I was expected to join the Brigadier in his compartment but in a friendly way he beckoned me to do so. Thereafter the train puffed out of the station and I fell asleep like a millionaire on his way to join a luxury cruise. I forget how many officers and other ranks were on the train, but I suppose there were about a thousand. The military machine had operated extremely smoothly, for which some of the credit must be ascribed to our Brigadier, unfussed and cheerful as he was, and more so to the many private soldiers. A lot in war depends upon the goodwill of the cannon fodder and in all my thirty-two years service I seldom saw it otherwise. God bless you, Private Atkins, for all that you have done!

In due course we embarked from lighters into a cross-channel ship of some kind. The sea was a flat calm, no one was seasick, all kinds of precautions were taken to preserve the blackout and we all had life-jackets. But I did not care, for I slept soundly on mine as a pillow. We slept on the floor of the saloon, till awoken by bugles and told by the tannoy that breakfast would be ready in ten minutes time. Disembarkation was then to follow at an unspecified port. Everybody guessed – and the crew were happy to tell us – that it would be Cherbourg.

In Cherbourg a totally different atmosphere seemed to prevail. The change was instantly perceptible, though it is hard to explain in the afterlight why; but it struck one at once, looking from the deck of our ship towards the jetty. The port seemed to be deserted except for a few British soldiers in battledress and a British staff officer. The Brigadier went ashore to speak to the British staff officer and the troops disembarked. The ship's crew began to unload cargo from the holds. An unshaven French official of some kind was urinating against a wall. I asked him how *la guerre* was getting on. "*Nous sommes vaincus*" was his simple reply. It seemed a bad start for a great war and I asked him to explain, but his reply was too voluble for my vocabulary, except for the word *trahison*, which he constantly repeated. I took this to imply treachery, but I only obtained a hazy notion of who had betrayed whom.

Soon the Brigadier made it known that we could not entrain for an hour or two and that in the meanwhile the troops, whether armed or not, must be dispersed in case there was an air-raid. He said that we would be entraining in cattle trucks of the type known to soldiers in the 1914–1918 War. He told me to see that the ones allotted to the officers were properly equipped, though with what he did not say. Each vehicle bore a notice saying in French that it was intended to hold forty men or eight horses. I could see that the journey from Cherbourg to the Front would be quite a different kettle of fish from the first class carriage from Waterloo to Southampton. But I was determined to see that the best was made of it, if only to repay the Brigadier's confidence in having me on his staff.

It was soon clear that the Brigadier and the other members of his staff had done much more than I had. Some sort of order was sorting itself out from amongst the chaos. The OC Troops was making provision for the troops, while it was left to me to make provision for the Brigadier and his staff only.

At that moment I happened to see Driver Reeves, who had been my groom before the war. He had become my Batman when the war began and he and I had both gone on leave together at the beginning of May. He had also come back, of his own accord, a few days early when he heard the BBC News. Prompted to some extent by him, I commandeered some bales of straw to sleep on. I reflected, as we bundled them into the train, that in the piping days of peace I had sometimes gone down to the stables after dinner to see how my horse was getting on, and found Driver Reeves, still fully dressed, fast asleep, lying in the straw alongside the horse. Perhaps that is where he got the idea of collecting straw in Cherbourg. It certainly made us all very comfortable and I got a good mark for foresight from my companions during our ensuing journey.

Most of the soldiers had their own knives, forks, spoons and tin mugs among their personal kit, but it was only after a lot of trouble that I managed to collect enough crockery and cutlery for our party in the headquarters cattle truck. I obtained it from the NAAFI canteen in Cherbourg and for this I had to sign. (Six months later, back in England, I was sent a bill for the lot from the NAAFI central office and I had a long haggle to square it up.)

Another officer on the Brigadier's staff had somehow got rations for all aboard the train and Reeves and I got hold of an army cooking stove and a couple of army tables. Drink proved a difficult question. It was generally believed that water out of French taps was undrinkable and it was obvious that, if wine or beer were bought for all concerned, there would be a lot of drunks on board – even if we could overcome the difficulty of paying for the stuff. However, a British army water cart was produced by the Embarkation Staff and the soldiers all filled their water bottles from this. Many men had also, of course, provided themselves with bottles of beer. As I had somehow become Honorary Mess Secretary of the Headquarters cattle truck, I felt I ought to get something more interesting to drink than water. Luckily there was an *estaminet* not far from the place where our train was marshalled and Reeves and I went over to it. I had no French money and I had run out of English currency, except for an iron ration of half-crowns that I was determined to keep against a real emergency. However, the old French woman in the *estaminet* said she would "trust a British Officer", and I gave her a cheque on Cox & Kings's Bank in Pall Mall. When France capitulated to the Germans about a month later, I was afraid I had done this poor woman down, but in some mysterious manner the cheque was duly presented and appeared in my bank statement after the fall of France.

No one seemed to know when our train would start and the Brigadier, supposing (quite wrongly) that as a Sapper I knew all about railways, sent me to enquire from the engine driver. Three or four French railway officials and a British Staff Officer stood parleying on the platform near the engine and it soon became apparent that the driver and the fireman were both very reluctant to start the journey. It was, they said, too dangerous. We would be shot up by German aircraft flying overhead. And anyway there was not enough coal on board to get all the way to Brussels. The fireman also was not entirely sober.

I could not play much part in all this palaver, and it was certainly not my duty to do so, but I *did* feel some responsibility for coming back to the Brigadier with an answer of some sort about when the train was going to start. The only answer that I could believe to be satisfactory was that the train was going to start quite soon. In this way I got mildly involved in the argument. It was not long before I found myself manoeuvred into a position where I was required to answer the following question: "What does your Brigadier want us to do in the circumstances?" I was by then thoroughly roused, so angry in fact that I retorted hotly in schoolboy French: "*Le Général a donné l'ordre que vous faites marcher le train tout de suite.*" I am not sure how many mistakes there were in this.

Of course the Brigadier had given no such order and it dawned on me that he might now blame me if all the melancholy consequences foretold by the engine driver actually came true. But I was too angry to care and spoke with tongues of fire in voluble but very bad French. This seemed to clinch the deal and the British Staff Officer suggested that I go back to the Brigadier and tell him that the train would soon start.

We all got aboard and the train started with a succession of terrific jolts and rumbled off into the countryside. No one had a map and it was impossible to tell where we were going. After an hour or two it got dark. The batmen in our cattle truck had laid on a very respectable meal of bread, butter and bully beef, which we washed down with *vin ordinaire*, and I soon discovered that the batmen had not done too badly either. They were all very jolly and fell asleep while the train rumbled on into the night. Perhaps the engine driver had had a tot or two also.

During the night we stopped at several places and trains coming the other way, chock full of refugees, sometimes stopped alongside us. We heard the most terrible stories of disaster and collapse at the Front. They all said that Brussels was occupied by the Germans, that the Germans would be in Paris in a fortnight, and that God knows what should be done. I tried to hearten them up in broken French, saying, "*Les anglais sont arrivés.*" They seemed to scoff at that. I had hoped that we were doing rather better, but evidently we were not.

Soon after daylight the train stopped with a succession of jolts, and I peered out of our cattle truck to see what had happened. We were standing in some country district, with fields all round. In the distance lay a trunk road with a few white houses by it. I told one of the officers, who was waking up in our cattle truck, to tell the Brigadier that I was going to see the cause of the halt.

Several other men got out of the train and we all walked up to the engine. The fireman and the driver had both departed. I told an NCO, who was standing by, to wait until I came back and I went with one of the others up to the level-crossing to see what had happened. At the level-crossing the gates were closed across the line. I saw that the gatekeeper's cottage was shut up and the curtains drawn. I banged at the door and presently an old woman peered out of an upper window. I asked her where the gatekeeper was and she explained that he, his wife and his children had departed with the pram earlier in the morning. They thought it too dangerous to remain where they were, but she did not know where they had gone. They had implored her to go with them, but she said she could not manage to walk very far and, thinking she might hinder them, she had stayed behind. She seemed to be a most unselfish old woman. I asked her if any trains had gone by, and she said none had gone in our direction. She believed the Germans were in Brussels. I asked how far it was to Brussels and she told me. I forget what she said but it was not very far and I guessed we must be inside Belgium.

Just at that moment I heard the sound of distant motor traffic coming down the road from the direction of Brussels. I wondered whether it would turn out to be a convoy of German armoured cars. Presently two motor-cyclists came roaring into sight, and I thought they must be German because they looked so menacing! However, when they got closer, I could see they were British and I stopped them. I asked where they were going. One of them said they were with an ammunition convoy that had gone up towards the Front the evening before to deliver ammunition. They were now returning empty to fetch more. They said that no battle had been joined, as far as they knew, and the Germans were still a good way away. I asked what unit they belonged to, but they were hesitant to say because of security.

When the convoy itself arrived, there was a young officer in charge, whom I knew by sight, from the RASC ammunition column of 2 Division. I asked him if it would be possible to turn his convoy round and take all these troops up to the forward area and then start again on his proper duty? He was a sensible young man. He said he thought that would be OK by his CO. There was plenty of time, he said; they had a big convoy of lorries; how many men had we got?

It seemed they could take the lot of us if we piled pretty thick into the lorries; so I walked back to the Brigadier and told him what the score was. He said, "That's a good show. Let's all have breakfast while they are turning the convoy round."

The batmen had already started cooking breakfast and Reeves produced a cup of tea there and then. I told him it might be good diplomacy to offer one to

11

the Brigadier too. I remember that he replied, "What Sir? Hunt with the hare as well as the hounds?"

The batmen gave us a good breakfast and we abandoned the train. We got into the convoy, which had by then turned round, and motored back in an easterly direction. Eventually we got to some suitable place, where we debussed. The Brigadier and one or two officers, of whom I was one, walked off to Divisional Headquarters. This was pretty near where I wanted to be, so I thanked the Brigadier for having arranged all this and we parted on the best of terms.

EXTRACTS FROM LETTERS TO MY PARENTS

1. Written from the United Services Club, Pall Mall, London. 10 May, 1940.
Just a line to tell you where I am . I hope to catch a boat train tomorrow, and I am determined to get back to France somehow, come what may.

2. Written from Cherbourg, 12 May, 1940. (No address given)
I am writing from "somewhere in France", but censorship prevents me from saying where. It seems very difficult to "march to the sound of the guns". I wonder if it will be easier to get away from them? Don't attempt to write to me till I give you a more certain address.

3. Written from near Wavre (Belgium), 13 May, 1940. (HQ.RE 2 Div.BEF.)
Until further notice I believe this will be my address. I think letters will probably arrive: but don't attempt parcels. I am told I am likely to be promoted Major and given command of a company "somewhere in France", but I have not been told where. I shall certainly try my best to lead them properly. . . . "Briggy"* is in splendid form. He seems to thrive on excitement.

* "Briggy" was Lieutenant-Colonel R. R. Briggs, DSO, MC, RE, our CRE.

2

From Phoney to Real War

The Sappers had opened up shop with their main office in the conservatory of a house that looked like the dower house of a big château in whose grounds it stood. The conservatory contained orchids and palms growing everywhere. There was a funk hole in the coal cellar, which was accessible from the conservatory, but nobody had apparently had to use it. The château belonged to a tycoon in Brussels who must have commuted daily to board meetings and business luncheons. There was every sign of affluence, but the owner had departed.

"Hello!" exclaimed the Colonel when I entered. "You have come just in time. Nothing has happened so far, but tomorrow we will have a battle. I am just off to see the line. You had better come too."

The Colonel was a dark-haired cheerful East Anglian – the brother of a General Briggs of the Indian Army, who gave his name, after the War, to the Briggs Plan in Malaya. The Colonel was a very experienced Sapper from the First World War. Unlike most Sappers of his vintage, he had not been to the Shop.* He had been to London University and had an engineering degree. He was a good horseman, an expert shot, and had won a DSO and an MC in the First World War. He was consequently reckoned in 1919 good enough for a Regular Commission in the Royal Engineers. They certainly backed a winner in Briggy. He was extraordinarily shrewd, but unbelievably lazy over affairs that he thought did not matter. Over things he thought important he was ferociously active. Seeing the Front he evidently regarded as important and we

* The colloquial name for the Royal Military Academy in Woolwich. Not to be confused with the Royal Military College, Sandhurst.

set off straightaway in his staff car. It was a Humber saloon and very unsuitable really for that sort of purpose, but it was all we had. A light armoured car would have been much better, but I doubt if such things then existed.

The front of 2 Division joined the French line on the right and stretched northwards along the River Dyle, through Wavre, made famous by Blücher's celebrated order after the Battle of Ligny in 1815. To the north of 2 Division's area was the area of General Alexander's 1 Division. North of that again, and in Louvain, was General Montgomery's 3 Division.

The Germans were not in contact with the BEF on this day (13 May), but further south, had we but known it, they had crossed the River Meuse near Sedan and Dinant, both places being north of where the Maginot Line ended. All our people seemed cheerful and we saw our three Field Company Commanders, who told us that their men were busy preparing the bridges over the River Dyle for demolition. We did not actually visit any of the bridges because there was not time to do so, though later I wished I had. We would then have seen what a trifling obstacle the River Dyle really was. That was to become important later.

Next morning there were several air raids and we took to the cellars once or twice. We heard encouraging reports later about the successes of our Hurricanes in combat with the Germans, though I never actually saw an air battle myself. The German Army was approaching and a beautiful sunny day was spent in tension. Our Officers' Mess arrangements were only very second-class, and we did not get proper meals. This was because during the phoney war we had employed an elderly French matron to cook for us, and she was no longer present. Urged by the Colonel, I went out and bought a couple of bottles of red wine from a Belgian *estaminet*. I paid for these with some of my iron ration of English half-crowns. Next day the *estaminet* was wrecked by a bomb, but the proprietor had gone, leaving the till open. I could no doubt have recovered my half-crowns, but it never entered my head to do so, nor did the rows of bottles on the shelves lure any of the regular soldiers to looting. The Regular Army of those days was well disciplined and would have given a good account of itself if it had been better equipped.

By that evening Divisional Headquarters was stirred by excitement and streams of intelligence summaries came pouring in. There were so many of them that our Intelligence Officer was unable to sort the sense from the nonsense. Most of them went unread. Our Intelligence Officer was rather a character. After attending Bristol University, he took a Direct Regular Commission in the Sappers. He was pious, very earnest, highly intelligent and perhaps rather a radical. I sometimes wondered whether I was right to burden him with so many highly secret documents. But he was so well-qualified an engineer that I preferred to give him the benefit of the doubt during the phoney war. Apparently, when he heard the news that the Germans had attacked the

14

Low Countries he was so incensed by their perfidy that his fighting spirit exceeded that of any of us and he retired in due time as a Lieutenant-Colonel.

All kinds of rumours were rife. There was so much intelligence coming from GHQ behind us, and so little coming from the Front, that practically any rumour from any direction could find corroboration in one of many reports in the Intelligence Summaries. Everyone was on tenterhooks awaiting the battle. The 'Top Brass', as was the custom in those days, were kept firmly at their desks by bureaucracy, and Bob Courtice, who was acting as Adjutant, was told by Briggy "to keep the bloody paper under control". I was more or less spare to run errands for the Colonel, which I rather enjoyed, because it gave me considerable freedom of action. I used to borrow the Colonel's saloon car and I was driven in state by his Lance-Corporal driver.

Towards evening the paper machine generated a notion that the demolition of the bridge in Wavre had not been successful. The Sappers in those days had no wireless, and dispatch riders, whom we had sent repeatedly with requests for reports about the bridge in Wavre, came back with unsatisfactory replies. This uncertainty prevailed for too long and Briggy got fed up with waiting.

"You must go off on a motorbike," he said. "Have a look at this bridge yourself and come back and tell me whether it's properly blown up or not."

So I departed on a motorbike into the gloom. First I went to the Headquarters of 5 Field Company a few miles from Wavre where Major Armitage commanded. He did not seem to be sure himself whether the demolition at Wavre was adequate or not. He explained, however, that the River Dyle in Wavre was little more than a trickle, that the masonry of the bridge was considerable and that whether the bridge were standing or flattened made very little difference; the gap would be full of masonry anyway.

Armitage and I were engaged in concocting a suitably phrased anodyne embodying this general theme to the Colonel when a dispatch rider arrived. He bore two messages, one from Bob Courtice, the other from the Intelligence Officer, both addressed to me.

To Henniker,

The bridge at WAVRE will (repeat will) be properly demolished.
The Colonel says that you (repeat YOU) are to see that this is done. Bad Luck!
Bob.

That seemed to settle it.

The second message, the one from the Intelligence Officer, announced that according to a French report the Germans had already used poisoned gas in the Ardennes, and that we must carry gas-masks 'at the alert'. It was only when I

15

read this aloud to those present that I remembered that my gas-mask was back at Headquarters. Knowing, as we do now, that gas was never used throughout the Second World War, we can see that we might have dismissed this message lightly. But then, with battle impending, and every sort of rumour current of the Germans' successes, with nerves on edge before a mortal trial of strength, it seemed we had received the news in the nick of time. Everyone fumbled to adjust his mask to the alert position except me. I felt my doom was imminent. I recount this at some length because the next act is typical. The dispatch rider, who had been a groom in Aldershot before the war, removed his own mask and offered it to me.

"Take this," he said. "Moving about on the bike I shall be all right."

Of course I could not accept, but it seemed to me then, as it does still, a most wonderfully unselfish gesture. Why should he risk his life for the sake of this careless officer? It showed a wonderful spirit.

Meanwhile the bridge at Wavre will (repeat will) be properly demolished, and what was Henniker to do about it? Clearly two things must be done. First, I must go and have a look at the thing myself, and, secondly, some men must be warned to complete the demolition as soon as possible if it turned out that anything remained to be done.

Armitage had a subaltern called Pat Hunter-Gordon, who had been to the bridge in Wavre and had in fact been responsible for blowing it up. His view was that not much that was useful could be done. The bridge had leapt into the air from the river bed and returned as a pile of rubble to the river bed again. The French expression *Faire sauter le pont* (Make the bridge jump) exactly describes what had happened. All that could be done now was to make it jump again. However, the rubble apparently consisted of very large pieces and, after discussing it with Pat, we decided to reduce them to dust and ashes. While, therefore, I went to look at the bridge, Pat Hunter-Gordon undertook to dig out some men to prepare more demolition charges so that a minimum of time would be spent on the actual site, which we expected might soon be under enemy observation – if not under fire.

I accordingly set off again on my motorbike in the direction of the bridge. By then it was night – pitch black and headlights were taboo. It was difficult to find the way, but at length I entered the outskirts of Wavre. Several buildings were burning and the *pavé* streets were deserted.

In 2 Division we did not then signpost our Headquarters because there was a general belief that enemy agents or fifth columnists abounded. These latter were said to be dropped by the Germans by parachute disguised as monks, or nuns, with tommy guns and hand grenades under their clothing. This was quite untrue.

After much searching in Wavre, I found a Company HQ of The Royal Scots who provided the garrison of the town. Except for a sentry crouching in the doorway all were asleep, but I roused the Company Commander.

"I want to see the bridge in Wavre," I said. "Has it been properly blown up?"

"Who the hell are you anyway?" demanded the sleepy Company Commander. He evidently thought me an enemy agent, though I was not dressed as a monk or a nun.

Luckily he had a subaltern called Thorburn, later killed in Burma, with whom I had been a schoolboy long before, who was prepared to vouch for me. Together we walked towards the bridge, followed by Thorburn's platoon runner, carrying his rifle at the ready. We turned into an alleyway, with Thorburn slightly ahead of me. He made as if to tap at a window to awaken someone within. Suddenly a bren was fired, a long burst apparently aimed at Thorburn from inside the window. I saw a flash and the bullets splattering into the wall behind our heads. We crouched in the alleyway and there was a scuffle in the house as the sleepers awoke. They were coming out to finish us off with bayonets. Thorburn recognized the voices.

"For Christ's sake don't fire that bloody bren," he shouted.

"Sorry Sir," came the reply in accents clearly denoting an origin north of the Tweed. "I thought you were a bunch of Jerries," he concluded.

Thorburn had a good deal to say about all this to his men and he lost interest in the bridge. However, he ultimately sent a couple of them to escort me to it.

It was not easy to see in the dark, but the impression I got was that the river bed was stony and nearly dry. The roadway of the bridge lay in two or three huge pieces, each the size of a billiard table, the whole thing being only a few inches below the roadway from which we viewed it. Across the bridge there was a square and, in the background, hills with what looked like camp fires, presumably German camp fires, burning on them. The escort fired a few bursts of bren across the wrecked bridge to hearten themselves and returned to their guardroom. I had nothing to do until Pat Hunter-Gordon and his men came with the demolition charges. Time passed on leaded footsteps. Who would arrive first – Pat or the Germans? And how was I to return to Briggy, having failed to organize the total destruction of the bridge at Wavre? It was a miserable interlude.

As it was getting light next morning Armitage and Pat, with a few Sappers, appeared. Pat had a number of explosive charges cleverly made on wooden frames that fitted to the remains of the girders under the old decking of the bridge. Just as we began to fix these in place there was an air raid. Dive bombers, Stukas, made a dead set at the bridge, as though they had the same idea as us. We all dived for cover and several houses in the square collapsed in flames. It was here I saw my first battle casualty of the war, a mother with a baby at her breast was killed in the wreckage of a small shop. Presently the Stukas departed and Pat led his men back to work. People were popping off rifles and automatics promiscuously from both sides of the river. I never saw any Germans, but they were not far away.

Pat and his men had the worst of it. Except when German aircraft passed low overhead, often under five hundred feet up, they continued working at their posts. There were a fair number of Stuka attacks which, in retrospect, were not very effective, but at the time they seemed extraordinarily unfriendly. The roar of the aircraft, the whine of the falling bombs, the explosions, the deep rumble of rubble and the crackle of burning roofs are sounds that will live in my mind for ever.

At length all was ready and we took cover. Pat pressed down the exploder handle and there was a terrific explosion. The wreckage of the bridge jumped into the air. Stones, brickbats and bits of steel whistled all over the town, but the main bulk of the bridge eventually settled back more or less where it had come from, only in much smaller pieces. Armitage wrote a signal to Divisional HQ saying that the bridge at Wavre had been totally (repeat totally) demolished and I took the signal back to the Colonel. Honour was satisfied and none of us had been killed. I threw myself on a bed, fully dressed, and slept till teatime.

It was not the done thing in those days – perhaps it is still not the done thing today – to call a movement backwards a retreat. It was always called a withdrawal. No one was ashamed of the retreat from Mons in 1914; indeed it was clothed in the aura of glory. The retreat to Corunna by Sir John Moore is an epic of British military skill, and the retreat to the lines of Torres Vedras by Wellington was always regarded as a far-sighted and cunning manoeuvre. But in 1940, when the French front was penetrated beyond repair at Sedan, the BEF did not retreat, it withdrew.

The first I heard about this withdrawal was at about 7 or 8 o'clock in the evening. There was to be a Divisional Order Group at which the General would give out his orders. The Colonel took me with him to make notes, while he followed the plans given out on a large-scale map.

We assembled in the drawing room of the HQ Château, seated on Louis Quinze chairs or on army benches, each according to his rank and station. Most of those present wore a more serious look than they were wont to do on similar occasions during peacetime manoeuvres. Two of the Brigadiers, I noticed, had sent Staff Officers instead of appearing themselves.

Presently the GSO I, a Gunner Colonel who was well known for his equitational skill at pre-war horse shows, entered the room. With him was a Brigadier Davidson, also a Gunner, who had been with our Division in peacetime, but who had since been promoted elsewhere. We were soon told the explanation. Our General, whose name was Lloyd, had gone sick and was being evacuated to England. The story was that he had gone with two Staff Officers to a Conference at HQ I Corps, which was then commanded by

Lieutenant-General Barker.* At the conference, so we were told, our General had had a heart attack and fainted, though what actually happened I do not know. Anyway he did not return and Brigadier Davidson, who then commanded the Artillery of I Corps, was sent to command 2 Division till some more permanent incumbent could be found.

Before the war I had had a close-up view of most of the up-and-coming Generals of the British and Indian Armies – Auchinleck, Alexander, Dill, Wavell, Wilson and others, and I had always looked long and carefully at them, saying to myself: "Which of these chaps will be any good when the inevitable war begins?" It would only be candid to say that I had always put our General Lloyd very high on the list. Yet when the real test came his health gave way; so now we were in the hands of Brigadier Davidson, sitting at a table near the grand piano in the Château. On one side of him sat the GSO I, on the other the AQMG, who was the Chief Administrative Officer in the Division. It was now Brigadier Davidson's task to give verbal orders for 2 Division's withdrawal from the River Dyle to the River Escaut, sometimes called the Scheldt.

One of the secrets of a successful Order Group is to know how much or how little to say. Brigadier Davidson was a highly skilled, staff-trained officer. He could undoubtedly have told everyone, from the summit down to the lowest platoon commander, exactly what he ought to do, and his Order Group went into extraordinary detail accordingly. He must have spoken for half an hour or more.

People began to ask questions, which in turn led to digressions. At one point something approaching argument was entered into, and the conversation became general. Even I, a Captain at the back of the room, offered an opinion, not on the employment of the Sappers, about which I might be presumed to know something, but about the Divisional Cavalry Regiment! Nobody even frowned and the suggestion was accepted! When the Order Group was finished, neither my Colonel nor I were quite certain what we had to do. I expect some of the others also had doubts. It seemed to me a strange Order Group.

The reader must not feel inclined to censure Brigadier Davidson for the rambling nature of this presentation. He had had no time to prepare for the event. It was as though a member of a Dining Club had been told at the end of the Annual Dinner that the Guest Speaker had fainted and would he please deliver the expected oration on Ceramic Pottery from the Guest Speaker's notes (herewith). Loud applause as the diner stood up. He did his best in a very difficult situation and the withdrawal did in fact happen in the manner required, despite a few hiccups on the way.

I do not remember much of the actual move back from the Dyle, but I

* Not the General Barker who commanded a Corps in Italy in 1944.

19

remember very clearly a hiccup over the demolition of the bridge at a place called Ath on the River Dendre. There was doubt in the minds of the Top Brass whether proper arrangements had been made to blow up this important bridge.

It is not difficult, in a technical sense, to blow up a bridge. All you require is sufficient men with suitable tools to bore a hole into the roots of the bridge and into this hole you put an explosive charge. You connect this explosive charge to a fuse and light it. In theory nothing could be simpler, but in practice many things can go wrong, mostly due to human rather than mechanical error. The men to do the work may not arrive in time to bore the holes before the enemy arrives to prevent them. There may be a shortage of explosives, in which case the thing goes off like a damp squib. But much the most likely thing to go wrong is something to do with the timing of the whole affair. What you want to achieve is to blow up the bridge when your last man has come over it to the home side, but before the enemy arrives. This is the time-honoured difficulty. Even Horatius had the bridge hewn down behind him "in the brave days of old", so that he had to swim the Tiber. There are many examples in military history of bridges being seized intact by treachery or guile. The Channel Tunnel will be very difficult when the day comes!

The bridge at Ath provided most of the necessary ingredients for this sort of confusion. The Sapper Field Company detailed to prepare the demolition had had a strenuous time and Briggy had doubts whether they had the manpower left to do the job. He was also not quite certain whether the lorries of explosive had ever reached them. Finally, no one at Divisional HQ was certain that anyone had been formally appointed to give the order to blow the bridge when all was ready. The Colonel therefore sent me to Ath to try and tie up these loose ends.

It was a fine sunny morning. The roads were packed with refugees, pathetic columns of despair, stretching like serpents along the undulating roads as far as the eye could see. The children were a most pathetic sight, the horses coming a close second. Every now and then an enemy aircraft, or a flight of them, would roar down the length of the road machine-gunning the column. As the aircraft passed, the column seemed to flatten like corn in the wind. Struggling to get past the refugees, either forwards or backwards, were troops of three nations – French, British and Belgian. Mostly, except the British, they had horsedrawn transport.

Being on a motorbike, I was able to make my way past these columns on the road and, after about an hour, I arrived at Ath. The bridge was a little outside the town and by the time I got there a kind of deadly hush had come upon the scene. Gone were the refugees. Gone were the columns of troops. No one was in sight; even the birds had flown. They had all flown and there was no sign of life whatever. All had succumbed to a creeping paralysis and it was as quiet as

20

death. I dismounted from my motorbike, as it were on tip-toe, and turned it round, ready for a rapid retreat.

The bridge was visible a few hundred yards down the road and it occurred to me that it might be on the point of demolition with the defenders taking cover to avoid the falling debris. I looked anxiously for some cover for myself and saw, to my relief, an armoured car from the Divisional Cavalry Regiment, the 4th/7th Dragoon Guards.

Sitting in a deck chair was the CO of the Regiment. He was reading *The Times* with a teacup in the other hand. He was a man of medium build, I should think in the mid-forties. His cap was pushed back and a pair of earphones were resting loosely round his neck. He had a sallow complexion and a neatly clipped moustache. He wore field boots and well cut breeches, as though his horse were waiting for him in the stables. He was, in fact, the embodiment of a cavalry officer of the old school – perhaps a bit of a Blimp. Near him, looking rather anxious, was a young subaltern of one of our Field Companies.

"What's your trouble?" inquired the Colonel, looking up.

I told him my mission and he said he believed everything was under control.

"We still have a troop of armoured cars on the other side of the river," he said. "But the enemy are not far off."

He offered me a teacup, similar to his own, which a trooper from the armoured car brought on a tray. I thanked him and took a sip, wondering if it were hot. It was excellent. I could not help remarking on the likeness between this scene and similar ones on manoeuvres.

"Yes," said the Colonel. "It's just like manoeuvres only now it really matters."*

For the first time I thought how odd it was to be actually in the presence of the enemy and that quite soon one might get killed oneself. But I positively did not feel frightened, partly, I suppose, because of the confidence this calm and level-headed Colonel exuded, and partly because my mind was totally occupied by the arrangements for blowing up the bridge. It overwhelmed all other feelings. I felt responsible for seeing that the demolition happened properly, and I felt much fortified by the sight of this cool Colonel who seemed so confident. In contrast, I noticed some slit trenches nearby in which there were a few men wearing their steel helmets and all clearly in mortal terror. I can now see that it is when one has not enough to think about in a battle that fear begins to take a hold. These men had been waiting a long time with nothing to think about but impending danger. Very difficult to resist.

Every now and then the CO spoke on his wireless and soon afterwards some mortar bombs pitched near us. The Germans could not now be more than four or five hundred yards away at the most. The CO was speaking to his rearguard

* His name was Lieutenant-Colonel L. E. Misa.

troop commander, who told him that there were some enemy in sight. The Colonel replied on his wireless; "Well you had better drive them away." At the same time, however, he said to the young Sapper Officer who was standing near us, "You must go up to your Sergeant on the bridge. It won't be long before I shall have to tell Bobby to come back to this side of the river." The Sapper Subaltern and I then walked off together in the direction of the bridge.

There was really quite a lot of mortar fire coming down now and we were both afraid lest some of these mortar bombs, crashing in the vicinity of the bridge, might cut the electric cables whereby the bridge was to be blown up. Soon, however, the armoured cars started retreating over the bridge. They must have had the order from the Colonel. Three or four of them came and the young officer in command of them waved cheerfully to us, saying he would tell his CO that he had got all the troops to our side of the river and might the order now be given to blow it up. Evidently he had a satisfactory reply and he said to me, "The CO says its OK now to poop it off." He waved and led his troop towards the rear.

The Sappers did whatever was necessary and we crouched in a trench that had been prepared for the occasion. There was a deafening explosion and the entire bridge sprang into the air. It was a good big river and it left an impossible obstacle for the Germans to cross without building a new bridge. I went back to the Colonel and asked him to send a message over his wireless to Divisional HQ to say what had happened. It was a satisfactory demolition and I said I would take the message home and confirm it to HQ by word of mouth.

When I got back to Briggy he was delighted and went over to speak to the main HQ, who were not very far away in a farmyard. Bob told me that they had not been so lucky with one of the other bridges. He told me that one of the Company Commanders on another bridge had had a hair-raising experience. There was no proper liaison at his bridge and no proper orders, so he went across the river on a push-bike but could find no sign of the Germans anywhere. He was returning on his push-bike and was pedalling over the crown of the bridge when he saw on the home side his own sergeant and a staff officer of some sort trying the exploder. The Sapper Company Commander luckily was an active man and threw himself over the parapet of the bridge and into the river, expecting it to blow up immediately. By extraordinary luck there had been some failure in the operation of the exploder and it was not till he got ashore that the bridge did blow up. The Company Commander then got out of the river, having lost his bicycle, and walked back to have some fairly straight talking to his sergeant. He then remembered that his suitcase, containing all his dry clothes, was on the other side of the river. He spent a wet and unpleasant day until he was reunited with something dry to wear.

A lull for 2 Division came one or two days later, when we were just west of

Tourcoing, and the Colonel agreed to release me to take command of 253 Field Company in 3 Division.

It was 23 May when I left HQ 2 Division and I was very sad to say goodbye. I had been Adjutant for nearly three years and of course I knew them all extremely well. I had no idea where my new Command was and no one at HQ 2 Division had any idea either. Moreover, I had no vehicle in which to travel. Naturally Briggy did not want any of his vehicles to go, and he said, "Try your luck with Sergeant Heather." Sergeant Heather was our transport sergeant, a splendid character who had been a long time with one of the Field Companies in 2 Division before the war. He and I, in days gone by, had practised on motor-cycles over Laffan's Plain and the Long Valley in Aldershot. I told him I wanted transport to get to 253 Field Company and I asked him if he could spare me a vehicle of some kind. I also asked if he knew where the Company was. He had no idea where 253 Field Company was; he had been about a bit, but had not seen it.

"But," he said, "there is no difficulty about transport. I've got a *bakhshee** French Citröen, which is a good runner. You'd better take that."

I bundled my possessions into the Citröen, thanked Sergeant Heather, and bade farewell to Reeves. (I should very much like to have taken both these men with me. They were splendid men and I am glad to say they both survived the war.)

I knew more or less the way back to HQ I Corps, which was a step in the right direction, and I motored away with a light heart. After a bit of searching I found the Chief Engineer's office, located in an infants' school. Some of the Staff were sitting in tiny chairs suitable for infants only and the whole aspect was mildly absurd. The maps, however, were the first I had seen that showed the full extent of the Allied débâcle. There was a complete breakthrough on our right, in the French sector, and it was evident that the BEF was nearly surrounded. No one in the Chief Engineer's office had the faintest idea where 3 Division was, and they only had a hazy idea where HQ II Corps was; but they gave me a map and I went off in my Citröen, forcing my way through columns of traffic, mostly refugees. Eventually, more by luck than anything else, I found II Corps' Military Police HQ.

The change in atmosphere when I got there was refreshing. They looked clean, tidy and efficient, with a smart sentry at the door. Inside I met an officer whom I happened to know and inquired the way to the Chief Engineer's office. He pointed it out on my map and I found it set up in a large country house. The Chief Engineer, Brigadier Phipps, had a desk in what must have been the study of the owner. He was calm and not unduly perturbed. He had time to give me a straightforward picture of how the battle was going. He made no bones about

* *Bakhshee*: A corrupted Hindustani word, much used in the British Army of those days, meaning surplus.

the unpromising outlook, but he told me he had known it much worse in March, 1918. He then showed me where 253 Company was to be found and he pointed on the map to a hillock, indicating that if the Germans were in possession of that hillock it would be prudent to move the Company HQ to somewhere that would not be overlooked by it. I took this to heart.

I then set off in my little Citröen to HQ 3 Division where, on Phipps's advice, I first called upon the Commander of the Royal Engineers. He was Lieutenant-Colonel Desmond Harrison, a cheerful little Irishman, who had formerly commanded 5 Field Company in 2 Division. He asked me how they were getting on and I told him that as far as I had seen they were all in good heart.

It was quickly borne in upon me that HQ 3 Division was in a sounder state than HQ 2 Division. I was surprised that even the General, General Montgomery, wanted to see *me*, a very junior officer, before I went to command a mere Company.

I had never met Montgomery before, but I knew he was called 'Monty' and I had heard on the grapevine all kinds of stories about him. His original military thinking had attracted me, but the autocratic way in which he seemed to sack anybody who displeased him filled me with apprehension. I had, as a matter of fact, had a dream some time before that I was going to be promoted Major and get command of a Field Company in his Division, and it seemed odd that this dream might now come true. In my dream all had gone wrong. My appearance was even now very much against me. I had been riding my motor-bike the previous day when the column was blitzed and I had jumped into the ditch and got soaked to the waist. The only trousers that I could get to replace my breeches was a pair of corduroys, which happened to be in my kitbag. I was still wearing these when I was ushered into the presence of the General. Incidentally, I rather think that it was I who set the fashion for wearing corduroy trousers in uniform. They became almost universal later.

Monty never raised an eyebrow. He sat me on a chair in front of his desk and asked the sort of questions one might have expected had we all been in Aldershot. He then told me about the military situation, bad as it was. Finally he told me about the Field Company I was going to command, ending with these words, "You go to your Company," he said, "and tell your men that you have spoken to me and that I have told you that we, in 3 Division, are the best troops in the world. There is nothing to be afraid of in the Germans. We shall see them off. All that the soldiers must do is to *do what they are told*." He had a trick of repeating key sentences and he repeated this last sentence several times. "They must do what they are told."

Desmond Harrison then told his Adjutant to take me to my new command and I was able to give him my Citröen car. I never heard what he did with it.

The Adjutant of 3 Division was Dick Walker whom I had known out hunting with the RE Drag before the war. He was a high-class horseman and a high-class oarsman too, a Member of the Leander Club. As we went along he was able to tell me something about the Company I was going to command. It was a Territorial Unit raised in St Helens, between Liverpool and Manchester, and it had been commanded by a man who was a Public Works contractor in the Liverpool area. Among the subalterns had been his younger brother, who had been killed before his eyes only a few days earlier. This had, not unnaturally, unsettled the OC very much indeed and it was thought best to remove him and post him elsewhere. This had been decided upon some days previously and during the interregnum the Second-in-Command, Otto Phibbs, a regular who had been with me in the Training Battalion at Chatham in about 1937, had been acting as OC. The thought was that he would not stay with me for long, as Desmond Harrison wanted him for another appointment.

Dick Walker knew the way to 253 Company and after about half an hour's drive he halted at a small farmhouse. As I got out of the car I caught a glimpse of the hillock that Brigadier Phipps had told me about, but I did nothing at the moment. Two subalterns emerged from the front door and I overheard one of them say to the other, "Christ! A bloody Regular".

This was not exactly a propitious welcome, but Otto Phibbs' appearance almost immediately was reassuring. He was a large, sturdy man and we had always been very friendly. "This lot," he said, "are first class chaps. Rather like the Royal Enclosure at Ascot. Very high hat and difficult to get into."

I was now what is called a Field Officer, that is to say a Major, but I was not wearing a Major's crown, only my Captain's pips. It seemed unlucky to put on a Major's crown before actually taking command of a Field Company, and now, of course, there was no Major's crown handy; so I managed for the rest of the campaign with my three Captain's pips. That did not seem to make much difference and Otto saluted me in a way he never would have done if we had still both been Captains. He also addressed me as "Sir" in spite of his genial grin.

I told Otto I would first like to meet as many people as possible and he at once introduced me to the young officers whose initial reaction to my appearance I had overheard.

The first to be introduced was Bruce Tompkinson. He was a tall, clean-shaven young man with reddish, well-brushed hair. His forehead was high and his face thin and open-air life had given him a bronze complexion. He had a serious, intelligent face, but you found that on very little provocation it lit up suddenly with a smile that suffused his eyes and mouth. He shook hands with a firm grip and I got the impression of a powerful young rugger player in very good physical condition. He was the son of a successful builder in Liverpool, and had joined the Territorial Army at the time of Munich.

The next to be introduced was Douglas Murray. He was short, thick-set and dark. He was a bit older than Bruce and had a gloomy countenance, but I later found that when shelled or mortared he was wont to omit some inaudible jest with a dry chuckle. He was not such an extrovert as Bruce, and perhaps not so quick on the uptake. He was the son of a sea captain from Fleetwood and he, too, had joined the Territorial Army in 1938. I sustained (rightly) the impression that both these young men were reliable though perhaps not very experienced in military matters.

The third subaltern was Tom Cochrane, whom I shall introduce now though I did not meet him until later in the afternoon. Tom was a regular officer on paper, but in fact he was no more than an army Cadet destined for regular service when the war began. He had probably received less formal training than Bruce or Douglas, but I was told he had been recommended for a Military Cross in Louvain a few days ago. He was young and pink-faced like a schoolboy, artistic, musical and intelligent, the son of a Captain in the Royal Navy with the tradition of service bred in his bones. It was only later that I appreciated his sterling worth, and perhaps I caught him at a bad moment, for he was wearing carpet slippers.

Next I must introduce the Quartermaster-Sergeant. He was known by his friends in the ranks as Digger. Quartermaster-Sergeants of the Royal Engineers of those days were always promoted from among the horse transport drivers, that is to say they dated from the days of the horses. He was short, bow-legged and sallow, requiring a shave at least twice a day, but he was now quite respectably shaved, although it was the afternoon. He was a regular non-commissioned officer of the best type. He understood the Army and how to do things and to get things done, and he was always willing to put his knowledge to the general good. If ever we wanted rations, petrol, ammunition, explosives, or any other military commodity – even a dirty joke – Digger could be relied upon to produce it. He had an immensely kind heart and must have helped many young soldiers in their bewilderment on enlistment. I will not introduce any more of them now because they do not come into the story till later.

Otto seemed to think the Germans were some way away. I asked him to see if he could get the Company paraded for us to see one another. He gave the necessary orders and in due course the men were paraded by their vehicles under the shade of the trees of a wood where they were leaguered. Many of them worked in Pilkington's Glass factory. There were a few from the coal mines, some from municipal employment, others from industry and private enterprise of various sorts. I could see at once that they viewed me with profound distrust and I confess to have been puzzled by this, my first command. Few of the Other Ranks except Digger, had shaved for some days. Many of them had puppies or livestock of some kind and every other vehicle seemed to contain a gramophone and a considerable collection of ladies' hats and other apparel. Everyone was cheerful; some perhaps were not quite sober.

The fact that Belgium was about to collapse, that France was tottering and that we were all of us more or less surrounded appeared to ruffle nobody. It seemed to me that most of the livestock had been collected to prevent it starving in neglect, and the millinery was probably picked up from deserted shops. It had not, I thought, been collected by organized coercion, so I said nothing. In their cheerfulness I had much to be thankful for.

I shook hands with most of the men and some said a word or two with that delightful Lancashire accent that makes their humour, with which they are very well endowed, all the more whimsical. We have had a number of reunions since those days and events have been called back to mind.

"Do you remember," asked ex-Sapper Holloway at one of those reunions, "what you said to No 1 Section in that wood?"

"No," I replied.

"You said, 'Whole Company's got to shave.' No one had ever said anything like that before. We thought you was daft."

"And did you shave?" I asked.

"No," he replied. "We did nowt about it, even when you had Corporal Tilley reduced to the ranks."

I think I must have tried to take a tough line over some matters, but in the turmoil of getting home all the records were subsequently lost. Many men redeemed themselves and King's Regulations revealed, when I consulted them later, that some of my sentences were invalid. Anyway I had been wasting my breath. The Germans could not get the better of them. How could I?

In the meantime, however, their haphazard methods caused me great anxiety. It was quite impossible to rely upon anyone being awoken at any particular time in the morning. In a properly conducted unit there is a guard mounted and one man, at least, is awake in his turn. He it is who rouses his relief after two hours and hands to him a list of early calls to be made, so that the cooks and others are roused at the appropriate times. In 253 Field Company the sentry settled down to a comfortable snooze for the night, when it got dark, and nobody stirred till God knows when next morning. During my first night with the Company I woke half a dozen times, thinking the Germans were upon us, and at 6 o'clock it was I who roused the sentry and the cooks. This was just as well, because, with my field-glasses, I could see that the wooded hillock that the Chief Engineer had spoken about was not as it had been the night before. Some trees were being felled. You could see the tree-tops tumble. From this I deduced that the Germans had occupied the place and were building a look-out post in the trees. Soon we should cop it, so I had the Company HQ moved from the farmhouse to a sunken road nearby. There were many grumbles about "That bloody Major mucking everybody about", but I took no heed. The move was hardly complete before shell-bursts straddled the farmhouse and the next one hit it. My stock as a competent person, even if bloody-minded, went up from that moment. They saw there was some sense in what I ordered and that it was not just 'regular army bull' – a phrase, incidentally, that had not then been coined.

After breakfast I went with Bruce to see two of the bridges that his Section had prepared for demolition, and then went on to see two more of Tom Cochrane's, and one of Douglas Murray's. At each bridge I questioned everybody to make sure that they all knew what they were required to do, and to make sure that there was enough explosive in each. There was no doubt that everybody understood the demolition business and had been well trained by Desmond Harrison and my predecessor during the phoney war. When I got back to Company HQ Otto told me that I was required at Brigade HQ by the Brigadier and thither I went to a Brigade Order Group.

At that time 253 Field Company was under command of 9 Infantry Brigade, commanded by a stout-hearted old warrior called Brigadier Robb. He was a good soldier and handled the brigade coolly and well throughout the retreat. For this he received the DSO at the end of the campaign, but he was a bit old for the job and went to command the Senior Officers' School when we got back to England. (Brigadier Horrocks, who later became very well known, replaced Brigadier Robb.) However on 24 May it was Robb at the helm. The Commanding Officers of the Infantry Battalions, the Gunners, and I (of the Sappers) lined up before him. It was clear that Robb was not at all pleased.

"The Belgian Mayor of the local town," he said, "says he will be thankful when the Germans arrive in a day or two, as looting will then cease. This is a shocking disgrace and I want it stopped at once." He thumped the table and glared round sternly.

The Commanding Officers of the three Infantry Battalions, with one accord, protested the innocence of their men. But I had seen all the ladies' hats and gramophones in the lorries of 253 Field Company, so I lay low, like Tar Baby, and said nothing.

The phenomenon of looting on active service by soldiers is very old. There was a lot of looting by Sir John Moore's troops during the retreat to Corunna and Wellington habitually had a gallows erected in every town he occupied to deal with looters. Kitchener court-martialled and shot a British Officer in South Africa, during the Boer War, for looting, though in the 1914–18 War looting was not punishable by death. In the Second World War there were very few offences for which a British Soldier could be sentenced to death, and looting was not one of them. Moreover, in the field imprisonment is not likely to stop looting. It is no good sending offenders back to base for a stretch of detention or prison, because prison is exactly what they would like. It is far better to be in prison at base than in the front line. By good example, and when morale is high, the British soldier responds to every call, the greatest dangers are overcome and heroic deeds are done. But that is quite different from trying to stop petty looting during a retreat.

In 9 Infantry Brigade there did not seem to be any way of stopping it. On the whole, when troops are kept busy they do not bother much about looting. When victory lies ahead the troops can see that it does not pay to loot, because they will not then be welcomed, and what the victors want is to be welcomed by the civilian population whom they are conquering. The Germans dealt with looting differently. They issued to the troops large sums of money in bogus bank notes, manufactured in Germany, and gave them to the soldiers on pay day. They could then buy what they wanted and were not personally corrupted. But in actual fact it was still looting, but in another guise. Of course every officer at Brigadier Robb's Order Group knew this and when Robb had delivered himself of his rebuke he probably felt he had done the best he could. He then went on to explain the next move of the Brigade – backwards, of course.

The Germans had, apparently, penetrated well behind both flanks of the BEF and it had been decided that the time had come to withdraw to the next position in rear, which was the Franco–Belgian frontier. We had occupied and fortified it throughout the winter during the phoney war, but, by some twist of fate, we, in 3 Division, were now to occupy a length of line prepared by 4 Division. They were known to have built many block-houses and pillboxes, but we did not know where they were. It would therefore be 253 Company's task to go back with Brigade HQ to discover where these fortifications were and then, with my carpenters, to make a lot of signposts and stick them up so that when the infantry withdrew it would be quite easy for them to find where they had to go.

These orders had the merit of absolute simplicity and I told Otto, when I got back, to collect everybody together, except a few small groups of men needed at each bridge to blow it up, and to bring them to a meeting point that we chose from a map. There was, however, a serious difficulty. There was a lorryload of maps to be distributed to the Brigade and all the maps had tracings to be slid over them. But the tracings with the fortifications were on a different scale from the maps! It was not dead easy to see how to sort this out. However, the withdrawal would not begin till nightfall, so we had time on our side.

Looking back on it, I remember that even as a mere Company Commander I generally knew by teatime each day what I would be required to do next day. Monty must therefore have made up his mind by about midday, and Brooke, who commanded the Corps, must have made up his in the early morning. Lord Gort, C-in-C BEF, must have made up his mind the previous day and as he was under the command of the French, who never seemed to make up their minds about anything, he must have had to make his plans on very indifferent and often totally confusing information.

I discovered later that the first idea of possible evacuation was considered by Gort on 19 May, Ironside having suggested collecting small boats two days earlier. Pownall phoned the War Office on 19 May to suggest men being evacuated and Ironside was sent to France that night to instruct Gort to move south-west and not towards the coast. On the following day, however, the Cabinet decided on precautionary measures, and Gort persuaded Ironside that evacuation was probably necessary. Eden authorized withdrawal to the beaches on 26 May, at which time operation *Dynamo*★ officially began, although some 20,000 men had already been taken off, largely non-combatants, etc.

From this it is evident that Gort was thinking a long way ahead of London and those who got back with the BEF should remain eternally grateful to him for acting so wisely. But I question whether he got much thanks at the time for his prudence.

★ Operation *Dynamo* was the code name used for the evacuation of the BEF by sea, using small boats.

3

The Retreat Continues

By the time I got back to the place chosen off the map for Brigade HQ I found quite a number of Brigade HQ personnel had assembled. It was not long before representatives from the Brigade units were beginning to trickle in, demanding maps of their sectors. Fortunately a draughtsman in 253 Field Company, whom I had brought with me, found in the lorryload of maps a few traced sheets that *did* fit the huge piles of maps. Working hand in hand with the Brigade Intelligence people, it was possible to give to each unit a few valid traces for its pile of maps. It was far from the perfect answer, but it was the best that we could do.

Otto got 253 Company back to the position without enemy interference and we set our carpenters to work in an abandoned sawmill making signposts. Someone found out how to work the circular saws in the sawmill, which had been evacuated, and someone else found a sack of nails. There was plenty of space and we had little difficulty in producing several production lines of signposts for the Military Police to put in place.

There had been, since before the war, a system of vehicle signs for every type of unit in the BEF and the final markings of the signposts and placing them in position was mostly done by the Military Police. It was not a very difficult business and I was pleased after the campaign to recommend for a mention in despatches the draughtsman who found in the lorryload of maps the few traces that fitted. It was a good bit of work on his part and we could never have achieved what we did if it had not been for him. I always tried, when making recommendations for mentions in despatches, to include one or two for administrative achievements. Combatant awards, such as Military Medals, were in a different category and the only men I thought eligible were those who risked their lives in the process. We had our fair share of them too.

By the time all this had been done it was late at night, and before sunrise each of the officers had taken his men to his affiliated battalion to do whatever they could to help prepare their defensive positions. Each battalion had its own ideas, so I told my officers to do the best they could and left it all to them. In the process of going round and supervising all this, Tom and I stumbled upon a cunning defensive plan which I will describe in a little more detail.

Tom was supporting The Royal Ulster Rifles and one of their Companies had, in the middle of its position, a large carpet factory overlooking a patch of rough ground about the size of a football pitch. The Company Commander asked Tom to make a series of loopholes along the ground-floor wall of the factory rather like the gun emplacements in the side of an ancient, wooden man-of-war. It seemed to both Tom and me that this would give to the Germans a good indication of where this Company of Ulster Rifles were. They had but to look at the wall of the factory from the far end of the open space and see every single rifleman's position marked by a loophole. We thought that a better plan might be devised and we suggested to the Company Commander that he look at a row of houses that ran out at right-angles to the factory from one corner of it. From this row of houses one could enfilade anybody crossing the open ground, and it was quite an easy business to burrow through these houses, all the way along them, and to set up on tables in the upper rooms, well back from the windows, firing positions for automatic weapons overlooking the open space across which the Germans were bound to advance. The Company Commander had a receptive mind and said, "Yes, not a bad idea, but I'll just ask the Colonel." By luck, almost at that moment, the Colonel arrived. The Colonel's name was Fergus Knox. I can see him now, considering the matter. When I explained our plan and told him it was quite easy to put into effect, his eyes lit up like those of a bank robber when he hears the clink of a till. In theory, the way to do the job was with a compressor to make holes through the houses. But of course the compressor would not start. Luckily the walls were thin and the buildings pretty old. The whole place was deserted and it was very easily done with hand tools. I heard afterwards that it turned out to be an enormous success. The Germans, when they saw the factory, started firing at the loopholes as we had foreseen they would. When they reckoned they had settled with the people behind the loopholes they walked nonchalantly across the open ground and received a belting from the upper windows of the row of houses.

In all this business one thing soon became apparent – namely that nobody in 9 Infantry Brigade had the slightest intention of occupying any of the pillboxes that had been built during the phoney war by the troops who had planned the defences there. What all these men seemed to think, after actually being in touch with the enemy and being fired at by him, was that it was much better to be out in the open than in a blockhouse. I felt that too; concealment made a far stronger appeal than protection.

By about 6 o'clock in the evening everyone had had a full day and it seemed likely that the Germans would have closed up on our positions by next morning, so I called off the work. While the men were having tea, I got someone in the Company, who was said to be a great entertainer, to gather those in the Company with histrionic ability and we had an evening concert. I doubt if any other unit in the British Army in the front line had a Company concert at this time during the retreat, but it seemed to be the only way to prevent all the men from vanishing into the city of Lille and perhaps disappearing for ever! It was in some way comparable, on a more vulgar scale, with the Duchess of Richmond's Ball on the night before the Battle of Quatre Bras. On that occasion Wellington had all his officers at the Ball when he heard that Napoleon had crossed the Sambre. He could give them orders there and then and tell them where to go. In the same way I had all 253 Company assembled in one place and available for orders. During the night orders came from Desmond Harrison saying that we were to prepare some bridges for demolition further in rear and in the small hours I gave orders to Bruce, Douglas and Tom. However, before describing that, perhaps I should here give some idea of the quarters that Otto had chosen for the soldiers, for the officers and for the Company office.

The Company was billeted in a large school. It really was a first-class place, with a kitchen and a dining hall and a lot of large classrooms in which there was plenty of room for the men to lie down and sleep. The men were very comfortable indeed. Otto had chosen for the officers and the Company office a new and well fitted house nearby, which must have belonged to some young, newly-married couple. We called it 'The Love-Nest'. The owners had departed and we luxuriated in the baby-blue tiled bathroom and ate our meals off Delft china from a polished table. (The cellar was stocked with many bottles and the cupboards were stocked with preserves but we left these untouched.) The sheets on my bed, a double one, were violet and the room was furnished with a blue bidet with chromium taps and a hand basin. The first night there I threw myself down on the bed, fully dressed, and slept for several hours, but with my boots off. The walls were lined with mirrors and when I awoke I wondered who the Hell it was I saw in the mirror sprawled on a double bed.

My Batman, whom I had inherited from the previous OC of the Company, brought me a cup of tea and told me the Adjutant was downstairs and wanted to see me. It turned out that Monty intended to present medals to a number of men that afternoon. One of them was Tom Cochrane, who had been awarded the MC before I joined the Company. Sergeant Powell was to receive a DCM, and a couple of Sappers the Military Medal. They were to be paraded near

33

Brigade HQ at 3 o'clock in the afternoon, dressed in their best, smart and soldier-like. The cares of battle were thrust from my mind; all my energies were directed to getting hold of some clean battledresses, which the Company Quartermaster-Sergeant coped with most creditably.

I assembled my men at the right time and place looking reasonably respectable and saw to my surprise, about a mile away behind the German lines, a captive balloon with a basket beneath it from which an observer with field-glasses was clearly visible searching the horizon in our direction. There was apparently no ack-ack artillery about and the best that could be done was to fire some twenty-five pounders in the right direction, hoping to frighten the balloonist. It had this effect and the enemy lowered the balloon.

Soon Monty arrived and presented the medals, standing in the glorious sunshine. He summoned all of us to close up round him, where we could hear what he had to say. By then it was not officially known that evacuation was being planned from the beaches of Dunkirk.

"Go back to your units," he said. "Tell them you have seen me and these are my instructions. We are 3 Division and we can give these Germans a bloody nose if they come near us. In a year or two we shall be ready to tan the hide off them. That's certain. But today everyone has only one thing to do and that is to do exactly what they are told. Nothing will be too difficult if we all pull together. Nothing." With that he departed to tell the same tale to somebody else in the Division. We now know that it all worked out exactly as he said. Nothing was too difficult and the Germans seldom molested us.

We, in 253 Company, did not remain in this defensive position round Lille for long, as orders had come for us to prepare some more bridges in rear for demolition. There had been some mix-up with the French or Belgians – I am not sure which – and these bridges had fallen between two stools and were left unallotted to anyone.

I went first to see how Bruce was getting on and then planned to go to see Murray at one of his. Bruce had a straightforward task, with plenty of explosives available, and a staunch British Major with an infantry company as bridge garrison. I was just about to leave Bruce when a dispatch rider came from Douglas Murray saying he was in great difficulty and would I come at once, so I went over to where one of his bridges was.

It was an important bridge on a trunk road over a wide river. As I have said there is no technical difficulty in blowing up a bridge if you have lots of explosive. We were lucky in this respect, because Desmond Harrison always made very good arrangements and we were never short of explosives throughout the campaign. There is, however, as I have said, often difficulty in deciding when to do the blowing up. All the difficulties prepared by the umpires on manoeuvres presented themselves here at Douglas Murray's bridge in real life. The CO of the batallion providing the immediate garrison on the bridge was carried off on a stretcher as I arrived. He had had a nervous breakdown, I was told. The Adjutant of the battalion was not fully conversant with his CO's plans. The CO was apparently a careful, diligent man who never delegated anything to anyone and he had never told his Adjutant what his intentions were.

When I arrived the Germans were mortaring the bridge and as the mortar bombs fell they frequently cut the electric cables whereby the charges would be blown. Douglas and his men had repaired these cables several times as best they could, but Douglas felt that if he left it much longer all repairs would become impossible. On top of this a French General had arrived and forbade the firing of the demolition. He told me that he had a light motorized division on the far bank, though exactly where he did not seem to know. I pleaded with him in indifferent French, but he was adamant. I went across the bridge myself on a motor-bike to try and discover the score, but I scuttled back, like a rabbit to its burrow, having nearly run head on into a German armoured car whose crew were luckily brewing up at the side of the road. My recollection is that they roared with laughter and never fired an aimed shot, though a few automatic shots were fired unaimed.

When I got back the mortar fire was almost continuous and very accurate. The French General had gone, but his words were still ringing in my mind: "The bridge must not be blown". And now the decision must be mine alone and what decision should I make? Here was an important decision in a real war. It seemed to offer me the chance, either way, of going down in history as the prize idiot of the campaign. It was no time for philosophical debate and I gave the order to blow up the bridge and damn the consequences. Suddenly a British staff car roared into view from the rear and who should appear but Monty, Desmond Harrison and Horrocks, who was still a Lieutenant-Colonel commanding the Middlesex Regiment. Monty stepped out and immediately said, "Hello Henniker, how are you getting on?" I explained to him the situation as best I could, wondering whether he would be furious at my having decided to blow up the bridge. I managed to stop Douglas from actually pressing the exploder while Monty had time to think. He thought for a moment and a stonk of mortar fire came down all round us. Monty never ducked his head but said calmly, "Right ho! Blow it up and never mind the Frenchman."

We sent the car back a few hundred yards and we ourselves sheltered behind a wall, while the debris of the bridge fell in splinters around us. We then went to look at the wreckage. In the middle of the swirling torrent (the bridge had incorporated a sluice gate) lay a slab of concrete as large as a billiard table and on top of this, blinking in amazement, was the largest pig I have ever seen.

"Someone," remarked Monty, as he walked towards his car, "will have pork chops for supper."

35

Before saying goodbye, I could not refrain from observing that this was the first occasion in my military service that I had been glad to see a General.

Monty made an oracular pronouncement. "Yes," he said. "One of the arts of high command is to be at the proper place at the proper time." And he swept away, no doubt to be at some other place at the proper time.

Whatever it was that brought the pig to its unfortunate situation I never discovered, but the event seems so improbable in the afterlight that I am prompted to mention it, particularly as there were credible witnesses present in Horrocks, Desmond and Monty.

The withdrawal in earnest to Dunkirk began, as far as we were concerned in 253 Field Company, at about 7.30 in the evening of 26 May when Desmond Harrison called for the Company Commanders to give us our orders. It had been decided, he told us, to extricate the BEF from France by hook or by crook, by which was implied the men with such arms and equipment as they could carry and nothing else. I went back to the Company and explained this to the officers and the senior NCOs. Otto Phibbs and the CSM and most of the administrative personnel were to leave at once with only their small packs and firearms. I was astonished to see how quickly the other lorries were also loaded and the convoy was lined up and pointing the right way. Within less than half an hour I was able to give the order to march.

During the hours of darkness there was not much traffic on the road because the civilian refugee traffic had dried up. The people, in exhaustion, had left the roads. It was warm and fine and they just collapsed in the fields on either side of the road in utter wretchedness. One could not help being terribly sorry for them, but there was nothing we could do to help them. We struggled along these unsigned roads with our very indifferent maps, among places peopled by the ghosts of the armies of 1914–18 – Ploegsteert Wood, Neuve Eglise, Poperinghe – and so in a northerly direction.

As soon as the dawn broke innumerable human beings seemed to come to life and get on to the road. There were three rows of traffic everywhere, and sometimes four along our road: French artillery dragged by horses; refugees pushing prams, riding on carts and on foot; military lorries streaming northwards towards the sea and occasionally British convoys bringing up ammunition in the other direction. The sound of battle was clearly audible to the right and to the left. We were moving along a narrow corridor with the Germans pressing on both sides to close the corridor.

Shortly after dawn there was a German air raid. A flight of Stukas flew up and down the road, bombing and machine-gunning the column. The columns of traffic stopped. Horses stampeded, women and children screamed, two lorries in front of us burst into flames and anyone still in a vehicle jumped into the nearest ditch. By some miraculous chance not a single vehicle of our Company was damaged in any way.

36

We had orders to build light folding-boat bridges at two places on the route, in case the road bridges were either destroyed by air raids or sabotage; so I told our people that I would send the Company HQ to a small town called Krombeke marked on the map. There the Company HQ would stay for the time being. I said I would decide later what to do on the merits of the case. I saw Bruce and Tom start work on their bridges and I then followed the Company to Krombeke.

The sky began to be overcast about midday and the tall church silhouetted against the clouds in Krombeke had a Red Cross flag hanging from the steeple. Ambulances lined up in queues to discharge the wounded into a hospital nearby. Soon it started to drizzle but later it poured down in torrents, adding the sound of thunder to the noise of not very distant gunfire. A private soldier, a Gunner with a staff car, came to me in the town to say that his Major was a casualty in the hospital and that he had all his kit in the car. He wanted me to advise him what he ought to do. I told him to stay where he was, near our Company HQ, for the time being and that I would look after him. In the meantime, having nothing else to do, I walked over to the hospital to see if I could discover the Major. I found him delirious, very seriously wounded, and I told his driver to take his kit to him in the hospital. He then joined my Company and eventually got back to England with us.

About that time I heard from Bruce and Tom that they had completed their bridges and I told them to come to Krombeke with their sections, leaving a few men and an NCO on each bridge to maintain it. The NCOs must be the judges of when it was time for them to withdraw and I gave them a route to follow. They turned up two days later in good spirits. They had done very well.

Presently a dispatch rider came with a message from Desmond Harrison telling me to stay in Krombeke and await orders. There was then very little to do except watch the traffic going by. It was a singularly demoralizing process, watching this retreating rabble. Everybody who passed told hair-raising stories of how the Germans were just round the corner.

While at Krombeke I got to know one of my NCOs called Sergeant Powell.* At that time I did not know him at all, but I came to know him very well later. He was a regular soldier, a stout-hearted man from Belfast, not exactly what you would call an intellectual, but steady, good-natured and efficient. We were standing talking on the pavement in front of the Company HQ, which was a deserted shop not far from a crossroads. There was a military policeman directing traffic, whom I supposed someone had put there to try and turn the utter confusion into something a bit more methodical. Sergeant Powell and I watched him for a few minutes and I noticed a convoy of trucks belonging to 2 Division, which I had only left a few days before. Among them I saw some

* Died 1978.

Sappers whom I recognized, and one or two of the men waved to me. I then noticed that the military policeman directed one part of their company to go left at the crossroads and the rest to go to the right. It seemed very odd and I said to Sergeant Powell, "See if you can find out what that chap's doing. I think he's making a box-up."

Sergeant Powell went off and came back with the military policeman almost by the scruff of the neck. He explained to me that the man was as drunk as a coot. What he thought he was doing God only knows. Sergeant Powell pushed him upstairs and into one of the upper rooms of our shop and locked him in. I asked what he was going to do with the man. He replied casually, "Oh, I'll let him out before we quit altogether, Sir." The drunkard was lucky. Sergeant Powell was a sensible man and not the type to forget and leave him there. He too returned with us to England.

The continual stream of soldiers drifting to the rear – many of them deserters, some without arms or equipment – were in sharp contrast to the regular convoys of troops who were clearly moving under orders. I felt that perhaps I ought to collect the stragglers and form them up into some cohesive group to defend the town. It occurred to me that I might set them to dig some defensive trenches with farm implements to accommodate the disciplined infantry who would presumably withdraw on foot very soon. I accordingly decided to walk round the town to make some plans.

When I came near the hospital I saw a few men who were already digging, but they seemed to have chosen an odd place to dig trenches. They were digging inside the grounds of the hospital, without any field of fire. I stopped a moment to watch them, trying to fathom their intentions. Presently a cortège emerged from the hospital, led by a padre in a white surplice, and followed by about twenty men in pairs carrying stretchers. The cortège halted near the trenches, the stretcher-bearers tipped the corpses, tied up in army blankets, into the trenches, the padre said his prayers and the cortège departed, leaving the gravediggers to crack obscene jokes, as I suppose grave diggers often do. The padre remained standing thoughtfully, and I spoke to him. He told me that he and the medical staff of the hospital proposed to remain in Krombeke, at their posts in the hospital, when the Germans arrived. I thought they faced their fate with magnificent calm and I took the padre's home address to tell his family when – and if – I got home.

Shortly after this the French *curé* came along the pavement towards his church. He stopped and addressed me. He told me he had been a combatant officer in the First World War, wounded and gassed, and he had hoped never to see another war. I asked him what he proposed to do now, for the town would be in the hands of the Germans within twenty-four hours at the outside.

"Nearly all my flock have fled," he said. "But my church will remain. The people will come back and they will need me. My duty is here."

He smiled very kindly and added peacefully that it was I, not he, who suffered the greater strain. He told me then what I was beginning to learn myself, that uncertainty about one's duty causes much worse tension than actual danger. He raised his hand, uttered a blessing in Latin and we shook hands. He was a good soul, like the padre whom I had seen bury the dead, and like the hospital staff who were to stay at their posts. I somehow felt comforted by making their acquaintances. Their fate seemed to me much worse than ours in 253 Company.

That evening I had a warning order from Desmond Harrison telling me to have the Company ready to move at first light next morning because he expected to have orders for us during the night. Desmond was a thoughtful CRE and easy to work for. He thought ahead.

At 4 o'clock the following morning, that is 28 May, I moved the Company just out of town to a small farmhouse half a mile away, where the dismal process of retreat was not in view of all the men. I ought to have done it much sooner. Sergeant Powell, who was acting CSM, made them wash and shave and we got the cooks to make some breakfast. This had a salutary and moral effect upon all of us. But, best of all, we also received orders to move. As soon as inaction had ceased and the turmoil of movement began again, all the depressing thoughts of last night were cast away and we went to our work almost with light hearts.

Desmond Harrison's orders were to take over some new demolitions prepared by another Division and we moved the Company to a clean little village lying on the edge of the marshes surrounded by the complicated waterways and canals of northern Belgium. The subalterns led their men to take over their demolitions, which had evidently been prepared during the last few days. Two of them at least had been prepared by the Belgians, the others by somebody else, who was unidentifiable. We could not really tell for certain whether these last had been prepared at all. No one was with them. Those done by the Belgians each had with them a few Belgian soldiers, all in shabby uniforms and unshaven. But nonetheless the Belgians seemed to know what had to be done and they assured me that their demolitions were properly prepared. It did not seem that we could do very much and I judged it better value to give the troops a peaceful time till the call came. However, that was not to be. One of Monty's staff officers arrived and told me that the Belgian troops were reported to have faded away and there was no one defending the sector. Accordingly I got my Company to patrol the canal bank between the bridges that were prepared for demolition. When night came the enemy must have been tired too, for they gave us no trouble and we had a quiet night. Many of us got some sleep.

Next morning the news of the Belgian capitulation reached us on the French wireless. I then began to have very severe doubts in my mind as to whether the

Belgian demolitions had been properly prepared by the Belgian engineers. It seemed possible that, knowing full well that their country did not intend to fight, they might have spared their bridges. They might have used sand – a sort of face-saving demolition. These thoughts were passing through my mind when Desmond Harrison turned up in his staff car with an enormous keg of gunpowder. Goodness knows where he had got it from. He seemed very cheerful and said in an Irish way, "You had better stick this in with the Belgian stuff, and when it's time to pull the plug you'll have a better chance of doing some good." He also said that one of the demolitions had to be done "on time, at 10 o'clock in the morning".

Just before 10 some infantry came back over the river line. They were British infantry, not belonging to 3 Division. I never knew where they came from, but they believed they were the last people over the bridge. When it was 10 o'clock we blew up the bridges. I counted four or five. I was most relieved to hear the detonations. Through a slit in a wall behind which I was standing, I saw the nearest bridge fly into a thousand pieces and disintegrate in a cloud of smoke. At this moment a Belgian engineer appeared, as if from nowhere, and said, "At any rate the last job I did for my Army before it surrendered was well and truly done."

I must say there appeared to be quite a number of Belgians who were extremely ashamed of the part their country had played in the battle. Many of them came to our units saying they wished to fight for the Allies and would we enrol them. When it came to the point of embarking into ships a few days later they were not so keen about it. This was very understandable, but they were a great help to us for the remaining few days of the campaign.

We shortly received orders to prepare more bridges for demolition, this time in a sector held by the French. We set to work and a French lieutenant-colonel appeared. He was a very different kettle of fish from the French General who was so ineffective on the previous occasion. This chap seemed to know what he was doing and said he would leave one of his officers as a liaison between us and his troops. These were the only French troops I saw during the whole campaign who seemed to have any intention of doing anything other than get back to their homes and their families. The French liaison officer was a tough little man, small and squat, with a square face, a flattened nose and a prominent jaw with two days' growth of beard. He told me he had been wounded twice, fighting the Riffs in Africa. He thought the Germans were really not so very remarkable. Their long suit, he said, was that "They have proper orders and know what to do". I formed an impression then that the French are admirable as individuals, but as a nation they are very hard to get along with.

A long time elapsed before the French were ready for their bridges to be demolished and as the afternoon wore on the German artillery started to shell us. The French said they must not be demolished until the German advanced

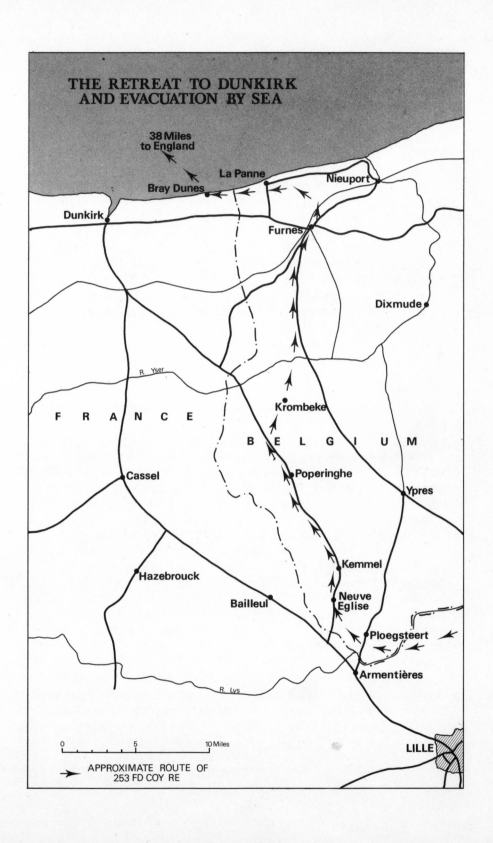

THE RETREAT TO DUNKIRK
AND EVACUATION BY SEA

38 Miles
to England

La Panne

Nieuport

Bray Dunes

Dunkirk

Furnes

Dixmude

R. Yser

Krombeke

F R A N C E

B E L G I U M

Cassel

Poperinghe

Ypres

Hazebrouck

Kemmel

Bailleul

Neuve
Eglise

Ploegsteert

Armentières

R. Lys

0   5   10 Miles

LILLE

APPROXIMATE ROUTE OF
253 FD COY RE

units actually appeared on the other side of the river. But it became increasingly obvious that the splinters of the shells, bursting round about, would cut the leads to the charges and prevent the bridge from being blown at all. I cross-questioned this Frenchman very searchingly to discover why he was so keen to delay. At last he said, "All right! You may blow it now. I wanted to wait for the enemy to come so that you would not think me afraid, firing the bridge and running away." It showed a splendid spirit, but a not very perfect understanding of the mechanics of a successful demolition! I have no idea where the French troops got to next. They vanished into thin air.

After this I received a verbal message from Desmond Harrison to take my Company at once to a place called Furnes not far from the point where the frontier between Belgium and France hits the sea. The men had all had breakfast so we got into our transport and battled through the streams of refugees and other traffic towards Furnes. It was a small town with a red church and a high steeple standing in a shady churchyard. I forget exactly how it came about, but we soon found ourselves assembled in the churchyard with our lorries parked outside in the square. There were men and vehicles from the other two Field Companies of 3 Division, and the more cumbersome vehicles of the Field Park Company. The OC of 17 Field Company was a Regular Officer and senior to me, but it was reported that he had been killed that afternoon. The OC of 246 Field Company was also a regular and senior to me, but he was out on a reconnaissance somewhere and the OC of 15 Field Park Company was only a Captain, so I was evidently the Head Boy of all those present.

It is a splendid thing, as I had recently discovered, to command a Field Company, but it is much better to command what is now called a regiment, and here was I, still wearing my Captain's pips, in command of a thousand men and many vehicles. Unhappily there was a fly, not in the ointment, but overhead. Five hundred feet above the town was a light German aeroplane wheeling about lazily in the clear blue sky. It had been a moot question in 2 Division whether to shoot at German aeroplanes with small-arms fire or not. On the one hand you draw attention to your own position by firing at the aeroplanes above; on the other hand, even a rifle bullet through the fabric of a wing would teach the pilot not to sneeze in church. I adhered to this latter school and I hoped 3 Division would not disapprove if I gave orders for everyone to shoot at the aeroplane. All the troops fired, which evidently frightened the aeronaut more than somewhat, but not before he had told his artillery friends that in Furnes there sat a splendid target.

Shells soon began to land here and there. One or two men sustained horrifying wounds and a couple of lorries went up in palls of black smoke. An officer said to me, "Don't you think, Sir, we ought to quit?" Here I was presented with another of those wretched questions for which one might be sacked if one got the answer wrong. I thought of the boy who "stood on the burning deck whence all but he had fled". Had he fled too, he would not have earned immortal glory, but perhaps his situation was not quite on all fours with mine. It seemed pretty clear, however, that if we remained here much longer, there would not be many of us left to reap the glory. So, with a good deal of heart-searching at quitting the place where I had been told to go, and doing so in the face of the enemy, I gave the Nelsonian order "Follow me" and left a couple of motor-cyclists in the crypt of the church in case anyone came along wondering where we had gone.

I then led a column of vehicles, loaded with troops, out of the town and we went down a long *pavé* road with poplar trees on either side, more or less in the direction of Dunkirk. When we had gone about half a mile I stopped the column and, looking round, I soon noticed what had hitherto escaped me: namely that a hundred yards to our left, in a field, was a totally deserted French or Belgian anti-aircraft battery which presently excited the interest of a German flight of dive-bombers. Having given a splendid display of flying they departed and were followed by another flight that concentrated on us alongside. I expect their display was equally impressive, but we were more interested in the ditch by the roadside.

Anyone who has been dive-bombed will confirm that the roar of the aeroplanes, the whistle of the bombs and the explosions around one create a most demoralizing effect. One of our lorries was set on fire but otherwise I do not think anyone was any the worse. But I felt very dubious about whether I had done the right thing, bringing the men away from the church (where we had been ordered to go) and not even bringing them to a better place. I was wondering what I ought to do when I heard the whining of the tyres of a vehicle tearing along the cobbled road. It was a staff car with a pennant flying. The car stopped and an ADC, a subaltern in the Ulster Rifles, came running towards me. "The General," he announced, "wants a word with you."

It sounded most ominous and the General was undoubtedly Monty. My luck seemed to be out. However, when I got to the car Monty was as cool as a cucumber. He remembered who I was and asked what I was doing. I told him the situation, expecting, as I always did until I got to know him better, that he would be furious because I had disobeyed orders. However, what he actually said was, "Well done! Well done! When did you last have a meal?" I told him that we had had breakfast and, looking at my watch, I saw it was about 6 o'clock. "Get into the car," he said. "Get into the car," and he made room for me to sit beside him, while the ADC produced a mug of tea from a thermos flask. I sipped it gratefully. "That makes you feel better, doesn't it?" he asked. I told him it certainly did. "Then take the men off to that little farmhouse over there," he said, pointing, "and get the cookers going and give them tea too. Then you will all feel better." Picking up his map he said, "You go along to 9

Brigade HQ and see if there are any orders for you."

I fumbled for my map, searching my haversack, but it was not there. It was back in the ditch where I had been crouching. I seemed to have boobed again. "Never mind," he said. "Never mind. Take my map. I've got another," and he handed me one from the floor of the car. I thought to myself what a wonderful little man this is. He might have been irritated, or cross, or even violently angry. But he was none of those things. He somehow restored my self-confidence and put me back on top of my form. It was an example in good manners for which I have always been grateful. I was becoming one of his greatest admirers.

Following Monty's advice, I dispersed 253 Field Company in the large field where the farmhouse stood and sent word to the other Companies to do likewise. We put our lorries higgledy-piggledy all over the field and dug slit trenches near them. (In actual fact I do not think we did much digging, but it was a good thing for everybody to have something to do to occupy his mind.) I was just about to go to HQ 9 Infantry Brigade when one of Desmond Harrison's Field Engineers, a young Lieutenant Donaldson, arrived on a motor-bike. He had been to the church in Furnes and had been sent on to us. He bore verbal orders from Desmond Harrison himself. As far as we were concerned in 253 Company, our orders were to go with him to the Suffolk Regiment in 8 Infantry Brigade, which was defending the Dunkirk perimeter and was having a bad time. 253 Company was to reinforce the Suffolks and the other companies were to reinforce other infantry battalions which they would be shown.

The vehicles were to be destroyed. It had been the intention from the start that only the troops and their personal arms and equipment would be preserved and everything else in the way of military impedimenta would be destroyed. But it seemed foolish to smash up all our lorries and then set off on foot to God knows where, when we might so much more easily use the lorries. I therefore left Digger, the Quartermaster-Sergeant, with the vehicles and told him not to destroy the lorries until I told him to. In the meantime I thought it best to preserve them in case there was some change of plan.*

With Sergeant Powell's help I assembled the Company, following Donaldson on foot, with one file on either side of the road, ready to jump into the ditch if enemy aircraft approached. That occurred almost at once. We jumped many times. In the confusion word somehow got round among the men that we were marching to the coast to embark in ships for England, Home and Beauty. The Company therefore marched with a light step. Donaldson on his motor-bike led the way.

* When we eventually destroyed the vehicles, the drivers, who had tended them so well, were much moved by the experience. They detested it, and what they would have thought if the transport had been horses and not lorries I cannot imagine.

44

The march turned out to be a long one with many air-raid interruptions. The noise of gunfire on the coast was terrific. Ships were firing at aeroplanes; they were also firing at ground targets. German batteries on shore were firing at the ships and our own artillery were firing at the enemy. Bruce, who was near me, remarked that "all hell's let loose", and an apt phrase it seemed to be. It sounded as though we were marching to a certain death, unless you happened to believe, as I did, that it takes hundreds of rounds of gunfire to kill anyone, particularly when most of it is aimed at aeroplanes in the sky. But it was difficult to put that idea across to the troops. The best one could do was to look cheerful – or try to.

Presently we turned off the main road and, because we had marched for about an hour, I halted the Company and told them to sit down. I tried to explain the situation as best I could to the men. I told them that we were to reinforce an infantry battalion and that later we would no doubt be withdrawn and would have to march to the sea and embark, though I did not know how this would be done. I told them also, very self-consciously, that it would be a good thing to pray. I said, "We none of us know for certain whether we shall be brave in this battle or not. We can do absolutely nothing about that. But if we pray to God that we conduct ourselves with decency, loyalty and honour, there seems a fair chance that we will do our best." I reminded them that in many things in life, when you have done everything you can think of to do, saying a prayer is one more possibility. If it does good, so much the better. After we got back to England several of the men told me that this had been extremely helpful and one of them wrote to his local paper in St Helens to say so. I commend this to anybody who is in trouble. It is a simple way of buoying yourself up to do better. It all seemed very real in the presence of danger and it is hard to recapture the feeling now, sitting in a chair, over forty years later. Still, it is worth keeping the instrument sharp against further trouble.

By now it was pretty dark and we could often see tracer being fired into the sky by anti-aircraft guns. We could also see, straight ahead of us, occasional bursts of tracer being exchanged by ourselves and the enemy. Sometimes a star shell or a Very light would make the surrounding countryside flicker in a dazzling light. We were evidently destined to take part in a battle. Had I known then as much about battles as I learnt later, I would have realized that many of the weapons being fired were British and therefore, from our point of view, quite harmless. There was in fact only sporadic reaction from the Germans. *They* had no cause to worry. *They* knew they were on the winning side, and local victory for them was only a matter of time.

We continued our march for about twenty minutes and a white farmhouse loomed up in the darkness ahead. Donaldson told me that this was HQ 1 Suffolks, so I halted the Company outside and went in. (The Company all flopped down at the side of the road.) The Commanding Officer of 1 Suffolks was a tall, slim man named Miles. He was just about to give out his orders to his own officers, who were assembled in the farmhouse. The room had a large table and I was given a seat near one end of it. A petrol lantern on top of the sideboard gave sufficient light for it to be thought necessary to cover all the windows with army blankets to comply with the blackout regulations. It was extremely stuffy and Colonel Miles had rather a monotonous voice. Almost at once I fell asleep. I do not know how long I slept but I awoke in time to hear him say, as it were in conclusion to his orders, "Are there any questions?" A number of elementary questions occurred to me at once, but luckily many other people, who may not have been awake either, started asking questions too and I was able to piece together most of the story.

Apparently the Suffolks were holding a length of the front with a canal between them and the enemy. On their right was a Guards Battalion and we, that is 253 Field Company, were to take up our positions near the right boundary of the Suffolks. Our role was to launch a counter-attack against any penetration by the Germans across the canal on our front. 246 Field Company RE, our sister Company, was to perform a similar task for the Guards Battalion. I was never told where Donaldson took 17 Field Company or 15 Field Park Company but I do not think they were in the line with us. They were doing something on the beach – building loading ramps, I believe, out from the beach into the sea.

Eventually the various people seated round the table had asked all their questions, and I buttonholed the Adjutant, a tall, burly, dark-haired Captain called 'Tiny' Heal. He told me that the danger point in his opinion was a brick factory that I would see as soon as it became light. It was at the junction of the Suffolks and the Guards Battalion, and was easily recognizable by its tall chimney. Apparently the Furnes gasworks was immediately across the canal from the brickworks and therefore within the German position.

'Tiny' Heal produced two or three guides and very soon, considering that in 253 we had never done this sort of thing before, we were all dispersed to suitable positions to await the dawn. On Heal's advice I set up the Company HQ in a small farmhouse with a stone-flagged floor and a cowshed alongside. Leaving Sergeant Powell to settle the HQ Section into this place I went with a sapper as escort to see our various positions. Sometimes the night was still, sometimes there was a tremendous shindy of brens and machine-guns and Very lights being fired into the sky. Above there were no clouds and the pole star was clearly visible. This was just as well as hardly anybody in a Sapper Company in those days had a prismatic compass, and it would not have been difficult, in the pitch dark, to settle down preparing positions facing in the wrong direction. It was a warm night and most of the men fell asleep. I suspected there were no sentries and I prowled around on my own a good deal of the night, but I do not think I actually did much good. One thing I did feel sure about was that these men from Lancashire were a phlegmatic lot and I much admired the way in which they showed no intention of running away. They were physically and mentally robust and had we been trained for it I think we could have been a very good infantry company. Infantry duties, intelligently done, call for considerable thought and skill as well as a robust mentality.

Dawn came about 5 am, 'rosy-fingered' in the best Homeric style, to start another fine and sunny day. I walked round the position again and the men by then had woken up and were all quite cheerful, but many of them asked where breakfast would come from. I was not actually able to give any very reassuring replies, but I told them that the Quartermaster-Sergeant (Digger), who had remained back with the transport, was doing something about it.

As I walked round the position I could see the canal bank slightly raised above the flat water meadows. It was about three hundred yards to the front of Company HQ and above it, towards the left, I could see the upper works of barges moored to the bank. White flags had been tied in the rigging. The brickworks chimney, square at the base and tapering, rose from a cluster of small sheds on our side of the canal. Across, on the far bank, I could see the gasometers of the gasworks. There had been a great deal of shooting during the night and it seemed odd that none of the gasometers had blown up, but I believe it to be a fact that when a bullet punctures a gasometer it does not cause an explosion. The gas is under pressure inside and there is no air to enable the gas to burn. But I would not like to go firm on this as a prediction for the future!

When I got back to Company HQ I was delighted to find that Digger had appeared with a lorry in the farmyard loaded with cooked breakfasts all round, brought in containers. It was not a very difficult exercise to get these distributed among the men and the batmen soon got breakfast ready for the officers.

I became aware during breakfast that my clothes were soaking wet from having stumbled two or three times during the night into the ditches that separated the fields one from another. While changing my clothes the farmer came back to his own farmhouse and asked if he might milk his cows. Most of the cows had returned to their cowshed of their own accord, though stragglers remained grazing in the fields. I could not let the farmer wander round collecting them, for he would certainly have been shot. It was impossible to walk in the open anywhere, because someone fired at you from one side or the other. However, he soon saw my wet trousers hanging in front of the fire and asked if he could have them! I told him I was sorry but he couldn't, but I told him that when we left his farmhouse I would see that clothes of some sort were left for him. Eventually, when we took our departure, I left a pair of very good English-made riding breeches. They did not seem essential for a sea voyage and I hope he lived to enjoy them.

About this time one of the sappers made a remark that was to become famous throughout the Company, and which he has never succeeded in living down. He was, properly speaking, the Sanitary Man, whose lot in the Army was to keep the latrines clean. He had been an attendant in a public urinal in Liverpool before the war, and the duty of the Sanitary Man in wartime was straight up his street. He had done little, if any, military training, but now that the latrine situation did not warrant his specialist attention Bruce had put him in the front line as a rifleman. Some Germans became visible and, egged on by Bruce, he fired a hesitant shot at them. A stream of bullets came back from an automatic on the other side of the canal. Bruce and the Sanitary Man rapidly withdrew their heads behind cover. The Sanitary Man then remarked in his splendid Lancashire dialect, "Aye! That seems to have aggravated them."

On another occasion during the morning I happened to be near a young sapper whose name I discovered to be Robinson. (You must remember that at that time I knew very few of the men by sight even, and practically none by name.) I did not know that Robinson was the Accounts Clerk and normally worked in the Company Office attending to the men's pay. We were standing in a dry ditch with a thorn hedge between us and the enemy, and we suddenly saw five or six Germans on our side of the canal, running across our front from right to left. They wore packs on their backs and stooped forward to balance the packs. In this attitude they reminded me faintly of the appearance of ostriches running across the open spaces of Africa. They were only about two hundred yards away and it seemed they ought not to be allowed to run about like this in the open, so I said to Sapper Robinson, "Have a shot at them. You'll never have another chance like this."

Robinson's rifle was not loaded and he made very heavy weather of getting a clip of ammunition into the magazine. With a certain amount of help he got it loaded at last and he closed the bolt on a round in the chamber. He held the rifle in an odd manner and I had to help him steady it. The Germans conveniently remained in sight and at last he fired a shot. He nearly jumped out of his skin!

"Does shooting always take you that way?" I asked.

"Couldn't exactly say, Sir," he replied. "That's the first shot I've ever fired."

I then discovered his background. He had been called up on 1 May, 1940, and in a belief, inculcated in the Army by the great British Press, that soldiers do not need any training if you keep them on their civilian jobs, it was supposed that he could be the Accounts Clerk without any further training. As a result of this, he had been sent overseas to the BEF on 10 May and he had no training at all. He had been posted to 253 Comapny as a clerk and had arrived with the Company on the day before I did. Now on 29 May he was firing the first shot of his life at a formidable and well-trained enemy!

During the afternoon the Second-in-Command of the Suffolks came to my

Company HQ, saying that the Germans had crossed the canal in strength near the left-hand end of the Battalion front and we were to drive them back. The reader will remember that we were at the other end of the Suffolks' front, that is at the right hand end, so to counter-attack to the left hand was a considerable diagonal move across the open fields. We had made some plans for mortar and even artillery support in case we wanted to counter-attack against the brickworks, but this operation that we were now being asked to attempt was totally different.

The Second-in-Command said there was no time to waste and that we must "get on with it at once". I told Douglas Murray to fire at our objective – a tumble-down brick and tile shed – with his No 2 Section, while Bruce and I tried to advance with his No 1 Section on the objective by two different routes. Everything went quite well to begin with. There was not much fire from the Germans and what there was was rifle fire only and not well-aimed. However, when my lot had advanced about half the length of a football ground, a German automatic was brought to bear. I found I was the only man still standing. I shouted to the others to get up and come on and I walked across to the nearest man to see what the hell had happened. He was dead! The next one I came upon was badly wounded, lying in the standing corn. Soon a few stretcher-bearers from the Suffolks – the Sappers had none – came up and I record with gratitude that a chivalrous German ceased fire. The casualties were removed and I walked back to the ditch from which I had come, carrying one of our wounded men.

Bruce, however, by his route, had got to what I had set him as his objective, and I was able to join him there. We fired at a cluster of farm buildings where we believed the enemy still to be. Someone had a Boyes Anti-Tank Rifle. We fired this at the buildings and watched the broken tiles fall from the roof. Suddenly we saw about twenty Germans break and run from the building. They reached the canal bank and disappeared out of sight. Our counter-attack had succeeded and the Suffolks thanked us for what we had done. I suppose that if I had known more about Infantry tactics and if a Field Company had had wireless communication with other units in those days, it would have been possible to call on the Suffolks' mortars to assist our counter-attack. We might then have done the job without any casualties at all. I wish I had done better for these brave men.

4

A Worm's-Eye View
of a Miracle

The evacuation from Dunkirk of over three hundred thousand men was a miracle, however you look at it, and it is no coincidence that 26 May was observed in Britain as a day of National Prayer with a Service of Intercession at Westminster Abbey. To us in 253 Field Company, who only saw a fraction of the whole thing, it was also a miracle and I now record it as I saw it, very much in the words of an account I wrote, red hot, when we got home.

It was on the morning of 31 May that we had a warning order. Dick Walker, the Adjutant of the Divisional Engineers, came to the farmhouse that was our Company HQ looking exhausted as though he had had a difficult and very dangerous journey. I told the cook to give him a raw egg beaten up in some rum and milk in a tumbler, and I had one too. We both felt much better as a consequence. The news he bore was simple. We were to send back immediately to the beach all the men who seemed surplus. They were to go to a collecting point which Dick Walker described. The rest of the Company was to follow during the night under orders of the Suffolks.

Sergeant Powell, who had by then assumed the duties of Company Sergeant-Major, soon had a group of men paraded in the farmyard and one or two lorries that we had not destroyed were produced too. I went to bid these men good luck and was rather surprised to see my batman* among them. However, I made no comment, as though I had not noticed him. The men were, needless to say, in very good spirits.

When they had gone I asked Sergeant Powell if *he* had detailed the batman or

* This was not the Driver Reeves who had been so good to me in 2 Division. He had remained with Briggy and the others.

50

whether the batman himself had volunteered to leave me.

"Yes Sir," said Sergeant Powell cheerfully. "I sent him. He's not your type Sir, not robust enough. I've found you another man instead." Sergeant Powell then shot me a glance in a way he had when he was going to be insubordinate and said, "This chap's name is Meek, but he's not meek at all. He won't be the least frightened of you, Sir." Meek and I stuck together till the end of the war. He was a Lancashire lad with no frills but a heart of gold. Nothing was ever too much trouble for him and never did he consider himself. He was joined later, when we got to England, by a Driver Lowe, also from St Helens. He drove me for the remaining years of the war. I cannot forget these two men, nor can I ever repay the debt I owe them.*

When Dick Walker had departed I sent one of the subalterns to find the way to the beach that we would have to follow when the time came. Later in the afternoon a written order came from the Adjutant of the Suffolks. This order included a paragraph to say that a rear party of fifty men, half of whom would have to come from my Company and the other half from the Suffolks, was to take over the whole position after dark, while the rest of us were thinning out, starting at 10 pm. All were to be away by 10.30, except the rear party, and certain steps were to be taken to make sure the Germans were not aware of the fact that we were quitting.

I asked for volunteers for the twenty-five-man rear party, explaining the importance of what they would have to do, but making no secret of the hazardous nature of the job. There were too many volunteers and I weeded them out rather arbitrarily. This Company was certainly a most heartening unit to command. They did not know much about soldiering and, not being an Infantry Officer, I did not know very much about our present role either, but whenever I wanted something done there seemed to be plenty of men willing to do it. They were really magnificent.

When it was dark I went with a Warrant Officer of the Suffolks and together we deployed the rear party of fifty in the places that seemed best. It was an eerie business; all was dark and every bush or tree took on a sinister shape. A half-dead horse gave a convulsive plunge in a ditch as we approached and it nearly scared the life out of us. Occasionally a Very light was fired and we all froze in position lest a burst of automatic fire caught us. As a tactical exercise it was extremely simple and the whole proceeding only took half an hour, but it seemed pretty hazardous at the time. I said goodbye to each man in a whisper, thinking we might never meet again, but I am glad to say that most of them followed us to the beach where they remained till the appointed hour and all the Sappers got safely back to England.

The remainder of the Company, under their officers, withdrew silently to

* I attended L/Cpl Lowe's funeral in St Helens in November, 1983. He left a widow, a married son and three grandchildren. We exchanged Christmas cards in December 1984 and 1985.

the assembly point according to a timetable and we started marching along a narrow road more or less parallel with the sea. The sky was overcast and the night was warm. We could hear the constant sound of shelling from the beach and every now and then the drone of an aeroplane overhead. As we approached the outskirts of a village we came within the enemy's target area and shells pitched here and there with a flash and a crash, but we were a long column and few came very near me. One shell, however, pitched in Bruce's section, and I felt sure that many men would be killed, but luckily it fell in the front garden of a villa, and a solid wall between the garden and the pavement stopped most of the fragments. One man only was hit, but he seriously; his face was in ribbons with blood all over his battledress. Bruce was torn by his natural desire to succour his wounded man and his duty to lead the others. Fortunately there was no lack of men willing to carry the wounded man and the dilemma was solved. (The man was carried for three or four miles before being put in a boat, apparently at death's door. But he survived.) One of the things about Lancashire people is that they are extraordinarily tough. I believe that in everyday life they seldom go to a doctor unless they are very ill indeed and they do not give up work until they are physically incapable of carrying on.

The little town of La Panne was in a shambles, with telegraph wires tangled in the roads and rubble everywhere. The enemy shelling became more intense as we approached the beach, but we noticed that it was in concentrations on the crossroads and not strung out along the streets. By a combination of cunning and luck we progressed without casualties except for the incident I have just described. We went with one file on either side of the road until we came upon a Staff Officer standing in the middle of the road.

"The enemy is shelling like hell where this road emerges on the beach," he said. "You must turn off into the sand-dunes as soon as possible and continue like that." Whether he was out of breath or frightened I cannot say, but he was certainly extremely agitated and it was quickly evident that the advice he gave was sound. We therefore turned to the left, through a blackthorn hedge at the roadside and into the sand-dunes. Here we straggled along like a lost legion. According to the map we were close to the sea. We lost touch with the Suffolks and simply trudged up and down in the soft sand, slipping back one pace for every few paces we advanced.

I put one of the subalterns in front with a map to find the way for all to follow. Then, finding there was a tendency among the men to lie down and fall asleep, I took up a position in rear, at the back of the whole column, and picked up a pickhelve. I used this to wake up those who lay down and to drive them forward like cattle. It was certainly perfectly safe where we were and the chances of a shell pitching in the particular sand-dune one happened to be in oneself was extremely remote. We all just blundered on. Suddenly, and quite unexpectedly, we topped a rise and I heard a curious murmur from in front.

For some reason or other those near the rear began to hasten forward and I in the rearguard, like Xenophon of old, also hurried forward. Eventually rising to the top of the sand-dune I could hear the gentle ripple of the sea and saw the phosphorescent glow of breakers. A murmur went through the Company. "The sea, the sea," they cried and the rank and file scrambled up to their officers and wrung our hands as though we had worked some kind of miracle. (In Xenophon's day they embraced their officers and built a cairn as a monument.) Here was history being repeated for it was curiously like the story that many schoolboys must have flogged out from the *Anabasis*.

The tide was low and there was a wide expanse of grey sand visible. All over the sand, as dense as a holiday crowd at Blackpool, were human beings, dark figures in disorderly array drifting silently along the beach from right to left, that is to the west. It was the remnant of a defeated army at its most uninspiring moment. I halted the Company in the sand-dunes and went down to the sands to try and find somebody in authority. The orders we had been given made no specific mention of embarkation arrangements; they had been concerned more with how we vacated our defences. I had supposed there would be a Beachmaster and an Embarkation staff, but everyone I spoke to said they had seen no such body. For some reason we all spoke in whispers. The Germans, we knew, were very close and somehow the tension of the experience heightened the illusion of their closeness. Dunkirk was a few miles further along the beach to the west and, like safari ants, everyone, by common impulse, walked that way. You could see a few fires burning and a pall of smoke against the sky in the direction of Dunkirk.

By now it was about one-thirty in the morning – I remember looking at my watch – as the drone of an aeroplane became audible. It came nearer, flying so low that one could hear the slipstream in the rigging. It circled and dropped a flare, a red ball of fire below the fleeting clouds. There flashed through my mind a quotation from the Book of Revelation, "I saw a star fall from heaven unto the earth: and to him was given the key of the bottomless pit. And he opened the bottomless pit; and there arose a smoke out of the pit, as the smoke of a great furnace; and the sun and the air were darkened by reason of the smoke of the pit."* As if in answer to the flare from the aeroplane the Germans fired a series of red rockets from their positions inland. The scene was illuminated by flares in dazzling but ghostly light and we all expected a crash of bombs and shells amongst us. A few men began to run and the running was infectious. The whole multitude, many hundreds of men, began to run in futile helter-skelter along the shore. All was confusion and the Germans in the aircraft must have exulted at the sight. But no shells or bombs fell. Presently

* This quotation comes from The Book of Revelation, chapter nine, verses one and two, in the Authorized Version. In *The New English Bible* it does not make sense in this context. It rang so truly in my mind at the time that I looked it up as soon as I got home and recorded it there and then.

everyone was out of breath and stopped running. They shuffled dejectedly instead, still in the direction of Dunkirk.

I watched all this with a sinking heart – a terrible leaderless rabble. However, I also had to run in order to keep up with 253 Field Company and now I exhorted them to stick together as a formed body. I told them to follow me back to the sand-dunes, where we were less likely to suffer any casualties, though God only knew what the end of the whole story would be.

Gradually it became light and there, perhaps half a mile out from the shore, we could discern in the dawn a line of ships drawn up to receive the troops. They had risked the hazards of the sea and the fire of the enemy to rescue the Army. But there seemed no link between us. We then saw at the high-water mark, resting on the sand, a collection of small boats – rowing boats, assault boats, folding boats and carley floats – also all manner of small craft from the pleasure beaches and lidos of Britain. At this point the tide in the Channel runs out at least four hundred yards and in the dark the boats at high-water mark, near the sand-dunes, had escaped the notice of all but a very few people.

We also saw several improvised jetties running into the sea. They were formed by lorries driven out into the sea and abandoned head to tail. I believe these had been made under the inspiration of our own CRE, Desmond Harrison. A cat-walk of duck-boards had been laid along the tops of the lorries. Men, who had been standing in dejected rows in the sea, began to walk along the tops of the lorries. An officer and a sergeant-major appeared and began to try and organize regular queues to get on to these jetties.

It was only then that I saw the officer in charge. In the dark nobody had seen him and nobody knew he was there. Sergeant Powell, who was standing near me, said, "This seems all much more regular, Sir," and so it was. In the dark all had been confusion, but now some sort of cohesion began to be apparent.

I saw 'Tiny' Heal trying to make some arrangements to get his men and the boats together, so as to get men out to the ships. Here we, as Sappers, could clearly help. Sappers are all supposed to be trained as watermen and 253 Field Company may not have been very expert, but they must have done some watermanship training, so we commandeered boats and put Sapper crews aboard with orders to ferry to and fro in a regular shuttle service to the ships. It would be idle to say that thenceforth all was order, because in war nothing happens like clockwork, but we began to make some sort of progress. I told Tom Cochrane to get into a largish boat with a lot of RAMC personnel and try and get them off to the ships. As he got into a boat, to take charge of it, I could see how he hated being in a position to save himself while so many of his comrades had to take their chance on the beach. I had to give him a formal order to quit. His was a fine spirit.

It would also be wrong to say that there were no acts of indiscipline, for there certainly were, and I saw some myself; but these disreputable acts were

54

completely overshadowed by the steady, patient, common-sense behaviour of officers and men in their thousands. I thought the men of 253 Field Company were particularly well disciplined in obeying the orders I gave them. Men took their turns in the queues, the wounded men being sent first, and older men gave their places to younger ones. Morale began to rise.

For several hours this process went on uninterrupted and by 8 o'clock the number of men left behind on the beach was only a fraction of what there had been when it first got light. But at 8 o'clock the ships also weighed anchor and began to steam away. There was an air attack at this moment and some dive-bombers peeled off from their formation and dived down out of the sun upon the ships. I saw one of the ships hit many times and a gush of smoke and flame erupted from amidships. There was first a loud explosion, which was followed by a noise that one can only describe as 'a buzzing sound', like that of a wasp caught in a spider's web. The ship described a circle at a slow speed till she settled with only her masts and funnel-tops showing. Another ship blew up with a tremendous explosion and pieces of her were thrown into the air. One could hear pieces of wreckage hurtling overhead. They must have come a very long way.

Having strafed the ships the Stukas turned on us, flying up and down the beach at four or five hundred feet releasing their remaining bombs. It was most unpleasant for those in the target area, though those a bit further on, under the command of their officers and NCOs, fired back at the aircraft with rifles.

Most of 253 Field Company had embarked before the ships departed and I got Sergeant Powell to assemble those who remained. Bruce Tompkinson and Douglas Murray were still ashore and we counted the party of 253 Field Company, making three officers and twenty-five other ranks all told. I was weighing up in my mind a plan to get back to England simply by rowing there. For the time being, however, I decided to follow the general trend of those left behind and we walked – we could not really march because of the sand – in an orderly column along the beach towards Dunkirk, which we knew to be the hub of the evacuation movement.

We crossed the frontier into France after about a quarter of a mile. There was a pillbox on the beach protected by coils of rusty barbed-wire, with a loophole (unmanned) pointing eastwards. There was also a notice stating that 'It is prohibited to enter France without a passport'. "I wonder," remarked Bruce, "if the Germans will have passports with them." There was a gurgle of laughter from the soldiers, who seemed to be getting back their spirits in a remarkably dogged way. The Germans would be on top of us very soon and the quicker we got to Dunkirk, or made some arrangement for getting off the beach, the better.

In the village of Bray, just east of Dunkirk, there were signs of I Division. I think the troops were from the Duke of Wellington's Regiment, but I am not sure. We collected our party in the cellar of a house on the sea-front of Bray and I bid them sleep while Bruce and I went to see what could be done. Bray was in a hell of a mess. Once it had been a flourishing seaside resort with pretty villas, attractive cafés and little shops. Now it stank of death. Dead men and dead animals lay in the gutters; telegraph poles and telegraph wires lay tangled in the road and many windows were broken. There was a fusty smell of decay, rendered more intense by the sun which by now was beginning to make it very hot.

Bruce and I walked along the promenade till we came to the main access road to the beach from the hinterland. There, sitting on a deck chair, with a bren-gun in one hand and a mug of tea in the other, was Colonel Dan Perrott. He was a Sapper, the Commander of the Engineers' I Division. He had a rasping Irish brogue. He was a great character and later was killed in the Western Desert. There had just been an air raid and about a dozen Stukas had bombed the beach. Dan had not moved from his deck chair, for he was a man of amazing calm. "Young man," he said genially when the aircraft had gone, "I fire a lot of ammunition, but I don't seem to hit much." I could not resist it and said to him, "Perhaps, Sir, it's because you haven't got a game licence." He smiled and said, "Perhaps that is the reason, but they are also out of season."

Adopting a more serious air, he asked me how we got there and what we thought of doing to get back to England. I told him of our state of affairs and explained that most of the Company had already gone, and I asked if there was anything useful we could do, because it seemed to me that I Division must have some plan for evacuation and I wondered whether we could be woven into the plan. Dan was not very hopeful, so I broached to him my plan for "rowing to England". He thought that reasonable and he gave me formal permission to try. I now had a perfect right to try and get the remainder of my Company back to England in this rather unorthodox way.

I was myself a qualified Mate of the Royal Engineers Yacht Club and I felt confident that it would be possible to row the distance to England. I had somewhere about me a quarter-inch map which showed the south-east corner of England. It did not show Dunkirk but it showed enough for me to estimate how far it was from where we were now standing back to England. I reckoned it was about thirty to forty miles*, and the tides in the Channel run roughly east or west according to whether the tide is rising our falling. If, therefore, we merely drifted with the tide when it ran west, and then anchored when it turned in the reverse direction, we should without any rowing at all get a good way to the west. It was clear from the map that we had but to row a few miles to the north and we should ultimately hit the coast of England somewhere near Folkestone or Dover. And there we were and Bob's your Uncle!

* It is actually 38 miles.

56

We returned to our twenty-three men, showed the map to them and I explained the general idea. The fact that Bruce and Douglas and Sergeant Powell, whom the men respected, were prepared to risk taking this chance had a profound effect. I felt sure I had their backing. We kept the men together while Bruce and I looked for two suitable boats. It was not long before we found two good rowing boats each the size of a ship's lifeboat. (No motor boats remained.) These two rowing boats came from Teddington which was painted on the transom of each. We then sent the men into the town to find both food and water and receptacles in which to store it. There were actually plenty of tins of rations to be found on the beach and I suppose in the town we might easily have provisioned our boats with caviar and champagne, but I told the men not to bring alcohol because we would have a good deal to do later on. We discovered in some of the boats (many of which had been damaged by the bombing), navigational aids of various sorts – oars, rockets, anchors and so on. The only really important thing that we lacked was a chart, but my quarter-inch map was better than nothing.

In the early afternoon, probably about 3 o'clock, the tide was nearly high and was not very far from where our two boats were lying. A soldier at that moment appeared, driving a lorry along the beach for no visible reason. All the troops of I Division by then had gone and this soldier appeared apparently from nowhere. I hailed him and asked him what he was doing. He was very shaken and said he was lost, so we used his tow-rope to haul our two boats, in tandem, behind his lorry. He towed them as fast as he could towards the sea. The enemy were by then shelling the beach fairly intensively, and we collected one or two men who were lost. I feared lest the shell fire might puncture our boats. That would be fatal.

I remember seeing a dead Grenadier Guardsman lying in the sand with his boots polished, his battledress creased and his small pack folded neatly on his back. "Must have been a smart lad that, Sir," remarked Sergeant Powell appreciatively, and it occurred to me that in my then rather disreputable attire no one could say that of me!

I was keen to make a move for navigational reasons. The tide would soon begin to run in our direction and I told the lorry driver to drive his lorry into the sea until the two boats behind him floated. We then all got into the boats and I told the driver to drive on until the lorry was flooded with water and we would be ready to start our journey. He did this and climbed into our boat and I made a fresh count of how many we were. We were a party of three officers and over thirty other ranks in the two boats. We were joined shortly afterwards by three more men whom we found drifting aimlessly in a small boat about half a mile off shore. They had no oars and God knows what would have happened to them if we had not by chance come upon them. Bruce was in charge of one boat and I put Murray in charge of the other. I was the Captain Bligh, who sat in the leading boat with a loaded pistol in one hand ready for all emergencies.

From then onwards we began to grapple with another set of problems – the wind, the waves and the tides. Having sought my recreation in peacetime on many a summer's leave 'mucking about in boats', I felt fairly confident that I knew what I was doing. The tide was running in a westerly direction at a fair pace and we were soon opposite Dunkirk itself. It was beginning to get dark at about 9 pm and we came upon two rather more seaworthy boats drifting at large in the sea, so we rowed towards them and trans-shipped. We carried on in the new boats until it became clear that the tide was on the turn. When we were making no more progress in a westerly direction we anchored the whole armada with the anchors and ropes that we had brought with us. We all assembled in one boat and I dished out the rations in the best Captain Bligh style. We had provisions for two and a half days if we used them wisely and I reckoned we should get to the Thames estuary in four favourable tides, that is to say in about two days. With reasonable luck we had nothing whatever to worry about.

The tide turned at about 10.30 and, as we could make absolutely no progress until it turned again and began to run in a westerly direction, it seemed best to settle down for the night and get some sleep. We kept the two boats moored to one another and I told the men to sleep or watch the fireworks over Dunkirk, whichever they fancied. The fireworks were most impressive. There were star shells climbing into the sky; there were fires on land; there were the flashes of bursting shells in the town, and the flash of guns being fired in return. There was AA tracer rising into the cloudless night sky and, to crown it all, there was a tremendous fire burning among the oil tanks at the western end of the town of Dunkirk, with a great pall of smoke rising from them and drifting away towards the north-west.

In order to try and get some sleep myself I detailed a number of men in my boat to stay awake in turn, each for half an hour to watch for the turn of the tide. I explained how, when the tide became favourable, our boats would stream in a westerly direction and the land would appear over the starboard side instead of the port side (only I called them right and left). Soon the only sounds were the snoring of the sleepers and the gentle lapping of the sea on the forefoot of the boat. The cannonade ashore was comfortably remote and I slept till I was awoken by a Lancashire voice.

The tide turned early in the morning and we roused the crews of both boats. Douglas Murray and Sergeant Powell were still in the second boat, Bruce and I in the leading one. First we cast adrift the two original boats in which we had left the shore, and then, having stowed everything in a shipshape manner, we started pulling in a north-westerly direction. I calculated this might land us home on the 4 June though I was not thinking of joining the schoolboys at Eton for the occasion!

After we had been rowing for about two hours we were out of sight of land. We then saw what I took to be a Royal Naval pinnace pointing towards us. The sea was like glass and, as we got closer, the pinnace seemed to be either stationary or moving very slowly for she had no bow-wave. I then noticed a rope, or painter, trailing in the sea from a fairlead in the bows. This seemed to be extremely unseamanlike and I scanned the pinnace with my field-glasses. I then saw she had a white ensign at the stern and a two-pounder gun on the foredeck. There did not seem to be anyone on board her. We rowed towards her and found she was deserted, so we tied up astern and boarded her. We were still drifting with the tide more or less in the right direction, so we started to explore the pinnace. There was a meal half-eaten on a table and food and water in plenty aboard. A Lieutenant-Commander's jacket (RNVR) was hanging on the back of the stateroom door with his name on the tailor's tab inside it. There were many empty shell-cases on the foredeck and some empties from a rocket pistol. There were also a few pieces of army equipment – anklets, haversacks and so on – and an impressive patch of blood on the foredeck. In the wheelhouse there was a signal pad with a half-written signal with the words:

"16.15 hours, in action with enemy off Dunkirk."

There were many charts and a locker full of signal flags with an international code book to help use them. I tried the wheel but it spun round, disconnected from the steering gear.

Soon the Sappers began appearing on deck rigged out in sailors' clothing which they had found below. Without warning the engines suddenly started and we darted forward out of control in a huge circle. One of the Sappers, who was a mechanic by trade, had been fiddling with the engines in the engine room, and had started the diesel motors. We throttled down to a moderate speed and I discovered that it was possible to steer by inserting an iron bar in the rudder-head which was flush with the main deck aft. We accordingly transferred all our possessions from the rowing boats, retaining one of them as a tender.

We steamed for about an hour at a speed that I estimated at about ten knots. The estimate was made in a not very technical manner by dropping pieces of lavatory paper over the bow and timing them till we overtook them in the stern. We were really getting somewhere now and all we needed, apparently, was a bit of luck and the trick would be done. Morale rose rapidly. Presently the soldier posted as a lookout in the bows shouted, "Land ahead".

We all peered through the morning haze at what began to look like mud-flats with trees or telegraph poles on them, not unlike parts of the coast of Essex. When we got closer, however, we found that what we had taken to be mud-flats were the curved sides of two sunken ships, lying close to one another. The trees were the masts and rigging of another ship sunk beyond them. At this moment a box of oranges floated temptingly close and we brought it on board. It occurred to me that there might be survivors in the water too. The Almighty had made ample provision for us and it was our turn now to do something for others, so we started to cruise round the wrecks but found no one.

Out of the haze to the south-east a warship presently became visible. In our simple faith in the Royal Navy we knew it could not be German and after a while the white ensign became visible flying in the stern. When she was quite close an officer hailed us from the bridge. "What ship are you?" he cried.

There was a ribald chorus from the Sappers, who by now were in very high spirits. The Captain of the warship – her name which we could now read was HMS *Locust*, a China gunboat, I believe – must have thought he had come upon a naval mutiny. I was about to explain ourselves and our white ensign when all thoughts were frozen by the sight of a line of aircraft flying low on the horizon towards us out of the rising sun. I counted sixteen of them, all fighters. Most of us grovelled on the deck, adding to the general impression that we were a not very well managed ship's company. The officer on the bridge of HMS *Locust* shouted ironically through a megaphone, "It's alright chaps; they're all jerries." A squadron of Spitfires roared overhead at masthead height. These were the first RAF aircraft we had seen for some days. Little, however, did we know what we owed them.

When the confusion had been got under control, HMS *Locust* came alongside. The Captain, whose name I later learned was Costabadie*, spoke from his bridge. He told me where we were and asked if we wanted a tow. "Yes," I said, and soon we were all guests of Their Lordships. I have cursed myself ever since for this. I ought to have transferred the Sappers only and brought my pinnace home myself with a skeleton crew. It really would have been quite a worthy achievement, but in the first place I was not sure that there was sufficient fuel aboard our pinnace and, in the second, I did not know if there were minefields off the mouth of the Thames. I hardly felt justified in risking even a skeleton crew just to cut a dash with a Royal Naval pinnace.

We climbed aboard HMS *Locust* and our pinnace was taken in tow. The First Lieutenant, whose name I discovered was Holdsworth†, took the army officers into the wardroom where he gave us coffee and the sailors took the Sappers below. At this point my story ends in a most ignominious way, for when I had shaved I fell asleep and I do not know what happened till I awoke in Dover.

* I met Costabadie about two years later at Combined Operations HQ and we had lunch at my Club. I believe he died of TB a few years later.

† I tried to correspond with Holdsworth after the war but I believe there were two officers of that name, and I am not certain that I got the right one. RN Archives later sent me a note on their version of this affair. They wrote us off as Royal Artillery, presumably not realizing that *Quo Fas et Gloria Ducunt* is the motto of the Royal Engineers as well as the Gunners.

It must by then have been about midday. The Captain had gone ashore and a train was waiting. We were transferred to the train and I never saw HMS *Locust* again. As we walked along the platform innumerable kind citizens pressed on us every sort of gift we could possibly want – socks, tobacco, cigarettes and many tokens of thankfulness for the delivery of yet another trainload of soldiers. An elderly lady of the Womens' Voluntary Service said to me, "Would you like me to telephone to your parents?" I gave her the telephone number and by the time we had all got into the train the good lady came back. She said, "I rang up your home and spoke to your father, who gave you his greetings and asked me to tell you that they had almost repapered the whole house."

Such was the worm's eye view of Dunkirk.

EXTRACTS FROM LETTERS TO MY PARENTS

1. *Written from RE Mess, Aldershot, 4 June, 1940.*

   I gather you got my telephone message from Dover Station. You might think, from the reception we got all along the line, that we had won a famous victory. I suppose it will gradually dawn on the generous English people, who greeted us with food, socks, cigarettes and every sort of gift one could imagine, that it was no victory but a crashing defeat. One thing is certain: it was Divine Intervention that gave us fair weather. When I have had time to clear my mind I will write a proper letter. Meanwhile I must tell you of my enormous debt to my Officers and Men. I propose to pray for them every night.

2. *Written from Codford, Nr Warminster, Hants. (undated)*

   Have you been advised to evacuate Woodbridge? My advice would be: Don't Quit! The Belgians and French all blocked the roads, fleeing in their thousands. Now I expect they are struggling dejectedly back again. Put a Red Cross on the gate-post, and take in the wounded of both sides. I don't expect the Germans want to be wounded any more than we do!

3. *Written from an Uncertain Address – probably near Worthing. (undated)*

   We had a Church Parade this morning. The Vicar said all the right things and many of the men thanked me afterwards for having ordered the parade, as they would not have liked to go alone. They are splendid men and deserve to be a splendid Field Company – and will be!

5

Home Defence

After the evacuation of the BEF from Dunkirk, many units, including 253 Field Company, became scattered all over the British Isles. They had been embarked piecemeal in small craft of all kinds from the beaches and landed in many different ports in the UK. In retrospect it seems that the War Office reassembled the jigsaw into a coherent pattern with remarkable speed and precision.

Within a few days of returning, all the units of 3 Division began to collect on the outskirts of Salisbury Plain, every man who required it having been provided with a new set of uniform. I had personally spent two days in a camp in Aldershot where I had been given (free of charge) a new outfit of battledress from head to foot, including shaving kit, a hair brush and a toothbrush. Now for the first time I wore the rather despised battledress.

During the "phoney" war most Regular Officers continued to wear the conventional khaki jacket, Sam Browne belt, breeches and riding boots or puttees (according to their arm of the service). Khaki trousers, or "slacks" as they were called, might have been appropriate for Church Parades, but, as far as I remember, for little else. All these garments the Regular Officer had to buy for himself out of his pay, and most Commanding Officers insisted on their Officers buying them only from "approved" tailors, trading in the county Town or occasionally tailors in Chatham. For many years I bought my uniforms from a tailor in Ipswich,* but this was considered an idiosyncrasy.

* The son of my Ipswich tailor took his own boat from the River Orwell on several journeys across the Channel to the beaches of Dunkirk to bring back soldiers from the BEF. I am thankful that at the time I owed him no money.

Since mobilization in 1939 Other Ranks were compelled to wear battledress and a variety of fashions began to appear according to the foibles of the soldiers' CO.

During the phoney war a circular from GHQ appeared on Briggy's table. It pointed out that the battledress "blouse" was one of the few masculine forms of dress that made no provision for keeping the loins protected from draughts and was therefore likely to be a health hazard in the arctic chills of midwinter in France. The last paragraph of the circular invited COs to collect their subordinates' opinions on these matters. Briggy had not been very interested in all this and had left it to me to provide him with a draft for his reply. I accordingly sent copies of the circular to our Company Commanders, asking for their views. One of them, perhaps mischievously, suggested that "tails might be tacked on to the waist of the blouse, so as to provide warmth for the loins and kidneys of the wearer". It might also, he pointed out, "give the impression to beholders that the wearer was not really a soldier but was a participant in a fancy dress ball". The outbreak of the German Blitzkreig put a stop to all this debate and battledress became a matter of importance to the drill sergeants.

However, now home again in England, we were all more or less forced to wear the despised battledress and the drill sergeants (including those officers with a like mentality) began to devise means of ironing and starching and padding and creasing it so that it lost its only virtue – free movement. They were, of course, quite right – though I did not then agree – because an army that looks like a mudstained militia can seldom be trained to fight. There are notable exceptions of ragged armies fighting well, but, in general, it is unwise to build too much on exceptional experience. When an army is directly in contact with the enemy there are so many vital things to be done with absolute precision that Authority can safely neglect an insistence upon uniformity of dress. Wellington only once issued an order about dress and that was to forbid his troops wearing the uniform of the enemy, and Montgomery in Eighth Army led the fashion himself in unorthodoxy. But when an army is being trained for battle, out of contact with the enemy, an important quality to inculcate is pride in itself. This presupposes a certain degree of smartness in turnout, drill and movement. I was well aware of this in 1940 and at the risk of being thought old-fashioned I was determined to smarten up 253 Field Company.

Our experiences in France had shown me that there was nothing whatever wrong with my officers and men; they were first class material, brave, enduring and easily led. I felt sure that they were capable of attaining the greatest heights. There were, however, certain fundamental weaknesses that must be tackled.

The first problem to be tackled was what in industry is called "absentee-

63

ism". When we came back from Dunkirk short leave was granted to everyone. This, with 253 Field Company, was like releasing the goldfish into the river; the men vanished from sight and I could not be sure if, or when, they would ever return. Hardly a man did not somewhat overstay his leave and about a week elapsed after the official end of their leave before we could muster the whole Company. It was lucky the Germans could not follow us across the Channel. I therefore assembled the Company one day, before paying them, and addressed them straightly on this matter. I explained that some day we should have to embark in ships and sail again to fight the Germans in France. (France had not then fallen.) Before departing I should like to give everyone (say) forty-eight hours leave at home, but if I could not be sure that they would turn up at the end of forty-eight hours I could hardly be blamed for not taking the risk of letting them go. They saw this at once, and I warned everyone that any man who in future overstayed his leave without sufficient reason would be severely dealt with.

Soon after this event a Sapper "Blank" applied for leave, which I gave him, to get married. He returned a day late and Douglas Murray put him on a charge and I heard the case. He was a first-class man and he spoke in his own defence with engaging frankness. (You must remember the Lancashire accent.)

"It was like this, Sir," he said. "I got home Friday night and was married Saturday morning. Sunday I should have returned but I overslept, so I caught the first train Monday."

Forty-eight hours is a short honeymoon by any standards, and even the most strong-minded person sometimes oversleeps. But I had warned everyone that the penalty for overstaying leave would be severe, so with great heart-searching I awarded the maximum sentence I was empowered to award. I hated doing it, feeling as I did so that in his place I might easily have made the same mistake. However, I did it and years afterwards at a reunion in St Helens I had my reward. Sapper Blank and I met, each with a mug of beer.

"That was best day's work you ever did, Sir," he said. "You must have saved dozens of others."

We raised our mugs and drained them. What a generous spirit! And he was only one of many.

The next thing I pitched into was the guard that we mounted. Throughout the battle the guard had seldom protected us from surprise at night, because the sentries so often fell asleep. We could easily have been overpowered in our sleep by an adventurous enemy patrol on almost any night, and in a lesser sphere, too, the whole Company suffered. The men seldom had a proper breakfast in the mornings because the sentry who should have roused the cooks in time was asleep and did not do so.

It is not easy to draw the line between efficient guards and a mandarin approach to guard mounting. I discussed this with Sergeant Powell, whom by now I had made my Company Sergeant-Major. He saw every problem in black and white only. He recommended going the whole hog with guards, ceremony and all. Powell was much respected by the Sappers because they had seen him to be staunch in action and thoughtful for the men of the Company. I left the process of "sharpening up" the guard to him. He soon put things right and thereafter on exercises (and later in action) everyone could sleep peacefully at night, knowing that there was an alert sentry ready to raise the alarm if need be.

Within a few weeks we had been re-equipped entirely. Not only had our personal kit been replaced, but our vehicles and engineer equipment as well were up to scale. The vehicles we had left in France were not, in fact, all regulation military vehicles; many were civilian vehicles – bakers' vans and so on – pressed into the Service in 1939 and taken to France. But now we had the proper complement of military vehicles. The men were much impressed with this and I remember being impressed myself at the smooth way in which the process of re-equipment went. It was extraordinary how this raised our morale. The BEF might have had a beating, but the country was not beaten; we were now "as good as new" and ready for another foray.

It was an open secret that 3 Division was destined for France and we looked daily at the maps in the newspapers to try and guess where we should be sent. In spite of what was constantly said about the vigour of the French defence, I personally felt that the French were a broken reed. I did not much relish the prospect of fighting alongside them again. However, on 17 June we read in the papers that Marshal Pétain had asked for an Armistice.

Colonel Harrison came over with Monty to see us. The Company was paraded and Monty distributed medal ribbons to two or three men whom I had recommended for their outstanding fortitude in action. He spoke to the Company, saying just the right things, and when he had departed Desmond Harrison raised a laugh by remarking; "We are now in the final and it looks like being played on our home ground." This saying became nationwide, but I never discovered whether Desmond originated it himself, or whether he had, himself, picked it up from elsewhere. It would have been quite in keeping with his general character if he were, in fact, the originator.

Now that France had fallen we had two main tasks. First, home defence; secondly, to train ourselves afresh. People often think that there is nothing so good as battle to train an army for war. That is quite wrong. In battle there is little opportunity to correct mistakes; you simply pay for them. Also leaders and specialists go sick, or get killed, or get promoted, and others less skilled take their places, so that although everyone becomes more experienced during a campaign, the efficiency of most of the units taking part tends to decline, unless something is done about it.

We therefore set about re-training. To start with it was very easy. We had a first class Brigade Commander – Horrocks – who knew what he wanted, and we were well enough provided with weapons and engineer equipment to train with.

We had, so to speak, "remobilized" at Codford St Mary, near Salisbury, and we were soon moved to the South Coast to defend the beaches. We prepared the piers of Worthing, Brighton and Hove for demolition, lest the Germans chose to use them for the disembarkation of troops. From there we moved to the Cotswolds, to Chipping Sodbury, where we were inspected by General Alan Brooke who had taken command of Home Forces. I had a new Second-in-Command by then in place of Otto Phibbs who had been taken away to command another Company. The new man was called Rigby Wharton, today the Engineer of a Welsh Local Authority. He drilled the Company in preparation for Brooke's inspection while I was on two days' leave. I returned to the Company about half an hour before the General arrived and we gave him the "Advance in Review Order" and a "General Salute". As a result of Rigby's preparation, and assisted by a fine afternoon, we put on a convincing display in this and other ways. The General seemed impressed. At that time few other Sapper units could do as well.

From Chipping Sodbury we went to Wimple, near Exeter, where an ill-fate befell us. Half our rifles were taken away – I believe for the Home Guard – and it became more difficult to keep the men occupied. You cannot train Sappers to blow up bridges without a considerable area reserved for demolitions, nor can you practice building bridges without a suitable bridging site. In 1940 the various training areas that later became available for troop-training had not been made available. Everywhere we went to try and train we were "shooed" away. "Private Property", "Trespassers will be Prosecuted" were the watchwords. While we had rifles and vehicles we could do a great deal. We could practice the approach march to a defensive battle near the coast; we could practice deploying in a very short time; we could practice the procedure of repelling an invader and following him up, after a victory, to drive him back where he came from. But as soon as half the rifles were taken away from us it was like rehearsing a play on the understanding that the actors would never be required to act it. The whole thing became a farce.

We had to do something, if only to keep the men out of mischief, so we devised the idea of marching into Exeter after the pay parade on Fridays. This was a thirteen-mile tramp and we did it in five hours between 12 noon and 5 pm. By then the pubs and cinemas were open and we released the Company to enjoy the night life of Exeter till 11.30 pm, when we paraded and marched home, arriving at 5 am. As CSM Powell remarked, "They march in on hope and march home on alcohol." Everyone was respectably exercised after this and only minimum duties were necessary until the following Monday.

From Wimple we moved to Bridport where we spend Christmas, 1940. Here we had the task of laying mines on the beaches. These beach-mines, as they were called, were intended to delay the Germans as they crossed the beaches. They were dangerous things to handle and several fatal accidents marred our stay in Bridport. The worst accident involved a number of men and was a direct result of a soldier not doing as he was told. It illustrates a facet of army life that is seldom understood and I shall recite it at length.

The Army is often mocked by civilians and the Press for making trivial duties difficult by insisting on military red tape. The fatuous Colonel Blimp is depicted insisting that coal boxes should be burnished and that the nails in the soles of mens' boots should be polished. I was myself frequently cursed behind my back by the men for insisting on lorries being parked *exactly* where they should be, neither a few inches too far forward nor too far back. "What the Hell does it matter?" the drivers would say, and it was not easy to contradict them. But I knew in my heart that these things were essential to good order and military discipline. Our slapdash methods with parking lorries was the direct cause of serious trouble on the Dorset beaches.

We were ordered to chart a minefield, laid by some previous unit, on the cliffs overlooking the sea. During the morning a Driver X took the haversack lunches for the working party in the back of his lorry to the beach. The orders were that lorries should halt at Point A and those who dismounted should proceed along a marked pathway. Driver X, however, thought this was just red tape resulting in an unnecessarily long carry, so he parked his vehicle a bit nearer the working party than Point A. He then proceeded to walk directly towards the working party. In doing so, however, he entered an uncharted minefield and trod on a mine. He was mortally wounded, though he did not die at once. Corporal B, seeing the accident, ran towards the injured man to help him, but he too trod on a mine and lost both feet. Sappers G and H then ran together to help both B and Driver X. Sapper G trod on another mine and was instantly killed, but H managed to rescue Corporal B alive and reach Driver X who was by then dead. It was no consolation for me, as Bruce and I picked up the bits of human bodies and put them in a sack to take to Bridport, that none of this would have happened if Driver X had obeyed orders *exactly* when he parked his lorry.

I had stressed the need for doing things properly on many occasions and I had stressed the need for giving the reason why whenever possible. But here was an occasion when even that had failed. It was a most distressing event.

Driver X had a brother who came to see me that evening. I tried to say what little I could to console him. I have met him several times since. Time has mercifully healed the wound.

But casualties are not always as bad as that. The word casualty is applied in the Army to every change in man's estate. If he marries, the event is published in Orders as a "Casualty", so that the Paymaster may know to give him Marriage Allowance; if his wife presents him with a baby that too is published

67

in Orders as a "Casualty". So it came about that many quite harmless casualties took place. CSM Powell was promoted Regimental Sergeant-Major and went to 4 Divisional Engineers. Bruce was posted to India during 1941 and I too received promotion and so became a casualty.

It had been a happy, interesting time commanding 253 Field Company. The men were good-hearted, loyal, willing and very patient about my short-comings. That was the main reason why I had been so happy with them. Secondly, I liked command. Command is quite different from anything else. As a Company Commander, under a good Colonel, you have a pretty free hand. You will be told what to do, and perhaps there will be more than can be done easily, so you have to decentralize most things. That means choosing good subordinates. You have plenty to think about and plenty to supervise. A Company Commander is, therefore, busy without being immersed in detail. It is a delightful life and I look back upon my time with 253 Field Company as one of the highlights of thirty-two years of military service*. It was a sad day in October, 1941, that I bade farewell to the Company, shaking each man by the hand and thanking him personally for all he had done. Their inarticulate wishes of good luck, too, are things to treasure.

The British Army is often slow to realize the potential of a new weapon. The British invented the tank and a comparatively small band of enthusiasts demonstrated at the Battle of Cambrai in November, 1917, exactly how it could be used to win a surprising victory. But it was not until 1939–40 that any army made much use of the lesson, and then it was the Germans. The British had no good tanks in 1939, nor any useful anti-tank weapons. It is not easy to say precisely what quality of mind the British Generals lacked that they never saw how fame and fortune beckoned. They must have been blind, and those who led the way with airborne forces in Britain found many blind Generals to obstruct them on that path too.

Exactly who "invented" airborne forces is hard to say. The Russians demonstrated to an international gathering of army officers (including British) that a considerable force could be dropped by parachute as far back as 1936. The Germans used airborne forces with great success as an ancillary arm in Holland in 1940 and they captured Crete in 1941 using them alone. Yet when I joined HQ 1 Airborne Division in November, 1941, as Commander of the Royal Engineers (CRE) of the Division, it was quite obvious that no one had thought out how the Division should be organized, equipped or trained.

I must point out at once that I was not a volunteer. The first I heard about it was in Weymouth where 253 Field Company was stationed. I was told by telephone at teatime one day that I was to hand over the Company to Major G.

---

* The next best appointment I held was three years as Commander of a Gurkha Infantry Brigade during the Emergency in Malaya in the 1950s.

G. S. Clarke RE* and report to HQ Home Forces in London on the following day. Major Clarke had come from Home Forces and knew what job was in store for me when I arrived there, but he was bound by secrecy not to tell me, so I set off to London in ignorance.

I packed my belongings, which consisted of a suitcase and a roll of bedding, and went up to London by train. I had forgotten to ask Clarke where HQ Home Forces was situated, so I took a taxi from Waterloo to my Club, thinking I might meet someone there who knew. In Pall Mall I saw a young Captain of my acquaintance. He had been a schoolmaster in peacetime and now wore the cap badge of the Intelligence Corps. I bade the cabby draw up alongside him and I asked in a hushed whisper,

"Do you know where HQ Home Forces is?"

"Yes," he said cheerfully, "but I don't think I ought to tell you. Why do you want to know?"

I suppose he thought that I wanted to test his "security grading", or perhaps even to ensnare him into some breach of security, for he would say no more. The cabby, however, had overheard the conversation and suffered from no such inhibitions.

"'Ome Forces, is it?" he chipped in. "I'll take yer there right away."

We left my Intelligence Friend on the curb and were soon at a door in Storey's Gate. Here I produced my identity card and signed a book. I asked for the Chief Engineer and found myself bidden into the room of Major-General B. K. Young. He had been my Colonel when I first became Adjutant 2 Division in Aldershot in 1937, and he had no doubt engineered my appointment to 1 Airborne Division.

B. K. Young was one of those solid, straight, conscientious officers that one often finds in high places in the British Army. Academically he had been in the sixth form at school in about 1910; he had a good record in the First World War, winning a Military Cross and probably receiving a wound as well. His service between the wars had been in Aldershot, Gibraltar, Chatham and the War Office. He loved the Army but he had never been to the Staff College. He had a real understanding of the men and was much respected by them. He had been very patient with me, his Adjutant, in Aldershot. I owed him a lot and I was genuinely glad to see him dressed as a Major-General.

First he asked if I knew what I was required for, and I replied that I had no idea.

"You are to be CRE† of *the* Airborne Division," he said, adding that the Commander of the Division was one of the finest soldiers in the British Army.

---

* G. G. S. Clarke won the DSO later in the war.

† A CRE is a Lieutenant-Colonel, whereas I was still only an Acting Major. In a Division the CRE commanded in those days about 800 men.

He was Major-General F. A. M. Browning, commonly known as "Boy" Browning.

"Shall I have to parachute?" I asked rather apprehensively. I had often considered parachute jumping as a kind of nightmare. I could see that if one were in an aeroplane that was on fire one might be glad to get out of it with a parachute, but to jump voluntarily was not my idea of amusement.

"Parachute?" queried B. K. Young. "I don't know. But if Boy Browning asks you, you'll find it quite impossible to say no. Anyway I've told him you're the man for him, and I don't imagine you will let me down."

We then went in the lift to the basement. What a place to find an Airborne Division! Not only the basement, but the sub-basement. We followed a labyrinth of passages till we came to a door that B. K. recognized as Boy Browning's office.

Inside the office sat two officers: Browning and his GSOI, Lieutenant-Colonel Gordon Walch of the Loyal Regiment. Next door was the Chief Clerk, Mr Watson. I made number four. That was the total of HQ I Airborne Division, so I can truly say that I was "in at the start". Now I must introduce General Browning. He was one of the most remarkable men I have ever had the good fortune to meet.

He was in the early forties, tall, thin and handsome, with a healthy outdoor complexion and not a grey hair. His eyes seemed to look into one's soul, taking stock of one's very thoughts. As a young man he had been a first-class athlete and horseman; he had commanded everything in the Grenadier Guards from a platoon to a battalion. He had just arrived from commanding a Guards Brigade Group. In the First World War he had won a DSO at a very early age. He was a man of the world, married to Daphne du Maurier, the famous authoress. He was always immaculately dressed and highly intelligent. He had a presence that set him a head and shoulders above many of his contemporaries and I felt sure that everyone would look at him as he entered a room full of people. He was a stickler for saluting, drill, smartness and discipline, and he made it quite clear that the only kind of soldiers for whom he had any use were those who would go with him in these matters. He was formidable when you met him for the first time, but he had a magnetic charm that was irresistible. It was not long before everyone in I Airborne Division felt that they were in a good formation, led by a man who knew what he wanted. We all felt he would stick at nothing to defeat the enemy and would never ask us to go where he would not go himself. In conversation I never heard him speak abruptly to anyone; he was as courteous to a corporal as to a CO, yet everyone sprang at once to do his bidding and tried to be the first to do it.

A year or so later we had as head doctor in the Division a Colonel Eagger who had been a Gordon Highlander in the First World War and had qualified as a doctor in the 1920s. When he joined the Royal Army Medical Corps in 1939 he had been a successful GP in Exeter. He soon became a bit of an "Elder Statesman" at Divisional HQ and he and I became friendly. One day he said to me, "This General of ours might be hellish dangerous to serve with; he has but to say 'Go to Hell' and all the troops will march there willingly." In this the doctor was quite right; General Browning had us all bewitched. It was he who devised the maroon beret, now worn by airborne troops of many nations. It was he who devised the Divisional sign of Bellerophon riding on Pegasus and it was he who set the tone for airborne troops thereafter throughout the British Commonwealth and Empire.

Now we must return to the sub-basement under Storey's Gate. The General and I looked at one another for a few seconds.

"Where have we met before?" he asked.

Till then I was not aware that we had ever met anywhere, but now it dawned upon me. Seventeen years before, when he was Adjutant at Sandhurst and I was a cadet at Woolwich, I had visited Sandhurst with the "Shop" hockey team. We had arrived dressed in plain clothes to find the Sandhurst cadets on parade under the Adjutant. We should have stood up as the companies marched past, but we lay basking in the spring sunshine on the grass at the side of the parade ground and watched them. The Adjutant gave us a sound lesson in good manners which I expect we all remembered thereafter.

"We met, Sir," I replied, "when you were Adjutant at Sandhurst."

"Ah, yes," he said with a twinkle. "A rather regrettable incident." He held out his hand and clasped mine in a vice-like grip.

Next day we set out in one motor car to visit I Parachute Brigade HQ in Chesterfield. *The* Parachute Brigade – there was only one at the time – was commanded by another remarkable man called Richard Nelson Gale* who looked the complete Colonel Blimp, but he had a mind as sharp as a needle. He was also a shrewd thinker.

While at Chesterfield I met an embryo Sapper unit commanded by a man called Stephen Dorman who comes into this story later. I asked him what he thought Parachute Sappers would do in battle.

"I don't know," he replied. "Nobody knows, but it will have to be done with very little equipment."

When we sat down to dinner in the Brigade HQ Officers' Mess, Richard Gale asked the same question and I gave the same answer, but I was not satisfied with it. It seemed like a glimpse of the obvious, yet somehow I felt it was totally wrong, and I expressed this view also. Richard Gale was silent for a few seconds.

"I see your point," he said. "If it is agreed that the Sappers will never have much equipment, it will follow that we shall need very few Sappers. And that is

* Later General Sir Richard Gale.

certainly wrong. You will have plenty to think about." Here I lapsed into silence. Next day we went to the Parachute Training Centre.

The Parachute Training Centre was at Manchester and was commanded by Group Captain Harvey, with a Squadron Leader Newman and a wealthy baronet, Sir Nigel Norman, as assistants. Nigel Norman was a wartime airman only, but had learnt to be a pilot before the war. Had he been a bit younger he might have been one of the aces of the Battle of Britain. He shortly got command of 38 Wing RAF, with whom I Airborne Division worked very closely, and he came to live with us at Divisional HQ.

My first tasks were clearly to make recommendations for the establishment and equipment of the Engineer component of the Division, and then to get the War Office to agree to them. Having done that the troops and equipment had to be collected and, finally, everyone had to be trained. All this, however, hinged about the answer to the central question, "What do Airborne Sappers do?" And it was to this question that I addressed myself.

"What *do* Airborne Sappers do?" B. K. Young advised me not to put pen to paper in any way until I had a considered answer. My job was therefore to think. I do not know how great men think when they have to evolve original thought, but down in the sub-basement of Storey's Gate I found the foetid air more conducive to sleep than thought. General Browning occasionally asked how I was getting on and I had to admit that I had made very little progress in laying this particular egg.

"Then why not go and do a parachute course while you're thinking?" he asked.

B. K. Young had told me it would be impossible to resist this man, and so it was. Next day I went to Chesterfield for preliminary training – they called it "synthetic" training – for parachuting, to be followed by the actual jumps at Ringway. The whole course lasted about three weeks. Many parachutists have written descriptions of the sensations of a parachute jump, so I will not repeat them. I shall, instead, recall a few incidents that pass through my mind. (Twenty years later I revisited Ringway as a retired officer, and the memories still rang true.)

First I must say that I believe that any man who says he enjoys a parachute jump is boasting. It is a terrifying experience with only one thing to commend it – the elation when it is all over is stupendous. It is something which is quite unforgettable, and men clamour to repeat the experience, though I question if anyone knows why.

I remember clearly the pallid hue of the faces of the parachutists in the hangars waiting to emplane. The colour was accentuated by the neon lighting, but everyone felt just as scared as he looked. I remember the smell of acetone "dope" in the hangars. Aeroplanes of those days – Whitley Bombers they were – seemed to stink of "dope", an aroma not unlike that of fibre-glass in the

72

making. As we loafed about, waiting to jump, we were sick with fright, blue with funk and nauseated by the smell of "dope". I remember the men of the "stick" I used to jump with – four officers (of whom only two survived the war, the other two were killed in action in North Africa) and five private soldiers of 'C' Company, 3 Parachute Battalion. I salute them all.

There was a staggeringly pretty blonde with an estate car who gave us cups of tea in Tatton Park after landing. I remember too the WAAF girls who packed the parachutes. They worked at tables over thirty feet long, on which the parachute and harness was stretched. They worked with incredible speed beneath a notice that read, "Remember! A man's life depends on every parachute you pack." I do not know of any failure that could be traced to these girls.

After four or five jumps I was summoned to Storey's Gate for consultations. In the train I met Vincent de Ferranti who had joined us at Aldershot as a Captain in 1939. Now he was back in industry with his electrical firm. That night I had a room in his suite in the Savoy. Next night I spent partly in a train and partly, by courtesy of the General Post Office, on a sorting table in the GPO in Manchester. The only living souls awake in the station were postmen, who "delivered" me with the mail to Ringway next morning in time for an early parachute jump.

I remember celebrating the award of our parachute "wings". We first entertained our parachute instructor, a splendid RAF Flight-Sergeant who succeeded in infecting us with some of his own enthusiasm. We filled him with beer at a pub at lunchtime and in the evening we turned cartwheels in the foyer of the Midland Hotel in Manchester. The whole thing is dated by the Japanese attack on Pearl Harbor which occurred during the course. We heard about it on the 9 o'clock news in the Officers' Mess. At first there was a deadly silence, then a roar of laughter. What would psychologists make of that? For myself, I believe it was relief. The corner was turned; henceforth we should have a real ally. Russia was too enigmatic. It was "the end of the beginning".

During the course at Ringway many of us had discussed in the Mess and elsewhere the ways in which we thought an Airborne Division should operate. There were two conflicting views. One was that the men should be put down by parachute in small parties to operate behind the enemy lines, in which case the Sappers' task would be almost entirely sabotage, demolition and destruction. The contrary view was that the Division should be landed as a whole behind the enemy lines and operate against the rear echelon of the enemy. If this were the role of the Division, the Divisional Engineers would have to be organized, trained and equipped to do all the conventional things done by Sappers – building bridges, landing grounds, roads; laying and lifting mines; water supply; and, if things went wrong and retreat were necessary, demolitions. Logic led one to the former proposition – small parties behind the enemy lines

– because there were not enough parachute aircraft available for anything else. Military instinct, however, which is quite unpredictable, led one to believe in the other proposition, namely that the Division would operate as a whole or in brigade strength and the Divisional Engineers would have to do all the conventional sapper tricks to help them. In fact, under this code, the only difference between the sappers of an airborne division and those of an infantry division was the manner of their transport to battle. Their equipment would have to be specially designed and light, because of carrying it by air, but their training should emulate the conventional in every other way.

I discussed all this with General Browning. He was determined to overcome all the difficulties of shortages of aircraft. He assured me I was right in the general assumption that we must be prepared to operate as a division, and the Sappers must be organised accordingly. This was a simple directive, and when one considers that it was born in a sub-basement in Whitehall, future generations may think Boy Browning had the seeds of genius.

A few months later a pamphlet was published by the War Office embodying translations of the numerous German documents captured in Crete. The German airborne troops who landed there came, apparently, loaded with written orders, directives, lists of stores and other documents. Although they captured the island, it had been a closely run race and many Germans had been killed or made prisoner in the process. A vast amount of literature had fallen into our hands. From this I discovered what orders had been given to the German sappers before emplaning for the capture of Crete. They had two main tasks: one was to work very closely with the infantry, carrying special devices for overcoming defence works – pill boxes and the like. The bulk of the German sappers, however, were to act as a general reserve for the force. I wondered, as I read the pamphlet, whether the CO of the German airborne engineers had thought out this policy himself or whether he had been bulldozed into it by the General Staff. I thought that I should very much like to meet him so that we could thrash it out together. After the war I did meet him and he told me he had wanted to discuss all this with *me*. His name was Witzig, a brave and competent officer who led the German airborne attack in 1940 on the Dutch Fort of Eben Email near Maastricht. His success here had confirmed Witzig in the belief that "storm-trooping" was the role of airborne engineers. With this I was only partly in agreement, but I should have liked to have discussed it with him in 1942 and not in 1955.

In the light of experience in North Africa, Sicily and Italy, many of us evolved theories of our own on the employment of airborne forces, and my own is to be found later in this book. It was written in Italy in 1943 and I gave a copy to General Down, who then commanded I Airborne Division, and I sent another to the Chief Engineer of Eighth Army. Neither of them was much

74

impressed, but I remained unrepentant to the end. Mainly, I think, the fault was that I never expressed it properly.

However, in 1941, with General Browning's views coinciding with my own, I stitched the coveted parachute "wings" on to my jackets and proceeded to tackle the formation of I Airborne Divisional Engineers. First I had to win the battle about who was to command them. The orthodox Sapper view was that the CRE – that is myself, still only a Major – was responsible to the Divisional Commander for all Engineer affairs within the Division. To that extent I wanted undisputed control of the Divisional Engineers' activities, but in order to save administrative and staff "overheads" the Sapper units would be administered by the Brigades with which they worked. Administration included moving the Sapper units by air – for which I had no staff – and I was therefore prepared to concede parachute training and glider training to the Brigades also. All other training I claimed as my own prerogative. This was a difficult proposition to put before the Staff in a convincing manner, and it had to be convincing because every Brigadier believed that the Sappers were his in every way and that the CRE was a Technical Staff Officer only.

In the early days of the Second World War most Commanders of Divisional Engineers encountered this difficulty in some form or other. Moreover, with I Airborne Division there were only sufficient aircraft to lift a small proportion of one Brigade, so that my "Sapper view" was difficult to substantiate. However, even from the basement of Storey's Gate General Browning wanted various Engineer projects executed on Salisbury Plain at once. I told him that the only way to get them done without argument was to give me full control of all the Engineer resources available and leave it to me. I hold it to Browning's credit that his quick perception led him to agree to this answer at once. I was – in his opinion at any rate – responsible for the raising and training of the Divisional Engineers and must thereafter be allowed to direct their activities. I now had the powers that I thought necessary to collect about me a suitable Engineer component to the Division. I had every intention of letting my Sappers work with their Brigades as much as possible, but, with Browning's backing, I was to be the judge of when it was possible.

In November, 1941, there was a small nucleus of Sappers in I Parachute Brigade under Captain Stephen Dorman, whom I have introduced to the reader already. The intention was to expand this nucleus into a Sapper unit to be called I Parachute Squadron RE, and I had to decide if Stephen Dorman was the man to do the job. I was at once impressed by his sincerity and upright character. As I looked at his open countenance I said to myself, "Here is a man who will work himself to the bone to achieve what is wanted." What I doubted was whether he actually knew enough about the Royal Engineers, whether, in fact, he had sufficient military background to give him sound judgement. He was a temporary soldier, only about 23, and his experience of life was mostly of

75

school and technical school. On the one hand, the conception of a Parachute Engineer unit was a new one to all of us. It also required an original approach, unhampered by preconceived notions. On the other hand, even new problems are often similar to old ones and experience is useful. Stephen Dorman was a well qualified engineer, he had seen active service in Norway, he was inventive, he was enthusiastic and he had absolute integrity. I felt at once that I liked him personally and that is an important point in choosing a subordinate. But by itself it is not enough. Here was a difficult decision, but it must be resolved quickly. He looked me full in the face across the table at which we sat.

"I can see what you're thinking," he said. "You are wondering if I'll do."

"Yes," I replied, meeting candour with candour. "And I want till tomorrow to make up my mind."

"So be it," he said quietly, "but I can tell you this. I know in my own mind that I can raise and train a Parachute Squadron better than anyone else."

He rose from his chair, put on his cap and saluted before he withdrew. I can see him still, tall, clean-shaven, with a freckled face and ginger curly hair. But it was his eyes that struck me; they had in them a transparent honesty that was irresistible. To cut a long story short, I told him next day that he was my man. Looking back on it, I have often thought I decided wrongly.

Stephen Dorman was missing, believed killed, after a patrol in North Africa in 1942 when commanding I Parachute Squadron, RE. He had collected about him an admirable company of officers and men and he had inspired everyone with his own enthusiasm. As an individual there could not be a man of better metal; as a subaltern he would have been outstanding, and as a captain he would have been above the average; but as a major, raising a unit from scratch, it was his lack of experience that hampered him throughout. A small unit like a squadron very quickly reflects the character of its commander, and Stephen Dorman's I Parachute Squadron was always brilliantly amateur. It never looked nor behaved like a good professional, and, against a first-class enemy, amateur genius is very seriously handicapped.

What I ought to have done was to make Stephen Dorman Second-in-Command and put a well-trained, resourceful, enthusiastic, young Regular in command. The unit would then have had the best of both worlds, the professional poise and the streak of genius. It would have been a better unit and would have suffered fewer casualties in North Africa. Perhaps Stephen himself would have survived to rise to a high rank by sheer personality and ability. It is a great mistake to advance a man too quickly, but I did not realize it then. However, having appointed him Officer Commanding I Parachute Squadron I managed to persuade Douglas Murray, whom I had left in 253 Field Company, to join him as his Second-in-Command. So much for I Parachute Squadron. They were a wonderful lot of men.

The next unit to which I turned my attention was 9 Field Company RE. This unit was with an independent Infantry Brigade. The Brigade was commanded by a Brigadier Hopkinson, whom I met in the sub-basement in Whitehall strapped up in plaster. He had injured his back doing a parachute jump. He told me that 9 Field Company was full of men who wished to "opt out" of becoming airborne. They would not have to become parachutists because Hopkinson's brigade was to be a gliderborne brigade, termed I Air Landing Brigade. Hopkinson was of the opinion that the Officer Commanding 9 Field Company was, himself, not very enthusiastic about the new role. At that time no one could be blamed for being unenthusiastic for a novel role that might condemn one to everlasting training without a chance of getting into action. It was a matter of opinion whether airborne was a good bet or not.

General Browning went to visit 9 Field Company near Newbury, taking me with him, in early January, 1942. It was a frosty morning and a guard, blue with cold and tension, was lined up to welcome him. The guard was smart and so was the Officer Commanding. 9 Field Company was a prewar regular company with a high proportion of regular soldiers in it. It had been in the BEF and had distinguished itself in the retreat to Dunkirk under a Major Houghton RE. The present CO had joined the Company in England and, as he had himself been a subaltern in it at Colchester before the war, it seemed a suitable appointment. We went round the billets, peering into cookhouses, stores, latrines and everywhere. It was a thorough-going "London District" sort of inspection. We watched the men at work, training in various ways in the grounds of the billets, and we watched them being served their midday meal.

On the way home General Browning said to me, "What did you think of that lot?"

I told him I thought it a first-class foundation on which to build a gliderborne unit: good men, steady discipline and a long tradition of service.

"But what about all these chaps who want to leave?" he asked. "And does their CO believe in this airborne business?"

I was not sure. The Officer Commanding was certainly a good officer and it is distasteful to get rid of a man, especially when he is a good man. But if he does not believe in what he is doing he cannot pull his weight.

"You've got a good chap there, but he's not happy," was General Browning's opinion. "He'll do very well somewhere else. I advise you to get rid of him and if you want any help just let me know."

The upshot was that I found that a Major Eric Kyte, whom I knew very well, was available and he was posted to the Company. The existing Officer Commanding was posted away and received the news with dignity. The interview at which we parted company was a bleak, correct and painful one. I was beginning to learn some of the unpleasant aspects of command.

Major Kyte was one of the best natural leaders I have ever known. The officers and men became devoted to him; he had brains, enthusiasm and personal magnetism. The list of those wanting to leave the Company dwindled rapidly to five or six men who were too old or not fit enough, and 9 Field Company remained throughout the war one of the best minor units of the British Army. From that day they have never looked back.*

The third unit I had to attend to was 261 Field Park Company RE. This was a pre-war territorial Company, raised in the West Country. The Officer Commanding was a Major Sir John Redwood Bt, and his Second-in-Command was a Captain Chivers, a building contractor from Bath. Quite different qualities were required for this unit from either I Parachute Squadron or 9 Field Company. The main requirement of a Field Park Company was great technical skill and this unit certainly contained many high-class civilian artisans. Moreover, they had always feared that in an Infantry division their skills and heavy equipment might preclude their ever coming to grips with the enemy and this change to the airborne role seemed to them a lucky chance. The men felt that hereafter skilled craftmanship would not be counted a bar to adventure. The Field Park Company, therefore, presented few if any worries. All they required was lighter equipment, if it could be found, and all they asked was a chance to go up in gliders at the first opportunity. Many also qualified as parachutists. Major Redwood was well able to manage these things. He left the Company through "natural causes" after about a year and Chivers was promoted and commanded from then until the end of the war. I was not quite sure that the youthful Chivers would be able to do it, but in the event he did it very well.

While on the subject of forming up the Divisional Engineers I will anticipate and mention the forming of 2 Parachute Squadron and 3 Parachute Squadron.

Early in 1942 2 Parachute Brigade was formed under Brigadier Down, who had formerly been the CO of I Parachute Battalion. This Brigade needed a Sapper Squadron and a new method of raising it was devised. A good territorial Field Company in Northern Ireland was selected and "converted" into 2 Parachute Squadron. Any officer or man who did not like the prospect could "opt out" and go to another unit. I therefore went over to Northern Ireland and had the Company assembled to tell them about it.

I took with me my driver, Driver Lowe, who had come from 253 Field Company. I thought – rightly as it turned out – that he would be a good recruiter. The men were assembled in a dining hall and I told them of the proposal. Following Gideon's example,† I dwelt more on the hardships than

---

* 9 Field Company, under their present title of 9 Parachute Squadron, served with distinction in the Falklands Campaign in 1982, and I met some of them on a military occasion near Bristol shortly after their return. Talking with their officers and men afterwards, I recognized with joy that many of the old virtues, traditions and customs observed in my day were still honoured by the sons, even grandsons, of the men I had known so long ago.

† See Judges VII, verse 3 et seq.

78

the joys. I told them of the discipline required of a parachutist, of the spit and polish, the drill, the physical training, the route marches and all the things most calculated to discourage the faint-hearted. The men listened in stony silence until I had finished. I then told them they could have a few days to discuss the prospects among themselves, but that as a matter of interest I should like to see how they felt at that moment by a show of hands. Almost everyone in the room put his hand up signifying his willingness to become a parachutist. It was a wonderful spirit.

In the event many men had to be rejected on medical grounds, but there remained a first-class nucleus with an *esprit de corps* and a Territorial Army tradition second to none. The Sergeant-Major was a particular character. A middle-aged man, a pre-war Territorial and far too old for the job, he asked to be allowed to remain as Company Sergeant-Major when the unit was converted. With many misgivings I gave the necessary permission and the CSM came over with the others to I Airborne Division in Bulford. He remained with the unit till the end of the war, a most outstanding success and a tribute to his own stout heart. He was a GPO Engineer by trade. Their Officer Commanding was a tall, thin Major from the Territorial Army named Paul Baker. He overcame the "teething troubles" of conversion to the new roles, but had the misfortune to suffer a serious motor accident in North Africa before going into action.

3 Parachute Squadron was raised in the same way from a Field Company stationed in the Midlands. I gave command of it to a Captain Roseveare, who had joined 253 Field Company during the summer of 1941, and of whom I had formed a high opinion. This unit ultimately joined 6 Airborne Division and I lost touch with them, but Roseveare won a DSO in the field in Normandy, so that choice was evidently justified.

Meanwhile we required more officers and men. To get them the War Office sent a circular to all RE units in the United Kingdom inviting volunteers to report at various centres for interview. I saw all the officers myself and asked them all why they wanted to join Airborne Forces. They gave all kinds of reasons. Most of them were tired of training and wanted a chance to fight. They thought that Airborne Forces offered the best prospect. Some, however, were in various kinds of trouble and thought that a parachute jump might get them out of it. Many had an inferiority complex and believed that if they went through the parachute training they would prove to themselves and their friends that they were as good as the next man. One man told me he had been Chief-of-Staff to Franco's main opponent in the Spanish Civil War, and felt his present lot beneath his dignity. When I cross-questioned him about the course of the war in Spain he seemed so hazy about it that I suspected his whole story. I turned him down and have often wondered what became of him. Then there were a lot of men who only came to the interview in order to have a spree away from their units.

Usually I had with me the Officer Commanding the unit for whom we were selecting men, but sometimes I did it alone. Later, when the numbers became too great, I decentralized the selection of other ranks, but officers I always interviewed myself until we went abroad.

The kind of man you want for parachuting is the kind of man that everyone else wants, the man whom Oliver Cromwell described as one "who knows what he fights for and loves what he knows". He is not flamboyant; he is not a thug with knives and pistols in his waist best. He is a straightforward, biddable citizen who realizes that one must accept discipline, make sacrifices and learn the skills required of a soldier. Physically he must be robust, and experience taught us that men of medium height (say 5'10") and well proportioned were less liable to injury than very tall men or very short ones. Fat men were unlikely to pass the tests physically, though many had their hearts in the right place. You want men who have initiative and you can do a lot to foster this by showing that you thoroughly approve of those who display initiative. For a year or so, that is in 1942 and early 1943, it was easy to find good men for I Airborne Division. When we got to Africa in 1943 it was more difficult. The men in combatant units there had seen plenty of fighting and were content to remain with their friends. When we got back to England at Christmas time in 1943 the best type of man knew he was already going to see active service in the invasion of Europe and was not volunteering for further adventure.

In these ways we formed up Parachute Squadrons, each of about 200 men, 9 Field Company RE (Airborne) of about 250 and 261 Field Park Company RE of about 200. Next, we had to pay heed to their equipment. At that time the only way to drop equipment by parachute was to pack it into a light cylindrical container, about the size of a Post Office pillar box, which was dropped by the aircraft from its bomb rack. All engineer equipment had to be no larger than would fit the container. There was, however, the possibility of reinforcing parachute troops with gliders and these were of three sizes. There was the Hengist (replaced later by the American Waco) capable of carrying nine men; the Horsa, a wooden thing whose belly would carry a jeep (jeeps were not in existence in England till late 1942), or about eighteen men; and the Hamilcar, a veritable colossus that would take an anti-tank gun and its towing jeep.

Power tools are always an aid to engineering, so we looked to procuring power tools that would fit into these various carriers. For the Parachute Squadrons we obtained some petrol-driven saws, like the things you see municipal gardners using to lop branches from trees, and some petrol-driven machines that operate a road-breaker on the lines of a pneumatic drill. Both these would fit into the pillar-box-type container.

For gliderborne equipment we relied on the designs produced by Colonel

1.   The Author in 1954

2. The Bruneval Raid: the objective

3. Parachute Packers of the Women's Auxiliary Air Force

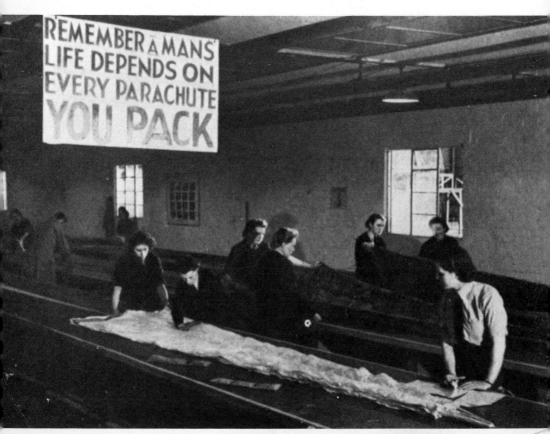

Shorrock, a brick manufacturer turned Royal Electrical and Mechanical Engineer. He designed a series of trailers capable of being pulled by a jeep, each having mounted on it some type of machine-lathes, grinders, electric generators and so on. We also broke down the Bailey bridge into Horsa-loads and I, myself, went aloft in 1942 with the first gliders carrying a complete bridge. We could not get a suitable bulldozer. The firm of Aveling Barford in Lincolnshire made what was called a "Calf-dozer", a small bulldozer that would have suited us admirably, but under some Government agreement they were forbidden to manufacture it for us. We therefore relied upon American production, but only two machines, both tractors without blades, were available for us. For material such as sand, cement, bricks and so on, as opposed to equipment, we decided to rely on local resources wherever we had to operate.

Thus, from small beginnings we built up the skeleton of what I had in mind. One man cannot do everything and, indeed, he should not try; it is better to rely upon subordinates. My main subordinates I have introduced to the reader. I had chosen them with great care and they could be relied upon to do all that was possible. My task was to encourage and help them, and occasionally to inject new ideas of which in those days I had many. Some were good, some were not; but I do not think we let many good ideas go begging. Nor did we back many bad ones. One bad one, however, I forced through against opposition, and I must end this chapter with a paragraph about it.

It seemed to me that our main lack was transport after landing and I therefore conceived the idea of folding motor scooters for officers and dispatch riders, and folding bicycles for the rank and file. The scooters were not really man enough for the work and I shall never forget how, when quietly descending by parachute myself, I saw with horror my motor scooter flash past me at a very great speed, having escaped from the rigging of its parachute. After it had nearly killed me on the way down, I had to carry the carcass across a ploughed field to the road on arrival. The bicyles were good in theory, but, in the event, their transport in England, Africa and Italy by other means – ship, train, lorry, etc – presented 9 Field Company with an administrative burden that far outweighed their occasional uses as pedal cycles. They were, however, quite a feature of inspections by visiting Generals. General Alexander insisted on riding one on the parade ground in North Africa, and HM King George VI was anxious to try one when he inspected the Division in England in 1944. It happened that the road was wet and, as the folding bicycles had no rear mudguard, the rider would get splashed with mud up his back from waist to crown. Somebody luckily remembered this in time and His Majesty was persuaded to take the bicycle on trust without personal trial.

EXTRACTS FROM LETTERS TO MY PARENTS

Written from 253 Field Company RE, Bridport, Dorset, November, 1940

I had a curious experience yesterday. A Sapper brought me a jam pot full of money, asking me to take care of it for him. He had about £30, and I enquired how he got it. He replied without hesitation or shame: "I won it gambling while on guard." Can you imagine *that* in Chatham or Aldershot? I asked if he gambled a lot, and he said: "Oh yes, Sir. Why not? We all do at home."

Written from 253 Field Company RE, Piddlehinton, Dorset, 15 December, 1940

We had a splendid drama over the office typewriter. It was out of order for a long time and I told the Second-in-Command to hurry up and get it repaired. The Ordnance people sent it back saying "Beyond Repair". Then a slick City gent came to the camp to seek business in repairing typewriters. He took it away and was seen no more till the police caught him having sold our typewriter. So we tried again with the manufacturer in (I think) Wolverhampton. After a long wait we had a letter saying it was mended and was coming back by train. The railway station wrote saying it had arrived; and the Second-in-Command sent a driver in a vehicle to fetch it. It was a beastly night – sleet and snow – and I felt sorry for the driver, lumbering off into the night. About 10 pm the police telephoned. The lorry had skidded off the road and crashed into a telegraph pole. "Was anyone hurt?" I asked. "No, Sir", was the reply. "No one hurt. Only an old typewriter in the back smashed beyond hope of recovery". TABLEAU!

Written from RAF Ringway, Manchester, 14 December, 1941

Since I have been up here I have done a course in parachuting of all things! I have jumped twice from a balloon and five times from an aeroplane. The balloon is rather cold-blooded: even at 500 feet you can hear the people talking on the ground. Breaking the rules, I glanced at the countryside from the balloon and saw a fox, and I heard the hounds. Even in those circumstances I thought "Lucky fox!" He was spared the balloon. . . . You ought to see me in parachute dress, with a rubber hat, a camouflage smock and rubber boots. I accidentally saw myself in a mirror and, apart from a greenish-yellow tinge of the cheeks, due to the imminence of a jump, I looked the most ferocious thug I had ever before seen. But when one has landed safely, one has but one desire and that is to thank God.

Written from Salisbury Plain on about 15 January, 1943

We had a quiet Christmas here. But I believe the troops had all the fun and food we could give them. Their Christmas dinners were terrific – goose and pork, followed by plum pudding and a pint of beer each. Next morning, Boxing Day, I took all the RE of the division for a route march across the Plain to work off the effects of Christmas. For this march I borrowed a horse. There is a saturnine old farmer whom I often see riding round his farm. He is always very grumpy when spoken to but no harm could be done by asking if I could borrow his horse, so I went to beard him in his den on Christmas Day. He was sitting like Scrooge in his parlour counting up some coins by candlelight. When I asked if he would lend me his horse he flatly said, "No". However, I said nothing; and he said I would not be able to manage the horse. Later he said the horse wasn't good enough for an officer. Then suddenly he changed completely and said, "Alright, I'll lend him; when do you want it?" I told him 8.30 on Boxing Day, but when I went for it, Scrooge was still in bed and there was no sign of life. So I went into the stable, saddled the horse and rode away. When I returned he was stumping angrily round his farmyard. I complimented him on his horse, thanked him for the ride and asked what I owed him for the hire. He said 1/– for the man who turned it out. When I told him I had saddled it myself he said, "Well keep your shilling and if ever you want to ride again I hope you'll take my horse. You can have it whenever you like." After that he became quite affable in a grumpy kind of way. He said he'd known various military commanders, who had been in Bulford for many years, but the only one he was sorry to see the last of was Lt-Colonel (now General) Wavell. I sent him 50 cigarettes on New Year's Eve and best wishes for 1943; so perhaps I shall be privileged to join General Wavell in Scrooge's list of officers whom he has been sorry to see the last of.

6

Two Operations
1942

The Headquarters of I Airborne Division had not long been established in Bulford before a raid on German-occupied France was planned and executed. At Bruneval, near Fécamp, a peculiar radar* appliance had been seen by an RAF reconnaissance aircraft, and more information was required about it. A conference was called at Admiral Mountbatten's Headquarters – Combined Operations Headquarters – at 3A Richmond Terrace, off Whitehall. General Browning, Gordon Walch and I attended this conference on behalf of I Airborne Division and Admiral Mountbatten presided. An important scientist was also present. We sat at a long mahogany table with the Admiral at the head. Browning, Walch and I sat on one side and the scientist and two or three sailors and airmen on the other. Among the sailors was a young Commander of the Royal Australian Navy, appropriately named Commander Cook. There were also a number of lesser scientists and technical people, some in uniform, others in plain clothes.

The Admiral explained the significance of the strange radar appliance at Bruneval and circulated a number of photographs taken by low-flying aircraft. The apparatus was thought to be used for locating ships or aircraft, or both, at night, using a scientific principle that was novel to most of us. It was mounted on the roof of a small building and consisted of a large black bowl, perhaps four feet in diameter, mounted on a pedestal. Near the apparatus was a white villa such as rich men have by the seaside, with tracks running to the apparatus and to a number of slit trenches or earthworks that were visible in the photograph.

* Radar was still called RDF or Radio Direction Finding in 1942.

The installation stood on the cliffs overlooking the sea, with a track or roadway leading down to a cove between two prominent cliffs nearby.

The outline plan, proposed by Mountbatten, was to drop a party of parachutists near the white villa. Their first task was to overpower the German guard and radar operators. Next, they must remove a few vital parts from the appliance for inspection in England, and, having done so, they must make their way down by the track through the cliffs to the cove where ships would be waiting to evacuate them with their booty and with any prisoners they had captured. He told us that the Admiralty had ships available for the enterprise and that the Air Ministry would make available a Squadron of Whitley bombers from Dishforth in Yorkshire. He counted on I Airborne Division to provide the parachutists.

This was the first time I had been present at anything like this and I soon saw how easily a simple idea can inflate itself with complications. Every member of the team wants to be sure that it is not he who lets the side down and therefore each one deems it necessary to have every detail duplicated and triplicated to ensure against all eventualities. The enemy are also credited with the powers of supermen, whereas in this raid their exact numbers were known and even some of their names. It was believed, however, that enemy armoured cars might make evacuation hazardous and that the ships returning the parachutists to England, if they ever got to Bruneval, would be under attack by the Luftwaffe on the return voyage. It was even suggested that a pocket battleship from Brest might join in as well! Everyone present was keen to make a success of the operation but, had it not been for Mountbatten's firmness, they soon would have made the preparations so complicated that Great Britain in 1942 would have been incapable of raising the necessary resources.

The planning of any operation, however great or small, hinges on judgement. There is no rule by which one can say for certain that such and such eventualities *will* occur, but that others will not. The man in charge must judge what is essential, what is desirable and what is a luxury. He will certainly have to draw the line at a lower level of perfection than many of his advisers recommend and he thus runs grave risks of forfeiting their confidence. Yet it must be done, and the sooner his judgement is established the better.

In this field Mountbatten was a great success. He had been in action against the Germans himself and was not a mere practitioner of theory. We instinctively felt that this man knew what he was talking about. Moreover, he talked fluently and well. He had enthusiasm for the fight; he had a commanding personality and everyone felt that it would be useless to oppose him unless supported by first-class reasoning. He exuded and inspired confidence, and I believe the others at the table felt, as I did, that we were in the presence of a man of considerable stature. It was not long before the outline plan was forged.

The parachute force would consist of about a company of infantry, reinforced by ten or a dozen Sappers as technicians*, under an officer. Another company of infantry would be landed from the sea to secure the embarkation beach, and on this basis the logistics of the whole enterprise were built. A Whitley bomber would carry ten parachutists, and an assault landing craft, of which a few existed in 1942, would carry a platoon of infantry. Fourteen aircraft and five landing craft would therefore be required. The landing craft were so slow that they would have to be brought from England on the davits of a parent ship, fitted for the purpose, and lowered into the sea near the landing beach. Moonlight was needed by the bombers to find the parachute dropping zone and a still night was necessary for parachutes to descend; a moon was also required for the seaborne force to be able to locate the exact beach from seaward. A rising tide was essential to avoid stranding the landing craft and everything must be timed so that the expedition, as it returned by sea, should get within home-based fighter cover before dawn broke and exposed the vessels to German air attack. One of the experts present had the meteorological information available and could advise on times of high water, moonrise, sunrise and so on. It was not long before it was ascertained on which days the conditions of moon and tide would suit and the conference was adjourned with orders to study their particular problems and to report again in three days' time.

As far as I was concerned the engineer aspects of the operation were easy to comprehend though difficult to execute. First, I must choose the right officer to command the Sapper party. (I was, myself, ruled out by General Browning as I was thought to know too many secrets.) The choice of men was limited by the few trained Sapper parachutists who existed at that time – perhaps fifty men in Stephen Dorman's embryo I Parachute Squadron RE. I chose a subaltern called Dennis Vernon, and there could not have been a better choice. He was intelligent, athletic and keen. He chose his own men and I never had the slightest doubts about their ability to do what was needed.

Next, the Sappers had to be trained in the primary task of recognizing the essential parts of the apparatus and removing them. This was, in fact, quite easy to do because the scientists were in no doubt about what was required. They wanted the aerial, which was likely to be a small antenna-like object at the centre of the bowl on the roof of the building, and they wanted the "Cathode ray tube", which was what today we call the "screen" of a a television set, and which was certain to be in the building beneath the apparatus. The technical difficulties do not appear formidable now, forty years later, when everyone is familiar with radar and television. In those days, however, television was a novelty. It had only begun to be available in the Home Counties just before the

* Later it was thought necessary to include a technical Flight-Sergeant Cox of the RAF in addition. He was rightly awarded a Military Medal for his part in the raid.

war. I had myself seen TV near Aldershot in 1939 but the majority of the population had never seen it. The terms "aerial" and "screen", as referred to radar, were mere figures of speech to most people. Moreover, everything connected with radar was secret and it was almost impossible to get anyone to show us an installation, so that we could see these mysterious aerials and cathode ray tubes for ourselves. However, this difficulty was resolved at the next meeting when a Colonel Schonlan attended. He was an important big-wig in the electronics field and he could open the treasure house of knowledge for us. A visit to a similar British installation was arranged.

Thirdly, I had to assemble some suitable equipment for the Sappers. They could not in those days jump with more than three or four pounds weight of equipment with them besides their arms and ammunition. Even the provision of ten light automatics in 1942 was not easy in the Sappers! There existed no suitable pocket container for carrying explosive detonators when parachuting. We devised a cylindrical plastic case that resembled the magazine of a revolver to hold one detonator in each chamber. This later became standard equipment. These detonators were required for mines and booby traps. The mines were to be laid on the road leading to the beach to delay any of the German armoured cars that might be alerted on the first news of the attack. Even one enemy armoured car positioned on the track leading down to the beach would hamper the evacuation and a troop of them might make the re-embarkation impossible. The booby traps were to be left in the intestines of the radar apparatus to add to the Germans' troubles when sorting out the wreckage later. A few burglars' tools – jemmies, hacksaws, files and so on – would be needed to prise open any doors found locked and to extract the required parts from apparatus. Finally, we resolved to give Vernon a camera and some flashlight bulbs to photograph the German radar installation if he got a chance.

Lastly, I was not only responsible for training the Sappers in their technical tasks, I was also responsible for preparing a training ground for the whole parachute force on Salisbury Plain.

The Commander of the parachute force was to be Major John Frost of 2 Parachute Battalion with a selected detachment from his own Company. A Staff Officer from the Headquarters of I Parachute Brigade, Major Bromley-Martin, was to co-ordinate training. Captain Cook, RAN, was to command the Royal Naval arrangements, and Nigel Norman was to supervise the RAF plan. The whole expedition was to be formally commanded by the Naval Commander-in-Chief at Portsmouth, so there was a tangible man in charge with a recognizable chain of command from the brain-centre to the periphery of the organization. All this was thrashed out at our second meeting. A selection of dates was chosen at the same time and training began at once.

The collection of equipment proved a difficult business. In those days the whole British Army was short of equipment and, in any event, equipment of the type we wanted was far from orthodox. Security – or secrecy as it was then called – added to the difficulties. The reasoning was as follows: German agents in Britain might get to know that equipment was being assembled for a parachute raid and they might hear that Sappers were having special training in radar appliances. They might connect these things with any photographic reconnaissance that had been observed at Bruneval and by observing some movement of shipping they might uncover the whole plan. It was therefore deemed risky to put our requirements through the ordinary procurement channels of the Royal Army Ordnance Corps. This was an error in planning, but it was done in good faith. It involved me personally in the details of procurement of all our equipment and I had to chase all over England to collect the various things needed. I only just assembled them in time. Had the equipment been collected by the RAOC, it would have been in the hands of the troops much sooner and there would have been less anxiety about whether the troops would have time to learn how to use it.

Two humorous events arose out of the search for equipment. The first concerned the collection of time bombs. I found that an organization existed, known as the Special Operations Executive (SOE*) which had a small factory in a country house outside London where they manufactured time bombs. I accordingly got permission to visit SOE to collect some of its products. On my way back to Salisbury Plain I noticed a number of policemen at Waterloo Station, including two constables standing at the barrier entrance to the platform of my train. It happened that the Assistant Quartermaster-General of the Division, Lieutenant-Colonel Goschen (later Lord Goschen), was travelling in plain clothes on the same train and we approached the barrier together. As we passed the constable stopped Johnnie Goschen, assuming him to be a civilian commuter, and made him open his large black box for their inspection. There were many apologies by the constables when they found it only contained a duplicator. I asked the policemen why the search was being made and they told me that they were looking for a "man with a time bomb"! I wondered what they would have said if I had been in plain clothes too and they had searched my canvas grip and found it was full of them!

The second event occurred in Manchester. I had to motor to the School of Military Engineering to procure some experimental anti-tank mines, which were light enough to be used on the operation. The SME was then located at Ripon and on the way back to Salisbury Plain, with the car full of explosives, I stopped the night at the Midland Hotel in Manchester and gave Driver Lowe ten bob to get a bus to his home nearby. With a good deal of heart-searching I left the car in a garage near the hotel. Next morning, emerging after breakfast, I was horrified to see fire hoses snaking along the pavements and smoke

* SOE was sometimes mockingly translated as "Stately 'Omes of England", an allusion to the grandiose mansions in which SOE chose to live.

hanging in a pall round the garage. I was in a panic lest my car, with its load of explosives, had been the cause of this conflagration. The consequences of my folly in leaving the car in a commercial garage hung heavily upon me.

"Are you looking for your car, Sir?" asked a fireman, standing on the pavement with a dripping hose in his hand.

"Yes," I replied, and gave its description.

"I think it must have been burnt completely," said the fireman, "for I have not seen it." My heart sank and visions of a court-martial arose before my eyes, but at that moment Driver Lowe also appeared.

"Did you want the car, Sir?" he said innocently, but obviously concealing something.

"Yes," I said anxiously, "where is it?"

"Up the side street," replied Lowe, pointing. "It's all O.K."

The explanation was simple. Lowe had bought some flowers for his mother with my ten bob and gone off to his home in the car, unknown to me. He had overslept and had only just got back. Seldom can a soldier's irregular conduct have been so beneficial to the reputation of his Commanding Officer. Thus all ended happily.

About ten days before the first suitable date for the operation there was a final meeting at Mountbatten's office in Richmond Terrace. At this meeting each of us who was responsible for planning gave an account of his stewardship. Johnnie Frost, who was more involved than anyone else, was not bidden to this conference. (The thought was that the parachutists might lose confidence in the plans if they heard a recital of our various doubts about them beforehand.) There was an elderly Colonel or Brigadier present who was to supply some of the troops going by sea to secure the embarkation beach. He made an ass of himself like this: In a final review of the latest photographs, someone present pointed to an object visible at the foot of the cliffs. He said that it looked to him like a machine-gun emplacement and what was being done to neutralize it? The truthful answer was that no one else had noticed it and nothing was being done. However, the elderly Colonel puffed into his Blimpish moustache and said with pomposity to Mountbatten, "My men won't be put off by that, Sir."

Mountbatten looked at him coolly for a couple of seconds and replied, "Quite so, Colonel. I take it you will be in the leading landing craft?"

The Colonel, who had no intention of being out of his bed "on the night", was punctured and we discussed ways and means of dealing with the supposed machine gun-emplacement. (It was not, in fact, manned on the night of the raid.)

The raid took place on the night of 27/28 February, 1942, and a vivid account of it is given by Hilary St George Saunders in his book *The Red Beret*, Chapter 3. The account describes the many failures in rehearsals, the postponements, the difficulties and doubts that beset Johnnie Frost, and the successful accomplishment of the raid when the time came. For myself, all I can add is my impressions of Johnnie Frost himself, who commanded the parachute force, and Wing-Commander Pickard who led the Squadron of Whitley bombers that carried the parachutists. Both men had exactly the right temperament for war – an intense application to the immediate problems, combined with a cheerful, phlegmatic exterior that inspired confidence in those about them. This temperament is immediately recognizable when in contact with the enemy. It shines like a flame in the dark, but it is not always recognized in peacetime. I can see Pickard now, standing on Thruxton airfield, near Basingstoke, talking to his pilots and crews. The moon had risen and the night was cold. He had his hands thrust into the pockets of his flying suit with his collar turned up. His voice was as steady and his manner as matter-of-fact as though he were briefing a rugger team before a station match. Johnnie Frost also had exactly the right blend of boldness on the one hand, and an accurate assessment on the other of what risks are acceptable. Any men with whom he served always knew instinctively that any expedition with him in the lead would be led from in front. Britain was well served in the Second World War by many men of high calibre in comparatively junior ranks like these two men.*

The success of the Bruneval raid was a welcome relief from the flood of ill news pouring in from elsewhere in those days. The reverses in Libya, the fall of Singapore and a catalogue of disasters in the Far East oppressed the nation. But in I Airborne Division we felt that we alone had been able to give the people of Britain a gleam of success for the moment and some hope of more to come.

By then the United States were properly in the war and there were many Americans in Britain. They brought a refreshing air of novelty to our problems. Whereas British soldiers seemed to see all the objections to anything new, such as airborne forces, the Americans seemed to dwell upon their possibilities. The British distrusted things "because they were new"; the Americans were intensely interested in them for the same reason.

The first innovation the American airborne troops brought was the Dakota aircraft, not just one or two aircraft but many squadrons of them. From these they jumped *en masse*. The British practice was for the aircraft, each containing ten parachutes, to fly in single file to the target, or at most in Vs of three aircraft. However slick the timing, the drop of, say, a battalion would take a considerable period of time. The Americans, on the other hand, flew a formation of twenty to fifty aircraft, each holding twenty-five men, to the dropping zone and 300 or 400 parachutists were therefore in the air at once. Tactically there were good arguments for both methods, but psychologically

* Johnnie Frost survived the war and is now retired. Pickard, alas, was killed before the war ended.

there was everything to be said for the American method.

"Of course," as Nigel Norman put it, "if you have a population of three hundred and fifty million and aircraft galore, you are bound to think nothing of staking thirty aeroplanes or a thousand men in a single throw."

On the other hand, the Americans were green in their training and tactical views. They were also soft physically. I remember the Chief Engineer of an American Corps remarking at a demonstration given by us near Bulford, "Gee, Colonel, if my men were half as fit as your's they would be twice as fit as they are now!"

All through the summer of 1942 we worked and trained in close co-operation with the American Airborne Troops. We all got on extremely well together. On one occasion there was an anxious alert late at night in Salisbury. A fight was reported between British and American troops in the streets. Many senior officers, including me, were awoken. It ended in not too bad a way. It turned out that the battle was not exclusively British *versus* American, as we feared. What had happened was that a joint Anglo-American Military Police Patrol had attempted to arrest a boisterous collection of American Airborne soldiers who were creating a disturbance in the streets. But a crowd of British Airborne troops arrived on the scene and, seeing the American being put under arrest, shouted "Up the Airborne!" and the Anglo–American "Airbornes" combined to over-power the Anglo-American Police. It was all disgraceful, but there was no rift in allied solidarity. Both American and British Headquarters thought it might well have been much worse. Only the Military Police of both nations suffered. They had to turn out twice as many Anglo-American Policemen every Saturday night thereafter.

Shortly after this incident, towards the end of September, 1942, Gordon Walch told me that word had come saying that HQ Combined Operations in London had another raid on occupied Europe in prospect, and that a Sapper Officer was required to visit Richmond Terrace and find out about the requirements. So I went up to London and was introduced to a Major on the staff of Combined Operations. He had been working on the project and explained the idea to me.

Apparently the Germans had commissioned a hydro-electric power station in Norway to produce a considerable quantity of a fluid called "Heavy Water", whose technical significance he either did not understand, or perhaps he did not wish to tell me about.* In any case I had never heard of it before. The power station was situated at a place called Rjuken in Norway on about the same latitude as the Orkneys. The outline of the plan was to fly twenty or thirty Sappers to the target area and land them either by glider or by parachute. They would be met there by a Norwegian agent who was already in England and

---

* The production of heavy water by the Germans was thought to be an essential step towards the production of atomic bombs for use on targets in England and Russia.

whom I met later. He would lead the Sappers to the power station where they were to break in and put the generating plant out of action for a long time. It was thought that there were a few sentries or "security guards" on duty there, but that no serious military attack would be required. Having put the power station out of action the British were to abandon their arms and their uniforms and make their way in plain clothes to Sweden, a neutral country where, at worst, they might be "interned for the duration" or repatriated to England through diplomatic intervention.

The Major had some air photographs of the power station, which he showed me. It was situated on the side of a mountain ridge. Water from a lake on one side of the mountains was conveyed in a tunnel through the ridge, whence it emerged several hundred feet above a river on the other side. At this point the water fell in two huge metal pipes to a turbine house below. Electricity was generated here and "heavy water" was made in a factory complex nearby. Not far from the power station there was a valley with a lake in it, near which the Major's photos showed a frozen, marshy area where gliders might be landed or parachutists drop. It was believed that the Germans were in no way alerted, and that the Norwegian agent could be got back to Rjuken before the raid was due. He would set up an electronic beacon whose pulses could guide the gliders and their tug aircraft to the landing zone. In a full moon it was thought there would be little difficulty in finding the landing zone, particularly with the help of the electronic beacon.

Sitting in the Major's office it did not look an impossible operation, but as the Major unfolded the idea I found myself disliking it more and more. Four fundamental objections began to build up in my mind. The first objection was that it seemed to me an illegal operation of war – the soldiers who were to carry arms in order to shoot sentries or guards and were then to escape in plain clothes were acting more as criminals than soldiers. If they were captured I did not think that they would be treated as prisoners of war. These legal niceties were quite outside my experience but my instinctive reaction was very unfavourable.

"O.K. Sir," said the Major. "We'd better go and see the boss. Perhaps he knows the answer to that one. Meanwhile what are your other three objections?"

I explained my other three objections to the Major. The first was that without knowing any of the technicalities of "heavy water", I doubted whether its existence was of sufficient significance to warrant the risks that would have to be taken. The Major assured me that the existence of "heavy water" was of the greatest significance for the war effort, though he did not himself pretend to know the whole story.

My third objection was that in my opinion the navigational and other difficulties connected with the flight to Norway were far beyond the capacity of the RAF to achieve. In several training exercises I had seen parachutists and gliderborne troops landed miles from the proper place in broad daylight. A flight to Rjuken, across four hundred miles of sea and over the mountains and valleys of Norway, was incomparably more difficult, even when assisted by the agent's homing beacon. I did not believe that any such flight could be done in the dark.

My last objection was more nebulous and ran as follows: Soldiers are required to fight as a body, to support one another and, if need be, to carry on "to the last man and the last round", as indeed they were prepared to do at Arnhem in 1944. Here, the proposal was that when things got too difficult all hands were to throw away their arms and uniforms and flee to a neutral country in plain clothes. If this were to be the conventional behaviour of I Airborne Division, then God help us all! I did not like the Major's project and wanted much more assurance than the Major was able to offer. We therefore tramped along the corridor to another officer. I cannot now remember exactly whose office it was.

A Senior Officer was sitting at his desk working and I got the impression that he was vexed at having to deal with a tiresome and unenthusiastic customer. However, he heard me out patiently and his reply ran on the lines given below.

"Your first objection, namely that this operation is an illegal one, I have investigated myself. I have legal advice from reliable experts in International Law, who assure me that the conception of this raid is entirely legal." He then went on to outline the legal position. He pointed out that all belligerents accept that it is a legal air operation to try and destroy an enemy military target, such as a munitions factory, by bombing it. In this raid we were to destroy the target, not with bombs dropped from the air, but by men landed from the air. So much for the legality in principle of this raid. Next, it is accepted by all belligerents that if an aircraft is hit over enemy-occupied territory the crew may bail out and try and avoid capture after landing. The aircrew, once on the ground, may cast away their RAF jackets and evade capture in their shirt-sleeves. If an airman comes upon a ploughman's jacket, hanging on a gatepost, it is legitimate to take it and wear it to improve his disguise as a civilian. Hundreds of RAF personnel had evaded capture and got to neutral countries in this manner, and probably Germans had too.

"So you see," he concluded. "You need have no fear about the legal nature of this raid. But, in any case, I shall make arrangements for a suitable Legal Adviser to visit your General and speak to any officers or men who ought to be briefed."

He then addressed himself to my second objection. He evidently did not know much about the technicalities of heavy water, but he assured me that scientists of all nations were intensely interested in its uses and it was essential that the enemy should be prevented from acquiring large quantities of it. (At a

93

later date I was introduced to a high-powered scientist who lived near our HQ in Bulford. I forget his name, but he convinced me of the importance of this raid, and I withdrew my objection on this score wholeheartedly.)

Next, he turned his attention to my belief that the RAF were incapable of delivering the parachute or gliderborne troops to the target area. I did not doubt their will to have a try, but I doubted their ability to navigate sufficiently accurately over so long a distance. I offered the opinion that a fishing vessel of some kind would be better, notwithstanding the long trek across country that would be needed from the coast to Rjuken. If a Norwegian guide would risk his life in the project, then that tended to convince me that the risk was acceptable to me too.

I suppose I struck the wrong note in the way I put this argument and he poured scorn on my doubts in the ability of the RAF to find the way from Scotland to Rjuken. He pointed out that the RAF had made successful bombing raids on countries as far away as Italy, and who the Hell was I to question such matters! I said I would have to discuss this aspect of the matter with General Browning and Group Captain Sir Nigel Norman. I decided not to air my final objection at this stage and I left him to go on with his work.

I knew that the Sappers would be as keen as mustard to undertake any warlike venture. We were all thoroughly fed up with training; all we wanted was a chance of action. The same applied to the RAF of 38 Wing with whom we were on very good terms. However, I knew General Browning would not let me lead this raid and I had no wish to launch any of my Sappers into a venture in which I only had qualified confidence myself.

I discussed all these matters, when I got home, with General Browning, Group Captain Sir Nigel Norman and a Wing-Commander Bruce Cooper who was available to attend to the RAF side of the operation. They listened patiently while I unfolded the Combined Operation's plan and we argued without rancour about the difficulties. The upshot was that we must get the best possible information available about all the military, scientific and legal factors that had a bearing on the matter. We thought that in view of the amount of equipment needed for the task in hand we would do better to mount a gliderborne raid rather than a parachute one. It was agreed that 38 Wing should apply to the Air Ministry for at least three Halifax bombers, which had much more endurance than the Whitleys with which they were at that time equipped. Special steps were to be made in picking suitable navigators for the aircraft and I was to select suitable volunteers from 9 Field Company and 21 Field Park Company. From there on Bruce Cooper and I worked in very close co-operation.

Bruce Cooper needs introduction at this stage. He was an able and experienced airman. He had commanded with distinction a Coastal Command Squadron and had gained extensive personal experience of flying over the ocean wastes of the Atlantic by day and by night, out of sight of land, for up to ten or fifteen hours. He was to be responsible for seeing that the RAF side of the operation was properly mounted and he said he would himself pilot one of the aircraft when the raid was made. I had come to know him very well in the previous few months and I had confidence in his sincerity and ability. (After the war it was painful to learn of his death in an accident, when flying as a test pilot from Boscombe Down.)

Here I will cut a long story short. Two glider-loads of men were chosen and trained. Extraordinary enthusiasm was evoked and I have seldom seen men more keyed up to succeed than were these men. Each glider contained a pilot and co-pilot and fourteen Sappers under an officer. The tug aircraft were to be Halifax bombers, in the flying of which three aircrews of 38 Wing RAF were given special training.

On 17 November, 1942, the whole party went by air to Wick in Scotland. Bruce Cooper was in charge of the RAF arrangements. I was in charge of the military arrangements. There were three Halifax aircraft and two Horsa gliders.

Here I must make a digression to tell the reader about some of the RAF difficulties in this operation. The first difficulty was brought about by distance. It was about 400 miles from Wick to the target in Norway. The aircraft had to set out weighed down with fuel to give them enough range to get home again after the raid. Moreover, the gliders had to jettison their undercarriages as soon as they were airborne, to reduce the drag behind the tug aircraft. Even then the aircraft had to be flown at nearly full throttle to maintain height and the engines needed careful handling. However one looked at it, there was very little in hand to allow for cruising over Norway searching for the right spot. Even to hit the right landfall after 400 miles of seaway was not easy in those days. Finally, even in moonlight, it was difficult to find the landing zone in a terrain serrated by mountains and valleys.

There was the possibility of ice forming on the wings of the aircraft or the gliders, or on the tow rope between them. In those days this was always a considerable hazard, particularly in winter. The conventional means of avoiding ice conditions was to steer clear of banks of cloud, to fly round, over or under them. But with the narrow margin of fuel, the difficulties of making the overloaded tug climb sufficiently and to avoid cloud were no easy matters.

From the enemy's point of view, nothing could be an easier target for night-fighters, or even anti-aircraft fire, than a bomber aircraft lumbering through the sky, towing a glider in the moonlight. Even the long daylight flight across the United Kingdom from Salisbury Plain to the North of Scotland with a loaded glider in tow was, in itself, quite an accomplishment and I, for one, was much relieved to find that the airmen could do it. I think they were themselves agreeably surprised.

We arrived at Wick in the early afternoon, though in those northern latitudes the darkness had already begun to draw in. It was cold, grey and windy, and as we circled to land we could see the North Sea breaking against the rocks on shore. A Norwegian meteorological expert who was on attachment at Wick for the operation opined that the next night and the one after that might be suitable for the raid and warning was sent by secret code to the agent in Norway.

Next morning, 18 November, the Met. reported that conditions were improving and that on the following night they were likely to be positively favourable; and Bruce Cooper decided not to attempt the raid that night (18/19 November). The raid, he said, would be carried out on the night 19/20 November. But it seemed to him expedient to make use of the 18/19 November to fly two of the Halifax aircraft, without gliders, across the sea to make a landfall and gain experience. The plan was to hit the Norwegian coast north of the proper landfall for the actual raid and then to fly south to Oslo and drop pamphlets as a blind. This later proved to be a sound ruse because next evening, when the aircraft approached for the raid itself, German fighters were alerted to patrol over Oslo several hundred miles from the actual target area.

Bruce decided to fly one of the Halifaxes himself. The other Halifax was to be flown by Squadron Leader Wilkinson, whom I knew to be a good pilot and who was keen for the operation.* It was agreed that I should fly with Wilkinson, sharing the dorsal gun turret with Sergeant Doig who was to be one of the glider pilots for the raid next evening. He and I had had some instruction as airgunners and Wilkinson was willing to accept that arrangement. We all hoped we might see the landing zone in the moonlight, even without the additional benefit of the guiding radar beacon. The agent was warned to lie low the first night and do nothing till the following one.

In those days a Halifax bomber seemed a huge aeroplane and we in the second flight watched the first aircraft take off. When its black silhouette had vanished into the gloom over the sea we clambered into the crew-space under the dorsal gun turret for take-off. As soon as we were airborne Squadron Leader Wilkinson ordered everyone to action stations.

The view from the dorsal gun turret was a memorable sight by any standards. Above, there hung the great dome of dark blue sky, with the stars and the moon standing out like diamonds set on a velvet cloth. Below, the carpet of clouds looked like a snow-clad mountain range, glistening in the light of a rising moon. Through occasional gaps in the clouds below we could see the sea, with the moon reflected in a silver streak. The aircraft purred with pent-up horse-power and from the exhaust pipes of the four engines there belched flaming tongues of fire. Looking forward I could see the perspex dome above

* Like many other brave men he lost his life on operations later in the war.

the navigator's seat and aft, the rear gunner's turret protruding above the tail with its two black flanking fins. I felt an extraordinary feeling of exhilaration, even as a passenger, and I swung my twin guns round in the moonlight to see that all was well. I had the utmost confidence in Wilkinson, whom I had known of old. He had been an Instructor before the war in the Cambridge University Air Squadron, and was a thoroughly capable man. I did, however, notice that whenever I switched on my intercom to acknowledge some comment from the Captain, I got a sizzling electric shock in the hand that held the instrument and in my head and ears.

Time passed and Sergeant Doig and I changed places occasionally. When not on duty I sat in the belly of the aircraft, only able to see the other people's feet. I reflected on the difficulty of getting out if one had to parachute into the sea and I wondered how long this great monster would float when once it had descended into the sea.* Soon it became bumpy and the aircraft pitched and tossed like a ship. Moreover, on my intercom, I sensed that all was not well. I could hear the Captain telling the Engineer to check petrol gauges and turn certain petrol cocks on and others off. By some extraordinary mischance this was the Engineer's first flight in a Halifax. (The proper man had gone sick at the last moment.) Presently I heard a conversation on the intercom, punctuated by electric shocks, like this:

"Which cock is it, Wilkie?"

"The one by the main spar. Be quick or we'll have an engine die on us."

"Is it the right-hand or left-hand cock?"

"The right-hand one, just behind the main spar. No, not *that* one, the other. And for God's sake be quick."

"Can't get it to budge, Sir."

"Turn the ******* thing the other way. What's happened?"

There was a splutter, the trim altered, and the aircraft began to shudder.

I climbed up into the dorsal gun turret to share the view with Sergeant Doig. I could just get my head between Doig's knees in the aperture of the dome. We were among the clouds and great whisps of what looked like cotton wool surged upon us. We were losing height and I could see that the port-side inboard engine had stopped. It lay inert and dead. I went back to the crew space in the belly and listened on the intercom.

The Navigator and Wilkinson were talking and I could tell that a tense moment had been reached. One engine had failed through over-heating and its opposite number on the starboard side was also hotter than it should be. Two questions were being discussed on the intercom: "Where are we now?" and "What should be done next?"

The Navigator was, I believe, by 1942 Bomber Command standards a well

---

* I was later told about ten minutes, though much depended on whether the petrol tanks were holed or not.

qualified man, but he had no aids beyond dead reckoning and celestial navigation. His opinion was that when we broke from the base of the clouds in which we were now flying we would see the Norwegian coastline at once and then we might charge into a mountain almost immediately. There was not much time to weigh the chances. The responsibility was Wilkinson's and he made up his mind on his own, bearing the responsibility as befitted his position. There was no fluster nor panic; the decision was taken calmly though swiftly.

"OK, Navigator," he said. "We shall turn for base."

I felt the aircraft bank and when I next climbed into the dorsal gun turret to relieve Sergeant Doig I could only see clouds above us and the black sea with its streak of moonlight beneath, and it did not look very far beneath us either.

Presently Wilkinson addressed me on the intercom. "I'm sorry," he said. "We can't carry out the plan intended, but you see the position." I did, and Wilkinson continued:

"We had no hope of completing the mission with only three engines. As it is, we shall have to jettison fuel in order to maintain height and we shall barely get back to Base."

We remained on a razor edge of expectancy and I prayed to the Almighty to give to Wilkinson and his crew the calmness and the skill needed. The prayer was answered and, after a freezing period of flying, we trundled across the Base runway and stopped in front of the hangers. About two hours later the other aircraft returned.

They had done better than we had. They had made a satisfactory landfall in Norway and had flown over the area of the Landing Zone. Bruce Cooper reported that the mountains and valleys in the moonlight looked "like the back of a tiger – stripes of dark and light", and that it was impossible to distinguish one valley from the next. However, he thought with the aid of the "homing signals" from the Norwegian agents on the night of the raid it would be possible to find the Landing Zone. Having cruised over the mountains for a few minutes he had gone on to Oslo and dropped the pamphlets. He expressed a good hope of success on the morrow.

We ate our bacon and eggs – a great rarity in the wartime days of rationing – and tumbled into bed in the small hours of the morning. After breakfast next day, Bruce, Wilkie and I discussed the prospects with the Station Commander, the Met. People, and others.

The Norwegian Met. expert predicted good conditions for the flight in the evening and Wing Commander Cooper confirmed his decisions to undertake the Operation that night. It was agreed that he and Wilkinson would fly one Halifax, while the other Halifax would be flown by Pilot Officer Parkinson RCAF. Both aircraft were reported as thoroughly serviceable. The Glider Pilots and the two RE Officers commanding the Raiding Party were in full agreement. With unanimity among the airmen, I formed the opinion that they were confident that they could get there and back, particularly when assisted by the guiding beacon of the Norwegian agents. Moreover, it had been borne in upon me that if the Germans succeeded in making atomic bombs, that was the end of Great Britain and certain defeat for the Allies. A secret signal was sent by Combined Operations HQ in London, alerting the Norwegian agents for the night.

After tea the time came to emplane. The raiding party – soldiers and airmen alike – were all confident of success and in good heart. I could not help reflecting that I was now in the same position as an Infantry CO despatching a trench raid into no-man's-land, but with more at stake and with much less control over events thereafter. It was not an experience I ever want to repeat.

The gliders became airborne while the tug aircraft still lumbered along the runway. Gradually each pair climbed into the evening sky and circled the airfield. The gliders jettisoned their landing wheels and the tug aircraft set a course over the sea. Only fragmentary signals from them were picked up by the watchers at Base. Only one aircraft – Bruce Cooper's– returned. We now know what happened.

One Halifax flew low, below the cloud base, hoping to climb over the Norwegian mountains as it approached the coast line. In fact it flew into a mountain side, killing all the occupants of the aircraft. The Horsa glider struck the mountain nearby and some of its occupants were killed, others were injured; some were unhurt, but very shaken.

Bruce Cooper, in the other Halifax, flew high and approached the Norwegian coast in clear conditions. It was found impossible to locate the Landing Zone. The "homing device" did not work. Shortage of fuel compelled them to turn for Base. The glider was still on the end of the rope. As they recrossed the coast of Norway they ran into a bank of icy cloud which they could not climb over. Ice formed on the tow rope and caused it to break in mid air. The glider landed on a mountain side and the Halifax returned to tell the tale.

The rest of the story must be briefly told, though it is painful to do so. The survivors fell into the hands of the Gestapo. They were executed in January, 1943, under a *Führer Befahl* (an order from Hitler himself) decreeing that all raiding parties were to be shot without trial. I can understand that many German officers and men might think – as at first I had done – that this raid was an illegal operation. But the decision to execute the participants was not made at a junior level. It was made by the Leader of the German Nation. He must have had the cognisance and perhaps even the approval of many senior German Commanders – including the German Commander in Chief of Norway. He had time and opportunity to consult the lawyers. He must have obtained the same judicial opinion as we did in London. It is hard to forgive these men.

"Operation Freshman" was an attempt to achieve what the experts thought necessary for our victory or even our survival. A second attempt was successfully made some time later by men of the Secret Operations Executive, using a fishing boat to cross the North Sea.*

In 1946, after the war, the German soldiers who had comprised the firing squad that shot our raiding party were tried by a British Military Court in Hamburg. Their defending council, a German lawyer, got in touch with me and asked if I would give evidence in court for the defence. I agreed to do so and was examined, cross-examined and re-examined.

I agreed that until I had been convinced by legal argument, I had some doubt myself about the legality of our operation,† and that I was only prepared to order my men to take part when legality was assured. From this the defence argued that the private soldiers in the firing squad had justification for assuming that before ordering his soldiers to fire, their own officer would have satisfied himself that he was acting within the law. The court presumably recognized the force of these arguments, because they did not award the sentence asked for by the prosecution.

---

* See page 94. But remember that in 1942 all the Top Brass was (rightly) primarily engaged in making successful plans for invading North Africa.

† One of the best accounts of this ill-fated operation that I have seen appeared in the *Royal Engineers Journal* Volume LX, dated March, 1946, written by QMS D. F. Cooper RE. After demobilization in 1946 he went into industry. He became a member of the Gas Council in 1964 and was awarded the OBE for his services to industry in 1978.

7

North Africa

The Allies landed in North Africa in the first part of November, 1942, with our I Parachute Brigade in the van of the invasion. Cynics remarked that "Never in the field of human conflict have so few been commanded by so many from so far away". Stephen Dorman and I Parachute Squadron were among the few and we occasionally heard how they were faring. General Browning and Nigel Norman went to visit them just before Christmas and brought back the sad news that Stephen was missing, believed killed, and that Douglas Murray was commanding in his stead. The unit was doing well and several officers and men had been awarded decorations including Douglas Murray.* It was all distant and fragmentary.

Those of us who were left behind in Bulford were itching to join the Parachute Brigade and get to grips with the war. We lived in almost indecent comfort. Our Headquarters was in Syzencote House, about four miles from the camp, and our billets were in houses about. "A" Mess was in a large house nearby. We had a good cook, ample rations and a batman each, so we fared far better than the civilian populations of towns and cities who suffered many privations and had to endure air raids as well. We were thus spectators of the war, occupying the best seats.

The reader will remember that I had not personally volunteered for Airborne Forces, but most of my companions had and they had done so for one reason only – they thought that it would get them into battle with the enemy more quickly than if they remained with conventional organizations. There

* He was awarded the MC.

was therefore a certain feeling of hollowness in our daily preoccupation of training the troops. The Sappers were apt to ask, "Training for what? Training for Welfare or training for Warfare?"

1942 had started badly on every front. The fall of Singapore in February was shocking and the capture of Tobruk in June was as bad. It is hard to say which was worse – to read of the disasters of our comrades or later to read of their successes without us – Alamein in October and the steady advance of Eight Army into Cyrenaica thereafter. Here was this little man Monty "hitting Rommel for six" in North Africa, apparently without need of airborne troops. And here were we, still training on Salisbury Plain. It was one of the hardest times I remember to keep the men's morale on the top line. Certainly we should have all gone to pieces but for the inspiration of General Browning and the pride he had given us in our airborne status. I remember a demonstration of equipment we gave for an American Airborne Division. We staged it in one of the hangars at Netheravon and I can still see in my mind's eye General Browning standing, tall and erect, beside a short, dark, Celtic-looking corporal of 9 Field Company. They were engaged in animated conversation. Later on I asked the corporal what he and the General had been talking about. He told me, concluding with the words, "He's really a very intelligent General, Sir."

That evening, during dinner, I asked the General if he'd enjoyed his chat with the corporal. The General said he had and added almost the identical words: "He's a very intelligent corporal!" I explained to the General that the opinion was mutual and I quote the incident now to illustrate one of the bonds that united us in Airborne Forces. It comes from officers taking the trouble to discuss things frankly with the men, but it only succeeds when both have the personality to command respect from one another. It is partly a matter of doing the right thing and partly a matter of being the right man.

Somehow 1942 passed and 1943 began. We continued to have hopes of getting to North Africa. Quite unexpectedly the news came. One evening in April I had a telephone message to go to Gordon's Walch's office. When I got there I found he had also summoned Major Bonham-Carter, a doctor in the RAMC, and together we saw him.

"Good news," he announced; and showed as a telegram.

"Lieutenant-Colonel Henniker and Major Bonham-Carter to report to A.F.H.Q. forthwith. EISENHOWER."

Eisenhower was the Supreme Allied commander in the North African theatre of war.

"You must be at this address," continued Gordon, showing me an address in North London, "by eight o'clock tomorrow morning."

Bonham-Carter and I swallowed our dinner, packed our bags and went up to London immediately so as to avoid all chance of delay. If the Supreme Commander had need of us, we felt we must not waste time. Punctually at eight o'clock we reported to the North London address and found it to be a sort of American booking office for service people flying to various parts of the world. An American Colonel was in charge and we showed him our telegram from General Eisenhower.

"Sorry, Colonel," he said, "but there's no ship for you today to North Africa. But if you'd like to go to the States you can fly there right now."

We expostulated on the urgency of our call but the American Colonel was adamant.

"No," he said. "No ship today. Come again tomorrow."

(Ship, in case the reader has not guessed it, meant aeroplane, and as we were greenhorns when it came to travelling on American aircraft the term was new to us.) Next day we reported and again got the same reply.

"Sorry Colonel," said the American. "No ship. There's a long waiting list. Come again tomorrow."

The next day we also drew a blank, so instead of going back to Bulford we went to my Club. It reminded me of trying to get to France in 1940. We sat down for lunch at one of the few unoccupied tables and presently the First Sea Lord, Admiral Pound, came and sat there too. I believe he seldom lunched at the Club, and we were lucky to meet him. He seemed a bit hard of hearing and when I haltingly broached the problem that beset us he merely replied, "No thanks. I don't take pepper."

However, the Chief of the Imperial General Staff had not minded when I had asked his help in getting to the battle in May, 1940, and I judged the First Sea Lord would not resent my asking his help three years later. So I raised my voice almost to a bellow and told him what I wanted.

"Well I don't think we can fit you up with a sea passage to North Africa," he said. "Murmansk, Archangel or Iceland would be simple, but not Algiers at the moment. You'd better have a word with General Simpson at the War Office."

General Simpson was a Sapper and we knew each other by sight. He was at that time Director of Movements or some such appointment, and it was he who organized the dispatch of reinforcements as required all over the world. He was also a member of the Club and I saw him having his lunch at another table.

"Come along to my office after lunch," he said affably. "I'll see what can be done."

Bonham-Carter and I went to his office and it was immediately obvious that he was busy with far more important matters than ours. We waited in an outer office, chatting with a young Major who told us of the difficulties of getting to North Africa. Sea transport went in convoy and their sailing dates were kept under the greatest secrecy because of the danger of submarine attack *en route*. It was quite impossible to tell us when the next one would sail. Air transport was run either by the American Air Force, and we had tried that

103

without success, or by the Royal Air Force who had practically nothing to offer. Even the Prime Minister had had difficulty getting a seat in a bomber to fly to Algiers. The Major saw no hope of us complying with Eisenhower's order. However, General Simpson had one more card to play.

"You might try seeing Miss I over the way," he said, as an afterthought. Civil air traffic was handled in the building next door to the War Office and we duly reported to Miss I in that building. Exactly what her job was I never discovered, nor, I regret to say, can I remember her name. We told her our troubles.

"That's quite easy," she said. "When do you want to go?"

We told her that the sooner we went the better.

"What about tomorrow?" she asked.

"That's OK by us," I replied.

"Good," she said. "Then there's time for a cup of tea."

At that moment an electric kettle in the empty hearth boiled and we all had cups of tea. While drinking it she explained what should be done. British Overseas Airways was apparently still operating a few civilian aircraft and she would book us into one of their aircraft the following day. Meanwhile we should go to the BOA Booking Office near Victoria Station. Taking a sheet of paper, she hastily typed and signed a note to BOA.

At the BOA Office we were met by a male receptionist.

"Where do you want to go?" he asked.

We told him and he did some telephoning behind the scenes.

"What authority have you?" he enquired, looking up from the telephone.

I waved the General's telegram and Miss I's note.

"Miss I's is the one that rings the bell here," he said, and resumed his telephoning.

Presently he put the receiver down with a radiant smile.

"Algiers," he said, "is impossible, but if Gibraltar will help I can fix you up within an hour."

I remember the date; it was 12 April, my mother's birthday.

A map of the world hung on a wall and anyone could see that if we got to Gibraltar we should be nearly there. Besides, as we got nearer the battle I guessed that we might find more competition to get away from it than towards it and our desire to progress towards the sound of the guns might be more favourably regarded. We closed with the Gibraltar offer and we were told to get passports quickly and return, dressed in plain clothes. Miss I knew how to get passports without delay, and a medical friend of Bonham-Carter's lent us each a jacket and trousers. Since clothing was rationed at that time, and could only be obtained against coupons, the gesture was a generous one. (I am glad to think we got the garments back to their owner.) We retained our khaki shirts and collars and in our passport photographs we looked like very shady types of "businessman", which was how we described ourselves.

During the night we went by train to an airfield in Cornwall and next day emplaned in a Dakota belonging to the Netherlands Airways (KLM) with a Dutch pilot and crew. We flew above the clouds in bright sunshine and landed at teatime on the banks of the Tagus. The airfield was crowded with civilian aircraft, including German ones.

After war-scarred Britain our overnight stop in Portugal was like a visit to the Caves of Aladdin. Sweets, fruit, food of all kinds, and drinks were to be had in plenty. Street lights lined the boulevards of Estoril and a polyglot crowd drank Irish whisky at the bar till the small hours of the morning. A flaxen German (100% Aryan) asked me about London: was the Bath Club still standing? He had left his top hat there in 1939. Would it be there still? I hope we were sufficiently sober to be reasonably discreet.

Next day we flew to Gibraltar. Clouds shrouded the Rock and we circled for a patch of blue sky. As we emerged into sunlight a view of the blue Mediterranean, dimpled with surf, unfolded beneath us. Looking out of the window of our Dakota I noticed that into our patch of sunshine about a hundred yards away a brown puff-ball of smoke had appeared. It was followed by another and then a third, rather closer. Gradually it dawned upon me that this was anti-aircraft fire. The pilot must have seen the puff-balls too, and made a diving turn. There was a crash towards the tail of the aeroplane and I thought the worst had happened. But it was only a tin box falling from the rack to the floor. A minute later we were on the runway at Gibraltar. The flak had been fired by the Spaniards when we accidentally transgressed into Spanish Moroccan air space.

In Gibraltar it was pouring with rain and we took a taxi. A Staff Officer at the Garrison Headquarters arranged for us to go to a transit camp nearby. He promised to send us on our way when it became possible. He explained that the signature "Eisenhower" meant nothing; it was merely a staff gambit to give the signal priority. The term AFHQ, he explained, embraced the whole North African continent. We might be required in Algiers, or Oran, or in Cairo. He would make enquiries which would take a few days.

"How will you enquire?" I asked.

"By wireless," he replied laconically.

"Then why will it take so long to get an answer?" I asked.

"Ah," he said, "that is one of the many wonders of science."

It was all extremely vague and when at length our orders came they were vague too. It was not certain whether we were required at Oran or Algiers. The two places were a long way apart (about 300 miles) and we asked our Staff Officer friend which was the easier to get to, for after three days in a transit camp we were becoming restless. "God knows," he said and advised us to go to the airfield and "thumb a lift" in the first aircraft going our way. This was our

105

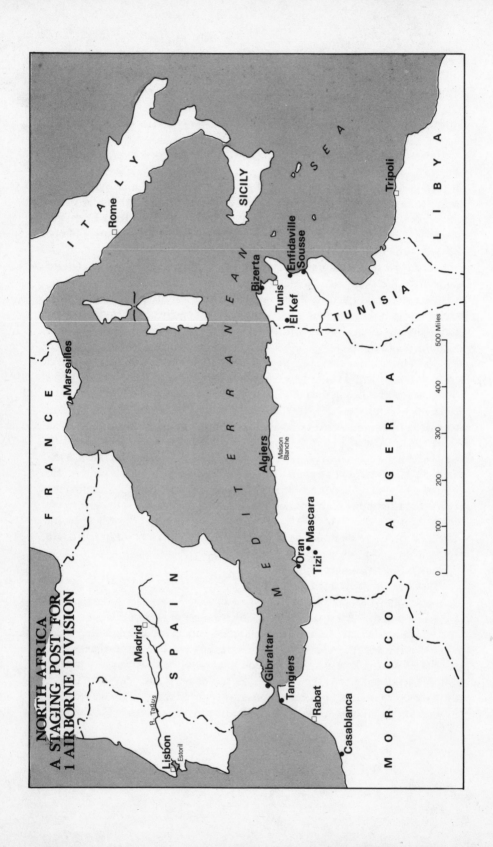

NORTH AFRICA
A STAGING POST FOR
1 AIRBORNE DIVISION

FRANCE

I T A L Y

Rome □

SICILY

S E A

LIBYA

Tripoli □

Bizerta •
Tunis •
El Kef •

Enfidaville •
Sousse

TUNISIA

Marseilles •

M E D I T E R R A N E A N

Algiers □
Maison
Blanche

ALGERIA

500 Miles

400

300

200

Oran •
Tizi •
Mascara

100

0

Madrid □

S P A I N

R. Tagus

Gibraltar •

Tangiers •

M O R O C C O

Rabat □

Casablanca •

Lisbon □
Estoril

first experience of military travel by American transport aircraft in the Mediterranean. We later got more proficient at it.

The proper drill was to go to the airfield with your luggage in your hand and watch for an aircraft whose engines were being started. You then asked the pilot where he was going. If the answer were satisfactory you bundled on board. While looking round the airfield, rather in the manner of a punter at the paddock of a point-to-point, we met our KLM pilot who had brought us out. He had been back to England and out again in the meantime. He agreed to the suggestion that one of his passengers might return our civilian jackets and trousers to their owner in London, and then a young officer of the Royal Navy joined us. He was carrying a diplomatic bag, which he waved in evidence, to London and was looking for a lift to England. The Dutchman offered to take him, diplomatic bag and all, and our flannel "bags" as well. Towards midday we found an American Dakota bound for Maison Blanche, the airport of Algiers. It was nearly empty except for a few passengers and some mail bags. The pilot welcomed us aboard.

Among the passengers was a Parachutist Major, a British Officer working as a Liaison Officer with the Americans. His Company of Parachutists was one of those flown out from England and dropped in North Africa without alighting *en route*. Apparently they had lost their way and found themselves over a deserted stretch of the North African coast. Circling round they saw an Arab on a pony and the Squadron Leader ordered his Squadron to orbit while he landed to ask the Arab the way. Having landed and taxied after the Arab, whose pony bolted in fright, he caught him with difficulty and asked the way to Oran. The Arab is reported to have pointed to the rising sun and said, "Straight on. You can't miss it."

Maison Blanche, the airport of Algiers, is about fifteen miles from the city and our aircraft added another dozen persons to the queue of service officers hoping for transport to AFHQ. Luckily we met an American General who we had entertained in our Mess in Bulford and who remembered me. He was on his way back to the States, though whether he had some better means of ensuring a passage than we had I never discovered. However, he had a staff car and a driver who took us to AFHQ without further delay.

Allied Forces HQ was situated in a large colonial-type house overlooking the city. American sentries at the gate stopped us to examine our credentials and while this was in progress no lesser personage than General Eisenhower himself appeared. He had been on a tour of the battlefield. It was then about 20 April, so the end of the war in Africa was almost in sight. The General had had a long day. He was, however, not too tired to grin at us as he returned our salutes and to tell an ADC to find out what we wanted. It was not long before I found my way to the office of Major-General B. K. Young who had become Deputy Chief Engineer of Allied Forces in North Africa.

B. K. Young was as mystified as we were why we were required at AFHQ, but he promised to make a search while we waited next door. After some delay he called us back. A young American Officer stood with a file of letters.

"Here's the signal," he said. "But the Colonel who signed it and who knows the background story flew to Cairo today. Would you care to follow him?"

"No," I replied. "I'm pretty sure we are required in North Africa. Perhaps the Colonel will by now have gone on to Calcutta."

"OK" said the genial young American. "I'll resume the search."

Eventually it turned out that I Airborne Division would soon be on its way by sea to North Africa. Meanwhile 4 parachute Brigade, under Brigadier Hackett, which had been raised in Egypt and trained in Palestine, was to join I Airborne Division in Tunisia. This 4 Parachute Brigade included 4 Parachute Squadron RE, and B. K. Young surmised that someone must have thought it necessary for me, as CRE, to have a look at them before embarking on the next phase of the war.

Although many aircraft would fly to Cairo, or even Jerusalem, and back within the time available, B. K. Young was of the opinion that it would be impossible to get formal approval in time to travel in one of them. He knew of no better way of travelling than simply "thumbing a lift" in an American transport 'plane. He suggested that I content myself with a visit to 18th Army Group HQ where Brigadier Basil Davey was the Chief Engineer.

"Meanwhile," concluded the General, "you'd better make your way down to the Aletti Hotel which is a sort of transit camp, and we will have dinner there."

This I was happy to do.

Over dinner "B.K" explained what I was beginning to suspect myself – namely that as we got nearer the battlefield the red tape that controlled who actually went there became less dense, and that from HQ 18 Army Group I ought not to find much of it left.

Algiers resounded all through our meal with the din of AA fire and the crash of bombs from a succession of German air raids. The meal was uninterrupted and I look back on it as a pleasant end to a long and tedious journey. (In parenthesis I might add that Bonham-Carter also fell on his feet when he met some big wig in the RAMC at Algiers.)

Next morning I thumbed my way in an American aeroplane to the airfield of El Kef. Basil Davey, the Chief Engineer – or Brigadier, Royal Engineers as he was called – sent a car to meet me and soon I was at the Headquarters of 18 Army group. It was an improvised Headquarters. When Monty's 8th Army from the East and Anderson's 1st British Army and the Americans from the West joined hands, some co-ordinating military influence was essential. There were political as well as military problems. The attitudes of the French colonists, the attitude of Metropolitan France, and plans for future operations all had to be taken into account. Political aims had to be reconciled with strategical ones in order to reap the harvest of military endeavour. At that time there were more British Forces involved than American ones. It was consequently arranged that the American General Eisenhower was "promoted out of sight" as the Supreme Commander handling policy and strategy, and three British officers were made Deputies who actually managed the sea, land and air forces in the Theatre. General Alexander was the Deputy Commander concerned with the land forces and had his Headquarters at El Kef.

I had met General Alexander many times. First in the early 30s when he commanded an Indian brigade on the North West Frontier and was then known as "The Boy Brigadier" because of his youthful appearance. Now in El Kef, when I saw him again, I recognized him at once.

Here I must make a digression to describe our meeting. Due to the American influence throughout the North African theatre of war it was customary to make "banks" of latrines without any partitions between the seats. The users sat huddled alongside one another like owls perched on the branch of a tree. But in Elf Kef I was surprised, on walking into an enclosure behind a canvas screen, to see a seven-seater latrine with one occupant – General Alexander, his red hat on the back of his head and a book in one hand.

"God Almighty!" I exclaimed involuntarily.

"On the contrary," came the bland reply. "The Deputy Supreme Commander."

We lived in tents in El Kef, located in a pine wood high above sea level. The air was fresh and cool all day; it did not rain and there were few if any flies. It seemed a sort of paradise. A conference was about to begin as I arrived. Basil Davey and his Staff Officer, Tony Jacobs, were to attend and they left me with some back numbers of *The Times* to read in their absence.

The object of the conference was to iron out the staff and administrative problems of re-grouping the 1st and 8th Armies for the final assault in North Africa. The 8th Army was stuck at Enfidaville. The Germans held the high ground, a sort of cliff presenting a precipitous face to 8th Army advancing from the south. I visited the area with Basil Davey and anyone could see the difficulty of dislodging the Germans from their commanding heights. The 1st Army and the Americans advancing from the West along the North African shore were also stuck, but they were held up by lack of resources rather than by the terrain. In theory the answer was obvious: to transfer formations from 8th Army sector to 1st Army sector with speed and secrecy. The practical difficulties were considerable – distance, bad roads and the detaching of whole formations of one army from their administrative "tail" and attaching it to another army. There was also a human problem with many unexpected manifestations.

The 8th Army under Montgomery had a *panache* and family spirit all of its own. It had fought from 1940 onwards continuously in the desert, as an independent entity. It had won staggering victories at El Alamein and beyond, and had (in its own estimation at any rate) borne the heat and burden of the war in the Mediterranean. The 1st Army under General Anderson, contemptuously referred to by Monty (according to legend) as "a good plain cook", came straight from England, pampered and untried, and had (according to 8th Army) made heavy weather of their part of the business. To weld these two Armies into a single whole was not a simple problem of arithmetic.

In General Alexander's Headquarters at El Kef were staff officers from both ends of the battlefield. Alexander himself was from the East, but many of his staff (including his Brigadier, Royal Engineers, Basil Davey) were from the 1st Army Front. Staff Officers from the East sat down to breakfast with the *Cairo Times*. Those from the West read the *London Times*. Those from the East went on leave to Cairo, where many had their families from prewar days. Those from the West saw no prospect of leave till the war was won.

I attended a troops' sing-song where a typical scene was presented. An officer of 1st Army was urging his men to be more aggressive in their patrols, to thrust deeper, to find out more about the enemy and to capture more German prisoners.

"In fact," concluded the Officer to the NCO setting out on the patrol, "I'll give you £1 for every prisoner you bring back."

By dint of great exertion the patrol brought back one prisoner and the NCO received his £1. Next evening another NCO was to command the patrol.

"Will you give *me* a pound for every prisoner I bring back, Sir?" he asked.

"Yes," replied the Officer and was amazed when the NCO returned with half a dozen.

"However did you collect all these German prisoners?" he asked.

"It was like this, Sir," replied the NCO. "I found an NCO of 8th Army selling them at five bob each."

I quote these things to emphasize that Alexander's task was not only one of strategy and administration; he had also to fuse two unlike materials into one. The success with which the whole matter was dealt with stands much to the credit of General Alexander and his staff in El Kef.

Such, then, was the background to the task that was in progress when I was there. I lived at the summit and was let into the secrets of the summit. I visited the battlefields and got something of the feel of the thing. I felt quite sure that 8th Army, although they did not admit it, were completely baffled by the change in terrain from the Libyan desert to the hilly country round Enfidaville. I was also sure that 1st Army, though lacking in glamour, was every bit as good as the 8th. All that was needed was someone who could fuse two unlike precious metals into one. Luckily for us, Alexander could do this extremely well.

While I was at El Kef I heard that 1 Airborne Division was now about to arrive at Oran. A glance at a map will show that although Oran and Tunis are on the same continent, Oran was almost as far from the fighting as was Salisbury Plain. However, the arrival of the Division made my presence in El Kef absurd, so I set about thumbing my way back to Algiers and thence to Oran.

On my way back to Oran I was stranded for two days on a US airfield waiting for a "ship" going my way. The Americans gave me a bed in a dormitory full of American Air Force Officers who were very kind and friendly in every way, but I was never more struck than then by the difference in our two nations. Superficially we spoke the same language and had the same ideals, but the similarity was superficial only. I always felt more affinity with a Free French Naval Commander, with whom I could only converse with difficulty, than with Americans, who spoke English. The Frenchman said he felt the same. "We have fought against one another or with one another so often that we have a common outlook on war," he said, and war was our main topic of conversation. On the second day we were joined by two Royal New Zealand Air Force Officers with a Beaufighter that had landed in difficulties. With these two and the Free Frenchman the time passed quickly.

We were all of us interested in observing this American camp from the inside. The food, of course, consisted of American rations, and we agreed that it had little taste and could be eaten without teeth. There was no bone, no gristle, and very little that was harder than a mashed potato.

A crowd of American Army Officers arrived one day by 'plane from an American armoured formation that had disgraced itself in an encounter with the Germans. Apparently the formation had consisted of nearly 100 tanks, all of which fell into the enemy's hands intact without a fight, and many men were taken prisoner. One of the officers who had escaped capture was a full colonel. He felt sure he would be court-martialled and punished severely. He told me all his woes in the most touching manner. I suppose it was protocol that made it impossible for him to confide in his subordinates. It is hard to recapture the atmosphere *now*, but I could plainly see *then* the terrible mental anguish he was suffering. A failure in battle is for any CO far worse than any physical injury. His distress fortified me to ask myself, "What can *I* do before the event to make sure I do not fail in battle as he has done?" The answer was clear. I determined to pray, morning and evening, for stability and good judgement when the chips are down. I wish I could say today that I always did so! The unlucky Colonel left next day. I never heard what became of him, but I suspect that the American military machine had very little mercy on him.

It seemed to me a very rigid machine in other ways too. They had notices in various parts of the camp saying *Speed not to exceed 5 mph*. In a British Military camp no one would be so foolish as to put up a notice like that, because no one would heed it. But when the American Military Police says 5 mph they mean 5 mph, and nobody exceeds that literal speed, not even the Commander-in-Chief.

Though strict in some ways they were lax about security. Before leaving England I had been told of the intended invasion of Sicily. When I was informed about it, I had to sign a paper to show that I realized the secret nature of the information I had been given and that it would be regarded as a court-martial offence if I were found to have divulged any of these secrets to unauthorized persons. The invasion of Sicily had the code name "Operation Husky" and the code name for the Island of Sicily was "Horrified". Any person to whom the secrets of "Operation Husky" had been thus formally entrusted was said in Intellegence jargon to have been "horrified". In this context an American Major, sitting next to me at lunch in the Mess, asked me, à propos of nothing in particular. "Have you been 'Horrified'?"

"Yes," I replied, wondering what he would say.

"That's good," he said. "Then we can talk freely."

He did not wait for me to comment, but at once embarked upon the plan of invasion and recounted his own views on it. At first I thought he was trying to test me to see if I was what he called "secure". I consequently listened without comment lest I committed a breach of security myself. However, he evidently had no such intention and prattled on. Eventually I stopped him and said, "You have told me a lot about these projected operations. How do you know that I have really been 'Horrified'? You only have my word for it, and we were strangers till a few hours ago. Besides, all these other officers at the table must have heard a good bit too. Are they all 'Horrified'?"

The poor chap was most upset. He told me he was an airline pilot in civil life and felt very strange in uniform. He hoped I would understand his indiscretion and would not give him away, which I promised not to do.

The Americans have travelled a long way since then. Even then, however, it was obvious that they really did mean business. The aircraft on the station often returned to base damaged in combat, and with wounded men among the air crew. Some did not come back at all. They did not wince or whine; it made them more determined. And the fact that both men and aircraft were apparently replaced within a few hours left me in no doubt that the Germans would find it very hard to get the better of them.

Eventually I arrived in Oran where I appeared to be the only British Army Officer. The Royal Navy had set themselves up in "Navy House" and I went there to see if they could tell me anything about the arrival of the convoy with 1 Airborne Division aboard. They very likely could, but were not willing to divulge secret information to a stranger whom they had never set eyes on before. Then I had a stroke of luck. I met a Royal Naval Lieutenant in the streets whom I had entertained as my guest at a guest-night in the Sapper

4.   The Heavy-Water Plant at Rjuken, Norway

5. The Primasole Bridge, Sicily, July, 1943

6. HM King George VI inspecting 1st Airborne Division in Lincolnshire, 1944. He is seen here talking to the author and Major Chivers.

Headquarters Mess in Chatham in 1937. He fortunately remembered me and as he was on his way to the harbour we went together and he found the American Embarkation Staff officer to whom he introduced me. From then on all was straightforward.

War has a curious likeness to fox-hunting. "The image of war without the guilt and only twenty-five per cent the danger" wrote Surtees on fox-hunting. (Had he lived in our generation he would have specified five and not twenty-five per cent.) In both war and fox-hunting you get into difficulties; you get lost, misled and frustrated. You get bored or excited, and frightened. You certainly get tired, even exhausted, and then it is easy to "give up". In fox-hunting you turn for home and miss the hunt of a lifetime, just through lack of grit. In war you get killed or captured through not standing fast to the end. If in fox-hunting you keep plodding on, using your eyes and ears, your luck usually turns. You round a bend in a lane and stumble upon hounds. In the twinkling of an eye you are on terms with the hounds and up with the huntsman. So it is in war; you must keep persevering. I had been stumbling aimlessly about Africa, lost, frustrated and despondent, but now, suddenly and unexpectedly, I rounded a bend and there lay four or five troopships about to tie up to the quayside, with hundreds of British soldiers lining the rails. I was back with 1 Airborne Division.

It was not the whole Division, but only part of it: 2 Parachute Brigade and some Divisional troops, including 9 Field Company and 261 Field Park Company. The rest of the Division was following in another convoy. There was plenty to do. The imminent disembarkation of these troops, several thousand men, had been kept such a secret that the American Headquarters in Oran had made no preparations whatever for their reception. They had, however, prepared to receive about 20,000 German prisoners of war, who had yet to be captured. We were told to make the best of the PoW cages. Brigadier Down, who was in command of the Brigade Group, might easily have taken offence at his beloved brigade being put behind bars, but he had the good sense to see there was no alternative and everyone took their cue from him.

Lack of transport was our first trouble. An airborne division never had very much transport, but what we had was in a convoy of freight ships that was not expected for several days. Brigadier Down, with his Deputy Assistant Quartermaster-General and I, called on the American Headquarters and met a Colonel-in-Charge.

"How much transportation do you want?" he asked. The DAQMG had a list of minimum requirements ready and produced it. The American looked at it for a minute in silence and I wondered what he would say.

"I reckon we could double that without it's being missed. Have you got the drivers?" he asked.

We had the drivers disembarking in the docks at that very moment. It was not long before the Brigade Group was fitted out with brand new American lorries in sufficient numbers to transport officers and men, except for a small party left to guard the baggage. We motored that afternoon to the prisoner-of-war camps allotted to us at a place called Tizi, some eighty kilometers inland.

Tizi was a small Arab village built of mud bricks on the edge of the Sahara; there was a sign post saying "Timbuctoo 1,800 kms". A vast PoW camp was set out in rectangles of barbed wire under the slopes of some rising ground. All was barren and sandy in colour. There was a guard hut, a flagpole with the Stars and Stripes and a few tents for the American guard company, some cooking apparatus in each cage and a row of bucket latrines. Each cage was intended for 1,000 men, one allotted to officers, another to warrant officers and sergeants, and the remaining cages to the rank and file. In a PoW camp you do not want to build up regimental *esprit de corps*; rather the reverse, you want to break up the organization so that the prisoners are more easy to manage. When treated as mere numbers they cease to be fighting units. The arrangement in Tizi had not been intended for preparing men for battle, but it was the best that could be done for us.

I went back to Oran next day to see the American Chief of the Service of Supplies to see what could be done about getting tools and materials from which we could make ablution benches, latrine shelters, grease traps, meat safes and all the paraphernalia of a camp in a hot climate. The Chief of the Service of Supplies was a tight-lipped tycoon with pince-nez glasses.

"Where is your *skedool* of requirements?" he asked. I showed him the rough notes I had prepared as a basis for argument, but as I had not the slightest idea what was available, whether it would be in the form of ready-made camp structures, or simply piles of timber, my lists were in outline only.

"That's no good here," said the tycoon. "You must get a regular *skedool*, giving every detail of what you want. If I approve the *skedool* you'll have what you require. Otherwise nothing doing."

"And bring it to me by midday tomorrow," he continued. "I leave for Algiers in the evening and except for me no one can approve it."

He was uncompromising and it was evident that we must make out a schedule of requirements as fast as possible.

We motored home and in the blazing afternoon sun my Field Engineer and I proceeded to make out a schedule of requirements of tools and materials. It looked like a mammoth American tennis tournament score sheet. Across the top was a list of items – nails, screws, sheets of corrugated iron and pieces of wood of various sizes. Down the left-hand side of the sheet was a list of structures, for each of which the material was wanted. By a feat of guesswork, judgement and arithmetic we made out a list of requirements covering several sheets of foolscap, and Sergeant Cooper, our HQ RE Sergeant, skilfully turned

114

it into a comprehensible Schedule of Requirements before nightfall.

That night it rained. It did not often rain in Tizi but when it did it pelted. The PoW camp had been sited in a slight hollow; when it rained the camp became the resevoir of a large catchment area. Everything was swamped. Rain water lapped the camp beds of those lucky enough to have them and the bedding of the rest got sodden in a few minutes. Boots, socks and clothing floated everywhere in a sea of mud; floating in it too was our precious *skedool*. When daylight came the rain had ceased, a bright sun shone to dry the scene, but the schedule had vanished. The typewriter, also, had mud in its intestines. It was a long drive to Oran and to have a replica of the schedule there by noon was next to impossible. There was only one course open: we dictated from memory a new schedule, much abbreviated, on to a few sheets of paper only – to be typed on the American typewriter in the guard house. It was done entirely by guesswork and memory. Even the addition of the figures in each column was approximate only. It was not worth the paper it was written on – not a single sheet! However, Sergeant Cooper gave it a magnificent cover-sheet to look like a Director's Annual Report and I took it to the Chief of the Service of Supplies in Oran.

The tycoon glanced at it.

"You sure have done a good job here," he said. "I wish our engineers could do that too. I approve the *skedool*."

He signed the list and gave it back. From then on lorries ran to and fro between Tizi and Oran, collecting all manner of tools, lumber, dunnage and building material generally. The Service of Supplies seemed far easier to cope with than any Royal Engineers' stores organization!

Here I must digress to say that there are two approaches to the handling of stores. You can cut the supply down to a minimum and then, with many clerks, control what you have. That was the British Army practice. Or you can supply great quantities of everything and then you hardly need to employ any controllers at all. That is the American system. The most economical in men and means probably lies between the two, but I would think that the nearer it can be made to the American system the better it is for everyone.

We worked hard in the Tizi area, preparing our camp structures, but men must have some free time and on Saturday afternoons many soldiers were sent into Oran in our transport. Though better than nothing, Oran was not a very exciting city and fell far short of the delights of Liverpool or Glasgow for which the troops hankered. But compared with Tizi it was paradise. In Tizi of a Saturday night one would see perhaps a thousand men surging to and fro along the one road that passed through the few dozen houses that constituted the village. We are told in the Book of Joshua that there was a harlot in Jericho, and possibly there was more than one in Tizi, but not many. Some of the soldiery, maddened by Algerian wine (which was both cheap and potent), may perhaps be pardoned for a certain amount of rough behaviour.

The detailed plans for the invasion of Sicily had not yet been agreed by the Commanders who would have to put them into operation. Those Commanders were still fighting the enemy in North Africa. But in 1 Airborne Division we were all quite sure what our roll would be in a general kind of way. We saw we would have to seize key defence works in the beach-head area and we might have to capture particular defiles, such as road bridges not far inland.

We had practiced all this in England before we left and an agreed stratagem had been worked out. The stratagem was as follows: first a small airborne force, which we called a *coup de main** party, must be landed by parachute or glider as close to the objective as possible, in order to seize it by surprise and stealth. If the objective were guns they were to be put out of action by firing a demolition charge in the barrel, after which they could be abandoned. If it were a bridge, the demolition arrangements prepared by the enemy must be removed or neutralized at once and more airborne troops must be landed as quickly as possible to reinforce the *coup de main* party so as to thwart the enemy's attempts to recapture the objective. The contest thus became a race: who would build up his strength on the objective first, the allied attackers or the enemy counter-attackers?

We held a number of exercises in the Tizi area, both with and without aircraft, to practice all this, and in the process two unforeseen factors became evident. The first was that the American gliders (called WACOs) which had been brought from the States in packing cases, would not be assembled in time unless urgent steps were taken. Secondly, the inaccuracy of the American pilots' navigation gave cause for misgivings. There was not much the Sappers could do about the navigation, but we could, I thought, do something to accelerate the assembly of the WACO gliders.

It did not seem reasonable to call upon the Sappers of the Parachute Squadrons – who would never use the WACOs – to help assemble them, but 9 Field Company and 261 Field Park Company seemed to me a reasonable proposition. But before proposing this to the Staff I consulted the OC of 9 Field Company.

I ought to have mentioned earlier that Major Eric Kyte had been whisked away from 9 Field Company a few weeks before we left for North Africa and I was told that I would have to replace him by a promotion from within my own command. The man I chose was his Second-in-Command, Captain Basil Beasley. He was young and inexperienced as a soldier, but he had a lot in his favour. In the first place he was an excellent practical engineer. He had served an apprenticeship with the General Electric Company and when war broke out

* I claim to have suggested this nomenclature at HQ 1 Airborne Division in Bulford, and I still think it a good one. I wonder whether it is still in use.

he was employed by the same organization as a qualified engineer, but had joined up at once. He had been an enthusiastic young platoon commander and Second-in-Command of 9 Field Company, but that is quite different from the wider view necessary in a Field Company Commander. However, he turned up trumps over assembling WACO gliders. He might so easily have shown some reluctance to take on a task like this, and, considering what a responsible task it was likely to be, it would not have been easy for me to force him into it. Suppose he had said, "No, Sir, I can't be responsible for an undertaking like this. I've never seen a WACO glider. I have no notion whether we could handle the tools or find the tradesmen required for the job. I will, of course, have a try if ordered, but I cannot be responsible for the result!" Instead, he said something like this: "Yes, Sir. Certainly we'll do it. We shall at least know that the gliders are properly bolted together." So that is what happened.

A platoon of 9 Field Company RE, under an officer called Roger Binyon (a relative of the poet), with some craftsmen from the Field Park company, was sent down to Oran to assemble WACO gliders under American supervision. Binyon had a flair for mass production and soon had an efficient production line going. But the Americans were not to be out-done by the Limeys and flew from America experienced gangs of fitters and riggers. Together, they soon got the matter in hand. However, the Sappers made quite a notable, though hitherto unrecorded, contribution. Alas, Roger Binyon was later killed at Arnhem.

Beasley did another rather remarkable job while we were still in the desert camps near Tizi. The camps were primitive and the only electric light available was provided by a few petrol-driven generators. These gave sufficient light for a few offices, guardrooms and so on, but none for messes, cook houses or any kind of recreation. Yet, striding across the vast expanse of desert, was an endless range of tall pylons, bearing notices in French and Arabic of *Danger de Mort, 33,000 volts**. I happened to remark to Beasley that it seemed ironical for us to sit in the dark when there was an almost unlimited supply of kilowatts in the cables overhead.

With his GEC training, this put Beasley on his mettle and he gave me a technical dissertation on what ought to be done. The upshot was that he and I went down to Oran and succeeded in running to ground the civilian boss of the French North African electricity enterprise, whose authority held sway over an area of prodigious size. He was at his private house, enjoying the shade from the burning sun during the hour of the siesta, and with schoolboy French and Beasley's professional know-how we made our request. He was a man of good sense and liberal intention; he was also a keen supporter of de Gaulle. He immediately set about telephoning to the appropriate people, and a middle-

* 33,000 volts seems child's play today, but in Africa in 1943 it was considered pretty formidable.

aged executive soon came round to the house. He received verbal instructions from the boss, the details of which passed over my head; but his co-operative intention was easily comprehended. The three of us – Beasley, the middle-aged executive and I – then left the boss to finish his siesta while we went to an office in the City to consider ways and means. We soon agreed that all we needed was a competent French engineer to come to the site, and for us to provide transport for the necessary equipment, and some Sapper technicians to erect it. At this stage I felt I had done all I could and I left them to get on with the job. In a few days electric light shone in all our camps and the kudos of the Royal Engineers was much enhanced. I later heard that Beasley was one of the few men who actually climbed to the top of a pylon and handled the 33,000 volts aloft. Without his know-how I doubt if we could ever have achieved all this and it is painful to relate that a month later Beasley was killed in action near Syracuse. Moloch is no respecter of persons and seems to devour the best ones first.

Our equipment, too, began to arrive from the UK and was sent up by single-line railway to a station near Tizi. I sent a Sapper Lance-Corporal to live at the railway station and act as Railway Transport Officer. His job was to recognize the British equipment and to identify from the markings which units it belonged to. He then had to send word to them by dispatch rider to collect it. Soon American equipment for the American engineers preparing the air-strips also began to arrive and the Lance-Corporal dealt happily with both national armies. The Americans, however, felt that Uncle Sam was not pulling his weight in this, and also established an RTO. But he was a Major! This put our excellent Lance-Corporal at a disadvantage and we had to "escalate" the post to an Officer's appointment. We sent a Lieutenant who played cards all day with his American opposite number, leaving the Lance-Corporal to get on with the job in his own way.

Here perhaps I should mention that a number of changes in the personnel of HQ 1 Airborne Division were taking place. The most important of these was the change of our General. General Browning, who was the architect and inspirer of the whole organization, was promoted and made the Commander of all Airborne Forces in England, in preparation for the day the Allies would invade North-West Europe. In his place Brigadier Hopkinson was promoted to command 1 Airborne Division.

Hopkinson was a short, stocky man with an active mind and body. His was an unusual background for a "Modern Major-General". He had served as a junior infantry officer in the First World War and left the Army soon after it ended. Exactly what he had done thereafter I am not sure, but it was usually supposed that he had gone into the steel industry and somehow persuaded the Turks to set up a giant steel works (or it may have been a power station) in Asia Minor, where he had remained to supervise the construction. He rejoined the

Army in 1939 and was posted to a new organization that eventually became known as Phantom. It was a communications and reconnaissance organization that enabled a Commander-in-Chief to get first-hand information from the front line on a wireless network controlled from his own HQ. Phantom grew enormously and became a great success. Perhaps Hopkinson – or "Hoppy" as he was called – might have done better to have stuck to Phantom, but, having joined Airborne Forces, he fell naturally into place as Commander of our Airlanding (or gliderborne) Brigade. From that he was promoted to command 1 Airborne Division just before the Division left the UK for Africa. And here he was in North Africa in command of us all.

I liked Hoppy personally. He was always friendly, but I found it hard, for some reason or other, to discuss military matters with him. I suspect that having been a big wig in civil engineering himself, he felt that he hardly needed *me* as an engineer adviser! In this he may have been quite right, but he seemed to apply the same aloofness to his Artillery adviser, who found the same difficulty as I did. Perhaps the fact was that Hoppy felt that both of us were rather narrow in our experience, and that he, as GOC, could command the Gunners and the Sappers without our interference. In training exercises bridges are not actually demolished nor are they often built. In the same way shell fire is not actually needed, and the enemy in an exercise cannot shoot at you. Both Gunners and Sappers therefore merely constituted yet another burden on the General's back in peacetime. Moreover, when transport aircraft are in short supply for exercises, there is a tendency to allow the Gunners and Sappers alike to be left behind or to travel by road. Instead, an assumption is made that when the real thing happens all will somehow be different. We both found this an unhappy period. However, we both agreed that it was no good belly-aching and we decided that we must get on as best we could.

After some weeks in Tizi the Divisional HQ was established in a small French colonial town called Mascara. We had our offices and a few senior officers accommodated in a large, partly-built hotel, while the remaining personnel were billeted in schools and houses in the town. It became very hot and I took to camping on the flat roof, where a stork on a nest lived on top of a chimney pot. Each morning when we awoke we eyed one another with curiosity. The nest was about sixty feet above ground level and I wondered how the stork would teach its young to fly from that height. Unhappily we did not remain long enough in Mascara to see the chicks' first attempts.

Almost at once the water supply gave us cause for concern because the water from the taps of the hotel was often odoriferous and many complaints were made. Our chief doctor, Eagger, and I went to call on the French equivalent of the Borough Surveyor to see what could be done. We met him in his pyjamas, enjoying a siesta. He clapped his hands and a boy appeared with an iced drink for us. (It did not stink.) He explained the situation regarding the water supply

119

and demonstrated what a wonderfully graphic tongue French is, particularly when describing horror!

"The water supply," he explained, "comes from springs in the hills and is brought to Mascara in pipes and is distributed to most of the civilized houses." (Pause for this to sink in.) "But in a town you have to have sewers too." (Another pause.) "But digging trenches in the rock-like ground is *très laborieuse*, so we make one lot of trenches do for both lots of pipes, and the supply pipes and the sewers are only a few centimetres apart."

The Frenchman assumed a demeanour of the utmost gloom as he watched our looks of horror. But suddenly his eyes gleamed and his face lit up with joy as he continued.

"But during *une époque normale* no danger is to be apprehended, for the water pipes are under pressure and the sewers are not; so if any leak occurs, it is the fresh water that comes out and enters the sewers and not *vice versa. Comprennez?*"

We both said we understood, but Eagger, whose French was no less elementary than mine, inquired whether the present very hot weather constituted *une époque normale.*

"The hot days, yes," replied the Frenchman. "But the many extra mouths – British soldiers' mouths – are very abnormal. In consequence the water pipes are often empty but the sewers are full. Therefore, there might be a vacuum in the water pipes." (He halted to let this idea sink in.) "And," he continued, "Nature abhors a vacuum and the sewers begin to blow out their contents, while the water pipes suck in that which surrounds them." Here he produced the most soul-searching sounds of sucking and puffing with his lips in case we did not understand. He could hardly have been more explicit and we certainly understood why the tap water was so foul.

"Then what," I enquired, "do you think we should do to supply our troops with drinking water?"

The Frenchman shrugged his shoulders.

"I am a municipal engineer," he explained, "not a military engineer. I must leave that to you two *Officiers Britanniques.*" Here he smiled a seraphic smile as though no further parley were necessary.

However, we had learnt what we principally wanted. We now knew where the springs and the reservoirs were and thereafter we sent water carts to fetch five gallons of water per head per day which we treated with chloride of lime. We stored water therafter in empty wine casks, supplied from Oran, and a few Sappers dished it out as required.

EXTRACTS FROM LETTERS TO MY PARENTS

Written from the United Service Club, Pall Mall, London 10 April, 1943
    This is to wish you many happy returns of your birthday. I tried to get you an

120

umbrella from a reputable maker in the Haymarket, but I was told "none available" but I got you a dual purpose one – partly umbrella, partly parasol – from a humble source: the Railway Lost Property Office. I am told the GPO boggles at umbrellas, so it may not come. I also told my batman to send off a couple of packages of my surplus clothes.

Written from a "Foreign Shore" 18 April, 1943 (Algiers)

I have not yet discovered my own address – or the censorship rules that apply here. It will therefore be best to say that all goes well and that I will write soon. Did you get the umbrella? (Later I had an answer saying "Yes. It is splendid but I am sorry for the owner who lost it").

Written from near Oran, 29 April, 1943

I have now got a comprehensible address! I think you may find a postmark on the envelope! We get the most extraordinary weather here. Yesterday morning it was as hot as hell, by noon it was cold; in the evening the sun shone and rain sluiced down almost simultaneously. You got wet and sunburnt at the same time; but it is much better than India. There appears no need to wear a *solar topee*. We wear our berets without sunstroke. Vast spaces here are covered with a blue flower. Cornflower or linseed or something. In the distance they look like lakes, reflecting the blue sky.

Written from near Oran, 6 May, 1943

We are kept busy and interested. There is a lot of interest in North Africa apart from military affairs. It is a mixture of India, France and the Holy Land. The towns are mostly French but divided into an Arab and a European quarter, though some of the smaller ones are mixed. The French seem very ignorant of the origins of the native Arab population. I have spoken to well-educated Frenchmen who seem to have no idea, and are not even interested. My guess is that originally there was a dark-skinned indigenous race which has since been overrun by Phoenicians, Carthaginians, Romans, Berbers, Arabs of Arabia, Turks and French. Today, other than the French, they seem to be mostly Muslims; and they have the same curious gift of artistry in the choice of sites for mosques and tombs that one knows from Indian experience. The towns carry an aroma like Indian bazaars. The Arabs – called "A-rabs" by the Americans – are excellent cultivators of their very fertile land. They are also fine thieves!

Written from near Oran, 14 May, 1943

Mosquitoes have started to bite. The French apparently just suffer malaria and don't care! I shall practice Indian precautions (mosquito net and long trousers after dark etc.) My office is in a large building with tiled floor. Nice and cool; but the lavatory stinks like Hell. *Très Français, je crois.*

121

Written from near Oran, 11 June, 1943

We have a new address. I have not had a letter for ages. Are you using the correct one? B.N.A.F. stands for British North African Forces. . . . The local harvest has been plentiful and is now all "gathered in". Oranges and lemons are finished, but cherries are plentiful. . . . There is a gunner Colonel in the next door office. He is now using his telephone; but you might think he was shouting direct to Cairo! The troops call him the "Whispering Baritone".

Written from near Oran, 12 June, 1943

By some freak in the postal arrangements I have been given two air letter cards this week so here is a second letter within two days. There is a stork that has a nest on the roof. I too have a nest on the roof in the form of my camp bed. So in the early morning the stork and I look at one another, each with a fish-like eye. The stork has a wife and two children. He himself goes off to work at sunrise and occasionally, having forgotten something, he drops in to see his wife and dashes off again. The two children are nearly able to fly. The first flight will be an exciting one. For either the birds are on the roof, or they are in midair, sixty feet above the ground. When interested or indignant the stork makes a noise like a boy with a stick on a paling.

8

The Invasion of Sicily

In due course all German resistance in North Africa was beaten down by the combined efforts of the British 1st and 8th Armies and their American Allies in North Africa. Our Airborne Division prepared to move over an enormous distance from Mascara to a series of camps not far from Sousse on the Western Mediterranean coast. We had privately hoped that we might be needed to help finish off the North African war and some years later those who survived were surprised to find themselves awarded the North African Star; but, in point of fact, at Oran we were almost as far from the fighting as we would have been had we remained on Salisbury Plain. However, I suppose the Top Brass in London and Washington got some sort of comfort from the knowledge that if the worst happened in Africa there was on the African Continent a reinforcement of considerable potential available. Hence our medals.

At last the time came, however, for us to move to the zone from which the attack on Sicily was to be mounted. Partly we travelled by air, partly by train and partly by road. I went by road, taking with me a subaltern as well as Sapper Meek (my batman) and Driver Lowe. The subaltern was from 1 Parachute Squadron. He had fought in Tunisia and he was able to show me some of the scenes of their exploits. We motored each day along the coast road, resting during the heat of the day to bathe in the warm sea and to prepare a meal. In the evenings we pitched our beds and mosquito nets near the staff car and smoked and yarned into the night. It was an enjoyable journey, travelling for three or four days, and it was heartening as we travelled to see the increasing numbers of landing craft, assault ships and troop transports being assembled in every harbour along the coast. The invasion force was evidently going to be a powerful one.

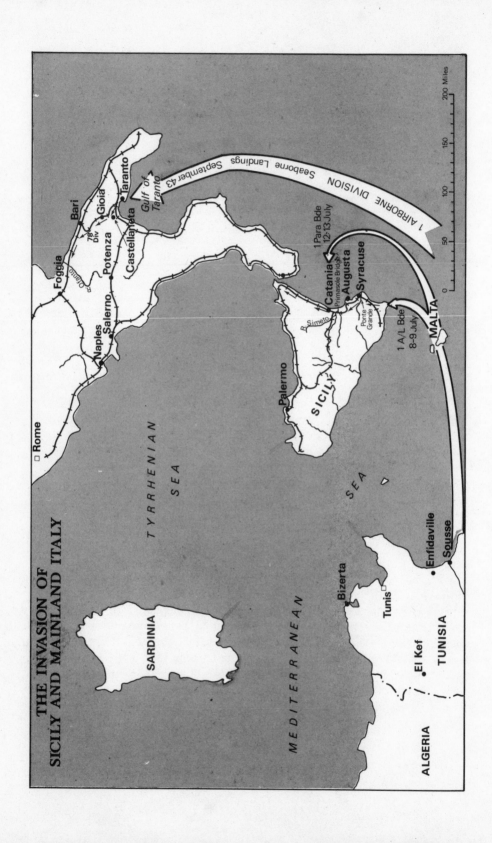

THE INVASION OF
SICILY AND MAINLAND ITALY

□ Rome

TYRRHENIAN

SEA

Foggia

Naples

Salerno

Potenza

Castellaneta

78
Div

R. Otranto

Bari

Gioia

Taranto

Gulf of
Taranto

I AIRBORNE DIVISION Seaborne Landings September 43

1 Para Bde
12-13 July

Catania
Primasole Bridge

Augusta

Syracuse

R. Simeto

Ponte
Grande

Palermo

SICILY

1 A/L Bde
8-9 July

MALTA □

SEA

SARDINIA

MEDITERRANEAN

Bizerta

Tunis □

TUNISIA

El Kef

ALGERIA

Enfidaville

Sousse

0   50   100   150   200 Miles

Our new location was a few miles south of the little seaport town of Sousse. Divisional HQ was in an olive grove and the Brigade camps were similarly situated. About five miles to the south, in open country, the Americans had made a number of airstrips from which the operation was to be launched. These were lettered A to K. On them the gliders were set out in herringbone fashion with tow ropes snaking along the ground to the points where they would be hooked to the tug aircraft. I never fully understood the drill in this process of getting several hundred gliders airborne in a short time, but anyone could see at a glance that a lot of thought had been put into it and in the event it went like clockwork.

Meanwhile the plan for the invasion of Sicily had by now been settled and the part to be played by 1 Airborne Division is easily stated. A seaborne assault was to be made by the British and American ground forces simultaneously on the south coast of the island, but I shall concern myself with the actions of the British contingent only. The 8th Army spearhead was to be 5 Division, landing in the small hours of the morning of 10 July, 1943, on the south-east corner of the island. This Division was to come ashore with minimum impedimenta and march towards Syracuse. The capture of Syracuse was essential to our purpose, as without its harbour the heavy equipment and supplies necessary for the campaign could not be unloaded from the ships. But to capture the port and town of Syracuse 5 Division would have to cross an arm of the sea just south of the town. This arm of the sea was bridged by the Ponte Grande Bridge and it was the principal task of 1 Air Landing Brigade to capture this bridge intact. It was therefore planned to land 1 Air Landing Brigade within striking distance of this bridge during the moonlit night of 9/10 July. The bridge itself was to be captured by a *coup de main* party and the rest of the Brigade was to assemble there to hold it intact against all comers. There were secondary and subsidiary tasks as well, but the capture of the Ponte Grande was the outstanding priority.

Similarly, south of the port of Augusta another airborne landing was planned. This was to be undertaken by 2 Parachute Brigade. It was hoped to do it soon after the capture of Syracuse, that is on the night of 11/12 July. In the event this operation was not necessary as Augusta was not contested.

North of Augusta and south of the town of Catania there was a complex of airfields known collectively as "Catania Airfield". These airfields were a key to the island, for the possessor of them could dominate the whole island with land-based fighter aircraft. It was certain that the enemy would fight for them and it was evident that he would do so along the river line of the River Simeto. The main road crosses this river by the Primasole Bridge and the capture of this was the main task of 1 Parachute Brigade, who were to be dropped on the night of 13/14 July.

We had all studied the aerial photographs of this and the most elaborate and detailed plans were made. My recollection is that there were 109 American Dakota aircraft available, operated by US Airforce pilots, seven RAF Halifax aircraft and twenty Albemarles, RAF-manned. These had to provide transport for the airborne troops. It was therefore decided that on the first night (9/10 July) they were not to come within range of the anti-aircraft batteries on shore. They were to cast off their gliders while over the sea, but near enough to glide ashore. On the second and subsequent assaults with the parachutists they would have to take their luck and the flight plan sought to avoid AA battery positions as far as possible.

There were many opinions about the correct composition of the airborne force. There were insufficient aircraft or gliders to carry the whole lot of us. Ruthless pruning was essential. It needed the judgement of Solomon to strike the right balance and there was not much time for haggling. I remember a Major of the Royal Army Medical Corps claiming that he foresaw many casualties being sustained that involved fractured faces and jaws and that he, as a dentist, was clearly more important than a Chaplain to pray for the dead. He must therefore have a place in the order of battle.

The redeeming feature of all this controversy was that there was no nonsense about "demarcation". Nobody said "I can't go; I'm a pastry cook!" or "I can't go as my driving licence has expired!" Everyone was as keen as mustard to get into the thick of it. There were no faint hearts in 1 Airborne Division.

As far as the Sappers were concerned, I felt that our allotment of seats gave us a fair chance of doing what had to be done, and when the Commander of the Air Landing Brigade asked me if I'd fly with his Brigade HQ I was delighted.

My batman, Sapper Meek, was very cross because I would not beg for a place for him too, but I did beg for (and obtained) a seat for a signaller with a wireless set, a splendid Corporal Thomas. Here I must say something about our signal arrangements.

Today one sees children carrying transistor sets weighing no more than a box of chocolates and policemen with radio transmitters in their pockets. But it was not like that in 1943. In those days it was rare to see any kind of wireless set that a man could carry on his back, and by the time he had loaded himself with a battery to last for a day's work he needed a vehicle to carry it all – and that meant one more glider. What went wrong for me was the radio frequency allotted to the Sappers. Radio frequencies were a sensitive subject. They were never divulged by Division or Brigade HQ until the last moment, and wireless silence was maintained until the battle was joined. It was therefore too late when Corporal Thomas switched on his set and found himself on a frequency used by no less than Radio Roma! It pumped out the news with infinite volume for 23 hours a day, coupled with music, propoganda and drama. No one had the slightest chance of hearing what Corporal Thomas or I had to say for ourselves. And Corporal Thomas's set weighed as much as a sack of coal. At least our common tribulation put Corporal Thomas and me on very good terms thereafter, and it was a great joy to meet him after the war on an Ipswich railway platform. We both had hard words to say about 1 Airborne Division Signals – but most unfairly, as was explained to me long after the war.

It was 5 pm on 9 July, 1943, when the gliderborne force was to be ready to take the air. I spent the afternoon getting my hair cut and writing some "Handing-over Notes" for my successor in case I was killed. By the merest chance I found these notes the other day. They are curiously matter-of-fact and say who I thought fit for promotion to replace any Company or Platoon Commander, should my successor have to make promotions before he knew the personalities. I did not make a will – I had nothing to leave! I did, however, tell my Adjutant (Willie Taylor, who after the war transferred to the Royal Scots Fusiliers) that if I was killed he might dispose of my visible effects in any way he chose. I supposed he might have liked some books I carried. I had a copy of the plays of Shakespeare and I read the lot several times during the war, though I have forgotten what most of the plays are about. I only remember those which I had been made to study at school. I also had copies of *War and Peace*, *Vanity Fair*, Macaulay's *Essays* and a translation of the *Odyssey*. Willie might have the lot.

In due course I went with my steel helmet on my head and my kit bag on my back and with a loaded pistol in my belt to the rendezvous appointed. Corporal Thomas had gone to another place, for he was to fly in a different glider and we were to meet in Sicily near the Ponte Grande. I was allotted to a glider with a Scottish pilot* and an American co-pilot. The Scot was a draughtsman in civil life and had been in HQ 3 Division when I was with 253 Field Company, so we were no strangers. The senior officer in the glider was Colonel Jones, the Deputy Commander of the Air Landing Brigade. The rest consisted of one or two staff officers, including the Brigade Chaplain, and a number of signallers with their wireless sets. There were a few soldiers of the Brigade HQ Defence Platoon. We were twenty men including the pilots.

The fierce African sun had begun to dip as we motored to the landing strip where we were to emplane. The tug aircraft and gliders were laid out in a herringbone pattern with their tow ropes snaking on the ground between them. A breeze had sprung up and I had the feeling that a dust-storm was not far away. Our glider was No 10 in the rank. It was an American WACO, a high-wing monoplane with the wing above the fuselage. It was not long before someone noticed that one of the struts under the port wing was slightly buckled. The glider pilots were divided in opinion about the seriousness of the damage and wondered what to do. As an engineer I was invited by Colonel

* His name was Andrews. He emigrated to Canada after the war. We lost touch for many years, but within a month of my writing this chapter he found my address and sent me, for my comments, *his* Memoirs covering the same events in Sicily.

Jones to give an opinion on the matter. I was glad to be able to tell them all that 9 Field Company had had a hand in assembling the gliders and I was quite sure that if anything had been seriously wrong they would have got it corrected. Everyone seemed to be reassured and Colonel Jones made some heartening comments that put everyone in good spirits. I think "Jonah", as we called Colonel Jones, was much to be admired for this attitude.

A long delay was expected before anything happened, so I walked along the line to have a chat with some Sappers whom I knew were detailed for another glider not far distant from ours. I found them with their Sergeant sitting in the shade of the wing. Many of the men had their eyes closed and were evidently praying silently. We all knew that these must be the last hours for some of us and I expect even the staunchest hearts must have felt some apprehension. Oddly enough, my own worst fear was that I had perhaps made some faulty decision in the preparation of our plans and be the cause of some crashing failure this very night. This sort of anxiety must, of course, hit the General more severely than the Colonel, and the Colonel more severely than the private soldiers. I formed the opinion then, which I still hold, that very few men can go through a campaign and come out atheists, and I believe that prayer is a great help to those who believe in it. (What no one can say for certain is whether it will be the same next time!) Anyway, not far from where these soldiers were praying was an Army Chaplain. He sat on the wheel of his glider, his mind wrapped in the contents of a book on his knee. I have no notion of his name nor of his denomination, though I somehow sustained the impression that he was a Roman Catholic. I beckoned to him and he walked quietly towards us. Many of the men knelt spontaneously. He raised his hand in an attitude of benediction and said the Grace from II Corinthians XIII, verse 14. There was a surge towards the Chaplain and we all shook him by the hand and thanked him. The whole thing was absolutely spontaneous and I instantly felt more cheerful. The only explanation I can offer is that now there really was no other act that we could do to improve our lot and worry vanished as in a miracle!

The signal to emplane was given at about 6.45 pm. Engines roared, clouds of dust rose from the ground so that the pilots could see nothing but the dust ahead. Presently the tow rope ahead became taut and we lurched forward into the unknown. After many bumps our glider became airborne and rose above its tug. We were out of the dust and soon saw the wine dark sea beneath us.* But the wind must have freshened considerably, for there were white horses on the waves and a threatening darkness on the horizon. The glider jerked up and down on its tow rope and other gliders nearby seemed perilously close.

Soon we were over Malta, a devious route having been chosen to deceive the enemy. It was now dusk and the sun had set, but we could see waves breaking

---

* 'Wine dark sea' is Homer's phrase. It is very apt at dusk and dawn in the Mediterranean.

against the rocks of the island and our own motion was not unlike that of a ship at sea in a storm. The tug aircraft lit their navigation lights and the stars came out. I suppose there was a moon, for that was needed for the operation, but I do not remember seeing it. A long time seemed to elapse before we got anywhere near Sicily. We were late over the target, the reason being the strong headwind, which, of course, we could not feel. There was nothing we could do but pray that the pilots of the tug and the glider would not lose their heads. We were, to use a classical phrase, "at the mercy of the Gods"!

By about 11.30 pm the coastline of Sicily became visible, a dark outline against the silver sea, and then, from the shore, rising up like a fountain from the black cliffs, were rows of little lights that puzzled me. At first I thought that the lights were those of a rope railway mounting the cliffs of the island. Gradually, however, as we got nearer I saw the lights were the tracer shells of anti-aircraft fire. For some time they were not directed at us and they seemed to travel very slowly. Presently, however, a burst of fire was directed at us and then I saw the difference. The little lights seemed to crawl into the sky till they were near and then, quite suddenly, they flashed past the windows, very close and at a sickening speed. The tug aircraft turned sharply away. The tow rope gave us a fierce tug and the glider bounded up like a hooked salmon. It then flopped back and a box, containing a wireless battery on the floor beside me, jumped up and hit my knee as it fell back to the floor with a crash. More flak flashed past the windows and the glider seemed to be bouncing on the end of its rope. It was thoroughly demoralizing.

At some point in all this the tug aircraft cast off its tow and a deadly silence suddenly replaced the roar of engines. The flak seemed to leave us and follow the tug aircraft. We were gliding free through the night and the only sounds were the gentle murmur of the slipstream over the wings and the staccato speech of the Scottish pilot and his American mate. One was reading the altimeter, the other was heading for the cliffs.

"Four hundred . . . three-fifty . . . three hundred," chanted the Scottish pilot and I saw the luminous needle of his altimeter sink back round the clock.

"Can you make it?" asked his mate.

"Don't know," replied the Scot.

"Three hundred . . . two-fifty."

"We'll just make it!"

The glider jerked upwards, bounced down again, flashed past a searchlight, hit a tree, smashing the portside wing and spun to a halt almost overhanging the cliffs.

"God all-bloody mighty," exclaimed a private soldier behind me.

"And no one f . . . ing hurt."

He was quite right; no one *was* hurt. The glider (unlike a powered aircraft which is full of petrol) did not burst into flames. It simply crumpled up with a sound of breaking sticks. We scrambled out and started to put into effect the drill we had learnt, namely to form a defensive circle round the glider. On this occasion it was not easy, for we were in a vineyard with grapes growing up innumerable wires to about waist height.

I saw some Italians silhouetted against the searchlight, which was about 100 yards away. It was too dark to see much of what happened, but people fired their pistols and several hand-grenades were thrown. Presently the shooting stopped and a British private soldier, gibbering with fright, ran up to me and pointed a sten gun at my stomach and pressed the trigger. Fortunately he had forgotten to cock the mechanism and I owe my life to his forgetfulness. I cursed him heartily and told him for good measure to "stand to attention when talking to an officer". I must have been somewhat on edge myself because this is not the sort of remark I was wont to make to wartime soldiers, who were not regular soldiers but patriotic civilians doing their best in uniform. I then took a swift pace forwards to disarm him and fell flat on my face, having tripped over a vineyard wire at knee level.

The private soldier helped me untangle myself and Colonel Jones, who was not far away, told me that the Brigade Chaplain had been killed in the mêlée. Personally I think he was probably accidently killed by one of our own men, for the Italian searchlight crew had vanished from the scene. Oddly enough my admonition to "stand to attention when speaking to an officer" had a steadying effect upon everyone within earshot. It makes me think now, looking back on it, that Colonel Blimp was perhaps not such a fool as cartoonists make him out to be. Discipline, even in crisis, is not a bad thing.

The question then arose, what to do next? The glider pilots, who alone knew where we were, thought we must be on the south-east coast of Sicily all right, and not far from a small promontory called the Cap Murro di Porco. The presence of the searchlight, which had been doused by its crew before departing, and the sound of breakers to the south of us seemed to confirm this opinion. In the darkness nothing was visible but trees and vines and the stars above.

Colonel Jones and I peered at a map with a shaded torch and decided we must be about fifteen miles from our correct landing zone near Syracuse. If we stayed where we were we should be behind the Italian beach defences. Then we might harry them as they attempted to halt 8th Army who were due to begin landing in a few hours time. Alternatively, if we marched northwards we might rejoin the rest of the Brigade and be able to attack the enemy in accordance with the plan of campaign.

We settled on the latter course and straggled inland to where we found a railway line that tallied with our reading of the map. Now we knew exactly where we were and formed up in a more military fashion to follow the railway that led towards Syracuse. Colonel Jones took command of the Main Body –

sixteen officers and other ranks – while I commanded the Advanced Guard consisting of the two glider pilots with pistols and a private soldier of the Brigade Defence Platoon with a light automatic.

The sleepers of a railway are never the right distance apart to make walking easy, but we nonetheless made good progress. On either side of the line were many trees, growing olives and oranges, some apparently ripe ones. There were sounds of small-arms fire not far from the line and ahead we could hear the progress of an air raid, presumably over Syracuse. This combination of warlike sounds and the dark shadows among the trees on either side provided a forbidding prospect of danger, which was not actually justified. As the ex-weapon-training-officer of our Training Battalion in Chatham some five or six years previously, I had acquired the habit of identifying the sounds of various weapons and I could tell that most of the small-arms fire we could hear was produced by British Army weapons. There was apparently no enemy response and therefore presumably no enemy. In the dark it seemed that we might find ourselves ambushed by our friends and I was tickled by the idea that if we had a pipe band marching with us we might be recognized as British and be far safer.

Soon a real need for identification became evident, for we presently heard the sound of footfalls crunching over the railway ballast a short distance ahead. I halted the Advanced Guard and we took up positions behind trees on the left-hand side of the railway line. I gave whispered orders that no one was to fire unless I gave the order. Colonel Jones and his Main Body, about one hundred yards behind us, halted too and he and a private soldier came up to where we were. They came quietly, but evidently not quietly enough, for we heard the footfalls approaching from the other direction halt. They had evidently heard us just as we had heard them. Each party was prepared to ambush the other and a pitched battle between friends seemed to me imminent. Colonel Jones and I spoke in a whisper.

"Can you whistle a tune?" I asked, thinking of my pipe band.

"No," he said. "Can you?"

The Scots glider pilot, who was crouching near us, offered to try, and did. Soon we were all whistling the strains of *The Lincolnshire Poacher*. Presently a typically English voice came back from the other party.

"Actually we are South Staffords, not the Lincolns."

Liaison was achieved and everyone was jubilant. The other party, like us, was lost in the night, but together with them we were over thirty men, so we continued along the railway line together.

Soon we came upon a glider that had crashed through a wall onto the railway line. The occupants had gone and I was astonished at what they had brought with them from Africa – melons, fruit and several bottles of wine. We divided these delicacies appropriately and continued our march northwards. By about 1.30 am, as I walked in the lead, I discerned in the pale moonlight what looked like a pill box on the railway line a short way ahead. The signal lights of a station were visible beyond that and I soon heard the unmistakable sound of Italian voices. There was a scuffling of enemy feet as hurried deployment was made. We crept closer and a shot from a foreign weapon was fired at us. The pill box turned out to be a platelayers' shed on the left-hand side of the line. It was full of Italians. Colonel Jones shouted:

"Let's rush it. Fix bayonets everyone." There was a rattling of bayonets and scabbards and I drew my pistol.

"Charge!" shouted Colonel Jones, and we ran towards the enemy.

Being more fleet of foot than the others, and less heavily accoutred, I got there first. There was a bright flash at my feet and an explosion. Someone seemed to hit me a severe blow with an unseen club and I fell down, wondering what had happened and who had struck me such a blow. I slowly became aware that two or three Italian soldiers were standing over me with their hands above their heads, and another Italian was sprawled across my legs. Either someone must have trodden on a mine or someone must have thrown a hand-grenade. The sprawling Italian was dead and I had been wounded.

"Are you bad?" shouted Colonel Jones.

"I don't think so," I replied, getting to my feet.

I wriggled my fingers and toes to reassure myself, and by the light of Colonel Jones's torch I saw that my khaki shirt and trousers were torn and drenched in blood. A warm trickle coursed down my right side from hip to heel. Whatever had happened had cowed the enemy but wounded me and killed the Italian. It was like losing a pawn in exchange for a queen, tactically acceptable, but bad luck on the pawn.

A medical orderly wearing the badge of the South Staffords emerged from somewhere and tied first field dressings to my various wounds, of which there were seven. I owe this nameless man from the Potteries a great debt and I hope he sees these words. None of the wounds could be dressed again for two days and a broken arm remained untended for nearly a fortnight, yet nothing went septic. Apart from a negligible disability today, I live to tell the tale. By all the rules I ought to have died of gangrene on a foreign shore.

After this commotion we resumed our march. I remained with the Advanced Guard which was now accompanied by several prisoners of war. One of them offered to carry my haversack and acted as a railway porter. We called him Macaroni. He was particularly solicitous for my welfare and walked immediately behind me. He knew some English and told me that he had worked in Soho as a barber.

Soon we came to the railway station where a goods train was standing. I halted my Advanced Guard near the engine and sat on the step of the driver's cab in the glow from the fire box. I began to feel weak. The station lights started to swing and circle. I thought I was about to faint, but Macaroni had tapped some water from the engine and gave me a drink from the engine driver's billycan. This had a magical effect and my senses returned.

Tramp, tramp, tramp; I heard the footfalls of Colonel Jones's party, assaulting up the railway line behind us.

"For God's sake don't try and capture this station," I shouted. "We've got it."

The main body came quietly. There was a lot of talk among the prisoners about the enemy in the station. The only words I could catch were *Tedesci* (Germans) and some onomatopoeic sounds suggestive of machine-gun fire. As it was now getting light, Colonel Jones decided to leave the railway line and we followed a cart track that crossed the railway by a level crossing near where we stood. The track led through the olive groves to a white farmstead with a verandah in front and a cactus hedge a few yards to one side. One of the soldiers battered on the door and roused the occupants. A man of about forty-five opened the front door. He looked like a lawyer, a commuter perhaps, getting dressed before motoring into Syracuse, when disturbed by the tiresome British. He seemed more cross than alarmed and began to harangue us in broken English. He was not engaged in the war, he explained. This was his home and what right did we think we had to intrude? We explained to him that whether he had anything to do with the war was his affair.

"Your Mussolini," I said, "declared war on us. Your soldiers have tried to occupy our colony in Somaliland and they kicked our Abyssinian ally, Haile Selassie, out of Ethiopia. It is now my duty to tell you and your family to take refuge in the cellar."

The Italian grumbled a bit and unwillingly complied, while Colonel Jones and I entered the house. Colonel Jones gave the necessary orders and in a few minutes he had the ground floor set up as a skeleton Brigade HQ with a couple of Staff Officers. The others were brewing up breakfast for the troops elsewhere. I wished I had my Corporal Thomas handy with his wireless set to tell me what had happened to the detachment of 9 Field Company who I hoped were on the Ponte Grande by now. But even Colonel Jones and his Brigade HQ could make no contact with anyone, and we were evidently out of a job. However, the Italian prisoner, Macaroni, had not been idle. With unerring judgement he had found the kitchen and presently appeared with some plates of breakfast that I shared with the glider pilots.

After we had eaten, Macaroni pulled my razor and a mirror from my haversack and asked if I wanted a shave. I saw in the mirror that I certainly needed one and in a minute the Italian, who only a few hours ago I regarded as a deadly foe, was now wielding a razor within an eighth of an inch of my jugular vein. There was also another development. A heavy gun, situated the other side of a thick hedge nearby, had opened fire and it was not long before its fire began to be returned. One of the glider pilots, meanwhile, reported that

Colonel Jones with a few men had gone to see what was the cause of all the shelling. The answer was that there was an Italian coastal defence battery in action nearby and that the returning shells now landing near us must be fired from the sea by the Royal Navy.

I came out to see if I could help in any way but had difficulty hobbling even with a stick that lay in the porch. However, it did not seem to matter much because Colonel Jones soon returned with no less than ninety-six Italian gunners as prisoners of war! And the Navy having, as they thought, put the coast defence battery out of action, had ceased firing. On top of this the sun was now shining brightly and the Italian prisoners of war from the Battery were bringing with them into captivity many baskets of fruit, with plenty left over for us. Life was becoming quite tolerable again and I fell asleep.

By the time I awoke, feeling much better, the advanced troops of the British 5th Division were within earshot and the unmistakable rattle of British light automatic fire was plainly audible. We were able to get in touch with them. They received all our prisoners except Macaroni whom I retained for the time being.

It was not long before Colonel Jones and I found our way to the HQ of the leading Brigade of the 8th Army. The Commander was a Brigadier Cooke Collis. His mother and my mother had been friends for many years before the war, and his younger sister had been a playmate of mine when we were schoolchildren. To this Brigade had fallen the task of capturing Syracuse and naturally he was very interested in the Ponte Grande Bridge. Was it still intact? Would it carry tanks? He wanted to know and he had not heard.

"Find me some transport," I said, "and I'll jolly soon find out and tell you."

Transport was, however, a difficulty. The leading Brigade had come over the beaches in the small hours of the morning and the men were pushing trolleys to carry ammunition and rations. The space for vehicles in the landing craft allotted had been kept for guns, tanks and a few heavy lorries for petrol and reserve ammunition. Cooke Collis couldn't give me the jeep that I wanted. He said jocularly, "The Lord must provide," and that is almost exactly what happened. At that moment there emerged from apparently nowhere a Sapper of 9 Field Company (Sapper Stokes) on a motorbike with a side car. I knew him by sight, for he was the OC's driver, that is Beasley's driver. Beasley had fitted him and his motor-bike into a Horsa glider that was planned to land near the Ponte Grande Bridge. Stokes must have information about it, I thought, and I cross-questioned him.

He had, apparently, been landed more or less in the proper place and he had got to the bridge alright. It had been captured intact; Beasley was there and Sapper Stokes had seen the Italian demolition charges detached from the bridge and dropped in the water beneath. The Italian troops in the vicinity had counter-attacked the small body of British troops who had captured the bridge and Beasley had been killed. As far as Stokes knew, Beasley had pronounced the bridge as fit to carry tanks just before he was killed. The British defenders from the Air Landing Brigade were few and very short of ammunition and he was not sure whether the small garrison of the bridge had managed to survive or not.

I told Cooke Collis all this and said I'd go with Sapper Stokes and his motorbike and side-car and see if I could get him some more up-to-date information. First, though, I thought I must try and find the nearest RE unit to give them what information I had about the bridge and I was told that a Field Company was nearby, so thither I went in Stokes's side-car. This was luxury indeed. Everyone else was slogging along on foot, yet here was I with Sapper Stokes and a motorbike to cart me about in luxury. But what about Macaroni? Here I must make a few diversions. Macaroni had explained to me early in the morning that he was a sort of "Home Guard Soldier", and lived on a smallholding nearby. He was not the least interested in the war and he was certainly very helpful to me. He had not only shaved me, but later he had asked permission to return to his smallholding to fetch me a couple of eggs for breakfast. Now I had Sapper Stokes to look after me Macaroni was "surplus to establishment". What ought I to do with him? I decided to send him to his home, a free man. But first I bought his khaki-coloured trousers to replace my bloodstained ones for an English half-crown and I gave him my name and my parents' address in East Anglia. He then, with many smiles and best wishes, trotted off happily to his home in his underpants. He sent me a Christmas card *via* my parents' home several years later. He sent no address and all attempts I have made to get in touch with him since have been unsuccessful. Monty, incidentally, soon issued an 8th Army Order telling us all to release harmless Italian PoWs who were domiciled in the island. So I had acted according to orders after all. Sapper Stokes proved to be a splendid companion. It was as though St David had appeared at the Arms Park in Cardiff to referee a rugger match against Scotland. I had no doubts about the future and I addressed him thereafter as "Saint" Stokes.

It turned out also that the Sapper Field Company supporting Cooke Collis's Brigade was 38 Field Company, in which I had been Second-in-Command before the war in Aldershot, and I found I knew several of them still, including a Sergeant, who in my day had always refused to accept promotion as he preferred the work he did as Company Wheeler*. And by another curious chance the Officer Commanding the company was a Territorial Sapper called Major Charles Tomkinson, the younger brother of the Bruce Tomkinson who had been with me at Dunkirk. He seemed to have all the right ideas and he gave me a bottle of whisky.

* In days of horse transport the Wheeler was the expert in mending wagon wheels, shafts, springs and so on.

St Stokes and I then followed the leading troops of Cooke Collis's Brigade who were, I think, the Royal Scots Fusilliers. There was some Italian opposition, but not much. The worst difficulty was the heat of the day and the very long march that had been made by the infantry since landing over the beaches at 2 am that morning.

At about 4 pm when everyone was thoroughly weary, the leading troops emerged from the last of the olive groves on to an open plain a mile or a mile and a half from the town of Syracuse, which I could see quite plainly. The arm of the sea over which the Ponte Grande carried the road was also visible, but trees growing along its banks hid the bridge itself. There were a number of Airborne troops about, including a few from 9 Field Company. They told me the Ponte Grande had been captured by the few of our *coup de main* party who had arrived in the right place. There were barely enough Sappers present to lift off the Italian demolition charges attached to the bridge, but Major Beasley, who got to the bridge with a few more men, was able to detach the charges and drop them in the river. The Italian counterattack began shortly after that. A few men, including Beasley, were killed and quite a number were wounded. Those remaining ran out of ammunition and were driven off the bridge, but as far as they knew the Italians had not been able to renew the demolition charges and no one had heard any explosion to suggest that the bridge had been demolished or even damaged. No one I spoke to could say for certain whether tanks would be able to cross it. I pictured in my mind the anxious Chief Engineer of the Corps, who might perhaps still be in Malta, being questioned by the Top Brass – Monty, Alexander or even Eisenhower – whether our tanks would be able to get to Syracuse tonight or whether a new bridge would have to be built and how long that would take. And until some competent Engineer Officer had sent in a report from the site no answer could be given. Moreover, as I knew full well, our two parachute brigades were waiting in Sousse to assist the attacks upon Augusta and Catania and until the answers were known about the Ponte Grande bridge there could be no realistic decision made on when these two brigades should emplane, etc. etc. One way and another it was obvious to me that at the risk of thinking myself too important a cog in the machine, I must somehow get to this blasted bridge and see it for myself.

There were by now a few of our self-propelled guns and tanks arriving in the leading battalion's area and a battle for Syracuse was about to be launched.* A considerable time was likely to elapse before much happened, and there was nothing I could do in the meantime. There is nothing worse before a battle than to have nothing to do and I began to have gloomy thoughts about my broken arm and bloody field dressings on my legs. Ought I to go to the Royal Scots

* Among others present I met Lieutenant-Colonel Walch, who was still the Staff Officer of General Browning in London, though in what capacity he came to Sicily I cannot say. (I suspect he was impelled by a sense of duty to hitch-hike to the sound of the guns!)

Fusiliers' Regimental Aid Post? It could not be far away; and would I get worse or better if I did so? A crucial factor in this dilemma was that if I *did* get worse and remained on the sick list for a long time, someone else would get my job and I should probably linger at the Base for ages and ages. Having struggled so hard to get into the war again after Dunkirk, I did not want to get out of it. Such, I think, would have been the view of any of my companions in 1 Airborne Division in similar circumstances. However, my luck held and fortune smiled. As it were by magic, there appeared, walking towards me, Colonel Eagger, the head Medical Officer of our Division. I knew I could trust him.

I had last seen Eagger the day before on the airfield near Sousse. He was to be a passenger in one of the WACO gliders waiting to take off shortly after us. He was now approaching on foot from the rear along the main road. He was dressed in white shorts and a floppy sun hat such as those worn in that era by paid hands at Cowes on the yachts of the wealthy. I asked how he came to be kitted out in that strange way and he told me that the glider in which he and his companions had been was released by the American tug aircraft too far out to sea. They had touched down among some landing craft about a mile out from the shore, and were picked up by a Royal Naval vessel. He had been given these garments by the crew of the vessel that picked him up.

"Let me have a look at those bandages," he said almost at once and I discovered instantly that magic lies in the hands of a gifted doctor. His fingers somehow combined strength with a curious gentleness, such as I had never even dreamt existed.

"You ask my advice?" he questioned and, without awaiting my reply, he continued. "As a Medical Officer and your senior in rank, I must order you to report to the nearest Casualty Clearing Station, but as your friend I advise you to have none of it. I've got a sling in my haversack for your arm, and I expect you'll be OK till we get back to Africa. There are several of the best medicos from London in the General Hospital in Sousse to patch you up. Don't fret yourself."

Much relieved, we shared a swig from Charles Tomkinson's bottle of whisky and, when the attack on the Ponte Grande was about to begin, I told St Stokes to remain with the Battalion HQ, while I joined one of the leading companies.

There was a lot of gunfire and noise generally, but most of it came from our own side. Progress was slow, but I don't think there were many casualties. The Ponte Grande was eventually captured, but as I walked from objective to objective I thought how much better it would have been if our Airborne Brigade, instead of being spewed out in the dark all over the sea and the cliffs of Sicily, had been landed now, in the daylight and behind the weary troops with whom I now marched. These troops had marched on foot all the way from the beaches and still had a long way to go. Had we but landed from our gliders in daylight a mile or two in rear, we might now be giving speed and impetus by our freshness to this painful struggle of weary men. This train of thought sowed the seeds of an idea that gradually grew in my mind into what I called "The Right Idea". As one event followed another, I became more and more obsessed with the conviction that "The Right Idea" had not yet been devised.

When we got to the Ponte Grande there were many signs of the engagement that had taken place earlier that day. Corpses, articles of clothing and pieces of equipment were strewn all over the place, and a fair number of Airborne soldiers (most of them wounded) emerged from various places where they had taken cover when they ran out of ammunition. They had achieved their object nobly in capturing the bridge intact. The demolition charges had all been dropped in the water and the enemy had been too shaken to replace them. My Corporal Thomas was there with his wireless set and I asked how he had got on.

"Listen to this," he said switching on his set.

The full blare of Radio Roma shouted the futility of the wave-length we had been allotted. But it no longer mattered because I could now get a proper report back through the wireless network of Cooke Collis's Brigade. I forget what I reported, but it must have turned out to be reliable or someone would have cursed me heartily afterwards.

St Stokes and I spent the night with Charles Tomkinson's Company and next day we joined the remnants of 1 Airlanding Brigade in Syracuse. The Brigade Commander, Brigadier Hicks, a stalwart warrior from the First World War, told me that his orders now were to collect his brigade together as quickly as possible and remain in Syracuse as a reserve for the ground forces who would continue northwards towards Catania. I thus had a chance to find most of the survivors of 9 Field Company's detachment who had set off from Sousse two days before. Many had pitched in the sea. One glider load was known to have landed on the slopes of Mount Etna, north of Catania, and one man, we learnt several weeks later, had been picked up by a merchant ship sailing in convoy; but the convoy never called at Gibraltar and the astonished Sapper made a journey to Brazil or thereabouts and back to England *via* New York.* The only 9 Company wireless set to get to the Ponte Grande was Corporal Thomas's one, netted to Radio Roma.

The remnants of the Airlanding Brigade in Syracuse numbered very few. The gliders had landed all over the place, a high proportion in the sea. The General himself had been released into the sea. I suppose he was picked up by the Navy, but I did not see him again till we all got back to Sousse.

However, although it was not intended, the numerous small bodies of the Brigade that had landed dotted over the coastal areas of the island had caused great alarm among the Italian beach defenders. The main beach landings by 5

* By the time this Sapper had rejoined 1 Airborne Division in the UK I had already been posted elsewhere, so I only heard of his adventures by hearsay long after the event.

Infantry Division had met comparatively light opposition due to the efforts of all these determined small parties of Airborne troops. Had not even our little group – Colonel Jones and his small band – silenced a coast-defence battery and captured nearly a hundred prisoners? Was that not something? It was later that we counted our losses which were relatively very high.

Having survived so far, and feeling much better after a night's sleep, I decided to accompany the leading troops of 8th Army as far as Catania. I no doubt over-estimated my own importance in the scheme of affairs, but if I returned to North Africa and my own people I could contribute absolutely nothing, so I felt my decision to go on was the right one.

The good St Stokes, with his motor-bike and sidecar, was game for this, and we set off together accordingly. We attached ourselves to the HQ of the leading Division of 8th Army, and accompanied their CRE – a Lieutenant-Colonel whom I knew slightly from days gone by.

As I moved about the forward area, I was able to contrast his position with my own. Here was he, at his own Divisional HQ, with his Staff and his signallers about him. He could find out his General's intentions merely by walking a few yards to his tent. His engineer companies were easily visited personally, or spoken to by wireless, so that he could give orders or receive reports promptly. By contrast, here was I with no orders and my General was God knows where, recovering from a ducking in the sea. I now had no engineer troops, no Adjutant, no Staff, and only a wireless set irrevocably netted to the delights of Radio Roma.

However, I soon perceived that our planned parachute attack on Augusta by 2 Para Brigade would not be necessary because there was no opposition. It was also evident that our parachute attack by 1 Para Brigade upon Catania certainly would be needed, because of stiffening opposition (mostly German) building up ahead of us. As I knew our own airborne plans in detail, I thought that alone might be of some help to the ground forces.

The airborne plan for Catania hinged about capturing intact the Primasole Bridge so that 8th Army (particularly its tanks and artillery) could cross the River Simeto south of Catania without having to delay while they built a new bridge. The plan therefore began with a surprise attack by a *coup de main* parachute party, consisting of two platoons of 1 Para Battalion, reinforced by a detachment of my 1 Para Squadron RE, commanded by Douglas Murray, whose job was to remove the enemy demolition charges and to verify that the bridge was strong enough to carry tanks. *The coup de main* party was to be followed after a few minutes by the rest of 1 Para Brigade to neutralize some enemy anti-aircraft guns nearby and to capture some high ground overlooking the river. I knew that the Brigade Commander (Brigadier Lathbury) would get to the bridge as soon as he could, and that Murray would also do likewise. I therefore intended to get as far forward as possible with the ground forces and make contact with Lathbury or Murray as soon as I could.

The Airborne attack began before dawn on the night of 12/13 July, when the ground forces were still rather a long way away.

In outline the operation went extremely well, but far too small a proportion of the parachutists, who set off from Sousse, ever got to the right place in Sicily. The cause of this – as in our own case a few nights previously – was the inability of the airmen to get the whole Brigade to their proper dropping zones. It was easy to blame the Americans, who supplied most of the aircraft and aircrews, but in the afterlight it is unjust to do so. In the first place, most of the American airmen had never been trained in navigation of the kind required here. They were mainly civilian airways pilots, stout-hearted men of great flying experience, but at home they navigated by flying along beams, directed from the ground. In the Mediterranean area celestial navigation or map-reading were the order of the day. Moreover, on this occasion many of the aircraft got shot up by anti-aircraft fire from the guns of our own ships supporting the beach landings south of the island. Many aircraft lost the way completely. Some discharged their parachutists many miles from the right place, some in the sea. A few gave up and brought their parachutists back to Africa, having taken no part in the business whatsoever.

A few, however, including Brigadier Lathbury, commanding the Brigade, got to the bridge and captured it. Douglas Murray and a few Sappers got there too and were able to remove the demolition charges from the bridge structure and throw them into the river below. The job was done, but it was impossible to hold a regular bridgehead round the bridge because of insufficient troops. The best that was possible was to keep the bridge under fire in a no-man's-land between the German defenders and a number of isolated posts of the Para Brigade within sight of it. Like our own show at Syracuse it was good work but only due to the quality of the officers and men of 1 Para Brigade who managed to get there.

The good St Stokes and I, with our motor-bike and sidecar, could easily accompany the forward troops of 8th Army and, in due course, standing near to one of our tanks, I came within sight of the Primasole Bridge. It was a few hundred yards ahead of us. It was a large lattice girder bridge with the roadway across the river perhaps a hundred feet long. Through my field glasses I could see it was a powerful bridge and of a type whose exact carrying capacity could be calculated by any engineer with a ruler, the back of an envelope to write on, and an elementary knowledge of rigid body statics. Even without these amenities I felt justified in telling the tank commander – a junior officer who enquired my opinion – that it would support two elephants "copulating in the moonlight", and that he might take it as perfectly safe for one tank at a time to cross it in broad daylight. I expressed the view that the sooner he got there to prevent the Germans having another chance to blow it up the better. He reported parts of this information "over the blower" to his Squadron Commander and it was not long before there were signs of the advance continuing. But the Germans, with their customary resolution, began interfering with the plans.

I sat behind an earthy bank of some kind and watched spellbound. On the far side of the bridge the main road lay out of sight and from behind this cover emerged three or four German motor-cyclists, who reached the bridge and dismounted. One of our tanks opened fire and I was afraid it might hit and damage the bridge that had been so skilfully captured intact. So also, apparently, was his CO, who was within voice range.

"For God's sake," he shouted, "don't hit the bloody bridge. We want to drive over it presently."

Luckily the shell missed the bridge and small-arms fire from all sides opened up on the German motor-cyclists. A few German shells also came our way, but not very close to where I happened to be. Presently, the German motor-cyclists vanished from view and all firing subsided. Suddenly, from behind cover on the other side of the bridge emerged a German lorry followed by a light van of some kind. A flight of three German aircraft also roared across the landscape, flying low and squirting automatic fire at targets I could not see. The German lorry halted in the middle of the bridge and its crew of four or five men jumped out and ran back to the German side of the river, followed by a lot of small-arms fire from our people. Several of the Germans were hit and fell on the deck of the bridge, but some got back to the North bank and disappeared out of sight.

Almost immediately the German lorry exploded where it stood in the middle of the bridge. There was a shattering explosion and dust and debris flew in all directions. The bridge was enveloped in smoke. A large explosive charge – anti-tank mines I believe – must have been detonated by a delayed action fuse inside the lorry, but, when the dust settled, I could see the bridge was still standing. The German stratagem had been excellent in theory and was carried out with great dash and bravery, but the technical detail was faulty. None of the many pieces of the lorry that flew in all directions was sufficiently massive to wreck the steel-work of the bridge and the detonation of the mines in the belly of the lorry was too high above the roadway to damage that either. We had been lucky but not so the Germans. Several German soldiers lay fallen in the road; and that was all they had to show for it.

What next, I thought, will happen? But what did happen was a total surprise. From our side of the river a British Army jeep drove down the road towards the bridge. It had Red Cross markings on it and there were two men in it; one was in a white shirt and shorts wearing a white floppy hat. It was Colonel Eagger, and we all watched in amazement. Firing ceased from both sides as the jeep was halted near the middle of the brige. The doctor walked calmly towards the bodies lying there. Two or three of the bodies he evidently judged to be dead, but one was alive and he loaded it on to a stretcher that was fitted to his jeep and brought it back for treatment. There had been a total silence during this escapade, but when the doctor had vanished from view it was as though some invisible referee had given the order "Box on!" and all hell was let loose.

The bridge was later secured and firmly held. It carried heavy traffic thereafter. All Airborne forces were soon withdrawn from Sicily, and St Stokes and I returned to Syracuse harbour where we were embarked in a landing craft returning to North Africa. I found myself with Johnnie Frost of 2 Para Battalion and other Para COs in the wardroom. In spite of the Supreme Commander's orders that no alcoholic refreshment might be served in naval vessels carrying troops, Johnnie Frost got over that difficulty in his own indomitable way and we had an uneventful passage back to Sousse. St Stokes brought me back to Divisional HQ and returned to his own 9 Field Company camp nearby, leaving me much in his debt.*

EXTRACTS FROM LETTERS TO MY PARENTS

Written from near Sousse, 19 July, 1943

First, I have now had a large packet of your letters. So they have found their way here at last. I'm sure you will be surprised to hear that! Secondly, I find I have been reported "wounded" in Sicily. This is rather an exaggeration. I could have prevented it being reported, but I was assured by the doctors that if anything went wrong with the cure, it was as well to have it reported properly and then one gets a pension! A super, top-notch London doctor has just inspected me. He says that two bits of metal must be extracted later, but not to worry.

Written from near Sousse, 23 July, 1943

The doctors all seem quite pleased with my progress. I invited one of the younger ones to dinner in our Mess. I procured some Algerian wine which we drank. I felt like death next morning and I telephoned to my guest to ask how he was. He replied, "Look at your own tongue in the mirror. If it is blue you'll know I feel the same as you do." I looked and it was blue!

Written from near Sousse, 18 August, 1943

There are millions of tomatoes and lemons growing round here, also peaches, but the Arabs pick them while they are still unripe. It is curious how

---

* In about 1963 (twenty years later), my wife and I were walking up the lane to the letter box one Sunday afternoon, when a large car approached, coming the other way. The driver stopped and enquired: "Can you please tell me where Colonel Henniker lives?" Here was Saint Stokes himself. He came from Bristol and was visiting a relative who happened to live in the village. He still survives, over twenty years on from that.

we buy earthenware pots from the Arabs to keep water cool and they steal our metal ones to boil it in! . . . We have an Italian P.o.W. as a Mess waiter. He sings *Funiculi Funicula* beautifully. He comes from the Island of Lampedusa. He says, "Anyone can have Lampedusa. Whoever lives there is a prisoner in war or peace.". . . I have finished Shakespeare's plays. The last one was *The Tempest*, which may have been set near here. In the play the King of Naples married his daughter to the King of Tunis; and apparently there were local forests in those days. I am surprised that forests lasted so long. Even in Biblical times men were quarrelling about the economic consequences of husbandry *versus* nomadic life, more than 1000 years before Shakespeare's day. The nomads evidently won, for by Mohammed's day their ubiquitous goats and sheep had barked every tree in the Middle East and killed the lot. . . . In *The Tempest* comes your often used expression: "ancient and fish-like". I take it W.S. thought of it before you did!

9

The Invasion of Italy

From our adventures in Sicily there was much to be learnt, and many conferences and discussions followed. Some were official and formal, held at Divisional, Brigade and Regimental level; others were of a more informal nature. We were all extremely vexed by the appalling muddle we had experienced in one way or another. About one thing we were agreed: a better way must be devised for getting the Airborne troops to their glider or parachute landing zones. It was futile to launch a whole brigade into the air and only land a handful in the proper place. It was all very well to say that the American pilots of the Dakota aircraft must have more training in navigation, but when were they to get it? Practically every serviceable Dakota in the Mediterranean had been employed lifting the Airborne Forces to Sicily and their absence from their ordinary duties for over a week had upset conventional arrangements very seriously. Another idea put forward was that a pool of spare navigators should be formed so that when airborne operations were ordered every aircraft employed could carry a supernumerary navigator. There were insuperable manpower difficulties in this and, anyway, no results could be expected for a long time. Meanwhile, 1 Airborne Division would be sitting under the olive groves of Sousse doing nothing useful, while others, less favoured, bore the heat and burden of the war.

No officer in 1 Airborne Division doubted that we were privileged to command magnificent troops and we all felt confident that we could do better than anyone else in the world. All that we wanted was to get to grips with the Germans on equal terms and "give them stick" as quickly as possible.

As the reader will have perceived, the author of this chronicle had begun to harbour ideas of his own on how we might do much better. It seemed to me that, because of the element of surprise, quite a small-scale *coup de main* party would usually achieve the initial capture of a bridge or other critical objective. Sufficient good navigators could be mustered for this. The difficulty principally lay in getting sufficient ground forces to the scene in time to hold the objective afterwards. The outline of my theory was simple. 1 Airborne Division itself must be given the whole job: to seize the bridge (or whatever) from the air, and then launch an attack on the ground from the existing front line.

This presupposed Divisional HQ itself being on the ground in the first place. The main body of the Division must then be landed by glider or parachute close *behind* our leading troops, to fight their way to the objective. They would not take up valuable places in landing craft, of which there were never enough, nor need they clutter up road space between the beaches and the spearhead of the attack. They would arrive under the same RAF umbrella as everyone else. Every sort of navigational aid on the ground could be prepared for them. They might even be safely landed in daylight. The troops so landed would be physically fresh on the scene and, by hypothesis, they would supply an additional and unexpected momentum to the thrust of the main force.

I had seen for myself at both Syracuse and at Catania how this might have been done, and a year later I saw how it might perhaps have been repeated at Arnhem. In the olive grove in whose shade the Divisional HQ basked near Sousse, I wrote what I hoped would be regarded as a useful paper urging my idea, but it never got much of a hearing. It was not perhaps well enough argued and the proposition is irrelevant today anyway. But I still think it was worthy of consideration. However, things were destined to turn out quite differently.

What pressures were brought to bear on General Hopkinson I cannot say, but I suspect they were many and heavy. I cannot blame him for what he decided to do, but I found his decisions most distressing. He determined to rid himself and the Divisional HQ of the complications of having Gunner and Sapper Units as "divisional troops". He determined to fine them down and allot them all permanently to the three Parachute Brigades and to the Air Landing Brigade.

It was quite impossible to convince him that this policy might be mistaken, and not, I thought, helpful to add to his troubles by continual argument. He had, on his side, the evident facts that both at Syracuse and at the Primasole Bridge the Sapper contribution towards preventing the enemy from demolishing the bridges was carried out by very few men; that his Gunner Commander, who was killed in a glider crash on landing in Sicily, had been unable to make any contribution whatever; and that I, his Sapper Commander, merely made an adventurous exploit comparable to his own exploit of piloting a glider personally that was released by its tug into the sea. Neither of us had made a

145

significant contribution except to demonstrate (perhaps needlessly) that senior officers regarded themselves as no less expendable than anyone else.

A curt *diktat* was therefore soon promulgated to the effect that Gunner and Sapper Batteries, Companies and Squadrons were henceforth to be integral parts of the Brigades with which they usually worked. Henceforth they were to be in no way under the control of the Commander RA or the Commander RE. The two of us, in due course, would be replaced by junior technical staff officers when the staff arrangements could be made.

The Brigade Commanders were, of course, delighted to have their private armies increased in size, though two of them said to me privately that they had some reservations. All I could do was to hope that my wounds would heal quickly and that my professional fortunes might improve before I was given the chop. Soon all was rectified as though by magic.

Meanwhile, however, Major Beasley had been killed in Syracuse and the OC of 2 Parachute Squadron had suffered a severe road accident in a jeep in North Africa, so two successors had to be found. Both these were easy, because in 9 Field Company there was a very competent Second-in-Command called Robert McNeile; and for 2 Para Squadron there was still the capable Denis Vernon whom the reader may remember as Commander of the Sapper detachment that went with Johnnie Frost on the Bruneval Raid in February, 1942.

Vernon therefore needs no introduction, but McNeile does. He was – alas, now deceased – a man of exceptional academic accomplishment and outstanding organizational ability. He had been a scholar at Eton and he had taken a good degree at King's College, Cambridge. As an ex-Kingsman myself, I could understand – though never equal – his academic acumen, but I had several times seen the cheerful, humorous and unflustered manner in which he was able to wade through paper work, pick out what mattered and get it all accomplished in very quick time. I was sure he was an excellent choice for 9 Field Company.

From the end of our operations in Sicily in July until 6 September we "licked our wounds", as I have indicated above. We bathed in the Mediterranean, gave the units as much opportunity as possible to do training exercises in the foothills of the Atlas Mountains, out of the African heat, yet within recall in case of emergency.

It was on 6 September that the call came. One of the Sapper Squadrons was having a concert, or "sing-song party", to which they kindly invited me. During the programme my Adjutant arrived and told me I was required at once for a meeting, because an unexpected order for operations had been received. The General was about to address us. It was then 10.30 pm and I hurried back to Divisional HQ.

The Brigadiers were all assembled when I got back, and General Hopkinson presently arrived. He told us the Italians had sued for peace and that 1 Airborne Division was to leave the camps near Sousse and move to a "staging area" near Bizerta as soon as possible. They would then embark in HM ships and other vessels collected from "the seven seas" to sail for Taranto in the heel of Italy. There was no indication of what sort of welcome we would get in Taranto. We knew that the 8th Army had crossed the Straits of Messina a few days previously, but we did not know about the Allied landings which were planned to take place very shortly at Salerno, not far from Naples.

The General told us that 4 Parachute Brigade Group under Brigadier Hackett was to land in Taranto harbour first. It would be followed by 2 Parachute Brigade Group under Brigadier Down immediately afterwards, and we were informed that six cruisers (RN and US Navy) were being assembled for this. Advanced Divisional HQ was to land with the first wave of troops. About forty-eight hours later a second wave, consisting of the Airlanding Brigade and 1 Parachute Brigade, was to land in the same cruisers which would be operating as a shuttle service.

The idea was that the first wave would secure the town of Taranto and the harbour against all comers. Thereafter, offensive patrols would be organized to cause the Germans to believe that a much larger force had arrived than had actually done so.

The General, with most of his Staff and the Brigade Commanders, were very cock-a-hoop at the way events were apparently proving them right. Now, under the new dispensation, the Gunners and Sappers were conveniently slotted into the Brigade groups and there would therefore be no Gunner or Sapper plans to complicate the issue.

The General, seeing my troubled looks, said to me with a smile, "Never mind, Henniker. Something may turn up in the end for you to do, but you mustn't wriggle into the Advanced Divisional HQ. We shall want the space for others."

But then an unexpected event occurred. There was the rattle of a jeep engine on the track through the olive grove. The vehicle stopped and out of it stepped a tall Flag Lieutenant of the Royal Navy. He saluted formally and handed a note to the General. The note apparently came personally from Admiral Cunningham the Naval C-in-C in the Mediterranean. It said that priority must be given to getting the docks of Taranto into working order, repairing damage and preventing sabotage. He stressed the importance of repairing a swing bridge that carried a main road over the waterway connecting the inner and outer harbours. He ended by saying that extensive Engineer responsibilities for port operation were envisaged and he hoped the General would allot sufficient Engineer troops to see that work was started with foresight and energy.

There was a roar of laughter from everybody, including the General, who

147

pointed at me and asked, "What do you intend to do about that?" I was able to reply that if we reverted to conventional practice, whereby I (as his CRE) was allowed to command the engineer troops, I would do my best to see that the Admiral had his way, and that our own Brigade Commanders might rest assured that I would also give them whatever support events appeared to demand.

I was now back in business and we heard no more wrangling about how best to get engineer work done. The new Gunner Commander, who had by now arrived to replace his predecessor killed in Syracuse, was not so lucky. He was detailed to remain in Sousse in charge of Divisional Rear HQ.

It was fairly easy to decide what we as Engineers wanted for our expected work in Taranto, and in conference with the Sapper Unit Commanders we cooked up a priority list of what seemed essential. I was able to arrange that 9 Field Squadron with some specialist equipment and tradesmen from the 261 Field Park Company would disembark in Taranto very early on the list and I made McNeile responsible for organizing the docks as best he could.

We all moved to Bizerta next morning and embarkation began immediately. I had been able to give Squadron Commanders a fair idea of what they were likely to have to do and I left it to them to barter with the Captains of HM Ships to take as much plant as possible. Some were more successful than others, and 261 Field Park Company had the most astonishing luck of all. The OC found three or four empty American Dakota aircraft going to Taranto as soon as an airfield was available, so the most unlikely unit of all to go to operations by air was the only one that actually did so. Moreover, the Company Sergeant Major of the Field Park Company, who was left behind with the Company's Rear Party, found a merchant ship, half empty, in Sousse bound for Taranto independently. He managed to talk the Captain into taking all the remaining men and equipment of the Company.* We were, therefore, quite an effective engineer contingent to support the Division and do what was necessary in the port.

When we sailed from Bizerta Admiral Cunningham stood on the mole to take the salute and to wish us good luck. Dressed in spotless white uniform, he had exactly the right touch – the right appearance of resolution, confidence and dignity. The last thing men want to see when they go into battle is some smiling politician looking only for the votes of his audience. I personally felt that the Admiral would see to it that the German Air Force would not be allowed to attack us with impunity. He imparted an air of confidence.

It so happened that a private soldier of the Royal Marines, who was standing on the deck near me, was a man I had known in Chatham some years before.

* His name was Clayton. He joined the Royal Engineers from the Army Apprentice College in Chepstow in 1936. I had been his "Party Officer" in the Training Battalion in Chatham at that time. We knew each other well.

148

He and a Captain of Royal Marines had once helped me build some fences for the RE Drag Hunt, and we instantly recognized one another. Referring to the Admiral whom we had saluted, he said, "We're in good 'ands with 'im in command of the Fleet," and when I saw the Captain of our ship, HMS *Aurora*, I felt we had the right man there too. (He was Commodore Agnew RN.)

In a way a good man commanding a warship has an easier task than a similar man commanding a regiment. He can be seen and his voice can be heard even in the thick of action. He is in the same danger as everyone else and he has a privileged position that no Regimental Commander has had since he used to lead his men, riding on a horse, at full gallop towards the enemy.

It is popular nowadays to denigrate Lord Cardigan, who commanded the Light Brigade in the Crimean War. He had been ordered to charge and he did not falter. He led his men himself "into the valley of death" in full view of everyone. And here was Commodore Agnew among us, walking round the ship, making sure that everything that could be done for the safety of all of us was being done. I am sure we all felt a great feeling of confidence in him. What, of course, none of us knew was that at that moment the Italian Fleet was preparing to surrender "under the Guns of Malta". And I doubt if Commodore Agnew knew that either.

Our journey to Taranto was uneventful and we tied up alongside a jetty in the outer harbour. Dark-eyed Italians flitted silently in the moonlight like bats in the rafters of a barn, while outside the town we soon found ourselves at grips with a German Parachute Division.

Fighting between parachute troops on both sides has some of the characteristics of a "gentleman's war". Neither side had any artillery to speak of, nor any tanks. When a prisoner was taken by either side, the first question was, "How many jumps have *you* done?" We certainly much regretted having them against us and we all felt that in peacetime we would have had a great many interests in common. The ethos of both sides was the same: "Engage the enemy more closely."

Fighting was very soon joined on the outskirts of Taranto and it was no easy matter. We had no howitzers, but both sides were determined to win and both sides knew how to use the weapons they had.

I was shot at a few times here and there, but in general terms my main concern was with technical affairs, for I soon found myself the Chief Engineer of a province about the size of Plymouth to Newton Abbot. The main duties falling upon the Parachute Squadrons was mine lifting, de-lousing booby traps, water supply and reconnaissance; while 9 Field Company and the Field Park Company were mainly engaged in operating the docks and clearing rubble from the roads, where the Allied Air Forces had bombed the place. They also had to make provision for receiving the immense quantities of warlike stores of all kinds that soon began to arrive by sea.

Dealing with the swing bridge in the port of Taranto turned out to be easier than expected. There was an amenable Italian Admiral as Dockyard Superintendent. He had plenty of civilian labour, who were competent and willing, and he managed the swing bridge with a firm hand. The only hitch was at midday when he called a halt for the *siesta*. A road block a mile long then had to await the Admiral's pleasure. But a young Sapper Officer found a diversion and McNeile got the Italians to improve a ring road which has now (I am told) become part of the landscape of Taranto. Everyone then lived happily ever afterwards.

A railway station, that was soon labelled (by order of McNeile) "St Pancras for the North", became a main artery for getting supplies to the forward troops. But first of all a tunnel through which the railway ran had to be unblocked. The Italian railway people were as keen as we were to get the railway repair equipment working, but they had to be convinced by the Sappers that all mines and booby traps left by the Germans had been removed. The unblocking of the tunnel looked at first sight a formidable task. There was a locomotive lying on its side with a number of truck-loads of ballast scattered higgledy-piggledy roundabout. But when professional railway gangs with heavy-duty plant get going they can move mountains. What was required was for the Sappers to find and remove the mines and booby traps first. Here the training we had done in this sort of work paid a good dividend. We had no accidents and the railway was used more and more every day.

A curious railway incident took place on the night of 13/14 September. An Advanced Party of the Special Air Service Regiment had arrived from North Africa and a young Major came to see me. He told me he intended to try and send a platoon by train into German-occupied territory and release some Allied Prisoners of War from a "cage", near a branch line about one hundred miles north of Taranto.

At that time a somewhat Gilbertian situation existed as far as the railway was concerned. There was a station at a small town called Potenza which the Germans had used for marshalling military traffic coming from Germany and northern Italy; they had no objection to the Italian railway authorities running a shuttle train between Taranto and Potenza for ordinary commercial purposes. The plan therefore was to include some covered wagons in the shuttle to hide the SAS troops. Then, instead of merely returning to Taranto, the points near Potenza would be changed and the shuttle would chug up the branch line to the PoW cage where the Allied prisoners were imprisoned. The Italian prison guards were believed to be no longer interested and it was hoped that it would only be a matter of minutes to get the prisoners on board the shuttle and bring them all back to Taranto.

The trouble was that the Italian Railway Authority could not find an Italian engine driver willing to face the adventure. The SAS Major asked if I could help. I felt I certainly ought to try, but I wanted no repetition of the disastrous Norwegian raid described in Chapter 6.

He and I hustled to 261 Field Park Company's workshop, where I knew there were one or two ex-railwaymen from the Great Western Railway, who had been Territorials before the war. It was about tea-time, and a lot of men were queued up with "knife, fork and spoon", hoping for a meal. John Chivers (the OC) and his CSM happened to be in the offing; and the CSM soon came back to the office with a somewhat surprised young man, who had been an engine driver, shunting locomotives in Swindon in peacetime. He was an enterprising type, wide awake and all for the adventure. His only misgiving was lest a railway collision occurred in the process. The SAS Major, who was clearly a first-class officer, had foreseen that difficulty. The railway traffic-signal arrangements were still in operation – I was told they could even telephone to Rome! – and they were prepared to put a railway inspector on the footplate to accompany the train and interpret the signals for the Sapper engine driver. This seemed to me as good a safeguard of the journey that I could hope for, and I agreed to the project.

The Sapper engine driver swallowed his tea and the train departed from Taranto at about 7 pm. A bit of shunting had to be done in Potenza under the noses of the German Military Police, but it all went without a hitch. By the early morning the train had returned in triumph to Taranto with 150 jubilant Allied PoWs on board. The driver went back to his unit as though nothing had happened. I tried to get him some mark of particular recognition, but a long time after the event I gleaned that the recommendation had been turned down. Nothing of note had, of course, happened, and in the afterlight one is apt to look upon the whole thing as of little account. But I personally had a very soul-searching time while the engine driver was away.

I was filled with foreboding and gloom. Here was I, returning for a civilized meal as though it might be Aldershot in peacetime, and there was the cheerful Sapper engine driver, for whose fate I felt deeply conscious, embarked on a hare-brained enterprise with a lot of SAS desperados whose competence or judgment I could only judge from appearance. Suppose it all went wrong? How could I possibly write to his wife or his mother, with anything but shame that I had let him go, as though it were no more than a treasure hunt in aid of charity? It was a longish walk back to the Mess and I had plenty of time to reflect. How could I even tell my Adjutant what I had done? I hardly even knew the name of the SAS Major! All I could say was that he looked like a reliable man and he was risking his own life in the journey too. What more might I have done that I had *not* done? There had been very little time to do anything. I had acted on the spur of the moment; and now I felt I had perhaps been a fool. Yet what more *could* I have done? And could I do anything *now*?

151

"Yes", I suddenly thought. "There is one thing I *can* do." At that moment I looked across the road.

On the other pavement was a large church. I suppose there was some kind of blackout, but there was enough light to see there was a considerable congregation within. "Ah!" I thought. "That's what I have *not* done." Had I been going on the train myself, I knew I would have asked God's help in making the best arrangements possible. Perhaps it was not too late even now. But was it OK to go into a Roman Catholic Church? Except at an occasional wedding of a brother officer – which tends to be something of a social occasion – I had never been inside an RC church in my life. I had, in fact, always associated the Roman Catholic Church with Bloody Mary, the Inquisition, and the Spanish Armada. The Pope, in those days, I assumed to be almost a half-brother of Satan himself; and Mussolini, who everyone said was a very bad man, was probably a Roman Catholic too. What about it?

Just then, who should appear but one of our Airborne Chaplains whom I knew to be Church of England. He was of junior rank, perhaps a Captain, and a very young man. He saluted me and, seeing my mood, he enquired, "Are you lost, Sir? Perhaps I can direct you."

"No," I said. "I know the way, but I want to say a few prayers. Is it OK to go into this Roman Catholic Church?"

"Of course it's OK," he said. "There were Christians in Rome when our forefathers were wearing woad. I'll come in with you if you like."

I thanked him and we knelt at the back of the Church. No one took the slightest notice of us and presently we both emerged. My doubts began to fade away. A feeling of greater confidence in the SAS Major who was in charge of the train suffused my mind. Instead of tossing and turning in mental anguish all night I slept like a log and only just got back to the station in time to greet the returning train. I had learnt a lesson, but there was a sequel.

In the morning, having rejoiced with the SAS Major and the Sapper engine driver in Taranto Station, I thought that the least I could do was to re-enter the RC Church to thank God for the Blessing of His gift of Peace of Mind. The Church door was open and the Church was empty but for one young man. He was sitting in an attitude of deep contemplation with his eyes shut. I suppose he may have been 25, no older. He had fair hair, an open-necked shirt, faded by the sun to a colour to match his trousers, which were kept in place by a belt. Had the belt been of a regulation pattern, and his garments been of a genuine khaki shade, I would have put him down as a British Army deserter. He was certainly not a Southern Italian, but the "cut of his jib" – an expression commonly used by men of my father's generation – was definitely un-British. Curiosity got the better of piety and, as I sat a few yards behind him, I watched him intently, wondering who he could be. After a few minutes he got up and turned to walk out. Our eyes met and he went absolutely white. I could see his knees actually tremble. The penny dropped and I recognised him for what he was. He was German. I had seen a German aircraft shot down over the harbour only the previous evening. Three or four parachutes had blossomed beneath the wreck. This chap must be one of them. He must have taken refuge in the Church to sleep the night and now was about to try and get back to his own people.

What ought I to do? Our countries were at war. We were both in a foreign land and we were enemies. I was certainly as strong and as active as he; also I was armed, which he was not. But we were both in Church, each before his Maker. A quotation, much used by my form master at school, surged into my mind.

"But for the grace of God, there goes John Bradford."*

I watched the German leave the Church, but I did nothing. I have often wondered since if he survived the war. I hope he did.

In writing about our exploits in Italy I have failed to weave in a number of disjointed occurrences.

The first concerns the sinking in Taranto harbour of HMS *Abdiel*. This ship was a mine-layer and was provided by the Admiral because she was able to accommodate small military vehicles such as jeeps and light anti-tank guns. She was also extremely fast and could make swift journeys between North Africa and Taranto.

On her first trip her main cargo was a (Welsh) Para Battalion and some of the Divisional Artillery, less its Commander who was left behind. She slid into Taranto harbour after dark during the first night of our arrival. Two Royal Naval vessels and the US cruiser *Boise* had been unloaded and we were expecting another batch of arrivals.

There was suddenly a terrific explosion in the harbour and it was clear that a ship was sinking. My Adjutant and I jumped into a rowing boat and attempted to haul out of the water some of the many soldiers struggling to free themselves of their heavy equipment and get clear of a sheet of fuel oil that had been spewed out of the ship when she blew up. She had steamed over an acoustic mine missed by our Fleet minesweepers and in a few moments she blew up again as a result of an internal explosion. She broke into two pieces and sank in a few minutes.

We made two or three trips in the rowing boat but found on each occasion more and more corpses floating with their heads and feet under the water and only their buttocks protruding above the surface. The explanation was to be found in the misuse of life-belts issued to the troops against such an emergency. The life-belts consisted of a rubber ring, like the inner tube of a motor tyre, which went round the man's body. It could be inflated either by an

* John Bradford was a Bishop in the sixteenth century.

automatic device or by puffing into the tube with one's mouth. There was nothing defective about that, as the buoyancy of the ring was sufficient to keep a man afloat in spite of a steel helmet, army boots and webbing pouches full of ammunition. The trouble seemed to lie in the fact that the troops had been insufficiently briefed in how to fit the life-belts. The buoyant ring round the man's body was held in position by two adjustable tapes. To be effective the ring had to be fitted round the chest and close under the armpits, not round the waist. In its correct position, even if the man were unconscious, he floated with his head above water. In HMS *Aurora* steps had been taken by the naval ratings to see that we (the ignorant soldiery) all knew about this. Whether this necessary instruction had been given in HMS *Abdiel* I cannot say, but it was evident to my Adjutant and me that many of the corpses we hauled out of the water owed their deaths to the faulty fitting of their own life-belts. The belts were loose round the man's waist, and the weight of his boots and his tin hat kept his head and his feet under water – particularly if he were stunned.

This was a most disagreeable episode; a great many unnecessary lives were lost.

The next incident had a happy ending. It concerns the water supply. The water supply of Taranto came from three sources. First there was the Apulian aqueduct. It brought water from the Apennines, near Naples. Secondly, there was another, shorter, aqueduct that brought water from artesian wells and supplied the arsenal and the dockyard only. A third aqueduct brought water from some springs a few miles to the east of Taranto and could only supply a small section of the town.

Middle East Intelligence reports had suggested that if these three aqueducts – all of which emanated from territory held by the enemy – were cut by retreating Germans, the civil population, the dockyard and the British troops landing in Taranto would be in a bad way. My Intelligence Officer soon discovered that so far none of these possibilities had actually occurred, but it was more than likely that they would soon. The question I had to answer was: What were the Sappers going to do then?

The Parachute Squadrons all had orders from me to locate the aqueducts in their areas and to do what they could to store as much water as possible in the parts of them that lay within our territory. This they all did extremely efficiently, but it seemed likely that unless Naples were captured soon, a severe shortage of water might occur, particularly as very large British military forces were already heading by sea for Taranto. Fortunately a most unlikely discovery was made.

In the course of visiting the Sappers engaged in clearing mines in the railway tunnel mentioned above, I came across the CO of 5 (Scottish) Parachute Battalion in whose area the tunnel happened to be. We spoke about the local military situation and I asked him how his Battalion was managing for water.

"Oh! We're all right," he replied. "We have a trout stream just beyond those trees."

We looked at our maps, and I wondered whether he had gone mad or whether I had. There was no stream marked, but a short walk revealed that there really was a babbling brook, running under a culvert only a hundred yards away. I threw a dead leaf into the stream on one side of the road and watched it emerge almost at once on the downstream side. Arithmetic revealed a flow of sparkling water exceeding 350,000 gallons an hour!

The Colonel's trout stream became the main supply of water for the troops thereafter. Unhappily there were no trout! The Germans later cut the Apulian aqueduct – I think on 16 September – but the water trapped in it between that point and the City was sufficient to tide us over till the source was captured too, and the aqueduct mended.

Two other events, whose position in the sequence of affairs I cannot remember, must be recorded. They concern the deaths of two senior officers, and both I would say were unnecessary. The first was the mortal wound, received in action, by the Divisional Commander, General Hopkinson. I did not actually witness the event, but I was not very far away.

There was an airfield at a place called Gioia, much needed by the RAF, and it was certain that, when captured, we would find it dotted with German mines and booby traps. I wanted to make sure that there would be no delay on the part of the Sappers with 4 Parachute Brigade in tackling the work of "delousing", so I went up during the attack to see Major Hardiman, who commanded 4 Parachute Squadron. Our meeting point was to be near a small town called Castellaneta. It was stoutly defended by the Germans who had laid a fair number of mines in the roads nearby.

Before I reached our meeting point, it was clear from the demeanour of everyone I saw that the scene of actual battle was not far away. Men were wearing their steel helmets and looked rather serious. They tended to crouch when walking in the open, and only stood erect when under the cover of buildings or behind trees. I stopped and asked a young Gunner Officer standing at the roadside what the score was.

"The Divisional Commander," he said, "was up here and has been badly wounded. They have just taken him away. He looked pretty bad!"

He went on to explain – how accurately I cannot say – that the attack on Castellaneta had been held up, and the only contribution that the General could make – and a gallant one too – was to go and have a look for himself, in the process of which he was shot in the head by a burst of German machine gun fire. The young officer went on to explain, rather ruefully, that had the Commander of the Divisional Royal Artillery been present (instead of commanding the Rear Parties in North Africa) he might have been able to collect the few guns that we had with other Brigades to do what was necessary at Castellanata. Instead, all the General could do was metaphorically to wave his sword and say, "Follow me".

This failure on his part was one of the inevitable consequences that follow when a small Regular Army, like the British Army, is suddenly swollen into many Divisions for a World War. There were dozens of British Officers of the right age and calibre to command Battalions and even brigades, but to command a Division is quite a different matter.

Up to, and including, the rank of Lieutenant-Colonel, an officer really only deals with his own arm of the service – tanks, guns, infantry, engineers and so on. A Brigade Commander deals with matters from a rather wider background. He occasionally has a few guns and a few tanks and a few engineers, or whatever is allotted to him by "Higher Authority". It is only when he becomes a Major-General that he really has quite a lot of every arm to weave into his plan of action. He must therefore have at his side his head Gunner, Sapper, Tank man and so on to get the best results. It was only by the intervention of an Admiral that General Hopkinson happened to have his head Sapper in Italy at all. Then, if he did not like what was being done, he knew exactly who to blame! (I dare say I was lucky not to get the sack several times.)

General Hopkinson died that night and Brigadier Down, from 2 Para Brigade, stepped into his place. He did not remain with 1 Airborne Division for very long, for he was already earmarked to go to Burma to command an Indian Airborne Division; but it seemed to me, while he was with us, that he had a pretty good grasp of what to do. He was good at getting the best out of his subordinates and I found him very easy to work with.

The other senior officer to become a casualty was a notable Sapper Officer, then the Chief Engineer of 5 Corps, which was being rapidly brought to Italy through the port of Taranto. He was Brigadier M. R. Caldwell. He was a man of great character, well known in wide circles of the Army. He had fought in Flanders in the First World War as a subaltern in a Sapper Company in a Guards Division. He had been bitten by the bug that is bred in Caterham, Pirbright, and Wellington Barracks, London. He was a great disciplinarian and was known as "Hindenburg" or "Hindy". He was a man of terrific drive, and violent outbursts of wrath at what displeased him. People sought to displease him as seldom as possible. I suppose he was not a particularly experienced engineer, because, apart from the First World War, he had spent a lot of time on the Staff, but he was a very good judge of men, and could recognize a good man or a good idea when he saw them.

On arrival in Taranto he instantly saw the importance of the provisions we were trying to make to set up the skeleton of an efficient Engineer Base Depot suitable for a Corps, or even for an Army. He took an immediate liking to Robert McNeile, commanding 9 Field Company, and asked if he might use the 9 Field Company's Officers' Mess as his base till HQ 5 Corps was established.

He refused my invitation to live in our Divisional HQ Mess, saying it might cramp my style "having a second engineer opinion always breathing down your neck". I thought that considerate and very typical of him. However, 9 Field Company Officers did him proud and I saw a good deal of him.

I had known "Hindy" before the War and I took him all round our Divisional area in Taranto, showing him what we were doing and what were our plans for the future. He had many good ideas to offer and he was particularly interested in the Engineer Intelligence Summary that my Intelligence Officer was compiling.

My Intelligence Officer was a young man called Michael Green. I had told him that I was sure that the Top Brass at 5 Corps HQ, at 8th Army HQ, and at Army Group HQ, who were still mostly in Malta or North Africa, would be burning to know what engineer resources could be hoped for in Italy. Would it be possible, for instance, to find forward landing grounds for RAF fighters? Did we see any localities that might easily be opened up as emergency landing grounds? (It was extraordinary in those days how few Sappers, outside 1 Airborne Division, knew how long a runway was necessary for even the commonest type of aircraft.) What local supplies were available of sand, bricks, timber, steel and so on in the heel of Italy? Individual Airborne Sappers were continually unearthing gold mines such as these, and Michael Green got the idea around to the Squadrons to report their finds to him. As a result, he amassed a formidable compendium of Engineer Intelligence which we were able to supply to "Higher Authority". They were in the market for such information and "Hindy" gave us encouragement in working at this. Later on, I personally – quite unjustly – got a considerable pat on the back for our efforts.

Unfortunately "Hindy" had not really got enough to do, so that when a railway wagon full of explosives caught fire in Taranto docks, he was the first to dash from 9 Field Company's Officers' Mess to lead a fire-fighting party to tackle the blaze. The wagon blew up almost at once and "Hindy" was very badly burnt. I was told by the doctors that his burns exceeded the normal maximum that any man could hope to survive, but he lived for several days. I often visited him in hospital and one evening he seemed so vigorous that I felt sure he would be the exception that proves the general rule about what a man could stand. Alas, he died that night and when I heard the "Last Post" sounded, and the rifle shots fired over the grave, I felt it very deeply. The Army had lost a fine officer and I a bright star in my firmament.

Gradually more and more of the 8th Army were landed in Taranto and little by little we, with our lighter equipment and lesser artillery support, began to take a back seat. The war in the heel of Italy was becoming organized and our Airborne boys were rapidly becoming redundant, to use a modern catchword. First, 78 Division became a more workable proposition, with a full staff, lots of artillery and plenty of transport. But for some inexplicable omission they had

157

no sappers, and our 9 Field Company was lent to them to fill the gap. Here Robert McNeile pulled off a personal triumph.

The 78th Division was launched in the direction of Bari and Foggia on the Adriatic Coast; and soon they saw on their maps the River Ofanto, which was an obstacle to be crossed on the way. It was quite clear that the main road bridge was likely to be demolished by the Germans; and it was obvious also that if a ford could be found a few miles to either side of the main road it might be possible to get a force across the river and outflank the defenders. Here McNeile's classical education at Eton paid a notable dividend. He knew from his schooldays that Hannibal's defeat of the Romans in 216 BC at the Battle of Cannae was fought on the River Ofanto. It probably took place at Cannae only because there must have been a ford there, and McNeile saw marked on an Italian map that there was a railway station named Cannae in the appropriate place. He sold this idea to the leading Infantry Brigadier of 78 Division who thereupon sent off a reconaissance patrol with either McNeile in person, or one of his officers. A ford was found and the German defenders were duly discomforted.*

Soon after this event, the whole of our Division was extracted from the battle area and the date of our departure became a subject for speculation and betting. I was soon sent for by the Chief Engineer of 8th Army so that he could thank us for what we had done while in Italy.

I found the Chief Engineer, Brigadier Coxwell-Rogers, in his tent when I arrived about noon. After talking for a bit he looked at his watch and, seeing the time, he invited me to "A" Mess for lunch. The only people present were Monty, still commanding 8th Army, Coxwell-Rogers and a couple of ADCs. I sat between Coxwell-Rogers and Monty. We had a light but civilized meal, during the course of which Monty turned to me and said, "I hope you weren't too disappointed in Bulford when I refused to have you in command of a Parachute Brigade." I told him that of course I was furious at the time, but that now I had got over it and could listen to the reason why without re-opening any scars. "It's like this," he said. "When a man has commanded an Infantry Battalion with success, I *know* he won't make a mess of a Brigade. But, however good a Gunner or a Sapper may be, I cannot be *sure* that he won't make mistakes when he first commands an Infantry Brigade. So that's my rule. In peacetime if a man makes a mistake, he may learn from it; but in battle, mistakes cost men's lives and that won't do."†

Anyone can see the sense in that and our lunch was not spoilt.

* For his many excellent works in the heel of Italy I managed to get McNeile the MBE, and this masterpiece of deduction was one of the factors I cited.

† I eventually got command of an Infantry Brigade in 1952 during the Emergency in Malaya. I commanded it for three years. It is a near thing which is the more rewarding during active operations – to command an Infantry Brigade or a Field Company.

Presently Monty asked, as a sort of *ballon d'essai*, "Tell me now, how could I have used an Airborne Division in my battles in Africa?" This seemed a rather difficult topic; an officer of no account lecturing a full General, still wearing the laurels of victory, on how he might have done better. But with Monty there seemed to be no impropriety. We discussed it easily and perfectly naturally, as though we were discussing Wellington's battles in the Peninsular War. I only wished I had had the time to collect my thoughts on my newly proposed theories about Airborne Forces in battle and had been able to express them better. I missed a great opportunity which I often regretted later. Certainly I became convinced that Monty was a very great man, and I have held that opinion consistently.

Finally the day for our departure from Italy came. It was in early November. The autumn was cold and wet and we all hoped to get home for Christmas. The Divisional Engineers were put in charge of the embarkation arrangements. It all went extremely smoothly – perhaps because we were all doing what we all longed for, namely embarking for home. The last act, however, included a scene of mild comedy.

Towards the evening everything was on board except for two Airborne trailers. One belonged to the Signals, the other to the RAMC. The ship's First Officer said there was only room for one; the other must be left in Taranto. A Signals Officer approached my subaltern on the quay and explained that the signals trailer contained some highly important new wireless sets: "The only ones in existence for future operations in Northern Europe." As he spoke, a Medical Officer appeared. He explained that his trailer was full of medical equipment of the highest priority: "Lives will be lost if it remains in Italy." My subaltern sent for his Major. The signaller and the doctor each brought up their heavier artillery in the form of their colonels. In the end I was sent for to adjudicate. I heard the full story from both Colonels. Whichever trailer we left behind, it seemed we would lose the war. I decided in favour of the signals. Their trailer was loaded and the medical one remained on the quay.

Instantly a hoard of medical personnel gathered round the medical trailer. They burst open the seals and the wire binding, and started filling their battledress blouses with the precious contents. It was full of oranges! I turned triumphantly to both litigants and pointed out that my judgement had been sound.

"Yes," replied the Signals Colonel laconically. "You *were* right, ours contains champagne."

And when we tasted it long afterwards, I *knew* I had been right.

EXTRACTS FROM LETTERS TO MY PARENTS

Written from Taranto, 25 September, 1943

We have a change of scene. I write from Italy where we have been for some time. . . . Italy is full of fruit, mosquitoes, sandflies and of course, Italians. When entering a village, after driving the Germans out, the people throng us about and shower us with fruit – grapes, figs and now peaches. The blue grapes, I am told, are made into wine and are not of much interest as eaters; but some of the green ones are splendid. . . . The Italians seem very pleased to see us; but, like all organ-grinders, they smile at the best bidder.

Written from Taranto, 9 October, 1943 (to my sister)

I live in a captured German tent about the size of the dining room at home. I had a captured German army "People's Car", with an air-cooled engine under the back seat; but now orders have been given for all captured German vehicles to be returned to HQ. I now have an American thing called a Jeep. It has no doors and if you fall asleep you may fall overboard going round a corner.

Written from Taranto, 10 October, 1943

The other day two of my officers and I walked 48 miles in 23 hours. The 14th and 15th hours were the worst. We now feel all the better for it. . . . I still live in my German tent and a tame hen lays an egg in it just before dawn every day; but an Italian policeman, who guards our enclosure, creeps under the flies of the tent and steals the egg as soon as he hears the hen lay. . . . There are still millions of grapes on the vines, and figs on the trees. Nothing in Italy ever happens today. I have not learnt the Italian for "today"; but *domani* one learns in the first five minutes in the country. *Pronto* and *subito* mean "in the not too distant future".

Written from near Bari, 17 October, 1943

We are enjoying weather like April in England. "Oh to be in England etc. etc." Green grass and millions of crocuses. The grapes are nearly over. . . . I do not know how the Italians will take their declaration of war on the Germans. They will find it much more exciting than just being a "defeated nation"!

Written from near Bari, 21 October, 1943

Today I killed a snake in my tent. A Carabiniere pronounced it to be *vipri*, adding that there are *molto vipri* when it's *fremdo* or warm. I hope that now it's cold there are not *molto* still. (Some, perhaps, lying for warmth in my bed!). . . . Our Signal Officer bought some chocolate buns in Bari. He gave one to me. It was much better than any you have seen in England since 1939! Across the street from here there are two Italian women sitting in the sun, one picking the nits out of her neighbour's greasy hair!

Written from Taranto, 23 October 1943

I have not seen Naples, but I hear it is not so badly mauled as the BBC would have you think. . . . I sent you some chocolates. Did they arrive? We captured a German supply train filled with "goodies" for the German troops, including thousands of bottles of brandy. Our troops deserve congratulating. There was no looting. The brandy was issued with the rations! Sufficient to taste but not sufficient to make T. Atkins drunk. Amongst my share of the trainload was a German electric lighting set with which we now light the house where the HQ has its offices. We also had 75 Italian Army mules. I am teaching the Sappers to look after them, which they (the Sappers) much enjoy. Some of the mules follow their masters about like dogs. I'm sure the mules will come in useful when we get into the mountains. There are still a few sandflies.

Written from near Bari, 4 November, 1943

In November the Italians are to celebrate their victory over the Germans in 1918. They are also said to have struck a medal for their sailors who fought (and lost) the recent Battle of Matapan. . . . We see plenty of dried figs in the shops here. I can't think why the ships that come here with munitions for the Armies do not go home with dried fruit for Britain. They must, otherwise, I suppose, go home empty.

161

10

The Last Months with First Airborne Division

We landed in Glasgow before Christmas in 1943 and were given Christmas leave at once. My sister in the ATS was given leave too, and my parents did the best they could for us, but times were hard. It was very cold in East Anglia. There was little coal to heat the house – not through rationing or cost, I think, but simply that the coal merchants had none for sale. Food may have been short too but the worst aspect of all for my ageing parents was the expectation of invading North-West Europe. They feared this would be a repetition of the pages of casualties in *The Times*, as it had been in the War in Flanders 1914–1918.

My Mother, with her wonderful stoicism, seldom showed it, and hung holly and mistletoe round the picture rail in the study, but my Father was less successful in hiding his thoughts. One day when we were sawing wood in the shed he suddenly stopped and exclaimed: *"Post equitem sedet atra Cura."*★ Then, as an afterthought he added, "What do you suppose the *atra Cura* was?" I told him I always supposed it was nightfall, but I had never read it except as part of an imposition at school, aged 14.

"That's what all the schoolmasters tell us, and what I always thought myself. But now I know it was not the dark they feared, but the unknown dangers that frequent the night."

Thereafter he found a way of relieving his own anxiety by murmuring *atra Cura* under his breath, thinking my mother and sister would not understand it. But one day I saw a book of quotations on the table and I guessed my sister must have found the explanation.

★ A black care rides pillion behind the horseman. (Horace)

I gave him a bottle of the Signaller's champagne on Christmas Day, but he begged to be excused from opening it. "I shall keep it to drink with you on another day." We agreed to this proposition and eventually drank the Signaller's bottle in July, 1945.

When I returned to our Divisional HQ in Lincolnshire a few days after Christmas I found we had a new Divisional Commander, a Major-General R. E. Urquhart, a Highland Light Infantryman who had been a Staff Officer in 51 Highland Division at Alamein and later commanded an Infantry Brigade with great distinction. He was a fine man whom I soon began to admire and to like very much. He was a good practical soldier, with both feet on the ground, and not too much "airy-fairy nonsense" about him. We in the Airborne business had built up a kind of mumbo-jumbo, based partly on theory and partly on bitter experience, and it seemed to me that Roy Urquhart was just the man to distinguish the sense from the nonsense in our philosophy.

There were still some months to go before the invasion of North-West Europe was due to begin and of course the plans were all secret, and we did not know the place chosen for the landing, nor the proposed date for D-Day. We did, however, soon realize that we would play no part in the plans for D-Day. That was allotted to 6 Airborne Division, and it was obvious to us that we might be needed either as a reserve division that could quickly be brought over by air to the lodgement area if things went wrong, or we might be kept in reserve for whatever might befall thereafter.

It was thus quite clear that we should probably have to operate on a totally different basis from 6 Airborne. They had several months to plan with the airmen exactly the best way to do what was required. They could rehearse the parts they would have to play on D-Day and get it all worked up to a fine pitch. Moreover, their flight plan could be fairly simple. They would be flying for most of the way over southern England, where they all knew the way about; the cross-channel flight could hardly exceed a hundred miles and the chances of most of the parachutists and gliders arriving at their proper destinations were far better than anything we had experienced in Sicily. That they would have a stiff fight when they landed was more or less a certainty, but we knew they would be as determined in battle as we were, and I, for one, felt sure in my own mind that they would give a valiant account of themselves.

Our role would, however, be totally different. It was extremely unlikely that we could expect much warning of what we should have to do. Very little opportunity to rehearse our operation seemed likely and in my own mind the absolute *sine qua non* of our plans must be tempered by simplicity and speed. We knew the Germans were absolute masters at slipping out of our clutches after suffering a reverse. They had done so after Alamein; they had escaped from Sicily, and when we had beaten them in the lodgement area in France

163

they would do their best to extricate their formations and withdraw to some position – probably behind a wide river line – to fight again.

It seemed to me that our best chance was likely to occur if, after an Allied victory in the lodgement area, a state of chaos might arise in Germany, Belgium, Holland, or (less likely) in France. This might be comparable with the chaos that arose in Italy after the Italians defected in the previous September. This had given us our chance in Taranto, and we had been lucky to have the Royal Navy behind us to get us to the scene in time. Here in North-West Europe things would not be so easy. It requires a positive fleet of aircraft to launch an Airborne Division into battle and it is all complicated by the arrangements necessary to lay out the gliders. Moreover, the aircrews required to fly this fleet of aircraft are not all sitting waiting for the call; they are taking part in real operations every day and they cannot give their individual attention to planning for every possible emergency that may occur. Even getting a suitable map into the hands of everyone who wants one is equal in complexity with arranging an art show in the Royal Academy.

What seemed to me the best chance of doing any good after 21 Army Group had given the Germans a hammering in Normandy would be to use the Airborne Corps of three Airborne divisions – two American and our 1 Airborne Division – as a Mobile Reserve, and merely carry them in aeroplanes in a shuttle service to where they were wanted at 100 miles an hour as opposed to (say) 25 miles an hour open to the Germans in lorries. It seemed to me that as soon as one attempted a parachute or glider operation one inevitably got back to the mumbo-jumbo techniques that took so long to arrange. This pedestrian approach of mine was rather scorned by the pundits, so I did not voice it much.

However, we had plenty to do in Lincolnshire to get our own training on the top line again. We in the Sappers, for instance, had never built a Bailey Bridge! Bailey Bridges had hardly been invented when we left the UK for North Africa, and they were so rare that we thought ourselves lucky to have a couple of days to see what one looked like. And there was much else besides.

In due time D-Day arrived and on D + 2 a planning party from our HQ was flown over to Normandy in a Dakota and landed on a grass and expanded metal runway within a few hundred yards of the beach. It was a fascinating experience, and reassuring to witness the armada of ships, both Royal and Merchant Navies, the activity on the beaches and the signs of the battle only a few miles inland.

Within half an hour of landing we were assembled with some of the staff of 30 Corps. (General Horrocks was still recovering from a wound received in the Mediterranean theatre, and another General was acting for him.) I got the impression that this Corps Staff was incredibly efficient, and one would like to think that the Nationalised Industries are equally well served today.

Our meeting, as far as I remember, was to settle the outlines of getting 1

164

Airborne Division to Normandy to plug a hole in the unlikely event of the Germans being able to make one. In the hands of such an efficient Staff, the matter was easily settled. The Staff had other work to do and the whole conference only took about three-quarters of an hour. Our aeroplane would not start to take us home, so we spent the might in a bivouac area listening to the guns in the distance and the hum of aircraft overhead. There was a German air raid during the night, but not very close to us. As I was shaving next morning a Military Policeman standing near by told me this was not like he'd been accustomed to in the Western Desert.

"Out there, Sir," he said, "there ain't all these bloody Froggies about. They are far more bother than the Bedouins – and much more numerous."

We flew back to England, arriving about midday, and returned to Lincolnshire next morning.

After this initial planning experience we were summoned from Lincolnshire for many more. They mostly took place at HQ Airborne Corps, commanded by General Browning. This was set up in Moor Park in Hertfordshire. I do not know the extent to which he had any say in the operations we were required to plan, or whether the projects were just farmed out to him as exercises to be studied by his HQ by way of precautions. It soon, however, became apparent that by the time the plans had been made, events had usually occurred in Normandy that made them superfluous.

The fault, in my view, lay in the complexity of the plans considered. We studied a great many possible and impossible operations, and I found myself gradually getting more and more out of step with those I was working with. Never in my career had I been a "Yes-man", but I was finding to my dismay that I was rapidly becoming a positive "No-man". If anyone had asked my opinion on any of our plans my "gut reaction" would have been to reply: "Have nothing to do with it". Luckily no one *did* ask me my opinion, but I'm sure most of them felt that they would do better with another man in my place. I felt in my own heart that I was becoming a "bolshie officer". General Urquhart must have been aware of this too, though we never had a cross word.

Exactly how it came about I do not know, but on 10 August he said to me, "I think you've been too long in this Airborne business. You've been Airborne for nearly three years and it's time you had an innings with an Infantry Division in Normandy. I'll help you to get a decent appointment in 21 Army Group, but will you tell me which of these Sappers I've been offered in your place is the best one?" He showed me a list of names, one of whom was a Lieutenant-Colonel Eddie Myers. I had known him for many years. He was a most accomplished man. Before the War he had, among other things, been a most successful Point-to-Point rider; he was also a well-qualified engineer, very shrewd in outlook, and had recently been in Greece, having been dropped there by parachute to assist the Partisans. (There were two rival lots of

165

Partisans in Greece at that time, but I forget which lot Eddie was assigned to. However, he had been so highly regarded that he had been interviewed by Churchill and Eden, the Foreign Secretary, when he got back to England.) Anyway he was an obvious choice for CRE 1 Airborne Division.

I felt very sad at leaving 1 Airborne Division, and saying goodbye to the Sappers was a painful experience. They all said nice things that I did not deserve. My driver (Lance-Corporal Lowe) and my batman (Sapper Meek) both volunteered to come with me, so we packed our Red Berets, of which we were proud, and sent them to our homes. General Urquhart told me to take my jeep – he presumably foresaw that it would not be required in any of the operations being planned – and we motored to Deal and crossed in a Landing Craft to Arromanches. Here a Staff Officer sent us on to a Reinforcement Depot Camp near Bayeux* where we arrived in time for supper.

The Base Reinforcement Depot near Bayeux was the nearest approach to Hell on Earth that I had ever seen. There was absolutely nothing to do. Bored officers sat aimlessly in the sunshine, discussing the prospects of languishing there for ever, and because casualties had been mercifully light in comparison with 1914–18, the prospect of a life sentence seemed quite possible.

The most pathetic inmate of the Depot whom I came across was a Lieutenant-Colonel, who had been commanding the engineer units of an Infantry Division. This division had been "broken up" (as the expression was) because the actuaries at the War Office foresaw that the manpower of Great Britain could no longer keep it up to strength. I was told that the unfortunate man had been the boss of a family engineering firm in the Midlands before the war and, because he was a Captain in the Territorial Army, he had been called up in 1939. By now his firm had gone to the Devil in his absence while his rivals were all prospering mightily on War Department contracts. He was eating his heart out in this miserable Depot. Moreover, like me, he was only a temporary Lieutenant-Colonel and, after a statutory period of a few weeks in the Reinforcement Depot, he would revert to his real rank of Major – or even Captain – and suffer the loss of pay, status and prospects that awaited many of the inmates of the Depot.

I foresaw the same thing happening to me and I did not relish it. I did, however, hold one good card as a Regular Officer which perhaps he, poor chap, lacked. I happened to know both the Chief Engineer of 21 Army Group and his deputy, Major-General Tickell. After breakfast therefore, on our first day at the Depot, I sought out my driver and his jeep to go in search of HQ 21 Army Group where I imagined that General Tickell might be found.

We had luck and saw at the roadside a group of tents and a numbered notice board that told those in the know that this was the lair of the Deputy Chief

* At this distance in time I am not certain of the accuracy of this name for the camp, nor its exact location.

166

Engineer. We entered the enclosure and met a junior RE Staff Officer whom I had met in Italy. He recognized me and when I told him I wanted to see General Tickell – and why – he took a sympathetic view. He said he was pretty sure that Tickell, at this very moment, was trying to find a Lieutenant-Colonel to take over an important job on the Lines of Communication which the present incumbent was making a hash of. I asked him to go and tell the General that I was in the compound and would like to see him if he could spare the time.

I knew General Tickell of old, for when he was a mere Captain in 1924, he had been the Military Engineering Instructor in whose class I had sat at the Royal Military Academy (Woolwich) when a Cadet. No doubt I had been one of his most unpromising pupils, but if he were now "in a jam" over something important, he might be willing to take a risk on someone he knew rather than on a stranger.

The young Staff Officer said he would "have a go" on my behalf and after a few minutes he reappeared with a grin on his face. Contrary to expectation Tickell said he would see me at once. (I should, perhaps, say that this young man was a bright lad and perhaps that was why Tickell listened to him. I was much in his debt, and I am glad to say that later on I was able to do him a good turn in exchange.)

Soon I was standing in front of Tickell and I could see he was looking me up and down, wondering whether he had before him the kind of man he was looking for. We exchanged a few reminiscences of Woolwich days and I told him how I was situated now in durance vile at the Reinforcement Depot and how I got there. I had prayed to the Almighty, while waiting outside, to grant me ability to state my case properly and I told my tale as briefly as possible. Generall Tickell, however, was not only a man of quick intellect and great ability, he also had a kind heart and made up his mind at once.

"All right," he said conclusively, "I'll give you a go. I can find you something to do at once. It's not much of a job, but at the moment it happens to be very important and it will keep you out of mischief till the Chief Engineer finds you something better to do."

He then explained that the German Army in Normandy was now in a bad way. Any day now Rommel might withdraw, and when he began it was anybody's guess how far he would go before he attempted to occupy some defensive position and fight again.

"My guess," continued the General, "is that he may go back as far as the Rhine, blowing up all the bridges on the way."

The consequences of this were obvious. We would have to do many river-crossing operations requiring many hundreds of tons of bridging equipment of all kinds to replace those demolished by the retreating Germans.

"How many tons of Bailey Bridging equipment do you think you'll want, Sir?" I queried. "And what have you actually got in store?"

167

The General had all the figures in his head, and he explained how he had not as much Bailey equipment in store as he would like, because such unexpected quantities had already been used in tactical bridges in the battle area in Normandy and all this equipment was still in place on the ground.

"What I want you to do," he said, "is to dismantle all the Bailey Bridges that are no longer wanted in Normandy, get the equipment stacked in some central place and then send it forward to 21 Army Group. Speed is essential."

He went on to explain that the Chief Engineer of the Lines of Communication had troops and transport for doing the work, but he lacked the right man to take charge of the operation.

"So there you are," he concluded. "Have you any questions?"

I said I thought I had enough information to begin at once, and I thanked him profusely. Within a few hours, Lowe, Meek and I were at the HQ encampment of the Chief Engineer on the Lines of Communication. He was Brigadier Perry, whom I had known some years previously in India. He was much older than I was, having been in the First World War, but we had originally become friendly from a common love of horses and playing polo. He was a resourceful engineer with an unflappable temperament and he had now collected about him on the Lines of Communication some good technical Staff Officers, some of whom he at once introduced to me.

One of these, a young Captain, was put, as it were "at my disposal". He had evidently been planning ahead and it was not long before the two of us had an outline plan ready for Perry to sign to get work started. This gave us the necessary authority and the rest we could do without bothering him further.

Rommel was already starting to withdraw and was being chased by the Americans and ourselves. Paris was liberated on 25 August and Brussels was reached on 3 September. Already we were beginning to use equipment we had retrieved from Normandy.

When we first began this process we both thought that detailed lists of component parts of the bridges, down to lists of nuts and bolts, ought to be made, but it soon became apparent that on the Lines of Communication there was an organization that made all this unnecessary. All that was required of us was to make up convoys of lorries, each holding all the parts of one single bridge, with a general description of the bridge in the hands of the Convoy Commander. Thus a convoy of *x* lorries might be said to contain "One 200 foot, Class 40, Bailey Bridge" to be delivered to the Engineer Stores at such and such a location. When this convoy got to its location an Engineer Stores Unit unloaded the lorries and sorted out parts into appropriate heaps, so that any particular set of equipment could be easily assembled and despatched to a site ready for re-assembly. Perry told me that the Major whose job it was to do this work was extremely competent, but he agreed to my motoring almost to Brussels to make sure that all was well.

168

When I got to this place near Brussels I was much impressed by the Major in charge. He was of a most unusual type. He turned up on a motor-bike, dressed in a shabby Service Dress cap. He wore motoring goggles with powerful spectacles behind them. His uniform was casual and he wore no belt; his face was weatherbeaten, and he had the most cheerful countenance it is possible to imagine. He showed me round his stores and introduced me to some of his junior officers and NCOs. It struck me as an extremely efficient set-up, and, having congratulated him upon the masterful manner in which he and his men sorted out the chaos, I added, "I'm glad it is you and not I who has this job. It would drive me dotty in a very short time."

His reply was unexpected. "Ah yes, Sir," he said, "but having been a University Professor of Moral Philosophy for some years before the War, I have the advantage of being quite already!"*

We really did have, in our wartime Army, a wonderful collection of capable civilians, and I think, on the whole, that the War Office was extremely clever in choosing round pegs for round holes and square ones for square holes – this Major being a prime example of this.

When I got back to Perry's camp that evening I found a Posting Order awaiting me. I was posted to 43 (Wessex) Infantry Division in 30 Corps which was by then said to be near the Dutch frontier. The former occupant of the post was Lieutenant-Colonel Pike who had been wounded. He had been Commander Royal Engineers of the Division for over a year and had trained the Divisional Sappers in England before D-Day. The Division was known to be a very efficient one and was commanded by Major-General G. I. Thomas.

My joy on obtaining release from the Base Area was diluted by dismay. This was caused by the fact that I had once met General Thomas and had formed the opinion that he would be a very difficult master to serve. We had met at an indoor exercise at Ripon in 1942, before the North-West European Campaign had been considered in detail by anyone.

The Ripon exercise was to study some of the engineer problems likely to need solution during an advance from a future bridgehead across the English Channel into the heart of Germany. It was directed by Lieutenant-General Gammell, who no doubt hoped he would by then be commanding the Invasion Army.† There were three syndicates, each led by a Major-General commanding an Infantry Division in Home Forces. One of these generals was G. I. Thomas. I was one of many Sapper Officers who were officially "spectators" only, but many of whom – including me – were pressed into offering opinions on many technical matters.

It was at once evident that G. I. Thomas was a formidable personality. He

---

* He may have been teasing me over his academic subject, but the gist of his talk is authentic.
† In fact he was in the Middle East by 1944.

was a man of superior intellect, with a brain like a rapier. If any speaker, whether from one of the syndicates or from among the spectators, chanced to make an ill-considered statement, he might be sure that G. I. Thomas would mutilate and tear him to shreds in a manner that would be strongly disapproved of by the Royal Society for the Prevention of Cruelty to Animals. Everyone, including General Gammell, seemed to be in awe of him – and I was too! On one occasion the Director called upon me to suggest how Airborne Sappers might contribute to the solution of a problem set in the exercise. Fortunately for me, it was a matter that, in 1 Airborne Division, we had all frequently discussed among ourselves, and I was able to withstand G. I. Thomas's searching cross-examination which followed immediately. But it is one thing to talk sense about some matter that has been thoroughly thrashed out beforehand and quite another to do so as a newcomer when you do not even know the views of your own subordinates and whether they will stand behind you or join the other man who cross-questions you. The reader will, therefore, understand why I set off for my new appointment as CRE 43 (Wessex) Division with mixed feelings – feelings of joy, awe and challenge.

Without waiting for tea or supper myself, I told Lowe and Meek to get some food while I went to Perry and Tickell and the young man who had helped me so much with the dismantling of the bridges. All three of them wished me luck and General Tickell, who evidently knew of G. I. Thomas well, added with a wry smile, "You'll certainly need luck!"

By nightfall Lowe, Meek and I were motoring up a Red Ball route* towards Brussels and Meek in the back seat was feeding us on haversack rations with which he had armed himself from the Officers' Mess before starting. This was on 16 September, and early next morning the BBC was announcing that the 1st Allied Airborne Army had taken the air. The three of us had but a single thought. Can we get there in time to join up with them?

EXTRACTS FROM LETTERS TO MY PARENTS

Written from Lincolnshire, 23 January, 1944

Have you ever heard one man describe another, saying: "He hasn't got a clue"? It was apparently coined in the Western Desert by 8th Army. I heard it for the first time in Libya. It means that the man so described is a soldier who does not understand his business. Well, we have now got a new General, who you will be glad to hear is NOT one "who hasn't got a clue". His name is Urquhart – not the Tiger Urquhart whom I brought home to Woodbridge once – but a chap who fought from Alamein to Tunis with 51 Highland Division. He

---

* Red Ball routes were those marked on the French maps with a red line and a string of red blobs.

may not be a Sherlock Holmes, but he certainly *has* a clue and I'm sure we shall get on well together. He is *Sans Peur et sans Raproche*.

Written from Lincolnshire, 29 January, 1944

Yesterday evening, returning from an exercise with my driver, we stopped to get a meal at a pub in the Fens – near the Wash. I asked the landlady what she could do about it. "For the Airbornes I can do a lot," she said. She gave us roast chicken, poached egg and a glass of sherry each, for which she refused payment. I asked about rationing and she said "Rationing has not penetrated as far as this".

Written from Lincolnshire, 19 March, 1944

The King came to see us yesterday. He had lunch in the Mess and I was placed opposite him. He's very easy to talk to – a most attractive personality with a very natural sense of what I think should be called *fun*, rather than humour. The General, who was sitting next to him, told him where the butter came from, adding that it was you who actually made it. The King asked me what was the cow's name. I told him that: "My mother calls it Patricia; but Father calls it 'the Cow Pat!'" That went down well! So you see you have been Dairymaid to the King! After lunch the sun shone and we introduced to the King as many men as time allowed, doing various forms of training.

Written from Lincolnshire, 16 July, 1944

My driver, Lowe, has got married to a local girl. He always used to say that he was proof against that. I bought him a silver butter-dish for a present, with which he was delighted; and he says his wife is too.

Written from London, 17 July, 1944

I was in London today and heard my first buzz bomb in an office in Whitehall. The Alert sounded and I asked the young officer in the chair, "What do we do now?" He replied, "We do nothing, as they ring a bell when danger is imminent". After a short while they rang a bell, and I asked again, "What do we do now?" There was a deafening crash. The young officer did not rise from his chair, but said, "It's too late to do anything now, but you might like to look out of the window to try and see where it landed." Nothing was to be seen but some smoke a long way off. I suppose the inmates of Whitehall get to know from the sound where the things are heading for.

Written from near Bayeux, Normandy (Date illegible)

I said goodbye to my Sappers in 1 A/B Division. It was a painful parting. They are inarticulate creatures; but many of them stammered out such touching things that I almost burst into tears! My Adjutant told me that the officers were making me a presentation of some kind. This is forbidden by King's Regulations. I don't know what they planned, but I can no longer exercise any authority over them. They'll send it to Woodbridge, so please open it. . . . Did you see in *The Times* of Friday, 25th that I had got the OBE "for services in Italy". One of my Company Commanders got the MBE. It was the rank and file who did it all. As usual, they carried me over the marshes. And I know when I am lucky!

11

Operation
Market Garden

On 16 September General Horrocks, who commanded 30 Corps in which 43 Division was serving, addressed all his officers of the rank of Lieutenant-Colonel or above, telling them the role of 30 Corps in Operation Market Garden. This was the code name for the succession of operations culminating in the Arnhem battle. As I did not join 43 Division till the next day I did not hear this address, but was left to find out for myself what it was all about. This was not difficult, as Major Tom Evill RE had been present and was able to tell me about it.

Tom Evill was the Company Commander of 204 Field Company in the Division and had been acting as Commander of the Divisional Sappers since my predecessor had been wounded. He was a thick-set, intelligent and artistic man, who sprang from an old Monmouthshire family. He had not been at the Royal Military Academy, but had joined the Territorial Army as an officer after taking an honours degree in engineering at Cardiff University. Oddly enough, when he came to Chatham on probation before getting his Regular Commission in 1934 or 1935, I had been the Senior Subaltern in the Training Battalion and had been ordered by the CO of the Battalion to "keep an eye on this chap and report to me his suitability for a Regular Commission". I had duly reported that the Sappers would be missing a very promising young man if they did not take him. If ever a pudding was "proved by the eating", Tom Evill was! He had grown in stature in the ten years since we first met, and I liked the Engineer Plan he had made for the Divisional Engineers.

The general idea in Market Garden was to advance on a narrow front over a distance of about sixty miles from Hechtel, on the Belgian frontier with

173

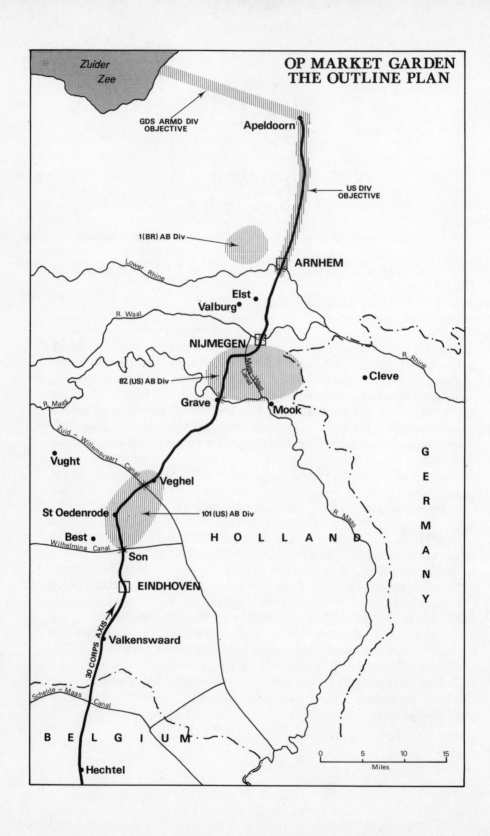

OP MARKET GARDEN
THE OUTLINE PLAN

Zuider Zee

GDS ARMD DIV OBJECTIVE

US DIV OBJECTIVE

Apeldoorn

1(BR) AB Div

Lower Rhine

ARNHEM

Elst

Valburg

R. Waal

NIJMEGEN

82 (US) AB Div

R. Rhine

Cleve

Maas - Waal Canal

Grave

Mook

R. Maas

Zuid – Willemsvaart Canal

Vught

Veghel

101 (US) AB Div

R. Maas

St Oedenrode

G E R M A N Y

Best

H O L L A N D

Wilhelmina Canal

Son

EINDHOVEN

Valkenswaard

30 CORPS AXIS

Schelde – Maas Canal

B E L G I U M

Hechtel

0   5   10   15
Miles

Holland, *via* Arnhem to the Zuider Zee. This would involve crossing three wide rivers: the Maas, the Waal and the Lower Rhine. This thrust was intended to cut off all the German forces in Western Holland and put 21 Army Group in a favourable position for another thrust on to the North German Plain in the heart of Germany. If this could be achieved quickly it offered a good chance to defeat Germany in 1944.

The three wide rivers mentioned above had bridges over them at Grave (Maas), at Nijmegen (Waal), and at Arnhem (Lower Rhine). The intention was to capture these bridges intact with Airborne Troops and relieve them as soon as possible with the Ground Forces of 30 Corps. There were, however, lesser rivers and canals to be crossed on the way and the Guards Armoured Division, which led 30 Corps, carried assault boats and Bailey Bridging equipment to cope with them. In addition to the equipment for crossing the smaller rivers and canals on our route, there were also 2,000 lorries* carrying bridging equipment to deal with any of the wide rivers in case the Airborne Troops failed to capture all of them intact. Much of this equipment was the fruit of my own harvesting in Normandy, and it was reassuring to know that every lorry-load would have had the blessing of the former Professor of Moral Philosophy and that not a nut nor a bolt was likely to be deficient in any particular. I hope someone thanked him for his systematic supervision of all this detail. He certainly deserved recognition of some kind and I hope he got it.

Tom Evill's engineer plan was simple. Each Field Company was to motor in the convoy of the Infantry Brigade to which it was affiliated. This would ensure that whatever task turned up there would be at least enough Sappers present to start whatever work might be needed. And because the most likely task would be to bridge any of the minor rivers, Tom had made provision for a fair dollop of bridging equipment to be within reach of the Field Company that might want it. Furthermore, he retained the Field Park Company under his own hand as extra manpower against an unforeseen emergency wherever it might arise. He had also made prudent arrangements with the Chief Engineer of 30 Corps for tapping the vast reserve of bridging equipment carried by the 2,000 lorries mentioned above.

Having explained his plans, Tom introduced me to General G. I. Thomas and the Staff at Divisional HQ. He also introduced me to the Sapper Staff that I inherited from my predecessor. The adjutant was Captain Gordon Lilley, a grand-nephew of a famous Sapper General, Sir Bindon Blood, who had made a name for himself on the North-West Frontier of India in 1897 and in the First World War. Gordon Lilley was not a Regular Officer, but had been a Territorial and had been Adjutant of 43 Divisional Engineers for a long time. He was extremely competent and I was very soon much in his debt. He will

---

* It must be remembered that in 1944 lorries were seldom capable of carrying more than 3-ton loads.

appear again in the story. Tom then departed to his own Field Company and left me to my own devices.

Following my own ideas, I asked Gordon to motor me round to the Sapper Companies in turn, who were dotted about over a considerable area, so that I could meet them and see if they were all as well briefed as Tom was. Here I had immediate proof of the high calibre of my Adjutant.

"Of course I can motor you round, Sir," he said, "but we would both be absent from Divisional HQ for a couple of hours at least and if G. I. Thomas wants anything from the Sappers during that time, it will go down very badly if both of us are absent simultaneously. May I therefore suggest I send one of the Field Engineers from the HQ to do the honours instead of me?"

This was good advice and I was grateful. There were evidently many things to be learnt in 43 Division! First, however, I had to try and learn the names of the Company Commanders and the designations of their Companies. In an Infantry Battalion the Companies are generally A, B, C and D, whatever the regiment, but in the Sappers each company has a number of its own, chosen in a totally irrational way. In 43 Division the Companies were Nos. 204, 260, 553 and 207, and, to make it more difficult, the Field Company numbers bore no relation to the numbers of the brigades with which they were normally grouped. Thus 260 Field Company was grouped with 129 Infantry Brigade and 553 Field Company with 130 Infantry Brigade and 204 Field Company with 214 Brigade. Of course after a few days this all became second nature, but to start with it was as difficult to learn as the Athanasian Creed. As we went round, the Field Engineer who was bear-leading me rattled it all off and I ended up confused. Fortunately I could learn names of people fairly easily, so I returned to Divisional HQ with a reasonably coherent picture in my mind of the officers and senior NCOs whom I had met. I got the impression that they were experienced troops. Their camps were tidy and clean, and their vehicles looked well maintained, though how adequate they were in bridge-building it was impossible to estimate. Their officers made no secret of it that they had done very little heavy bridging since leaving England, and of course there was not the slightest chance of us having any opportunity to "brush up bridging" before being launched into Operation Market Garden. I asked several of them how long they thought it might take to build various types of Bailey Bridge, but there were so many "ifs" and "buts" that I got no solid data to work upon. What would happen, I thought, if when I got back to Divisional HQ the General were to question me about this sort of thing?

In 1 Airborne Division I could have answered these questions from actual experience with the troops concerned. Here it would be difficult to give anything definite at all. Fortunately G. I. Thomas asked no such questions. He had other things to think about.

7. 43 Division Memorial near Caen. Designed by the Royal
   Engineers of 43 Division and erected on land presented
   by the French Government

8. "Bond Street", near Brunnsum, Holland, November, 1944

9. The Commander-in-Chief with Major-General Thomas, GOC 43 Division, Brunnsum, 25 November, 1944. The author is at rear centre.

10. The Humber Mark III Armoured Car, known as an Ark.

The Guards Armoured Division crossed the start line at Hechtel during the afternoon 17 September. In effect their task was to advance about sixty miles on a front of 600 yards, astride a single road. The Germans, however, had begun to react with their customary speed and methodical vigour, and fierce fighting soon ensued. This naturally produced delays on the route and, in spite of the very careful road-traffic arrangements, the most monumental road congestions were apt to build up. Experience, forty years later, on wider motorways shows us how quite a trifling obstruction, on one lane only, soon produces a long "tail-back" over miles of road, and the main axis of advance of the Guards Armoured Division was not even a dual carriageway. Quite apart from enemy action, which was stubborn, the breakdown of a single vehicle was apt to cause a traffic jam. It was difficult to get a breakdown lorry to the site and quite impossible to tow the defaulter off the road to somewhere it could be mended. And any return traffic – ambulances with wounded, for instance – trying to get back from the scene of battle was apt to cause chaos. A single German 88mm gun, concealed in the orchard of a roadside farmhouse and able to fire down the road was a difficulty that took infinite effort to overcome. The successful advance of the Guards, in spite of all this, was a most astonishing achievement. Eindhoven was captured by nightfall on 18 September and the outskirts of Nijmegen reached by 20 September. It was not until then that 43 Division was called upon to start moving up the axis behind the Guards Armoured Division. But, to keep the Division "in hand", G. I. Thomas had summoned all his Commanding Officers to a transit area near Hechtel. Here he would be able to give verbal orders as soon as the call came and meanwhile we discussed the possibilities of a number of operations that might become necessary. As far as I was concerned it was a good opportunity to make the acquaintance of the Brigade Commanders in the Division and most of the COs of Gunner and Infantry regiments as well. It also gave me something of the "feel" of working with G. I. Thomas. This was, in itself, quite an experience.*

One among several possible situations that G. I. Thomas envisaged was that the Guards Armoured Division might be completely halted by German opposition somewhere along the line between (say) Grave and Nijmegen. It might be impossible to mount any effective outflanking "hook" across country in that area, because of the paucity of the roads. Moreover, the soggy nature of the countryside in those parts was such that tanks got bogged down and were unable to operate if they left the roads. The suggestion therefore was to form a

---

* In the History of the 43rd Wessex Division at War 1944–45 (by General Essame, published by William Clowes & Sons Ltd, London), an account of one of General G. I. Thomas's exercises is given on page 113. It reads as follows: "The exercise reached the normal high standards of the Division. In fact, there were many present who would sooner have faced the fire of the enemy than the demolition of their unsound argument by the director of the exercise (General Thomas) . . . Real battles were much less tense; the enemy at least often gave more time to think and did not pounce on every error."

flotilla of Rhine barges on the River Maas, load an Infantry Brigade and a Regiment of tanks on board them and send the lot by river transport all the way to Arnhem. If they navigated during the night it seemed possible that they might get through absolutely unseen and undetected by the Germans.

From where I was sitting, I could see the faces of many of those taking part in the discussion. There was a look of horror on the faces of the conventional soldiers, the reliable, experienced warriors who had battled all the way from the beaches in Normandy to where we now sat, almost in Holland. There was also a gleam of delight amongst some of the other Commanding Officers, the kind of men who are occasionally to be found in every walk of life, men who like an original idea simply because it really is original. I could foresee how, if this plan were to be attempted, I myself and the Divisional Engineers would be deeply involved. It would be the Sappers who would be called upon to marshal the barges, to strengthen their decks if need be, and to play an important part in the loading and the navigation of the flotilla from Grave to Nijmegen, or even to Arnhem; It would not be difficult at this conference to be stampeded into agreeing to undertake all this before having had a preview of the conditions actually existing in the riparian territory ahead of us. Would barges exist there? What were the loading facilities? Were the barges self-propelled, or were tugs needed? Were the rivers tidal? What about the bargees? Would they help or were most of them Germans? There were many uncertainties, and I could see I should have to put forward the Sapper view of the proposition and that, whatever I said, I would get a severe cross-examination from those present. They would never dare to question G. I. Thomas, but they had no such inhibitions about teasing me, a stranger in their midst. For me it was immensely important to jump this fence in a collected manner, and not get hopelessly unseated at the first one. Luck, however, was on my side.

The previous evening, when I had met for the first time the Officer Commanding one of my Field Companies, a man called Tony Vinycomb, he had put forward exactly this idea himself. We discussed the possibilities with the map in front of us. We had both liked the idea in principle and would welcome a chance to "have a go". We had also agreed on the conditions we thought that must prevail before taking it on "in cold blood". After this it was not difficult, even when confronted by G. I. Thomas, to talk sense on this, my first opportunity to play some part in the affairs of 43 Division.

As it happened, however, the need never occurred, for on 21 September I was able to motor into Nijmegen in the conventional manner, the town having been recently occupied by the Guards Armoured Division. By the combined efforts of the Guards Armoured Division and 82 US Airborne Division the road bridge over the Waal had also been captured intact and the demolition charges which the Germans had fixed to it had been removed. About 400 yards to the west of the road bridge was a railway bridge which had been similarly dealt with.

The advance by Guards Armoured Division from Belgium as far as this had been a feat of arms by any standards and is well covered in many books, but I saw very little of this myself. So far, 43 Division was a follow-up Division and not a leading one and it is personal experiences that form the basis of this chronicle.

At this time Nijmegen had suffered negligible war damage. The houses, typically Dutch, were tidy and well painted and appeared to be the houses and shops of a prosperous community, though they had no doubt suffered under a draconian German occupation. The wide river, dimpling in the sunshine, swept under a long and graceful bowstring girder bridge. While standing on this bridge I met my opposite number, the Commander of the Divisional Engineers of the Guards Armoured Division. He was Lieutenant-Colonel C. P. Jones*, an old friend from Woolwich days who later became very distinguished. His Sappers had done extremely well in supporting the Guards Armoured Division in the long advance from Normandy, through France and Belgium to the middle of Holland where we now stood. He had seen the tactical situation that existed north of the River Waal on the low, marshy land stretching from Nijmegen to Arnhem, now visible about ten miles away. He told me that the leading tanks of the Guards' Armoured Division were a short distance away, on the other side of the river, and were meeting stiff resistance.

Having been on the scene for some time, he was much better informed than I was about the state of affairs in Arnhem. It was now about 3pm on 21 September and communications with 1 Airborne Division were tenuous, there being only a makeshift wireless link with the outside world by way of an Airborne Artillery Regiment in the Arnhem area and a 30 Corps Medium Regiment behind us. The BBC in London seemed, rather ironically, almost as well informed as we were. It was doubtful whether 2 Parachute Battalion was still holding out on the Arnhem Bridge, but it was believed they would not be able to hold it for much longer, even if they were still there. Most of 1 Airborne Division was believed to be hemmed into a shrinking perimeter in the western suburbs of Arnhem, north of the Lower Rhine, more or less opposite Driel.

We were both well aware that no time must be lost in getting to Arnhem by one route or another and Colonel Jones offered the opinion that if access to Arnhem proved impossible along the main road, direct, it might be possible to find an alternative route on the left-hand side of the main road, in the neighbourhood of Driel – or even a bit further to the west – and force a crossing of the Lower Rhine there. That task was likely to fall to the lot of 43 Division, so I was particularly interested in the matter. Having heard how the Guards Armoured Division and some American Parachutists of 82 US Airborne Division had crossed the river in Nijmegen in a most spirited way so recently, I

* Not to be confused with the Colonel Jones mentioned in Chapter 8.

felt it ought not to be impossible for us to try the same thing in Driel. There were, however, three obvious differences in the situation that faced us. First, there did not seem from the map to be a decent road to Driel, suitable for carrying the traffic required for such a wide river-crossing operation. The ferrying of a few tanks across into the Airborne perimeter did not seem to me to fulfil the requirement. What appeared to be wanted was a Bailey floating pontoon bridge that could carry the main axis for a Divisional operation. This would not be an easy affair, as the terrain on the north bank of the Lower Rhine in that area overlooked the river itself and most of the approach roads on the south bank as well. It looked as though any bridge, if it were possible to complete one by night (which I rather doubted), would be impossible to keep intact during the day, because of enemy gun fire. This seemed the second difficulty. The third was that, even if we got across the river at Driel, we were still not in Arnhem. However, it is a hopeless outlook for a Sapper to be pessimistic about attempting anything that is clearly desirable and I hoped that G. I. Thomas would manage to get the leading Brigade across the River Waal very soon and make it possible for the leading Field Company to get a look at the place for themselves. Naturally, I was determined to have a look for myself too!

While we were talking on the Nijmegen Bridge we saw a sortie of RAF aircraft attempting a re-supply mission over Arnhem. It was in broad daylight and was greeted by intense AA fire from the Germans. It was an incredibly valiant endeavour, and we saw many parachutes descend, but we also saw many aircraft hit. It was clear that the RAF had not got the mastery of the air-space over Arnhem, and when I got to where G. I. Thomas was giving orders to 214 Brigade, a short time later, I saw another example of how the air situation had so recently changed.

The orders were given in a village about five miles south of Nijmegen. It was thronged with jubilant children waving flags to greet the troops. Simultaneously a flight of German fighter-bombers roared overhead and gave a conflicting display of patriotic emotion. The orders for 214 Brigade were to hasten to Nijmegen, and cross the Waal by the railway bridge about quarter of a mile downstream of the main road bridge. From there they were to pass through the Guards' forward troops and make their way as fast as possible towards Arnhem, approaching from the Guards' south-east flank. I am quite sure this was the best possible thing to attempt. I refute the contention that any practicable method of making speedy progress was neglected. Divisional Advanced HQ followed close on the heels of 214 Brigade, so that it was not long before we were all intent, with one accord, to get to Arnhem and relieve 1 Airborne Division as soon as it was humanly possible.

The country between Nijmegen and Arnhem is low-lying and boggy. It was known as the Island. There was only one main road across it, and that led from

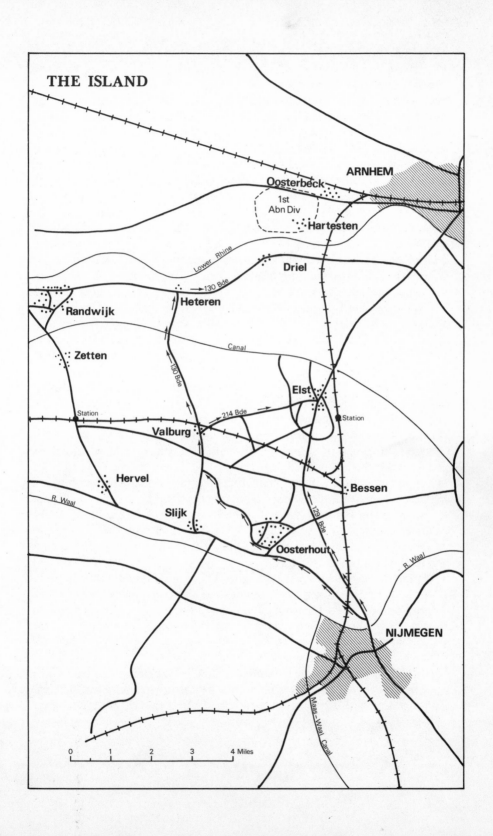

THE ISLAND

ARNHEM

Oosterbeck

1st
Abn Div

Hartesten

Lower Rhine

130 Bde

Driel

Heteren

Randwijk

Canal

Zetten

130 Bde

Elst

214 Bde

Station

Station

Valburg

Hervel

Bessen

R. Waal

Slijk

129 Bde

Oosterhout

R. Waal

NIJMEGEN

Maas-Waal Canal

0   1   2   3   4 Miles

Nijmegen, through Elst, to Arnhem. In 1944 this had a good surface, but it was not a first-class highway by modern standards. It had no dual carriageway, and although two civilian lorries could pass on it, there was not much to spare if two tanks or heavy military vehicles attempted to do so. In many places the road ran on an embankment, and if a vehicle approached too close to the shoulder of the road it might easily topple off the embankment and get stuck in the mud up to its axles.

On both sides of this main road there was a network of narrow roads and lanes used by farm vehicles. These minor roads had drainage ditches on both sides in which stagnant water lay. In all directions there were orchards with apple trees bearing fruit. The trees were twenty or thirty feet tall and, except from the tower of a church, it was seldom possible to see in any direction for more than a hundred yards, often less. There were many small farmhouses, with stables, cartsheds and outhouses nestling in among the trees and usually close to the road. This country was therefore ideal for defence – like the *bocage* in Normandy – and was not suitable for fast-moving mobile armoured warfare.

If a Squadron or Company Commander were to motor his unit incautiously along a road he was likely to fall into an ambush, because the Germans were dispersed in well-concealed and skilfully sited battle groups, each consisting of one or two tanks with an anti-tank gun and a small detachment of infantry. These battle groups were the outposts of stronger positions in the background.

The first an incautious Commander would know of trouble would be that his leading vehicle was hit at short range by an anti-tank gun concealed in a woodshed. There would be a traffic block at once; another vehicle would be knocked out, and the column halted. Casualties were inevitable and, if the column Commander were not one of them, he would have to do something about it under difficult conditions. Troops would have to be de-bussed and a minor battle would have to be fought, involving the use of mortars or smoke or both. If all went well the German battle group would be driven off, perhaps leaving a wrecked gun or vehicle that had to be got off the road to allow the column to proceed. Whatever the Top Brass might "burble" about "making all speed", it was, in fact, only possible to make progress by using ponderous and methodical tactics.

During the afternoon of 22 September 129 Brigade found it impossible to make further progress northwards astride the main road towards Elst, which was firmly held by the Germans. Tanks could not move off the main road to support the infantry, and movement by infantry on foot unsupported by tanks was equally unpromising. 214 Brigade was similarly spread out between Ousterhout and Driel and was likewise halted.

G.I. Thomas therefore ordered 130 Brigade to advance at first light on 23 September towards Driel in a left hook passing through Valburg and Heteren. The intention was to make contact with 1 Airborne Division who were encircled in a perimeter north of the river. He also ordered 214 Brigade to help 129 Brigade by mounting an attack against Elst from the west of the main road.

Dawn broke on 23 September in cold and driving rain and it was not till late afternoon that 130 Brigade overcame fierce enemy resistance and cleared Valburg. Until this was achieved it was impossible for 214 Brigade to start its attack upon Elst. This was because the only passable route in the right direction for 214 Brigade's tanks, carriers, anti-tank guns and mortars ran through the crossroads in the middle of Valburg. However, by 5 pm a start was made by 214 Brigade. Very heavy fighting developed and continued all night. At least two German heavy tanks were knocked out.

During this confused fighting, one of the Companies of 214 Brigade secured an insignificant, minor crossroads which, unknown to them, was a sensitive spot in the German communication system. Within an hour a miscellaneous assortment of German artillerymen and guns were captured. This apparently caused the enemy defenders of Elst to form a pessimistic opinion of their position. Their grip on the town was immediately weakened, much to the advantage of 129 Brigade trying to capture it.

Meanwhile, 130 Brigade had cleared itself of Valburg, so that contact could be made by 214 Brigade with the Polish Parachute Brigade that had been dropped south of the Lower Rhine on 21 September (that is D + 4 of the main operation). 214 Brigade was at once ordered to spend the night getting the Poles across the River to 1 Airborne's position, using a collection of DUKWs (amphibious lorries) and some assault boats (folding boats propelled by men with paddles like the Red Indian canoes in the films.) 204 Field Company were ordered to assist. The ferrying was supported by the 43 Divisional Artillery. The operation was not an unqualified success. The Neder Rhine is a very wide and swiftly flowing river and the Poles were not accustomed to boating operations. There were also language difficulties and many misunderstandings. Only about 200 Poles actually landed on the far bank and many of them, unknown to us, took their paddles with them when they left their boats. A considerable number of boats were also damaged beyond repair, all of which misfortunes added to our difficulties the next night. But this we were to find out later.

While all this was happening on the Island, other events were occurring elsewhere. In the first place the situation in Arnhem itself was by 23 September critical and getting worse. Colonel Frost, with his 2 Parachute Battalion supported by various detachments of other arms, had taken a heavy pounding. It seemed unlikely that they would be able to hold their position at the north end of the Arnhem Bridge for more than a matter of hours. The remainder of 1 Airborne Division had become encircled by German tanks and infantry in Hartesten, a suburb of the town, and were now short of ammunition and suffering heavy casualties. Furthermore, resupply by the RAF was becoming

A DIFFERENCE OF STRATEGIES

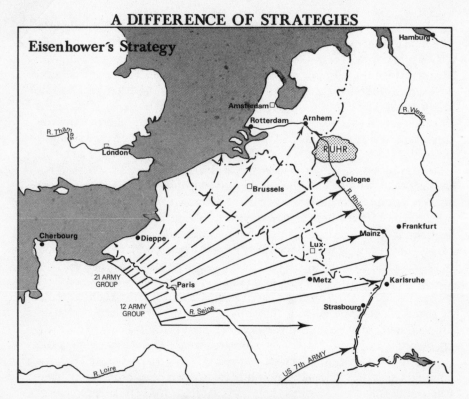

Eisenhower's Strategy

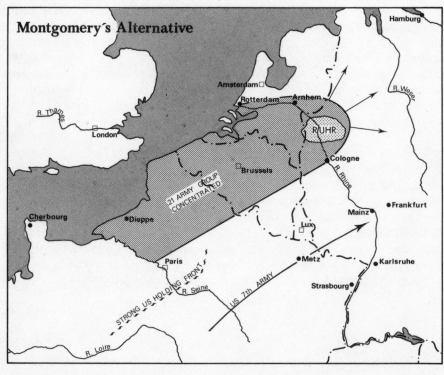

Montgomery's Alternative

almost impossible in spite of the heroism of the aircrews that attempted it.

Above all, however, the Germans, who had abandoned Normandy in haste and confusion, had played their remaining cards extremely well. They had lost a lot of men and material in the Falaise Battle but they had nonetheless virtually broken contact with their allied pursuers. By destroying the bridges behind them and fighting delaying actions with their rearguards they slipped from our clutches. As they withdrew they absorbed their own formations that lay behind them and by the time they had retreated to the frontiers of Germany they were able to turn and face us with something like a new army. While our maintenance depended on convoys of road vehicles stretching 300 miles or more from Normandy to Holland, passing over many temporary military bridges on the way, the German maintenance depended on the well-stocked larders of the Fatherland immediately behind them. What had formerly been an allied armoured fist had become the fingertips of an outstretched arm.

To add to our troubles our own supply line had been cut more than once by the Germans thirty-five miles behind us. This was not just a daring raid by desperadoes, but a full-blooded attack with tanks, artillery and determined infantry. Troops that we might have used to strengthen our efforts to reach Arnhem were now required to clear up the mess on our supply route behind us.

The appalling weather in England from D + 1 onwards played havoc with the airlift to Arnhem. The second lift, in itself a regrettable necessity, was prevented by fog till late on D + 2. Throughout the operation the airlift, due to bad weather, was piecemeal. The sovereign virtue of surprise was immediately forfeit, and without surprise success was forfeit too.

With hindsight, moreover, it now seems there was considerable delay in Eisenhower's HQ to settle what should be done after the German defeat in Normandy. Two possibilities appear to have been considered. A broad front policy – mainly American – was one possibility; a left-handed punch – mainly British, but assisted by American Airborne Troops – was the other. There was insufficient logistic support for both. The protagonists of both possibilities were men of outstanding character, determination and repute. They were supported by loyal and determined subordinates and it may be argued that Solomon himself would have been hard put to it to judge correctly between them. But no Solomon was present.

Eisenhower's HQ was still west of the Cherbourg peninsula. That may have been suitable for a Supreme Commander orchestrating the Allied navies, armies and airforces, as well as their political relations with the French, but it was far too distant from the battle front for a tactical Commander of the Land Forces, which Eisenhower had also become on 2 September. His signal communications, too, were apparently totally inadequate. His directives often took two or three days in transit, and sometimes they arrived in two parts – Part II a day before Part I.

Discussions about the future plans to be adopted after Rommel's defeat in Normandy appear to have begun on 20 August; yet on 17 September, when Market Garden began, they had still not been finally agreed. And, according to Field-Marshal Montgomery in his Memoirs (Page 282) the final decision was only taken on 23 September "exactly one month too late". By then the position in Arnhem was practically hopeless.

On the night of 22/23 September General Urquhart, commanding 1 Airborne Division, sent two officers by stealth across the River from his perimeter in Oosterbeck to get in touch with 30 Corps and tell the full story of their condition. The two officers were Eddie Myers, who had taken over from me in Lincolnshire about a month before, and Charles MacKenzie, whom the reader will remember as the Lieutenant-Colonel who had shown me his trout stream in Taranto. I happened to meet both these officers at Divisional HQ on the Island, but I was not present at any formal meetings they may have had with either General Horrocks, commanding 30 Corps, or with G. I. Thomas. I have little doubt, however, that the picture they painted on conditions prevailing in the 1 Airborne Division's perimeter was a very serious one. It must, I imagine, have contributed to the decision made by the Top Brass to abandon further attempts to cross the Lower Rhine in strength, but to evacuate the remnants of 1 Airborne Division instead. It therefore came about that a plan was made to effect this evacuation in two steps. The first step was to send one battalion of 43 Division (4th Dorsets) across the river into the Airborne perimeter to ensure holding it for another twenty-four hours, and then, during the following night, to evacuate everyone. As something of an afterthought, it was decided to add the remaining Polish Parachutists who had failed to get across the river the previous night.

The dispatch of 4th Dorsets and this Polish contingent was to be undertaken by 130 Brigade with 553 Field Company to man the boats. HQ 30 Corps promised to supply four more lorry-loads of assault boats for the purpose. The ferrying sites for the Dorsets and the Poles were chosen by 130 Brigade: the Poles opposite the eastern flank of the Airborne perimeter, the Dorsets about 200 yards to the west of that. The Poles were thought to have retained most of the boats they had used the previous night, but, presumably due to a language difficulty, it was not discovered until too late that many of the Poles disembarking the previous night had, as stated above, taken their paddles with them, leaving their comrades without boats or paddles.

From the start everything seemed to go wrong. The convoy of lorries carrying the boats to 130 Brigade took a wrong turning up a side road after crossing the railway bridge on to the Island and the first two lorries motored straight into the German lines where they were captured. The two following lorries, seeing the fate of those in front, tried to turn and get away, but they

186

slithered off the road and into a deep ditch alongside. None of the boats ever got to Brigade HQ, nor to 4th Dorsets.

Clouds had turned twilight into darkness and rain was falling when I met Lieutenant-Colonel Tilley, CO of 4th Dorsets. His own arrangements had been excellent and he was ready to begin the assault, but he had no boats. Meanwhile, some other boats were found with 5th Dorsets, who were not far off, and these were carried by hand to where 4th Dorsets wanted them. Colonel Tilley might well have made acrimonious complaints about his treatment, but what he actually said was, "Tell Brigade HQ that we shall do our best and please thank them for the help they have given us." What a man!

At about 11.30 pm sufficient boats had been collected for ferrying to begin. Each boat had two Sappers in charge of it, and ten Dorsets as the "nominal" passengers to be landed on the far bank of the river. I call them "nominal" because they had, in fact, to assist the two Sappers by wielding paddles too. It was, however, left to the two Sappers to get the empty boats back. With unskilled infantrymen manning so high a proportion of the paddles, the results were creditable but far from perfect. Each boat also had on board two boxes of ammunition and supplies for use on the far bank. It was not easy in the dark to keep any accurate account of how things were going.

Two factory buildings were burning on the wooded slopes rising from the water's edge on the far bank and a reflection of the flames illuminated the swirling waters of the river. As the boats crossed the patch of reflected light one had a glimpse of them and the toiling boatmen. But by the time they landed on the far bank they had passed out of sight again and when the Sappers reappeared with the empty boats they were often as much as 200 yards further downstream.

The enemy fire was prevented to a great extent by our covering fire, but every now and then a German machine-gunner would fire a burst of fire at a boat that was crossing. One such boat was a DUKW which someone had launched upstream of us. As it swirled downstream in front of us, a German spandau machine-gun was fired at it, a traversing burst of five or ten shots. The burst was aimed too high – the gunner could not possibly have seen his sights properly in the darkness – and the shots all missed the DUKW, but passed above it. But they were just the right height above the water to splatter us. I was standing on the flood bank of the river about ten feet above water level so as to get a better view of what was going on. A Corporal standing near me was hit in the head and fell dead, striking my feet, and the next shot hit another man standing on the other side of me. He was hit in the arm. He spun round, cursing, and without meaning it he hit me in the face with the muzzle of a sten gun that was in his hands. The two shots sounded like a tennis rally played close to the net. "Thud, thud," and the rest of the burst flew through the branches of the trees behind me. The whole episode was the fruit of bad arrangements and I felt that there was no single mind impressing its will on events. Ferrying continued until the dawn, when it became impossible to get a boat into the water without drawing withering fire. I do not think anyone could say precisely what result this gallant effort by 4th Dorsets and the Poles had achieved.

It was a bad night.

As soon as I got back to Divisional HQ Gordon Lilley told me that the Divisional Commander was about to give his orders for the final evacuation of 1 Airborne Division and the Dorsets from Arnhem. I was required to attend. Here, at last, I felt there was a chance of taking effective control and of doing something that might really help my friends in 1 Airborne.

G. I. Thomas gave his orders at 10 am. I had been up all night, but a time comes when one gets a sort of second wind. I did not feel the least bit tired but fully alert.

First he explained that there was to be a deception plan to distract the enemy's attention from what was about to happen. 130 Brigade was to manoeuvre early in the afternoon with a road convoy of bridging and pontoon lorries about three miles to the west of the evacuation site. It was hoped – rightly as it turned out – that the Germans would scurry off to meet this challenge which was only bluff. Next the evacuation of the Airborne Division was to be covered by the Divisional Artillery, supported by the "Pepperpot". This was a new phrase to me and I must explain it.

The Pepperpot was the brainchild of G. I. Thomas. The theory was as follows: By definition, each phase of an operation is undertaken by a different part of the whole Division, so there will always be, at any one time, a lot of men with no particular task to perform. The Pepperpot was therefore arranged to make use of all these men and every weapon that was otherwise idle. All that was required was for someone to organize the Pepperpot so that every idle man and weapon was ordered to open fire on a fixed line, aimed at anywhere enemy troops were known to exist. When this was properly done it was possible to ensure that one shot per minute would fall in every square yard of enemy territory within range. Even though not many hits might be achieved, there would certainly be a considerable psychological effect upon the enemy. (Interrogation of enemy prisoners after they had endured the Pepperpot showed that this was, in fact, the effect achieved.) This practice in 43 Division had been perfected and the Pepperpot was always organized and managed by the OC of 8th Middlesex Regiment, our Divisional Machine Gun Regiment. On this occasion he was also to arrange to have snipers posted on the raised river flood bank, overlooking the far side of the river, so that if ever an enemy weapon were fired in the dark in our direction it would be engaged at once by every armed man who saw the flash. (This was known to be effective in night operations and was ordered for this occasion.) It was quite clear that everyone understood all this exactly.

G. I. Thomas then went on to the tasks of other people and he soon turned to me, asking how I proposed to manage ferrying across the river. This was to be a leading role in the night's work and I had been warned not to be overawed by G. I. Thomas, "or you'll get hell from him forever more!" I realized that he would be a formidable cross-examiner and I determined to try and get the initiative by telling him *my* ideas and seeing his reaction, and not the other way round. I felt nervous to start with but got into my stride, using some notes I had made in discussion with Gordon Lilley beforehand.

I explained that we would have two Canadian Field Companies to help us, each using storm boats, that is, large punt-like boats propelled by outboard petrol motors, whereas our own Field Companies (260 and 253) would have assault boats which are collapsible boats propelled by two or four men each. I told him of the arrangements already made by Gordon Lilley to ensure that all four Field Companies, complete with their boats and equipment, arrived at the proper place at the proper time.

It was, however, soon evident that, in spite of G. I. Thomas's agile intellectual equipment and his experience and knowledge of military affairs, he was unbelievably ill-informed about the behaviour of boats in a swiftly flowing river. He was amazed, even shocked, to hear what a haphazard affair this ferrying operation was bound to be. He had apparently imagined that all you had to do was to put forty men into twenty boats – two men in each – and that thenceforth the boats would go to and fro across the river all night, bringing back ten or more passengers per boat each time. He looked at me with astonishment and increasing displeasure as I told my tale, but it seemed to me prudent to warn him of the worst before he heard of it from spectators the following morning.

The fact was, and still is, that watermanship in a wide and swift river is as much of a skill as cabinet-making or joinery. It is easy to say that you must keep your boat pointing upstream and slightly at an angle to the current and it will travel willingly across the river. But it is not easy to do this in the dark with another man beside you, who must play his part in accurate concert with you. And if the current is so strong that it needs more than two boatmen, even more co-ordination is required. If a single one of the boatmen fumbles or misses a stroke, the probability is that the boat will get broadside on to the current and get hopelessly out of control. Then the entire boatload will be in utter confusion and will not reach the far bank before it is a hundred yards downstream. (If the boat is shot at and someone is wounded, even worse may befall.)

You may launch the boat at A (in the drawing overleaf), but only the very skilled crews will arrive at B on the opposite bank. Most will arrive somewhere near C and on the return journey they may end up at D. They must then get their boats back to A again for the next trip.

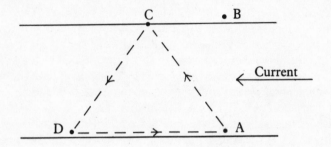

A further difficulty must be overcome when two kinds of boat are involved: the petrol-driven storm boats of the Canadians and the manhandled assault boats of our own Field Companies. The assault boats, being lighter than the storm boats, will be the first to get launched and started, but the storm boats, when once in the water and under way, will do many more trips. Collisions in the dark must be avoided and provision must also be made for rescue boats in case of accidents. However it is done, control by the officer in charge is not easy.

"Do you mean to tell me," chipped in G. I. Thomas, looking fiercer than ever, "that all this muddle is inevitable?" "No, Sir:" I replied. "I do not consider it inevitable because we have stout-hearted men to deal with, though they cannot have practised it very recently. Four things, however, I deem essential to success. First, the four Company Commanders concerned must have sufficient time before nightfall to get their men properly organized with crews and relief crews. Secondly, we must have two separate ferrying sites – about 200 yards apart. One for the Canadian storm boats, the other – downstream – for our own Field Companies. Thirdly, the Gunners must mark the two ferrying sites by firing anti-aircraft tracer bullets on fixed lines over the boundaries of each site. Finally, if the Gunners can spare him, a liaison officer near my Control Point on the river bank will be needed to give the enemy hell if he tries to intervene. All in all, I feel confident that if we do these four things properly our men will be able to do what we ask of them."

Paddy Boylan, who commanded the Divisional Artillery, nodded his assent to the last two points and even G. I. Thomas's severe expression seemed to soften slightly. I felt there was a sense of stern resolve among those present and I was reminded of one of my father's favourite quotations. They were words written by the Marquis of Montrose on the window of his prison the night before he was executed in 1650.

190

"He either fears his fate too much,
Or his deserts are small,
That puts it not unto the touch,
To win or lose it all."

When I went to the riverside in the evening I took Lowe with me, and a signaller who had become a new member of my warrior companions. He was Lance-Corporal Ashworth, who in peacetime had been a Post Office engineer. "He could, with a nail file, coax a wireless set to perform better than an expert radio fitter could achieve with a box of tools."* I could not have been in better company and we three stuck together till the end of hostilities.

All four Companies, with their equipment, were at the meeting point near Driel to receive the orders I had for them. It had stopped raining for once, and it was not windy. The current in the river seemed to me to have slackened slightly since last night. What I had to say was simple in concept. They all knew the importance of the occasion and they all knew they had the right equipment with them. A light bridge had to be put across a drainage canal between the unloading point on the road and the water's edge, but this was out of sight of the enemy and was already nearly finished. Tapes were laid across the fields to guide everyone to his place after dark and, as I moved about among them, I got a reassuring feeling that this was a sturdy and reliable bunch of men. A few asked questions and I was glad that I could give satisfactory replies. (My experience had taught me that British troops are very quick to sum up a situation before a battle and I got a strong feeling now that they, like me, formed a favourable impression of the omens.)

The men had an evening meal and time passed slowly. At 9.15 pm a subdued but purposeful activity began. There were few audible orders but everyone seemed to know what he had to do. The first boat was launched by 260 Field Company with a Lieutenant Bevin in charge of it. Simultaneously a regular tattoo of fire broke out from our side of the river. The Pepperpot began and no reply came from the Germans.

Within a few minutes there were several canvas assault boats launched. They vanished into the inky darkness. There was nothing to be seen and nothing seemed to be happening. I paced the shore concealing, I hope, the inevitable doubts that assailed me. Had the Sappers upset the boats and all gone silently to the bottom? Had they paddled their boats into waiting Germans, concealed on the far bank? Had the boats been washed downstream to God knows where? It was a tense interval and no man could have importuned his Maker more fervently than I did that night.

I do not know how long the interval was, but perhaps after ten or fifteen minutes, though it seemed longer, there came across the darkness the sound of

---

* This analogy came, thirty-nine years later, from Horace Lowe (late Lance-Corporal RE).

dipping paddles. Then I saw a boat. It held a dozen men. I could recognize their airborne-pattern helmets. What a welcome sight it was! First one boat, then another, then another. About sixty men, including many wounded, came ashore. The boats were hauled back to the starting point for another trip.

More and more boats were launched, and then I heard the first Canadian storm boat's motor start. First it spluttered, then it roared. Then a boat with a white, foaming, wake was visible, aiming for the far bank. Soon there was a regular procession of storm boats and a regular routine of ferrying began. The assault boats had got the first catch, but the Canadian storm boats got the greater haul. The ferrying of both kinds continued with unending zeal. A line of tramping "Airbornes" filed along the tapes from the landing points to where the Q Department received them. I met many old friends: General Urquhart, Eddie Myers and many Sappers tramped past in the dark. The plan was working.

In the small hours of the morning the current in the river quickened. Assault boats which at the beginning had been paddled by two men began to need four. Later six became necessary; still later it became almost impossible to manoeuvre them at all. I had to stop them, though the storm boats with their horsepower could still reap a fair return.

When dawn broke, things went less smoothly. There was no longer any flash to reveal where the enemy lay and fired from, and they became more daring. The boats on the river were now clearly visible and each trip was a hazardous journey. Little fountains of water marked where German mortar bombs had fallen, and the struggles of men in the water brought rescue boats to pull them out. This clearly could not be allowed to go on much longer.

Colonel Gadsden, who was controlling the gunfire, suggested trying with smoke. This worked well for a bit. (I heard later, from a prisoner captured, that the enemy thought – wrongly, of course – that the smoke was poison gas!) Soon, however, a morning breeze sprang up. The smoke was wafted away and I decided that we must stop. A young Canadian officer completed a trip with a storm boat, but nearly every man in the boat was wounded during the passage. He made one more trip with life belts, to leave them on the far bank for any swimmers to use – perhaps the next night. Tony Vinycomb, commanding 260 Field Company, also made a last trip as a passenger in a Canadian storm boat. He was an accomplished waterman and had made many successful trips in his own Company's assault boats. In a life hereafter he may well be invited to understudy his duties while Charon is on his annual holidays. On this last trip no more Airborne soldiers were found awaiting passage to the south bank. Colonel Gadsden and I spoke to G. I. Thomas on a field telephone and we called a halt to the operation.

This was no occasion for oratory, but I thanked the troops as they loaded their boats back into their lorries. We had suffered mercifully few casualties and had brought back nearly 2,500 men. The bearing of the Airborne Troops was exemplary and I felt as proud to have formerly been one of them as I was now proud to wear the Wessex Wyvern shoulder flash of 43 Division.

I am glad to say that a number of officers and men in both the British and the Canadian Field Companies who took part in this operation received recognition for the part they had played in it. The following extract from a letter I wrote home shortly after it reflects the views I formed about it at the time.

EXTRACT FROM A LETTER TO MY PARENTS

Written from near Nijmegen, British Liberation Army (Undated)

You ask if Monty gave me a medal. As it happened he was unwell, or something, on the day arranged, so G. I. Thomas presented the ribbon on his behalf. I now have more initials after my name than you presented before it. But anyway I don't deserve it. . . . The whole thing comes from the men. One makes the best arrangements one can for them but in the end everything depends (as the Duke of Wellington said long ago) upon "the good will of the private soldiers". It is they who do the deed that wins their CO the medal. This decoration is for the RE part in digging 1st Airborne out of Arnhem. As it all happened in the dark there was nothing I could do to influence what was happening. My wandering about in the dark made no difference whatever. I merely got my feet very wet! . . . The soldiers did as they were told – which took a lot of doing. I saw no one falter. They did exactly as they were required to do. Our losses were miraculously light – Thank God. It was Divine Intervention. "*Gaudeamus igitur Juvenes dum sumus.*"*

---

* Let us live then and be glad while young life's before us. . . ." Anonymous – *c.* 1267.

12

The Close Bridge Garrison

When the survivors of 1 Airborne Division had been evacuated from Arnhem the state of affairs on the Island seemed to change in the twinkling of an eye. While there were British troops still in Arnhem there was only one idea among us all – we must get across the river! Next morning we had evacuated 1 Airborne Division. We had shot our bolt and in our minds there was a void. What ought we to do *now*? Very likely something similar had happened on the other side of the river. While British troops were in Arnhem the enemy also had only one idea in mind: to annihilate the British in their perimeter. Next morning they found the perimeter empty. The struggle was over and what should *they* do next?

It was as though we had all been passengers on some giant pendulum. It swung us with gathering speed from Normandy to Brussels. Thereafter it seemed to lose momentum until it reached its zenith and halted at Arnhem. Some unknown law of Nature seemed to have willed it all.

I was certainly very much aware of this change of scene when I came to breakfast, rather late, after the night of ferrying described in the last chapter, but I was not alone in this awareness. The Mess Sergeant of "A" Mess hurried in to apologize for the breakfast table being disarrayed, the porridge being cold and the bacon finished, but he said that "a couple of eggs could be fried in no time". He then posed the question, "Where do you think we'll be tomorrow, Sir?" I had not the slightest idea, but in the back of my mind I thought of Napoleon's Mess Sergeant, serving the breakfast over one hundred years ago in the suburbs of Moscow. He may have posed the same question and he might have got the same reply: "God only knows." In the event we did not move

194

anywhere on 26 September, but by 5 pm on 28 September I had to tell Gordon Lilley to get our own Sapper HQ packed up quickly for a move to Nijmegen.

G. I. Thomas had sent for me in a hurry; a lot had happened very quickly. The interruptions on our axis behind us had had more effect than I was aware of. We were now short of artillery ammunition. There was anxiety about supplies of petrol and restrictions on movement had to be imposed to save it. Luckily we had captured vast quantities of German Army rations in Nijmegen and food was therefore plentiful. But British troops do not thrive on black pudding and "door-step" biscuits tasting of caraway seed; nor do generous supplies of Dutch cognac, gin and cigars take the place of spuds and bully beef. And if anything happened to the two bridges in Nijmegen – the main road bridge and the railway bridge – we might be short of German rations too.

Even as G. I. Thomas spoke to me in his caravan, I heard again what had now become a familiar sound – the crash of German shells fired into the Island from across the Lower Rhine. North of the river the land was high, overlooking the Island, and German observers on the far bank were well-placed to direct their artillery fire on any movement they saw in our midst. The Germans had begun to show a marked disposition to take the offensive and seek to drive us out of the Island. Intelligence sources informed us that the Germans in the Arnhem area had been reinforced. Two more Panzer Divisions (9 and 116) had arrived from Germany and a Panzer SS Brigade from the south had also been added to the opposition against us. We believed a new German General had arrived to command the troops across the river and it was already evident that he was a capable and energetic man. Whether we liked it or not, we were now on the defensive.

But we were none of us depressed. G. I. Thomas himself had been made responsible for the defence of the whole Island (including Nijmegen) and all the troops on the Island were now under his command. He therefore commanded five Infantry Brigades, an Armoured Brigade and four additional Artillery Regiments, which constituted a useful force. And having battled so hard himself to attack across the Island, no one knew better than he did how to defend it.

He looked his usual severe but confident self as he addressed me. He could not, he said, prevent the enemy making occasional successful sallies here and there, but he had reserves well placed to make a quick counterattack to drive them out again. And any counterattack we might make would be well supported by our now numerous artillery, provided our ammunition supply-line remained intact over the bridges in Nijmegen.

"And this," he said, glaring at me, "is where you come in. You, with your Divisional Engineers, are to be the nucleus of a 'Close Bridge Garrison' for Nijmegen. You will also have under your command two Batteries of 73 Anti-tank Regiment and B Company of 8th Middlesex Regiment [our Divisional Machine Gun Battalion]."

He made it quite clear, if it was not clear to me already, that my main responsibility was to ensure that no harm came to the bridges in Nijmegen. An enemy sally by an armoured column could be driven back again anywhere in the Island without much difficulty. But if one of those sallies got into Nijmegen, even for half an hour, it might be possible to blow up both bridges before our reserves could intervene.

"And that would be very serious," he said. "Hence your Close Bridge Garrison. Your job is to stop any enemy penetration from entering Nijmegen itself."

He pointed out, rather as an afterthought, that a sally by an armoured column was not the only threat. An attempt might be made by guile to introduce into Nijmegen a civilian lorry, loaded with dynamite hidden among sacks of potatoes, and contrive to wreck the bridge by detonating it on the bridge itself. Clearly, therefore, I must halt and search all traffic proceeding towards either of the bridges. This, he seemed to think, would be the main threat.

Time was short. I must get my garrison organized by nightfall at the latest, and Gordon Lilley had meanwhile arranged for the COs of every unit in my Close Bridge Garrison to meet me at the main road bridge in Nijmegen at 6.30 pm.

Before dismissing me, G. I. Thomas asked if I wanted to ask any questions. I said I had one question "What about Anti-Aircraft protection?" I asked. The answer was simple. There was already an AA Battery in Nijmegen. It had recently been reinforced. It operated in close co-operation with the RAF and the night fighters. It was not under his (G. I. Thomas's) command, nor mine. The Battery Commander took his orders from "higher authority". I suppose I ought to have known that already, and my question was taken more as a sign of amateur status than of prudence.

As I climbed down from his caravan he smiled faintly, wished me luck and said he'd come over next morning to see what I had arranged. I then hurried away and got to the meeting point for my Order Group just as the others were arriving.

It was still full daylight and the first thing that struck us all was the amount of Dutch civilian traffic using the bridge. It was said to be under intermittent enemy gunfire and, as proof of this, a salvo shortly whistled overhead and splashed into the river not far away. One of the Battery Commanders, who had been camped near by for some days, told me that a tall factory, visible about a quarter of a mile away, was now occupied by the enemy who had an observation post in it. The building had often been shelled by us and perhaps that was why the enemy shelling was now inaccurate. A Liaison Officer from the local Infantry Brigade confirmed all this. He said they were reserving their ammunition to give the factory a good dressing-down if there were any signs of a full-blown enemy attack being imminent.

I was personally struck by the width of the river. I should say it was about the same as the Thames by the Houses of Parliament. There were many signs that river traffic was considerable in more peaceful days and several of us remarked that it might even be possible for the Germans to send a naval pinnace armed with a torpedo to be fired at a pier of a bridge from a "considerable range".*

My Order Group did not take long. The only approaches suitable for an enemy armoured sally must be covered by anti-tank guns and machine guns. Road traffic must be halted and searched. Provision must be made for firing anti-tank guns up or down the river at a hypothetical enemy naval vessel approaching by day and I undertook to tackle the AA Battery Commander in order to obtain illumination of the river at night. There would be a bridge guard of Sappers on each bridge, with one Field Company in general reserve. We fixed a time for stand-to next morning and I asked if there were any questions. There were a few questions relating to "loose ends" that I ought to have "tied up" more securely. Several of those present urged me to arrange for illumination of the bridges by night, but several others said, "For God's sake don't, or they will bomb the bridges for a certainty." I told them to leave that to me.

After the O-Group I had a look at where our own clerks and draughtsmen had to work and live. It seemed to me to be a principle of command to visit my own office staff from time to time. They had been well chosen by my predecessor and gave most excellent service. They were managed by the Chief Clerk, a junior civil servant by profession who had worked in local government in Wiltshire. He had an interesting and responsible job in the HQ, far better than that of the Regimental Sergeant-Major. In a Gunner or Infantry Regiment the whole unit occupies a comparatively small area and the RSM is at the HQ that is at the hub of the whole thing. He plays an important part in the management of the whole Regiment. But the Sappers are spread over the whole Divisional Area which is far too wide a field for one man to get a proper grip of all the detailed matters that require the RSM's attention. Consequently, the Company Sergeant-Majors have the real jobs, while the RSM of the Divisional Engineers never seemed to me to have a worthwhile task. His promotion from Company Sergeant-Major to Regimental Sergeant-Major was a step up in pay but nothing more. Later on in the campaign I found a real job for the RSM, but I shall explain that later.

There were a few routine office duties to be done and when they were finished I went into the room where the cooks had served food and we had an

---

* We only held both banks of the river for a short distance in each direction from the bridges.

197

evening meal. Today, I suppose, someone would have turned on the radio or the TV, but in those days there was no TV and the only radio to be heard – and it was very popular – was the German singer known as Lilli Marlene*, but she came on later. Otherwise those off duty made their own amusements with chess, draughts or cards.

Living as we did so much in the open air, most of us fell asleep early, but I went out with one of the Field Engineers on a tour of my bailiwick to see that all was well. Just before we set off a report came from the AA Battery. The report said that a reply had been received to my request for illumination of the river. "Higher Authority" had ruled that unorthordox searchlight illumination was not allowed. The official view was that this was likely to do more harm than good. The searchlights were intended to illuminate the enemy aircraft in the sky. If, instead, they illuminated the river below, they would certainly make it easier for attacking bombers to find the target area and even the target itself. There was logic in support of both arguments – the AA Gunners' argument and my argument. So I let the matter rest. This was a mistake.

It was pitch dark when we left HQ and a very noisy air raid was in progress. The whistle and crash of falling bombs seemed unceasing. Several fires had broken out in the town. AA guns were firing in reply and searchlight beams were weaving in the sky in search of enemy bombers. However, neither bridge was hit, no military casualties were reported, sentries were alert wherever I went and Duty Officers were to be found at all unit headquarters. Eventually the raid was over and I went to bed fully clothed. I slept soundly.

An hour before dawn I was awake. No important messages had arrived during the night and stand-to would take place in half an hour's time. Stand-to is military jargon for "Stand to arms", or (more familiarly) "Pick up your arms and accoutrements and go to action stations". (The converse is "Stand down" or "Leave action stations and relax".) Both have been practised by soldiers since time immemorial†. For many reasons dawn is a favourite hour for standing-to and it is often a propitious hour for a CO to go and see for himself what, if anything, has happened during the night.

It was a fine morning, but the sun had not yet risen when I reached the road bridge. Troops were standing to, manning guns, and observation posts were at action stations. They were vigilant and alert. There had been a lot of damage done during the night by both air raids and gunfire, but there had been no military casualties and neither bridge had been hit. I motored across the Road Bridge and spoke to the Guard Commanders at both ends. Near one bank there was a young officer on duty – a cheerful young man with a quick and somewhat wry sense of humour. He emerged from under the deck of the bridge, where he

* Her real name was Lale Andersen. She died in 1983.

† See Judges VII, verse 19.

198

had been to make sure that no saboteur had got there by stealth during the night to set a time-bomb for our discomfort. He told me that a stick of bombs had been dropped during the night and narrowly missed the bridge. Water had been splashed all over the place but no damage had been done. I could see both banks dimly. These were sensitive locations and stood in shallow water. There was certainly no damage done anywhere to either bridge.

I was much relieved that we had got through the night without suffering damage and I very much liked a suggestion that Tony Abbott had made.

"How would it be, Sir," he said, "if we could get some amphibious lorries by tonight and fit their headlights on pivots as spot lights? We could then patrol the river with armed crews. If a German fishing boat came along we might even fight a naval action."

I do not think we could have got these precautions into operation the evening before – even if anyone had thought of them. But I determined to press for them as soon as G. I. Thomas arrived for his promised visit.

I was therefore in fairly good spirits when I got back to my HQ. But there was a surprise awaiting me. Gordon Lilley was on duty. He had in his hand the receiver of the civilian telephone that the Signals had fixed up for us. He was evidently on the phone to some important person.

"He's just come in, Sir," I heard him say. "I'll put him on the phone at once."

The speaker on the far end was none other than General Horrocks, commanding 30 Corps. He had received a garbled report from some underground source of the Dutch Resistance. The Dutch story was that both the railway bridge and the road bridge in Nijmegen had been destroyed during the night and he, the Corps Commander, wanted to know what had happened.

"There must be some mistake, Sir," I replied. "I have only just returned from the road bridge myself. Five minutes ago I motored across it. The men were all standing-to. There was no damage whatever to be seen on either bridge. There *must* be some mistake. . . ."

I was about to say more when the Intelligence Officer put his head round the curtain. He had the earphones of the command set on his head and the pressel switch in his hand*. I could see the matter was urgent and I asked the Corps Commander to wait a moment as I had Stop Press News.

"It's OC 204 Field Company on the blower, Sir," said the Intelligence Officer. "He reports that both bridges have been damaged – the railway bridge seriously, one pier in midstream having been destroyed. The road bridge is less seriously damaged. There is a hole, forty feet long, in the roadway and stretching across the road surface from one footwalk to the other. Both bridges are passable for pedestrians, but neither is possible for wheeled traffic. He says

* The pressel switch was a gadget enabling the operator to switch the set to Send or Receive, as required.

199

that eighty feet of Bailey Bridge would make a reasonable roadway repair for heavy vehicles and tanks on the road bridge. It would only take a few hours to do this."

General Horrocks could hardly be expected to rejoice over this tale of woe, but he took it very well. It might all have been much worse. I said I would see for myself what had happened and I would initiate repairs on the road bridge and report again shortly.

When I got back to the road bridge "all hands and the cook" were on deck. It was now broad daylight. I could plainly see both bridges. The middle pier of the railway bridge was utterly demolished and two bays of railway track, each about sixty feet long, sloped down into the water where the pier had formerly been. The damage to the road bridge was exactly as had been reported on the blower. Sappers were already working on the hole in the roadway. We had enough Bailey equipment to begin work, and if the Chief Engineer of 30 Corps could send immediately a few extra loads of equipment, repairs ought to be finished by midday.

No one knew for certain how the enemy had achieved all he had done. Nothing suspicious had been seen by the bridge guards at any time and the first news was the sound of bursting demolitions a few minutes ago. There had been no casualties. We received the explanation later.

Parties of German sailors, equipped as frogmen, had entered the river upstream. They had been trained in Venice for attacking warships at anchor. Each party was armed with a torpedo-shaped device that floated. It consisted of a naval magnetic mine with its magnetic activating fuse replaced by a time fuse and buoyancy tanks added at each end. The Germans brought two such devices to the road bridge. Among the occasional flotsam that is always to be found on a wide river, the Germans were able to conceal their mines, partially submerged. One party had no difficulty in finding their way successfully to the railway bridge and attaching a mine to the central pier of it. The others were less successful with the road bridge. Only one mine exploded. The other was recovered in about six feet of water where it ran aground. It was hauled out of the water by 260 Field Company, using the winch gear of a lorry. It was landed safely and Lieutenant Bridge, GC, RN, defused it.

Time switches were set by the frogmen before leaving to swim downstream. When they judged they were back again in German-held territory they came ashore. Unfortunately for them, they misjudged the distances and landed into the hands of 43 Divisional Reconnaissance Regiment to whom they proudly told their story. We all thought they were brave men and I was told that their chivalrous captors had congratulated them on their exploit. The frogmen willingly told their story, smoking their captors' cigarettes and warming themselves at their fire.

Soon after all this the Chief Engineer of 30 Corps, having received our report

200

on the repairs necessary, sent a Corps Field Engineer Regiment to do whatever was necessary. We ourselves had made a good beginning and the roadway of the road bridge was soon repaired and traffic flowed again.

G. I. Thomas came to see me the same morning. He had to cross the river from the Island in a Dutch ferry-boat organized by 204 Field Company. I said I was sorry to have disappointed him. His generous remark was, "Forget it! I do not blame you." He told me that he had heard independently the night before of my attempt to get the river illuminated by searchlights. He had backed the idea himself, but it was turned down "at a very high level". We never mentioned this episode again and I never followed up the timing of the Germans' movements, but I think they must have placed their charges before it was light. The time switches gave a delay of about two hours, so that when I myself had looked at the road bridge during Stand-to, the torpedo must have been grounded but submerged, and ticking quietly, waiting to explode later. Next night I had all the illuminations I wanted and the river looked like the scene of some fluvial torchlight festival.

The Germans were not to be deprived of their fun and during the nights following they pushed haystacks and logs into the river to float downstream towards the bridges. All these objects were reported by observers as nautical mines, midget submarines or frogmen. They drew fire from every possible weapon and ricochets off the water flew in all directions, making the river banks hazardous places for spectators.

Thus, for a second time, I had seen an imaginative German strategem, daringly carried out by the enemy, but brought to nought by imperfect technical details.

13

The Battle For
the Rhineland

When the Arnhem battle had died down one did not have to be a Clausewitz to see what ought to be done next. In the first place 21 Army Group in particular, and the Allies in general, needed the port of Antwerp. The lines of communication still stretched back to Normandy and all our wants had to come from there, mainly by road. This was a long haul and the round trip for each lorry was a slow one. The opening of the port of Antwerp for shipping was therefore the first necessity.

Next, we had got as far as the Rhine at Arnhem, but we had not crossed it, and without crossing it we could not reach the heart of Germany. We had momentarily gained surprise at Arnhem, but we had failed to keep it. Had we kept surprise, who can say what we might or might not have done? Having lost surprise, for whatever reason or reasons, a second bite at the same cherry did not look an attractive venture. It seemed that a better bet would be to increase our foothold along the west bank of the Rhine. We might then have a wide choice of bridging sites available – perhaps anywhere between (say) Arnhem and Cologne – and having the choice of options would automatically give us a commanding position.

There was therefore a dual and worthwhile winter occupation awaiting us, namely: 1. The opening of Antwerp to shorten our lines of communication, and 2. The clearing of the west bank of the Rhine, so as to acquire a wide option of crossing-places over that river for the spring offensive of 1945.

The achievement of these two winter aims would give us the initiative again and a firm base from which to exercise it. Moreover, as a bonus, during the winter we might develop some of the potential airfields of the Low Countries and restore our complete command of the skies above our armies. All that was required was to maintain the morale of the troops in Europe and the people at home. Both were well within our scope. There must be no costly failures or grandiose designs, but a succession of well-planned local offensives, using our mobility to concentrate our forces wherever the best prospects of gain offered. There was certain to be hard fighting during the winter, but we all felt that with Monty at the helm, and generals like Horrocks and G. I. Thomas in charge of operations, we would never be launched into any battle that we could not, by our own exertions, be sure of winning. It was disappointing that we had not achieved all that we might have hoped for in Market Garden, but, even so, in October, 1944, we were certainly on a far better wicket than the Germans. They had lost all their gains on their Western Front and most of them on their Eastern Front too. We and the Americans were hammering on their front door and the ferocious, unforgiving Russians were beginning to hammer at their back door also.

It was therefore no surprise to find that at the beginning of October plans for short leave (48 hours) in Brussels were beginning to appear on the scene, and plans for longer spells of leave in the UK (ten days was the rumour) for those who had landed on D-Day were within the bounds of possibility. As a newcomer to 43 Division – I had not landed in France till August – I could not expect to be eligible for these benefits for some time to come, but it was comforting to think that many of my Sappers could entertain high hopes of both quite soon.

On 2 October 43 Division was relieved on the Island by 82 American Airborne Division and one of their Battalions took over responsibility for the Close Bridge Garrison at Nijmegen. The CO of this battalion was one of the American officers whom I had met on Salisbury Plain before we went to North Africa. The first question he asked was, "What control do I have over the AA Battery here in Nijmegen?" I said that this was the first question I had myself asked and I explained the answer that I was given, namely that the AA Battery was a small cog in the air defence arrangements for the Low Countries and that I had no say in the matter whatever. I told him I had acquired a kind of "leverage" over the Major commanding in Nijmegen and I advised the American to struggle on with that. I wished him luck, but what actually happened, I never heard.

From the Island 43 Division was moved to an area south of Nijmegen between the River Maas and the German frontier. As a start we were mainly on the defensive, presumably because getting a grip on Antwerp was the first priority for 21 Army Group. Meanwhile, a defensive attitude elsewhere was all that could be attempted until Antwerp had been opened for our sea traffic.

The front line was close to the German frontier and until about a month ago military trains from Germany had been arriving at the station nearby,

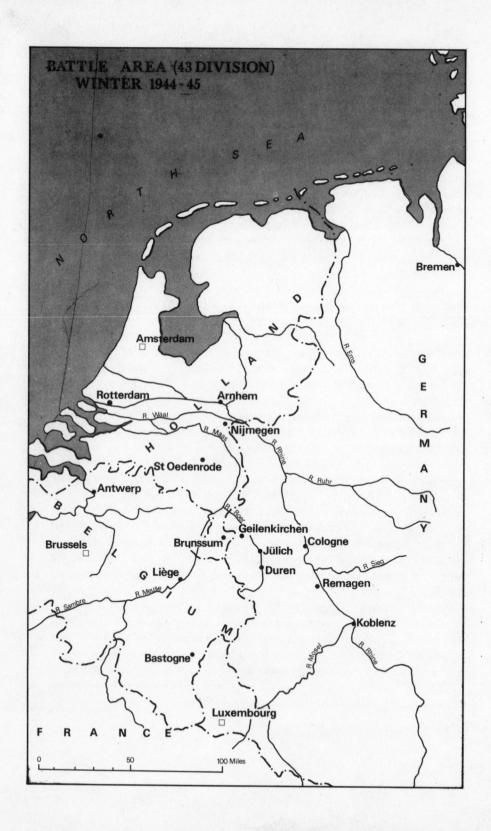

BATTLE AREA (43 DIVISION)
WINTER 1944-45

NORTH SEA

Bremen

Amsterdam

HOLLAND

GERMANY

R. Ems

Rotterdam

Arnhem

R. Waal

Nijmegen

R. Maas

R. Rhine

St Oedenrode

R. Ruhr

Antwerp

R. Roer

R. Roer

BELGIUM

Geilenkirchen

Cologne

Brunssum

Jülich

Brussels

Duren

R. Sieg

Liège

Remagen

R. Meuse

R. Sambre

Koblenz

Bastogne

R. Mosel

R. Rhine

Luxembourg

FRANCE

0   50   100 Miles

but it was now more or less in no-man's-land. The slit trenches taken over by our troops were mostly roofed by smashed wings and spars of American gliders that had been used in the capture of Nijmegen. About one hundred gliders in various collapsed attitudes were visible, and many silk parachutes still lay about on the ground. Almost every other soldier seemed to be wearing some part of one of them as a neck scarf. Patrolling was a regular nocturnal pursuit and little movement by day was possible without drawing fire. Behind the front lines, however, the Dutch were extremely hospitable and almost everyone not actually in a slit trench was taken under cover somewhere – in private houses, deserted industrial buildings, schools, farmhouses, stables and so on. The Dutch took the "Tommies" into their hearts as well as into their homes. Women would turn up, as it were for fatigues, to peel potatoes every day, saying that they had been ordered to do so by the Germans, but that they now did it as a pleasure. (They were mostly the womenfolk of an agricultural population, and although I am sure the "Tommies" gave them a share of their rations, the Dutch often in exchange gave them chickens, eggs and fruit out of the kindness of their hearts.)

We at Divisional HQ, however, were leading a fairly rugged life, still in tents, as G. I. Thomas had a "bee in his bonnet" about keeping out of inhabited places. He frequently urged me to direct my mind to the possibilities of digging with our bulldozers troglodyte underground abodes for everyone. The Divisional Staff, however, always urged me to make the most of the obvious limitations to this policy, and to resist to the utmost G. I. Thomas's insistence on living in the bleak discomfort of the fields.

I did my best in this, but the man to whom we were in the end indebted for G. I. Thomas's giving way was the GSO II of the Division. He was a Gunner Major, an ex-territorial from Merseyside: efficient, sensible, friendly and good-humoured. He was always polite and took great pains to spare us all the trouble he could. He never seemed to get tired; he was constantly on duty and the very high standard of staff work in HQ 43 Division's operational planning must have been due to Major R. S. Williams-Thomas, RA.

I personally endured a tent well into November, by which time it was really very cold and wet, but then, by chance, I came across a deserted 4-wheel German boat trailer of very modern design. It had torsion springing, deriving its resilience from the twisting of spring steel, and the wheels of the rear axle "tracked" exactly in the wake of the two front ones. I had it converted to a caravan for my office and bedroom. It was towed by the lorry that carried the electric lighting plant for Divisional HQ, so I never lacked a well-lit office and a reasonably comfortable bed.

The Sapper Field Companies were kept busy in their brigade areas doing minor engineer tasks to help the Infantry, though we did have a few larger Sapper projects. One was to build a bridge of fifty-foot span over a canal. It was required to shorten the journey for vehicles carrying reinforcements from a safe "harbour area", out of range of enemy artillery fire, up to the forward area where they would be needed if things hotted up on our sector of the front. I wanted this bridge designed to take forty-ton loads, and therefore fit for heavy tanks, but the Chief Engineer of 30 Corps said he could not spare any Bailey Bridge equipment. We were therefore restricted to the use of local materials, but four years of German occupation had denuded local resources of many of the materials we might have liked. Nor could we be sure how long we could count on for building it and we certainly did not want to leave it only half-built if we were hurriedly moved away.

I had now got on to reasonably cordial terms with G. I. Thomas and we discussed the matter calmly. We settled for building what was called a Class 30 bridge, that is, one capable of carrying all classes of military loads up to a maximum weight of 30 tons. It was vexatious having to make this restriction, and if we had been sure of about a fortnight for building (which in the end we had) we might have built a bridge for "All Military Loads".*

I gave the job of designing and building this bridge to 553 Field Company. The Major commanding this Company was a stout-hearted warrior, and volunteered to begin work within thirty-six hours, when I told him that we had found an abandoned timber yard a few miles away with some 12″ × 12″ baulks of timber in it, from which wooden trestles might be made. Someone else had observed a steel-fabricated building wrecked in an air raid, probably by the RAF, in which some very substantial rolled steel joists were available in the wreckage.

The Major did the only sensible thing and delegated the work to one of his platoons. The Subaltern commanding the platoon had recently become a casualty and had been replaced by a Second Lieutenant "straight out of the egg". He had probably never built a bridge in his life before, far less an improvised one to take thirty-ton loads. However, he was a cheerful young man, with self-confidence and common sense, who knew how to use the many tables printed in the various Royal Engineer text books of those days.

I went to the site next morning to see what was happening and found the young man bustling about unloading timber and steel, and I was reminded of the first bridge that I myself had ever built. It was in India in 1928, two days after my arrival in the country. (I was 22.) It was a Warren Girder Bridge about forty feet long. It had been designed by somebody else, to be built of wooden poles like telegraph poles. They were to be spliced together to give the forty-foot span. Distance pieces, also cut from telegraph poles, gave the girders depth and diagonal tie rods of 1½″ steel held it all together. I was introduced to the Sikh platoon commander who was to build it, and we considered the

---

* It was the search for materials that would have taken the time.

proposition together. He was fat, jolly and elderly, but very wise. He spoke no English, so we could only communicate by sign language. He took a measuring tape from his haversack and indicated that we should measure the gap. It then revealed that, whereas the drawings indicated a forty-foot bridge, the actual measurement of the gap was one foot longer. The Jemadar's wisdom had averted a monumental folly sixteen years ago by using a measuring tape and I was delighted to see that the young man in 1944 had a measuring tape in his hand too. While he checked the gap with the tape, I examined a drawing produced by a draughtsman from the back of a lorry. I also checked (with the young man's slide rule) a sheet of arithmetic that accompanied the drawing. It was soon quite obvious that the design was so simple that if there were no fundamental errors in the measurements nothing was likely to be wrong in the calculations. It was a joy to watch the work proceed, and I went to see progress whenever I could. The bridge was completed in very good time and the young man and I travelled as passengers in the first vehicle that went across it.*

I quote this event at some length because it illustrates a principle that tends to be forgotten in the complicated world of today, namely that if you have the right sort of men about you, the overcoming of technical difficulties becomes comparatively easy. And about thirty years later I met the same young man again. He had become in middle age the Chairman of a successful firm of civil engineering contractors in the west of England. And many of the other young men whom I had the privilege to command in those wartime days were just that same sort of young man. How lucky we were in the Services! There was talent everywhere.

At the beginning of November the Port of Antwerp came into full-scale operation and more divisions could be maintained in Holland and against the German defenders of the Siegfried Line. The 43 Division was therefore moved again some fifty miles south into the Province of Limburg and our Divisional HQ was set up in the town of Brunnsum. We were to provide protection for the left flank of an American thrust, based on their salient near Aachen, and aiming towards Cologne. Their first objectives were the German towns of Duren and Julich. Their attack was planned to begin on 18 November and our attack was geared to theirs, so we had a few days to plan for it.

Brunnsum was a colliery town, not unlike many of those in England, but not a bit like a Welsh valley coalfield, which is much steeper and more enclosed. As far as the troops were concerned there was much to be said for Brunnsum. The Dutch were, as everywhere, friendly and hospitable, and the pit-head baths for the miners made it possible for a whole regiment to get hot baths in one visit.

This was the first battle we were to fight almost entirely on German soil. We were now about to repay the Germans in the coin they had used all over

---

* The subaltern's name was FitzJohn.

Europe. It was, however, just as pitiful to see a poor German family, with their entire belongings in a wheelbarrow, leaving a burning home, as it had been to see this sight in France, Belgium or Holland. The only consolation was that if a pig were found in a pigsty it was now permitted by Army regulations to eat it for breakfast, which had not been allowed while we were in allied territory.

Divisional HQ was in billets for the first time. We had the offices in a school and our "A" Mess was in the house of a Roman Catholic priest, almost opposite his church. The priest led a spartan life, using only one small room himself, but he gave up the rest of the house to our use. In exchange our cooks fed him well and Brigadier Paddy Boylan, who was a devout Roman Catholic, saw that he was never short of a bottle or two on his sideboard: (Paddy, himself, was a regular worshipper in his Church most mornings before breakfast.) I had a bedroom in the house of a Dutch widow whose brother (or brother-in-law) worked next door as a pastry cook.

The first Sapper task in preparation for the forthcoming battle was to prepare tracks through a strip of pine woods for approach roads to the start line for the attack. The American troops who had previously held the front line were new arrivals in Europe and when one of their Brigadiers handed over his command post to his Wessex replacement, I heard him say, "Gee! I feel like a thousand dollars being quit of this goddam forest!"

The main tracks we made were called "Bond Street", "Regent Street" and "Strand". The local tree trunks were not suitable to make a proper surface (called a Corduroy Surface) and I had to ask the Chief Engineer 30 Corps to send us proper tree trunks, but we only received enough to do the worst places. I had hopes that the slag from the coal pits might be some use as road surface material, but it turned out to be useless and became a sea of mud very quickly.

Half a mile of one of these roads was a straight stretch across an expanse of well-drained arable land, ploughed and planted with roots. It was in an area of no-man's-land, unsuitable for occupation by either side, being on a gentle slope with no cover higher than a turnip. The Germans had sown it with anti-tank mines and the Americans had added many anti-personnel ones as a defensive measure against enemy patrols. No record of either existed. It was easy enough to clear the track of the roadway, but every now and then a German low-flying aircraft would appear with a roar over the skyline of trees and spray the Sappers among the turnips. Anyone who from instinct sprang aside was liable to jump on a mine and lose a foot or a leg, and if his friend was incautious in getting to his aid he was liable to suffer the same fate.

I had a most unpleasant experience of this sort of thing one morning while I was inspecting this track. Lowe was driving me in the Ark* and we were returning along this open stretch when three German aircraft in line ahead

* Popular name for a type of armoured car.

11. The Railway Bridge at Nijmegen, destroyed by German
frogmen on 30 September, 1944.

12. The Commander-in-Chief with Lieutenant-General
Horrocks and Major-General Thomas, February, 1945.

13.   The ruins of Cleve, February, 1945

14.   Xanten after its capture by 129 Brigade, 8 March, 1945

whisked over the treeline behind us and roared along the alignment, spraying us with cannon in a most unfriendly manner. Lowe jammed on the brakes, which probably saved us, for the shots flew over our heads and struck the road about fifty yards ahead of us. The whole attack only occupied a few seconds, but when I had collected my wits I saw a wretched Sapper who must have sprung from the alignment of the road and trodden on a mine. He lay amongst the turnips waving his tin hat and wimpering in pain and despair.

Natural instinct prompted me to jump out of the Ark to do what I could, but Lowe yelled at me. "Stop," he shouted. "I can see a mine just in front of you." Fingering amongst the roots, and guided by Lowe, who from the height of the Ark had a better view than I had, I was able to walk on virgin soil forwards to the wounded man. Meanwhile several Sappers appeared, apparently from nowhere, with a mine-detector and marked a clear passage to carry the unfortunate man back to the road. The worst part of this minor adventure was the pathetic cries from the wounded man as he watched my slow and cautious approach towards him. He was in terrible pain. "Please hurry, Sir. Please hurry," he kept repeating. Poor devil! He must have thought me an absolute swine to be so slow.

This experience instantly showed me the need to order a wide swathe to be cut in the turnips on either side of the track and get it all properly cleared of mines. A few days later, when the attack began, I have no doubt that convoys of lorries, bumbling along the track, must occasionally have been shot up by aircraft and everyone must have jumped for dispersal into the swathe in the turnips. But thank God it was by then swept. About 1400 mines had been lifted by our Divisional Sappers.

EXTRACTS FROM LETTERS TO MY PARENTS

Written from Nijmegen, Holland, 1 October, 1944

I am now in a school that was used by the Germans as an annexe to a hospital devoted to Dutch mothers expecting children by German soldiers and the school was evidently a storehouse. It is full of cupboards of drugs, German newspapers and pictures of Hitler. There are also stocks of German rations – frozen pork, brown bread and pots of honey. . . ! The other day a naughty German fired a shell which pitched within 5 yards of where I was standing. But it was a dud! *Deo Gratia.*

Written from near Nijmegen, 16 October, 1944

The King visited us today. I had the honour of being presented – in company with about 200 others! He's a splendid man. Most conscientious and painstaking. He has a good memory too. He remembered our last meeting in

Lincolnshire and your home-made butter! He must have had many thousands of officers and soldiers presented since then. I am sure he really does take an interest in everyone. God save the King! Wouldn't it have been awful if we'd lost this war! The boasting Hitler does not know what's coming to him!

Written from near Nijmegen, Holland, 21 October, 1944

At present I live even more simply than Diogenes. I don't know why he chose to live in a barrel, but I can't believe he was prompted by the reasons that make us all live in the peculiar way we do. I sleep in a tent and we have our meals in a lean-to against a lorry. The other day, who should walk into the Mess but George Howell. Last time we met was in *Whimbrel* in 1938, when I sailed him onto a sandbank on the south side of the Needles channel. The tide was falling and we spent the night there. Poor *Whimbrel* looked like a dead horse on a racecourse. But she did not break. I'll try and treat her better if I ever sail her again. . . . The Dutch are incredibly kind to us all.

Written from near Nijmegen, 12 November, 1944

Yesterday I was talking to an American, who pointed to a windmill and asked: "Is that a grist mill or a water pump?" Can you think of neater English for quite a complicated technical question? They seem to have a better command of Anglo-Saxon English than many of us do. But they also have some horrors. What do you think of *Activating* a division? or *Alerting* a regiment?

14

Battles of the
Rhineland

The battle that followed the preparations described in the last chapter was the first of a series that in retrospect seem very much alike. In Market Garden, for instance, the aim was almost unlimited; it aimed at total victory. But from November until March there was a series of battles that *in toto* merely aimed at clearing the enemy off the west bank of the Rhine. Until that was achieved we could not hope to deal the *coup de grâce*. From now onwards each battle was for limited objectives only. They were battles of attrition, each one aiming to nibble a relatively small portion off the flesh remaining on the bone. The most the enemy could achieve in any of them was to delay us and to postpone his final defeat. Unless we made some serious mistake, the enemy ought never to have a chance to tip the scales his way.

The Allies did, in fact, make a serious mistake and in consequence we gave the Germans a glimpse of hope which they snatched at in the Ardennes in December. But our mistake had not been fatal and our discomforts were only temporary. We were able to regain our balance and revert to attrition and to continue nibbling at the Rhineland until we had it all. Then we were free to cross the Rhine and start again with hopes of total victory.

It would be wrong to give the impression that the worst of the fighting was over. On the contrary, the fighting was just as fierce and the casualties just as grievous, but the kaleidoscope consisted of smaller pieces and my main memories of those months are of fatigue, worry and constant grinding toil. To describe all this in detail might please the author, who took part, but it would impose on the reader a burden that I prefer to spare him. My aim will therefore be to tell only of the brightly illuminated and vivid pieces of the kaleidoscope that happened to come within my view and to leave the rest to the reader's imagination. Some of the vivid pieces may seem trivial, but I believe they somehow reflect what it all felt like to one small cog in a vast machine.

This battle, whose preparations I described in the last chapter, began on 18 November. It began with the softening-up treatment by our Divisional Artillery and a pounding of his back area by guns of the heaviest calibres, thickened up by the Pepperpot whose nature I have explained. Most of the attacking Infantry came from their concentration areas some distance in rear. Some were carried on the backs of the tanks that were to support them from the Start Line forward. Some were carried in Armoured Troop Carrying vehicles and some travelled in a new kind of vehicle that now made its appearance for the first time. These were called "weasels".

A weasel was a small amphibious vehicle, with a propeller and a rudder for use when the weasel was required to swim. It also had wide tracks on each side, mounted on rubber bogey wheels for use on boggy ground. It became a useful, all-purpose beast of burden because it was able to slither its way across a sea of mud. For carrying up rations and ammunition, and for carrying back the wounded, it had no equal. It was easy to drive and the carrier platoons of the infantry battalions soon learned how to get the best out of them.

Our objectives for the first day were captured according to plan. An exceptional turnout of journalists, press photographers and BBC men lined the approach roads. Above all, the weather was fine. We were now on German soil and soon a lot of German prisoners were captured. I became aware for the first time that German troops *en masse* carried a peculiar odour, different from that of British or American troops. As a child in East Anglia during the First World War, I had noticed how troops, when out marching, "had a funny smell about them", and I remember some grown-up person explained the phenomenon by saying that it came from "the smell of the shaving soap they all use". I have since been told that the explanation is really to do with their diet, but, whatever the cause, there is no doubt about it that troops of every nation have a national aroma peculiar to themselves. Even the trenches occupied by one nation smell odd to the troops of another nation when they change hands.

Next day it rained. Zero hour was before dawn and the infantry must have had a miserable night. A few were in houses and sheds perhaps, but most of them simply dug themselves slit trenches and passed a night of doubt and sorrow as soldiers have done since the dawn of history. Roads and tracks became muddy from the rain too. Tanks milling about here and there, backing and filling, churned up the surfaces of roads and made pot holes everywhere, so that even on some of the main roads one splashed about in mud over the tops of one's boots. Progress became slow, but the miseries of the Germans were far worse than ours, and by the evening of the second day there were few objectives that we had not captured.

212

It was quite clear to me that it would not be long before my worst worries would arise from the state of the roads, and after three or four days the American advance, whose left flank we were protecting, slowed down and eventually fizzled out. I suspected that this was as much due to the weather, the mud and the general disintegration of the roads as to the German resistance. Later on there was frost to aggravate the damage. Frost produced a phenomenon constantly mentioned and bewailed by the few Germans with whom I spoke. *Frost scharden* they called it, or "frost damage".

Many of the roads in Germany were cobbled, the surfaces having been made by laying granite "sets", each the size of a large, square loaf of bread. The tapered faces were such that, when laid in moist sand, the road surface became slightly cambered to allow the rain to run into the kerbs, and a neat, curved pattern was also given to the surface as viewed by the traveller. I was told that this technique had been evolved by the military roadmakers of the Napoleonic era. So long as no frost occurred, the arch effect of the tapered sets, reinforced by the sand beneath, was perfectly adequate to carry normal civilian traffic – and up to a point to carry military traffic too. But a severe frost played all kinds of tricks. It froze the moisture in the sandy formation and distorted its cambered profile. The tapered sets lost the rigidity they had acquired from their arched formation and a single vehicle, passing along a stretch of frozen road, might act upon the arched camber as a ploughshare would act on a row of potatoes in a field. A regiment of tanks, driving along a frozen road, might do damage in a single pass comparable with the destruction of an earthquake.

In consequence of this – even without frost – a few days of mechanical winter warfare turned German highroads into vast rivers of mud in which lay innumerable granite sets in higgledy-piggledy disorder. And a few three-point turns by a tank might excavate a hole in which that tank would wallow helplessly till another tank could extract it by brute force.

In peacetime it was possible for local authorities to stop all traffic after a hard frost until more temperate weather allowed the cobbled roads to regain their pristine form; but in time of war such forebearance was totally unacceptable. Commanders-in-Chief would order operations to continue, despite the weather, and military engineers must do their best to keep the roads open. Only one option was open and that was to fill the potholes with brick-rubble and leave it to the traffic to pound it more or less flat.

Everywhere that the battle had flowed there remained a trail of buildings battered out of all recognition by aerial bombing or artillery fire. If the Sappers could be equipped with sufficient bulldozers, mechanical diggers and fleets of tipping lorries, there seemed to be a reasonable possibility of initiating a crude system of road repairs. First, the shattered buildings must be made into piles of brick-rubble, each pile the size of a haystack. Next the haystacks must be loaded by mechanical monsters into tipping lorries (tippers) and spread over the worst potholes. Finally, the surface of the road, which by now had acquired the appearance of a lunar landscape, must be roughly levelled by more bulldozers till traffic could move over it to roll it, even if only on low gear. The more rubble that was laid, and the more pulverising and rolling it was given, the less obstacles there were to road movement at a slow but steady pace. This was a rough, rude process, known in 43 Division's Sappers as "Opening a Rubble Factory for the Masses".

Those engineers brought up in the intellectual and rigorous disciplines of Archimedes and Euclid, or the inventive achievements of Telford and Brunel, were shocked by this departure from excellence. But Moloch had to have his fill. Quality must go to the Devil. Quantity was what Moloch demanded. Thus the Genie of Mass Production which had escaped from a bottle in the Automobile factories of the New World cast its baleful influence upon the engineers of the Old World too.

Speaking for myself, I did not mind the appearance of the Genie too much, because I lacked the intellectual stance of the dedicated engineer. I was, however, aware of how our best NCOs (who were often the most skilful craftsmen too) regarded all this with distrust. Our RSM remarked one evening how "this sloppy, haphazard outlook will ruin the Corps of Royal Engineers". In a way he was right, even as regards the entire country, let alone the Corps. The term *Made in England* soon ceased to be a guarantee of excellence. But due to the existence of a small band of brothers, of whom the RSM was a forefather, the term 'Sandhurst-Trained' has more or less taken its place.

In an odd manner the Rubble Factories for the Masses brought about a metamorphosis in the RSM's duties in 43 Division Engineers. I have remarked how he had a rotten job. I must now tell how it was changed by the Genie. The high productivity of the Rubble Factories, regardless of the low intrinsic quality of the product, necessitated quick and effective delivery thereof. Here I found for the RSM a responsible job.

Every day, in increasing quantities, there was a need for the delivery of engineer stores of all kinds including brick-rubble. There was a pressing need every day to guide many lorry-loads of material up to the Field Companies destined to use it, and the locations of Companies, and the sources of supply in mobile operations, were continually changing. It was therefore necessary every day, and sometimes twice a day, to inform a lot of people of new locations, and some of these locations could not be sent out by signal "in clear" for fear of giving useful information to the enemy. To get it all into code, to transmit the signals in code, and then decode them, was a considerable bureaucratic task which was apt to end in delay or error or both.

We therefore devised a "notational" address known as Stackpipe. The RSM would choose the site for Stackpipe and, being a wise old bird, he would find a spot near to the seat of action, but not too close. We could notify the location of

Stackpipe to a wide list of addressees without evil consequence if it accidently leaked to the enemy. The only visible military object to be seen at Stackpipe was a noticeboard. Lorry-loads of engineer equipment and stores destined for our Field Companies could always be sent to Stackpipe with surety, partly because it occasionally remained in the same place for several days and partly because the RSM located it at some suitable landmark that was easy to find. When lorries of equipment arrived he parked them somewhere reasonably safe where they would not attract fire. The intended recipient could be told to send a guide to collect and lead them from Stackpipe to any God-forsaken place where they were wanted.

The blessings of Stackpipe depended on the wisdom and judgement of the RSM, who became very cunning in its operation. It became a useful feature in 43 Divisional Engineers' set-up. It will reappear in this narrative. (The text-book solution was to use the Divisional Field Park Company's camp as a meeting point, but this had several disadvantages, one of which was that this Company was liable to become very inefficient if located as far forward as Stackpipe was required to be.)

Before ending this Chapter I must recall two events that may be of interest. They relate to a wood we had captured early on in this battle. It was a wood of about twenty acres, first captured by 7th Somerset Light Infantry. It was not far from a part of the Siegfried Line, on a forward slope facing it, with a shallow depression between them.

Brigades and battalions in the line were changed periodically and this wood was considered by all its successive occupants as a very unpleasant place. It was shelled frequently by the enemy in a random manner, first here, then there, but with no visible pattern or method, just sufficiently to keep people under strain and to cause random casualties. In peacetime the wood was probably well kept and might have been used for wild game of some kind, either for breeding pheasants or perhaps wild pigs, but now it was full of undergrowth and brambles and any rides or tracks were worn and rutted by infantry carriers and weasels bringing up rations and ammunition to the forward positions and observation points overlooking the Siegfried Line.

The weather was becoming extremely bad and Gordon Lilley, whom I had promoted to command 553 Field Company, asked me to go with him to visit this wood and see what we could do to help the hapless battalion occupying it.

The track we followed into the wood was a sea of mud. At every turn, of which there were many, the manoeuvering of weasels and infantry carriers had churned up the ground, making pits so large that one got wet to the thighs crossing them. There was thick wet undergrowth among the trees on both sides of the track and we had a choice of wading in the mud of the track or struggling among soaking brambles and undergrowth on either side of it.

We eventually got to the Battalion HQ which was in the kind of dug-out that

I believe had been commonplace on the Western Front in the First World War. There were duckboards on the floor and a sump (or pit) dug in one corner, from which a soldier was baling water with a bucket when we arrived. The CO was in remarkably good spirits considering the circumstances. He told us that they had recently captured a German soldier in the wood. He had apparently been left *in situ*, concealed in the wood with a wireless set near a track junction. Whenever a weasel or a few men passed the track junction the German tapped out a codesign in morse, and a stonk of mortar or artillery fire landed as directed by the German; but now the German was no more.

The Colonel offered to send a guide to lead us up to one of his company positions so as to get some idea of the difficulties he had to contend with in getting rations, ammunition and so on to his positions at the forward end of this great wood. Assuming there were no more Germans with wireless sets lurking in the undergrowth, our movements towards the forward positions were unlikely to bring down retribution on the luckless defenders of the position, so we felt quite justified in going with the guide, but it turned out to be an exhausting and quite a creepy excursion. The mud was of a particularly sticky type; it would haul a wellington boot off your foot like a bootjack and every now and then a few random mortar bombs would come whistling over and burst in the treetops. After one such stonk I could hear shouting in the distance and a few minutes later a weasel came back along the trail carrying a wounded man on a stretcher, wrapped in a blanket. I was told it had been purely fortuitous. He had gone to a latrine dug in the heart of the wood and totally concealed. Six mortar bombs had crashed into the wood – one here, one there, guided by no rhyme or reason – but one of them had burst immediately above him.

The ideal answer to the Colonel's troubles would have been a Company of Gurkhas with kukris to clear new paths through the undergrowth and a Company of Sepoys with mules that could use the paths without turning them into the rivers of mud that vehicles made. These amenities, however, neither Gordon Lilley nor I could provide just by waving a wand, but we agreed to sending a platoon of Sappers with matchets (which they could leave behind when they departed) to show the Infantry how they might help themselves. We also agreed to produce enough pit props from the Brunnsum coal mines to make one or two decent corduroy tracks wherever the CO required them. We recognized that work would mostly have to be done by night, lest the waving treetops during the felling of trees might be visible in the Siegfried Line. A certain amount of stealth would also be required to get God knows how many lorry-loads of pit props unseen to where they were wanted, but this too was not beyond the wit of man.

On our way back to Gordon Lilley's jeep we came in for another random stonk by the Germans. This time, instead of being a noise of explosions in the distance, it turned out to be a crashing of shellfire all around us. We spread-eagled on the ground (which was extremely muddy at this point), but the distant German, by a random chance, changed the fuse-setting and the shells began to explode above our heads in the treetops. A red-hot piece of metal went *whack* into the ground just between us. With one accord we jumped and ran about fifty yards to leave the stonk behind us.

When all this was over and we were on our feet again who should appear but the Regimental Sergeant-Major of the Battalion, bringing forward a squad of reinforcements who had arrived that morning from the Base. The RSM looked as though he might have just come from the parade ground at Sandhurst, whereas both of us were spattered with mud. He saluted smartly and showed no suspicion of the disdain that he was entitled to feel at saluting such scarecrows! It was a lesson in good manners.

Gordon Lilley's platoon worked in this unpleasant billet for about ten days until the Brigade was relieved by another. The newcomers in the wood naturally expected the Sappers to send a platoon to help them too and the provision of a platoon, continually in this wood, became something of a running sore. My Company Commanders complained because they never had sufficient men for all that had to be done and they thought this a waste of manpower. Rightly or wrongly, I remained adamant, but I frequently visited the place to judge whether it was acceptable to withdraw the platoon or not.

For some reason the enemy seemed reluctant to shell the roads leading to the wood, but remained quiescent for a long time, and road-users consequently became careless. But I always felt it was only a matter of time before interruptions began, and I believe I was one of the first to get into trouble. It happened as follows. The road passed along the upper slopes of the valley where it was visible from the Siegfried Line. It was nearly straight for about half a mile and it reminded me of the roads one sees on the Wiltshire Downs near Marlborough. It was undulating downland exposing wide vistas of country with few trees, no hedges and little cultivation – just grass and chalk.

Suddenly a shot was fired and a shell whizzed across the road only a few feet behind us. Lowe "trod on the gas" and we passed out of sight, but I determined to be more crafty on the return journey.

When the time came, we approached the danger spot varying our speed between very fast and dead slow. I kept a lookout for any gun-flash giving us warning to alter our speed. Either our tactics of altering speed had defeated the German gunner or he had gone away for his dinner, but no shot was fired. However, when I got home myself I spoke to our Chief Gunner who said he would tell one of his Batteries to do something about it, and next time I passed that way there was a prominent notice posted at the roadside:

BEWARE!
ENEMY SHELL-FIRE FOR 800 YDS.

217

The Gunners did, in fact, do better than that. They established a well-concealed Observation Point* from which an observer kept vigil. If an enemy shot was fired the observer saw the flash immediately and signalled to his guns where the gun-flash came from. This brought down retribution on the enemy before he had time to scuttle for safety. One successful *coup* was apparently sufficient to damp the Germans' ardour, and shelling temporarily ceased.

I suppose that long before Virgil sang of "Arms and the Man" the tactics of one side defeating the wiles of his enemy by devising counter-measures to silence him was well-known, and it seems likely that the same pattern will continue as long as man continues to be what he is – and always has been! Perhaps, however, it may be that megaton weapons will put an end to man himself in the meantime. What a miserable prospect man creates for himself! We who took part in the Second World War must count ourselves lucky that we were not born in time to take part in the frightfulness of the future nor the horrors of the trenches of Flanders in 1914–18. Then casualties and stress were so continuous that hundreds of healthy young men on both sides collapsed with shell-shock, even though they might survive physical wounds of the greatest gravity. We were never tested to such lengths as they were, and, speaking for myself, I only witnessed two cases of shell-shock between 1940–1945. But I thank God I was not called upon to answer the final test myself, for I am certain that for every man there is a limit of stress beyond which he cannot endure and no one can say in advance where the final limit lies.

Much must have been learnt about shell-shock in the First World War and more perhaps may be known about it today, but I am not conscious of ever having been formally instructed in the prevention or cure of it. The nearest that came within my experience was when, in my presence, a youngster broke down and blurted out that he could not endure it any longer. It was a face-to-face scene; we two alone were present. I had no idea what I ought to do. The decision had to be mine and mine alone. I was totally untutored. I took him to the rear in my car and we spoke not a word. I put him down at his own Company HQ, telling his Major I would give orders about it next morning. I bade the Major to pray for guidance, in the meanwhile saying I would do likewise. As it turned out the guidance came quickly, but not in the least as I expected.

A message came to me within an hour telling me that the Chief Engineer would be visiting HQ 43 Division next morning. He wanted to see as many of my Company Commanders as possible and he would want to meet G. I. Thomas too if that was possible. So we fixed a Meeting Point at Divisional HQ.

He arrived next day in a car that was polished like the bridal one at a society wedding. The Guard turned out; the CE saluted and I took him to G. I.

* I called this point Mizpah (a watchtower): see Genesis XXXI, v. 49. I doubt if anyone else did!

218

Thomas's caravan. I thought I'd better not stay to hear what they talked about, lest he wanted to tell the Chief Engineer that he was fed up with me and required a replacement by return of post!

The Chief Engineer, however, emerged in a few minutes and I introduced the Company Commanders to him, one by one, followed by the Adjutant, the RSM and one or two others. He seemed to be genial and he said the right things to each in turn. He had the proper touch with human beings. He was a ginger-haired, rubicund man from Ulster, with just a touch of the Belfast intonation.

"Your General," he said, when he had finished speaking to them, "is very pleased with what you are all doing. Well done! Stick to it! And if there is anything I can do for you, now's your chance to ask."

They none of them spoke, so he dismissed them in a cheerful manner. Then, turning to me he added: "And what about you? Are you satisfied with all your Officers?"

I told him I'd like to speak to him privately about one of them. We walked a few yards away and I told him all about the man I had seen the previous day.

"What sort of chap is he?" he asked.

"He ought to be jolly good, but he's useless," I said. "It's not fair on the others to carry a passenger who does not play his part. I would value your advice on what I ought to do next. This is a new experience."

"My friend," replied the CE, "I look at it this way. If this boy had been wounded in the arm or the leg, you would have sent him to hospital and written to his next of kin. But as he's been wounded up here," (he tapped his forehead) "I suppose you feel that the proper answer is to court-martial him. But I don't agree. Nor would it be lawful.★ You must send him to my HQ and I will deal with his troubles." He gave no indication of what he would do.

"I'm not sure that I entirely agree with you, sir," I answered, "but I'm certainly grateful."

The Chief Engineer was silent. He got back into his car. I thought that perhaps I had not been very tactful but he did not seem to mind, for as he settled in his car he lowered the window and spoke in a cheerful voice.

"There is something else, too, that I might be able to do for you, and I hope you *will* approve this time. I could send you a couple more bulldozers to use in one of your blasted Rubble Factories. Is *that* O.K.?"

"Yes, Sir," I replied emphatically. "Send them to Stackpipe, c/o 43 Divisional Engineers on the Wings of the Morning. They will have a Royal Welcome. And, as tomorrow is Sunday, I'll sing the *Te Deum* with renewed gusto."

I saluted and he departed. Many people seemed to think Pat Campbell rather a forbidding customer, but he always seemed to me a wise and friendly

★ From 1930 onwards only treachery and mutiny remained punishable by death. Only four men were executed between 1939 and 1945, three for mutiny, one for treachery.

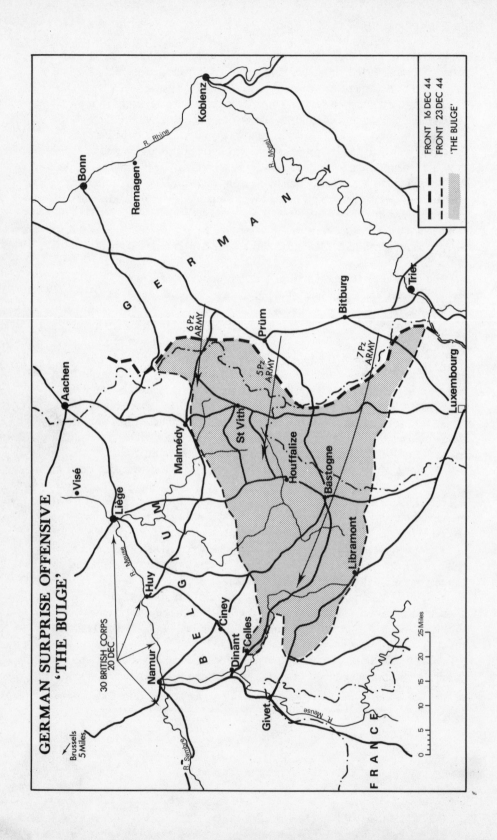

GERMAN SURPRISE OFFENSIVE 'THE BULGE'

FRONT 16 DEC 44
FRONT 23 DEC 44
'THE BULGE'

Bonn
Remagen
R. Rhine
Koblenz
R. Mosel
G E R M A N Y
Bitburg
Prüm
6 Pz ARMY
5 Pz ARMY
7 Pz ARMY
Trier
Luxembourg
Aachen
Visé
Liège
Malmédy
St Vith
Houffalize
Bastogne
Libramont
R. Meuse
Huy
B E L G I U M
Ciney
Namur
Dinant
Celles
30 BRITISH CORPS 20 DEC
Brussels 5 Miles
R. Sambre
Givet
R. Meuse
F R A N C E

0 5 10 15 20 25 Miles

man, and we got on reasonably well together.

Since those days I have often thought about this unpleasant experience. I have read that in many foreign armies any soldier who shows lack of endurance in the face of the enemy is shot out of hand, without the slightest compunction. I reject this approach utterly and I am thankful that the British Army will have none of it. On the other hand, is it justice to condone the action of an unreliable officer, who happily enjoys the privileges of his rank but cannot bring himself to share the risks that his men must endure continually?

It seems to me, in the afterlight, that this man was not of the right material, but a weak vessel, incapable of facing danger for more than a short time. He should never have been given a commission. Yet could that have been foreseen by whatever selection machinery may have existed in those days? Can it be foretold today? I rather question it.

Certainly, in my experience, most men have a threshold beyond which their endurance will not step, but I have a feeling, though not a certain conviction, that Nature gives no man warning. Today he faces peril without flinching, but tomorrow no one, least of all the man himself, can say whether or not he can still do it. It is all very mysterious. I fancy Religious Faith plays some part and that is why Christians are taught to say: "Lead us not into temptation, but deliver us from evil." All we can do is to pray for Deliverance.

"There are more things in heaven and earth, Horatio,

Than are dreamt of in your philosophy." *Hamlet*.

While we were engaged on the left wing of the Americans near Geilen-kirchen, the Germans had been cooking a surprise for us all elsewhere. Field-Marshal von Rundstedt had returned to his old haunts of 1940 and attacked the Americans in the Ardennes. He began on 16 December, attacking with the Fifth and Sixth Panzer Armies and the Seventh Army. Bad weather had grounded the Allied air forces and the German blow fell like a bolt from the blue. It struck the Americans, mainly on the US First Army Front, where the line was thinly held. Surprise was complete and US First Army crumbled under the blow. Within two days a wedge had been opened between the American First and Third Armies, and by 20 December it looked from the maps as though the enemy would soon be crossing the Meuse and the Sambre, and marching on the road to Brussels as Napoleon did in 1815.

Two months earlier, at Arnhem, we ourselves had sustained a considerable reverse and many Americans had adopted what one of my friends described as a "cocky sort of attitude, as though they were superior to any such weakness". Now the boot was on the other foot. It was the Americans who were in a muddle and it may have been too much to expect the British Press to refrain from crowing a bit. This crowing may have been only human nature, but it did not exactly bolster Allied solidarity.

At HQ 43 Division I do not think there was any unbecoming chortling because we were all of us aware that if the Germans had set up an offensive against 21 Army Group, immediately after Arnhem, they would have caught us at an awkward moment. Had they been able at that time to muster the resources now deployed against the Americans, it is difficult to exaggerate what damage they might have done. We all remembered clearly how weak we had been when in the Island. Antwerp was then still in German hands and our lines of communication stretched back to Normandy. They were only tenuously guarded and we had often been short of ammunition, petrol and stores of all kinds. Between D-Day and 1 October 43 Division alone had suffered nearly 8,000 casualties. The numbers had barely been replaced and we had had neither the time nor the opportunity to reabsorb them or to retrain ourselves to the standards required to fight first-class German divisions. We had been extremely lucky to have had a second chance. We had good reason to be thankful, but none to be "cocky". Now in December, however, we were "back in business" and, through the foresight of our leaders, we were on top of our form.

We heard on 20 December that Eisenhower had ordered Montgomery to take command of all troops – British and American – north of the German salient in the Ardennes, leaving the south to the Americans. We now know that this order was given by Eisenhower, on the telephone to Montgomery, at 10.30 am, but word was passed from mouth to mouth and very soon we all knew what had happened. We were electrified by the good news.

Monty himself appeared at the HQ of 214 Brigade, where he had arranged to meet the British 2 Army Commander (Dempsey) and the Commander 30 Corps (Horrocks). They retired to Brigadier Essame's caravan to make their plans and emerged after about forty-five minutes. Monty collected round him all those who were standing about and addressed them. Using a map pinned to a blackboard, he showed how he would position 30 Corps to halt the Germans and prevent them crossing the Meuse or the Sambre. It seemed clear to all who heard him that we would now have a real chance, in Monty's phrase, "to give the Germans a bloody nose". Thus was the confident gospel preached.

When I had last seen Monty (in Brunnsum) about ten days before, it had struck me that he seemed to have lost the "fire in his belly". At lunchtime with us in "A" Mess, he had ruminated aloud upon how he would pass what he described as "the evening of life". He would spend his days, he thought, in the Athenaeum, reading the papers and occasionally watching a test match at Lords. As he came out from the Mess, after lunch, returning to his car, he carried an umbrella! It seemed most unlike him. But now he was back in his usual style. He alone of the Army Group Commanders had been called upon by Eisenhower in a crisis to save the Allies from what might become a disaster. It was now his responsibility to make the plans and he had the opportunity to demonstrate the touch of genius that he knew he possessed. This was a setting where his particular manner exactly suited the occasion. Everyone wanted a lead and here was the only man who was clearly able to give it. No one now suggested that his manner was boastful or in bad taste. No one gave a damn about taste. What everyone wanted was victory and here was this self-confident cock-sparrow of a Limey simply itching to give it! Not until the crisis was over did people begin to take a different view of him.

We had prudently been pulled out of the line a few days previously and G. I. Thomas now held an Order Group in a new HQ in a small town not far from Liège. It was a very different sort of Order Group from the one I had attended in May, 1940, in HQ 2 Division. That one had been something of a shambles. This was typical of G. I. Thomas and thoroughly well-conducted. He prefaced it with the words: "The Boche has had the impertinence to attack and now we have a good chance to annihilate him." He then announced a simple plan.

The main body of 43 Division would remain concentrated north of the Meuse, poised to counterattack any enemy attempt to cross the river. The bridges at Huy, Liège and Visé were each to be held by what the Germans would call a "battle group," such as they had used so effectively against us on the Island. Our own battle groups were now to be provided by 43 Divisional Reconnaissance Regiment, reinforced by a few anti-tank guns and supported by field and medium artillery from afar.

G. I. Thomas gave to the Sappers three main tasks. First, we had orders to reconnoitre the river line from end to end of the Divisional front to verify that there were no crossing places other than those shown on the map. Secondly, we were to pull to our bank of the river any boats that might be useful to the enemy in an attempt to cross the river. Thirdly, we were to prepare for demolition the bridges at Huy, Liège and Visé, and at any other crossing places that our reconnaissance revealed. Express orders were given that "no detonators will be inserted in the charges until further orders".

The Sappers got to work on these tasks at once. I forget whether we found any bridges other than the main ones shown on the maps, but we immediately discovered that a misunderstanding existed regarding the responsibility for the bridge at Liège. The Americans had prepared this for demolition and had already inserted the detonators into the charges. There also existed an American command post for the defence of Liège itself with authority to blow up the bridge if necessary. This status had become almost a matter of national honour and prestige. The fact that German flying bombs were landing at frequent intervals in Liège aggravated the matter of honour. To abandon Liège might be interpreted as "succumbing to enemy pressure", which neither party would regard as honourable. After much argument, the matter was amicably settled and, in the words of the 43 Divisional History, "The United States retained Liège – and its flying bombs!"

The wisdom of forbidding the insertion of detonators into the demolition charges of the bridges was also hotly debated. On the one hand, if detonators were inserted there was an evident risk of some excited local commander prematurely demolishing a bridge that was still required. On the other hand, the time likely to be taken to insert detonators into a complex series of charges, spread over the girders of a large bridge, might be considerable, and failure in emergency was a possibility not to be excluded. The risks and possibilities could be argued to an Nth degree, and because both protagonists had received separate orders, rational control tended to be a subject for heated argument.

Fortunately the fighting qualities of the American soldiers, the solidarity of the Anglo-American Alliance and a wonderful improvement of the weather, made the whole question of demolitions utterly irrelevant. Bastogne was held by the Americans; flying conditions improved and the Allied air forces regained control of the air above us. Any hopes the Germans may have nursed of victory must soon have seemed to them illusory. Von Rundstedt had told his troops before his offensive that this was their last chance of victory in Europe and for a short time it must have seemed to them that Fortune smiled again. But now, as Christmas Day approached, we could see from the Situation Maps that their cascade of Fire and Sword had been halted. It was now our turn to rejoice and we shortly received the welcome signal: "Christmas will be celebrated on 25 December."

One hour's notice to move still remained the rule, but, even so, Christmas could also be celebrated. Nature seemed to breathe anew. The sun shone brightly by day; the moon by night peered down from a clear starlit sky. The cooks worked overtime. The NAAFI pulled out all the stops and the Belgians willingly gave up cafés and halls for soldiers' Christmas dinners. We sang the old carols and any appearance of a white surplice brought all men flocking to many altars, improvised from ammunition boxes and draped in Union Jacks or Army blankets. A few men had to remain on guard, minding AA guns and the like, but church parades did not have to be ordered. Men thronged to them. They thought their own thoughts, but as we knelt, shoulder to shoulder, on the hard and frosty grass each one of us experienced the unmistakable feeling of being "in love and charity with his neighbour". By chance Lance-Corporal Lowe and I happened to be side by side and when we stood up some unspoken urge, sweeping away both age and rank, prompted us to grasp each other's hands. Never before had I been so aware of the debt I owed him and I rejoice that until his death we occasionally met, but the same emotions seemed to make it impossible to speak till the spell was broken. (Oddly, perhaps, those same emotions seemed to grip our wives as well!)

The Holy Spirit was among us on that Christmas Day, but the war had still to be won. Naziism had to be anathematized.

Soon after Christmas we returned to the Brunnsum area, but due to the reorganization necessitated by the Ardennes affair we found ourselves in 12

Corps instead of 30 Corps. Moreover, G. I. Thomas had been given temporary command of 30 Corps while General Horrocks was on leave, and a Brigadier Rawlings (the Commander of 30 Corps Artillery) acted in G. I. Thomas's stead for a few weeks.

It might be supposed that the change in atmosphere from the flamboyant *panache* of 30 Corps to the more sedate directives of 12 Corps, and the change of coachmen from the hands of G. I. Thomas to those of a man with perhaps a more sensitive touch, might seem very agreeable to us at HQ 43 Division. But not so. We were accustomed to one set of conditions and now we had to become used to another set. It did not seem easy. For one thing we were in reserve, and it was apparently the view of the Top Brass that the enemy had more surprises in store. We were therefore bidden to give our minds to examining every possibility, however remote, that might conceivably befall. Everyone began to write Top Secret documents which engulfed us in paper for about a fortnight. I do not know how General Horrocks and G. I. Thomas would have dealt with the same situation, but I fancy it might have been different, and more our style.

Besides this change in atmosphere, it also became extremely cold. Without an enemy to battle with we had our work cut out to keep alive! The temperature recorded one night in my caravan by a centigrade thermometer was down to minus 20 degrees. A generous issue of sheepskin coats was made to all and sundry and we also tasted for the first time self-heating soup. Many precautions against frostbite had to be taken and, perhaps because everyone began to take less notice of the non-essential precautions of personal hygiene and more notice of the real ones, the sick rate almost vanished to nothing. We all looked rubicund; we all walked briskly to keep our feet warm; the soldiers threw snowballs at the Dutch children, who responded joyfully, and we all felt extremely fit. The Dutch, in their usual way, were hospitable and many friendships were made. In fact, only recently – nearly forty years later – I met an ex-43 Divisional Sapper whose wife (now a grandmother) was an ex-Brunnsum girl. She told me that there are many ex-Brunnsum brides now living in the United Kingdom.

After about a fortnight of "paper chase" we reverted to planning another offensive operation. It was named Operation Blackcock. It was to be another nibble at the enemy to reduce his foothold on the west bank of the Rhine. During this operation I made my first acquaintance with a newly weaned branch of the Royal Armoured Corps – 79 Armoured Division.

This Division grew up in East Anglia after Dunkirk under the command of a General Hobart, who had started his military career in the Sappers. Since then he had transferred to the Royal Tank Corps, but during his later career he had gone through a bad patch in the Home Guard. I do not know who rescued him from his plight and I never met him to speak to, but according to the Bush Telegraph – and I am sure it was in this instance reliable – he was a man of great ingenuity with a fertile quiverful of bright ideas for harnessing track vehicles so that many difficult technical tasks could be carried out by troops without dismounting from their armoured vehicles – i.e. tanks.

The armoured vehicles in 79 Armoured Division were collectively known as "funnies" and were manned by soldiers of more than one arm of the Service. There were, for instance, "funnies" that carried flame-throwing tanks – known as "crocodiles". There were others called "buffaloes" that could swim rivers, and others again called "flails" that could force a passage through a minefield. These were manned by men of the Royal Armoured Corps, the logic being that if you train (say) a bus driver to drive a flail tank to neutralize mines you teach him two new skills in one operation. But if you teach a Sapper to drive a tank you are likely to deprive him of a useful trade of (say) blacksmith or electrician at the same time. There were, however, many operations carried out by Sapper Units of 79 Division named "RE Assault Engineers" who specialized in Sapper work such as building bridges and doing demolitions from a heavy tank without dismounting. These vehicles were known as Armoured Vehicles RE (AVREs).

All these funnies (and many others) had demonstrated their value since the landings in Normandy, but it was not till Operation Blackcock that I had ever met "flails" on the battlefield. They, and the Canadian-manned Armoured Personnel Carriers, did a very good job in Operation Blackcock, but the "flails" had to work in difficult circumstances.

The weather was tricky throughout the operation. Sometimes the roads were flooded and the fields were so soggy that the flails were liable to get embogged. Sometimes the weather was extremely cold and the earth was frozen solid, like iron. In ice the flails were not always successful, because the mines were so solidly frozen that the thrashing of the flails did not always detonate the mines. It was therefore often necessary to back up the flails with conventional Sappers, who, with frozen fingers, had laboriously to lift mines (when their mine-detectors were able to detect them – which was not invariably). I was afraid our Field Companies might lose faith in these "funnies", but I need not have worried, for their good sense prevailed. Blackcock was an unpleasant, but nevertheless well-conceived, operation in which many prisoners and valuable real estate were captured without very serious losses on our part.

I think that all of us in 43 Divisional Engineers saw the potential of "Assault Engineers" and I determined to try and get them involved in every sort of engineer operation where the task could be done better by them than by conventional Sappers. By a mere chance such an opportunity arose on the last night of Blackcock. It was enlivened by a faintly comic incident.

One of the many air-photos available showed that in the middle of a main road in no-man's-land, near the final objective, there was a large crater. It would certainly have many mines and booby traps about it and it would certainly be covered by enemy artillery and small-arms fire. Much thought and argument was put into finding a workable method of crossing it. In the end the Field Company whose duty it would be to overcome the difficulty urged me to sponsor a plan of their own. I was not particularly keen on it myself, as the evidence, so I was told by my Intelligence Officer, was suspect. No patrol had ever got far enough down the road to see it. When I explained the plan to the Chief Engineer of 12 Corps, who had been my predecessor in 43 Division, he was frankly horrified.

"Too risky!" he said. "Too risky!"

I showed him the long Bailey Bridge that the Field Company had erected during the night. It stood on wooden skids, laid on the main road, concealed by a clump of trees, about half a mile from where the crater was shown. The idea was for an AVRE, lent for the occasion, to haul the bridge on its skids down the main road by night and push it across the crater. (A heavy counterweight on the tail of the bridge was designed to prevent the nose falling into the chasm as the bridge was launched.)

The night was bitterly cold. There was no moonlight and the Sapper Officer in charge of the enterprise went stealthily forth to reconnoitre the site in an armoured car. He returned after considerable delay, for he had covered the last part of the journey backwards in case he had to retreat hastily. He went backwards almost into the enemy lines, but he found no crater. It did not exist. The Intelligence Officer was right. The evidence was suspect. The spot on the air photograph was a speck of dust on the lens of the camera and there was a good deal of friendly jeering, of which I was the butt. I was told I ought to have forbidden the adventure, but I remain unrepentant. I always felt that if the young men who have to risk their lives in an enterprise are keen on any particular stratagem they should, if possible, be allowed a chance to try it. As it happened, I had prepared an alternative plan, which I kept up my sleeve. But I did not have to reveal it and it came in handy shortly afterwards.

When Blackcock was finished, a period of wireless silence was ordered. This was a stratagem concocted by the Intelligence people and the Signals. It was to allow 21 Army Group to concentrate and to redeploy the Divisions in new locations for another operation. During the silence, "spoof" transmitters were established where the real ones had been. They were intended to transmit a daily routine of traffic calculated to lull the enemy into the belief that nothing unusual was happening. This was a well tested deception plan and was always a success. I only mention it now because during the silence another event occurred that affected us all in 43 Division. General Horrocks came back from his leave to resume command of 30 Corps and G. I. Thomas returned to us. In spite of wireless silence – or perhaps because of it – the Bush Telegraph still operated, and word went round with a speed unrivalled by the wonders of modern radio. The war drums proclaimed the news (misquoting Robert Browning perhaps): "The lark's on the wing; The snail's on the thorn; G. I. Thomas is back – All's well with the world!"

EXTRACTS FROM LETTERS TO MY PARENTS

Written from Brunnsum, 16 November, 1944

We are now living in houses. Our office is in a Dutch Roman Catholic school, beautifully fitted out. I have had an office in schools in England, Africa, Italy, France, Belgium and Holland. The most squalid were the French ones, with the English a close second for squalor. They were always so dreary! Next Belgian, then African (French Colonial). The best were the Italian, with the Dutch about equal. The Dutch have in the front hall a Crucifix or an image of Christ. The Italians have a bust of Mussolini. Our HQ in Gioja had a bust of Mussolini which some solider with a sense of the ridiculous had painted to look particularly idiotic.

Written from Brunnsum, 21 November, 1944

One cannot help feeling pity for the Germans when one sees them faced with the same miseries that they inflicted on every other nation in North-West Europe – not to mention Poland and Russia. A family leaving its ruined home with all its property in a barrow is a pitiful sight whatever the nationality. Many of the English are as much to be pitied as anyone.

Written from Brunnsum, 21 November, 1944

I had to reconnoitre rather a dangerous area yesterday so I left my ARC [armoured car] to go on foot. But while I was away, four enemy mortar bombs pitched within a few yards of the car. L/Cpl Lowe, who knows no fear, was quite unmoved, but he told me that L/Cpl Ashworth (the wireless operator) who sat behind him kept "bowing like a mandarin in the presence of the Emperor." But he had a "nice cup o' char" ready when I got back. My Ark has a happy party aboard, but we are an assortment as varied as Noah's. I pray for the day when a dove brings back an olive branch.

15

The Rhineland Cleared
of the Enemy

In a few days we were back in 30 Corps and concentrated near Nijmegen again. A two-handled series of operations was to be conducted by 21 Army Group. The aim was to finish, at last, what the Ardennes affair had delayed – namely the expulsion of all German forces from the west side of the River Rhine. The idea was as follows: The American Ninth Army became part of 21 Army Group and Monty's command therefore included Second British Army, First Canadian Army and US Ninth Army. For the forthcoming operations Second British Army was denuded of Divisions and was given the task of planning the Assault Crossings of the Rhine which were to be undertaken as soon as we had complete control of our bank.

Meanwhile, First Canadian Army was given command of extra Divisions to make a total of four Canadian and nine British Divisions. With these they were ordered to carry out Operation Veritable. This Operation was based on the Nijmegen area south of the Rhine and was directed at the Reichswald Forest, the northern tip of the Siegfried Line and the Rhine riparian area as far as the town of Wesel. The Ninth US Army was to carry out a complementary Operation named Grenade. This was to spring from the vicinity of the River Roer and advance north-east to meet Operation Veritable in the vicinity of Wesel. (The boundary between these two armies was the line Geldern-Wesel.)

We, in 43 Division, were a part of 30 Corps and 30 Corps for this Operation was in First Canadian Army. That was the set-up: a pincer movement with First Canadian Army from the north-west and Ninth US Army from the south-west, converging on the Rhine opposite Wesel.

D-Day was set for 8 February but the enemy opened the Roer River barrages

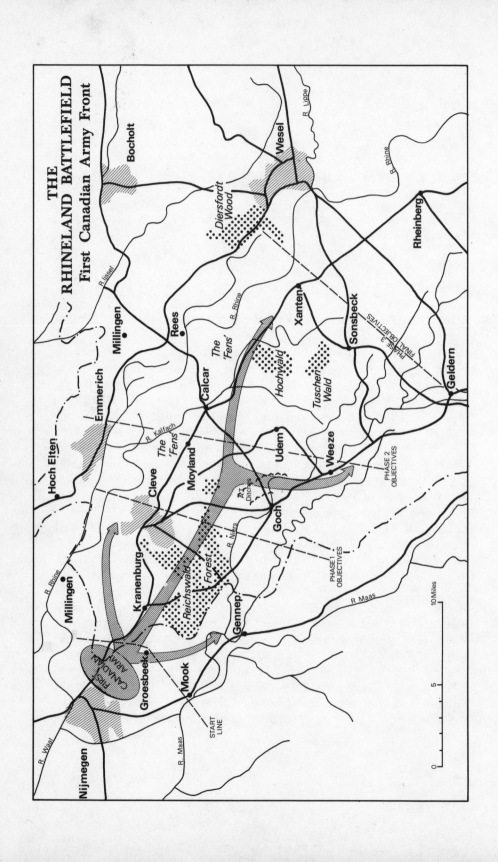

THE
RHINELAND BATTLEFIELD
First Canadian Army Front

Bocholt

R. Lippe

Wesel

R. Rhine

Rheinberg

Diersfordt
Wood

R. Jissel

Millingen

Rees

R. Rhine

The
'Fens'

Xanten

Sonsbeck

FINAL OBJECTIVES

Emmerich

Calcar

Hochwald

PHASE 3

Geldern

Hoch Elten

R. Kalfach

The
'Fens'

Moyland

Udem

Tuscher
Wald

Weeze

R. Rhine

Cleve

A.T.
Ditch

PHASE 2
OBJECTIVES

Millingen

Kranenburg

Goch

R. Niers

PHASE 1
OBJECTIVES

Reichswald

Forest

R. Maas

Nijmegen

Groesbeek

Mook

Gennep

FIRST
CANADIAN
Army

START
LINE

R. Waal

R. Maas

0   5   10 Miles

a few days earlier and flooded the Roer Valley. The Americans were unable to launch their half of the pincers till the floods subsided, so that until nature performed one of her miracles, removing the flood water, the Germans could take three or four divisions from the American front to re-enforce their divisions opposing us. The German intention was, no doubt, a classical military strategem that would have delighted Clausewitz. They hoped, while the floods lasted, to give us a mighty mauling and then turn on the Americans and maul them too. It did not, however, work out like that. We withstood the German mauling and paid them back in full and overflowing measure. When the Roer floods subsided about a fortnight later, the Americans had a much easier passage to the German back door than they could have expected. Thus both Veritable and Grenade together repeated for 21 Army Group a success on the same lines that Monty had planned in Normandy, though on a less prodigious scale. Whether anyone could foresee it in this light I cannot say, but this glimpse of the future may ease the reader's task in comprehending the moves that follow.

The Canadian Army planned Operation Veritable in three phases. In Phase I 30 Corps was to clear the Reichswald Forest of Germans and capture Cleve. In Phase II 30 Corps on the right and 2 Canadian Corps on the left were to advance up to the line Weeze-Emmerich. In Phase III a general advance was to be made to the line Geldern-Xanten and thence to make contact with the Americans who were the right-hand arm of the pincers.

Anyone could see that there was likely to be the most frightful congestion of traffic with so many divisions milling about in so small an area. But congestion, though frustrating, is better than loneliness, especially upon a battlefield against a numerous enemy. I certainly felt that this battle might be hell for us, but it would be much worse for the Germans.

The build-up for Veritable was colossal. We were supported by over 2,000 aircraft – 1,000 of the Tactical Air Force and 1,000 heavy bombers of Bomber Command. The Artillery support in guns, ammunition and firepower was on a lavish scale too.

It seemed to many of us, of whom I was one, that the Germans would have done better to withdraw all their troops west of the Rhine at once and keep them intact on the East Bank to repel the assault crossings that were sure to follow. But that was not in Hitler's nature. He ordered a fight to the last man and the last round and we knew he would be obeyed. We went into Operation Veritable with no illusions of an easy victory. We foresaw, and later experienced, a fierce and bitter struggle.

As Sappers we could see from the maps that there were unlikely to be many concentrated engineer works to be done; there was no wide river to be bridged. There were, however, many small bridges and culverts on our route, all of which we might expect to find demolished. Most of the roads were lined with trees, many of which we expected to find felled across the roads, with mines and booby traps concealed among the tangle of branches. Every forest track was likely to be sown with mines and on the verges of many roads we could expect to find anti-personnel mines cunningly concealed to catch the unwary. Well-concealed enemy automatics were to be expected to cover all these obstacles.

All this was obvious to every Field Company Commander and I knew I could rely on each one of them to do his best for the Brigade with which his Company was affiliated. My main preoccupations would be twofold. First, to make sure that the Field Companies' calls for engineer stores were promptly met. For this I could rely upon my Field Park Company Commander, who always kept his store cupboard well stocked, and the Stackpipe convention which we had by now got into working order. Secondly, I intended to keep in close touch with the day-to-day progress of the battle so that I was the first man (not the last!) to glimpse what might be required on the morrow. In theory it was the duty of the Field Engineers to be the CRE's "eyes and ears" in the forward zone, reporting the score to a "big white chief" wrapped deep in thought in HQRE. But in practice this kind of existence was not my *métier*. The wireless set at HQRE had to be constantly manned, day and night, by an officer, and both the Field Engineeers had to take their turns to save the Adjutant from collapsing from lack of sleep and exercise. All three of them worked extremely hard, and for the smooth running of the Divisional Engineers I was always much in their debt. They were best employed keeping the Adjutant sane!

For my part, I found the best sources of information were to be found in the forward areas – the more forward the better, up to a point beyond which no one could put his head above ground for fear of drawing aimed fire at it. It was only thus I ever saw the real world. It was extraordinary how often, coming from another world, I was able to perceive at once what the Sappers on the spot required, but which they, struggling to keep alive, had never foreseen. I also enjoyed two blessings that few Field Company Commanders had. The first was Lance-Corporal Lowe, who was apparently insensitive to fear or fatigue. He put me to shame in both respects. And secondly Lance-Corporal Ashworth. With G.I. Thomas's help, I procured a more powerful wireless set than I was entitled to. Due to these men I could then always get to wherever I ought to go and be able to communicate with HQRE, telling them what I thought should be done.

I am sure there were other ways of doing what I conceived to be my duty and I am doubtful whether the strain of such continuous activity would have been endurable for much longer. But while a man is still in his thirties he still has much of the resilience of youth, yet he has also lived long enough to acquire some of the wisdom and shrewdness that springs from experience. He enjoys the best of both worlds and should make the most of them.

One day, returning from a visit where a Field Company was working, we came across General Horrocks, whose car had broken down. It had become waterlogged driving on a main road that was flooded. He left it to his ADC and the driver to get it going again, while I gave him a lift in my jeep.

General Horrocks was a splendid leader. He had the right touch with everyone he met. He chatted to us as I drove him in the jeep and he told us how the battle was going. He spoke in a friendly and buoyant manner, asking the two Lance-Corporals about their homes and so on. You could not help liking the man. He certainly enjoyed Lowe's Lancashire humour, just as Lowe enjoyed the General's wit. I feel sure the episode has been repeated in many Merseyside pubs since then. Suddenly the General turned to me:

"And how's the wicked Wyvern?" he asked.

The Wyvern was the 43rd Divisional Sign, part dragon and part serpent. It dates back to the dark ages and appears in the Bayeux Tapestry. It has a bright eye, a sharp beak and a tongue like a rapier. It has wings, talons and a sting in its tail. It enshrines the traditions of the Anglo-Saxon warriors of old, and the mythical, pagan gods they worshipped. King Harold raised the emblem at Hastings and it epitomizes the valour in battle and the guile in council that every real warrior must have. It also epitomized G. I. Thomas!

I was able to reassure Horrocks that the wicked Wyvern was ready for whatever lay ahead.

"Another bloody clutch at the Boche?" he queried.

"Yes Sir," I replied. "You can almost hear the gnashing of its teeth from here."

At that moment a stonk of mortar fire pitched in the garden of a house nearby. Horrocks never batted an eyelid. He was evidently as much in his element under the fire of the enemy as at a high-level discussion among the Top Brass. I had seen for myself near Dunkirk that Monty also had this chameleon-like ability and I think it likely that History would reveal that there never was a real Captain of War without it.

The town of Cleve was captured on 12 February. It had been devastasted by Bomber Command and it is a matter of opinion whether the present inhabitants of the town would be happier if they still had their buildings of historic interest, or whether they prefer the better plumbing that replaced them. Our own Divisional HQ was in a lunatic asylum on the outskirts of the town. Until better arrangements were made, one might at any time see one unfortunate inmate, squatting on an empty ammunition box, fishing in a flowerbed with a rod and line. It was reliably reported that when one of our Staff Officers, who prided himself on his German, spoke to the lunatic, the conversation went as follows:

Staff Officer (in a patronizing tone of voice): "And how many fish have you caught today, my friend?"

Fisherman (Abruptly): "You're the third, *Herr Oberst*."

I had always hoped that after capturing Cleve we would get into more open country, where we could make better use of our preponderance of armour, but it did not work out like that. The country was still close woodlands and the Germans continued to offer the staunchest resistance possible. (I was told it was comparable with anything we had so far met.) Yet in the short time since Veritable began on 8 February, 43 Division alone had captured over 1000 prisoners. After the war a retired German Colonel who had been on the other side gave me an explanation of this fierce resistance combined with a high rate of surrender. He told me it was thuswise: the enemy against us were remnants of several Parachute divisions. These high-grade Airborne types were only the skeletons of their former enemy formations. The flesh on the skeletons was made up of the "poor and the maimed, the halt and the blind". While human endurance lasted, the Parachutists used their skills and their weapons to inflict the maximum possible casualties on us, but when the Parachutists were eventually overcome, they withdrew in good order, leaving the weaker brethren to surrender. They often surrendered in such large numbers that we, who were counting heads and not medically examining them, failed to realize how this came about. In the afterlight this explanation seems to make sense.

However, whatever the explanation, it was not until ten days later that 214 Brigade of 43 Division got to within sight of Goch, which lies only about ten miles from Cleve.

Goch was an important pin in the German defence structure. Five main roads converged on it and we had to capture the place to gain access to the country we wanted. It was again defended by a high-class skeleton of Parachute troops, made up to strength in rank and file by weaker brethren. A river ran through it and the defenders had vast opportunities for demolitions and obstacles of all kinds. The town had been bombed by Bomber Command and the destruction of buildings had been stupendous. But this did not lessen the possibilities for defence, as wrecked buildings lend themselves for use as weapon-pits in which anti-tank guns and automatic weapons and riflemen may be concealed.*

Although our foremost Infantry were not far away from the town, it was still out of sight because it lay beyond an escarpment, and until one reached the escarpment no one could see over its crest. Moreover, we had no recent air-photographs and only an outline plan had been made for its capture. This outline plan envisaged 43 Division pressing on as far as the escarpment and

* I heard recently (1985) that the Germans of 1945 were astonished that we never wrecked the bridge at Goch. While the Germans held Goch they were manifestly able to use the roads passing through the town so long as the bridge was intact. I can only think that we never dreamt that the bombing by RAF Bomber Command could have possibly left the bridge fit for use. Also, of course, we were short of air photos of Goch at that time.

then digging in. Thereafter, 15 Scottish Division, who were behind us, would pass through our lines and assault the town in a full-scale divisional attack. Early in the afternoon of 17 February, however, my Intelligence Officer brought me some newly arrived air-photographs, saying, "G. I. Thomas is expected back from a conference any minute now, where he is hatching a plot with 15 Scottish Division for the assault upon Goch."

"Let's have a look at the photos," I said.

The Intelligence Officer started laying the air-photos on the table, pinning them together and giving us a general bird's-eye view of Goch and its approaches. We examined them together. They showed that the enemy had undertaken a considerable number of road and bridge demolitions, but, above all, he had dug two long anti-tank ditches just below the escarpment. It was obvious that no full-scale attack could be made on the town until extensive engineer works had been completed to cope with the first anti-tank ditch. But who would be expected to do this work? Us, or 15 Scottish Divisional Engineers?

I guessed we should soon hear from G. I. Thomas, but in the meantime it might be prudent for us to attune our minds to the possibility of it being *our* next assignment. I therefore aired a private plan that I had been brooding over for some time, so that I could see the reaction it made on my own staff before putting it out as a formal order.

My thought ran like this: There seemed to be two options for crossing ditches such as these. One was to tackle them in daylight and under cover of artillery fire, with all the paraphernalia of Assault Engineers, mechanical equipment and conventional engineering. The other was to rely on darkness, stealth and silence, overcoming the obstacle with Sappers using hand tools, as their grandfathers did in days gone by. It might still be possible to overcome the obstacles without opposition, unknown to the enemy, by working silently in darkness. This is what I wanted to attempt now. It seemed to me probable that at this very moment the enemy would still be using the roads and that they would not complete the ditches across the roads until they were safely back across them. If, therefore, we were to start harassing the roads where they crossed the ditches continuously with artillery fire from now on, their Sappers might have difficulty in executing their final demolitions. This would be helping ourselves and hindering the enemy. We might then capture the line of the first ditch and work on it in darkness.

I was delighted to find that my small, but critical, audience was reasonably optimistic, so I told the Adjutant to send one of the Field Engineers to 204 Field Company to tell the Officer Commanding what I thought might be cooking. The young officer had barely mounted his motor-bike before G. I. Thomas returned from his conference and sent for me . He was in his caravan pouring over the same air-photographs of Goch.

"Have you seen this one?" he asked, pointing to the one in which the anti-tank ditch was plainly visible.

"Yes, Sir," I replied.

"Well," he continued, "I have made a good bargain with 15 Scottish Division this morning. *We* go as far as this first anti-tank ditch. 15 Scottish Division will then pass through us and will take on the very severe battle for the town which will certainly follow."

G. I. Thomas was visibly pleased with his bargain, and I was sure his troops would be thankful to be spared the severe fighting.

"But what, Sir," I asked, "is the *quid pro quo?*" I was certain that the Jocks would not take on the battle merely for the honour and glory.

"The *quid pro quo,*" he said, "is that we prepare six crossings over the first ditch by first light tomorrow morning, so that they get a fair start for their attack."

If ever there existed an occasion in real life when a man could be knocked over with a feather, this was it. Our leading troops had not reached the ditch. No one had seen it. We did not know what the banks were like, though the probability was that they were wet and muddy grassland, quite unfit for bearing traffic without a lot of preparation. And it would now be dark in a few hours' time!

G. I. Thomas was a good poker player. Looking into his eyes, I had no notion whether he realized he had made a rash promise and now regretted it, or whether he would blow up if I uttered any suggestion of surprise or bewilderment.

"All right, Sir," I said. "We'll do our best and I'll let you know in the morning what has happened."

"Good," he said. "I know there will be no failure."

I saluted and left the caravan. This was a compliment to me of no mean order, but, if it turned out to be merited, he would have no one to thank but my Sappers in general and the OC 204 Field Company in particular, for it was they who would have to do what was necessary.

Here I must introduce the new man who had recently replaced Major Tom Evill as OC 204 Field Company. Tom had been promoted to better things elsewhere and a Major Moore had taken his place. I had known Moore slightly in a former incarnation as a tall, thin, happy-go-lucky younger officer, who was known as "Streak" Moore because he was said to resemble one of those rashers of streaky bacon that were a regular feature at the breakfast table at Brompton Barracks, Chatham. I knew nothing of his work and I had only accepted him because he had recently married G. I. Thomas's niece, and I did not like to say no to his uncle-by-marriage when he asked me to take him. (I did not recognize it at the time, but I was dealt a straight flush without knowing it.)

236

I went back to my Adjutant and told him the news. I was surprised by his reply.

"Don't worry," he said. "If anyone can strike lucky, 'Streak' can. He'll get us out of the soup. You've got a good idea. 'Streak' will understand it and make the most of it."

I then told the Adjutant to summon two platoons (over one hundred men) from 260 Field Company to report for work with 204 Field Company tonight. They must be provided with picks and shovels. We must also provide three lorry-loads of sandbags for the Sappers to fill with earth where required. "Finally we must pray to God that the Germans will not get wind of what we are up to." I then set off to meet Streak Moore at HQ 214 Brigade, where I perceived that we had received the blessing of those "on the ground" – as well as those in Heaven!

When I got there I found that much had been done. The two platoons from 260 Field Company had arrived. The sandbags were due any minute at Stackpipe. A searchlight had been whistled up from somewhere by 214 Brigade and was in the process of setting up in order to provide "artifical moonlight" from a dip in the ground about a mile short of the ditch.* Best of all, the CO of the Somersets and Streak Moore were both enthusiastic for the enterprise. The only hitch was that no one had so far reached the ditch. But while it was one thing to criticise the slow advance as the minutes slipped away, it was quite another matter to be the leading soldier on the ground, wondering if what he thought he saw ahead of him was an enemy armoured car or not.

Streak Moore and I with a few Sappers set off on foot to follow the leading Infantry. It was pitch dark by now, and one felt a natural, but futile, inclination to walk on tip-toe. We eventually overtook the leading platoon. They were elated at their successful progress and were glad that their task was nearly done. We soon reached the ditch, and were thankful to find that the retreating enemy had not been able to crater the road we were on. The ditch was about thirty foot wide and fifteen foot deep, but it had not been cratered. Both sides of the road were nearly vertical, where both ends of the ditch reached the verges of the road.

Streak told a couple of Sappers with mine detectors to search for explosive devices, buried under the road ready to be exploded later by a time switch. None were discovered. Cautiously, using a torch, we peered at a footpath which seemed to run the length of the ditch. It was presumably intended for enemy patrols to move safely along it. There were many fresh footprints in the path and we felt reasonably safe using it.

The first task was to shore up the vertical sides of the road to prevent it from

* Artificial moonlight was produced by directing a beam of light on the underside of low clouds so that some light was reflected back to the earth below. The searchlights were usually mounted on a tank.

crumbling. Use by the enemy had already damaged it and 15 Scottish traffic would quickly pulverise it. Streak Moore set the two platoons from 260 Company on this. He and I, each with an escort of a few Sappers, set off along the ditch in opposite directions to look for more crossing places.

It was really perfectly safe walking along this well-trampled pathway at the bottom of a deep ditch, though it did not feel like that! I was reminded of an occasion in Central India when another young officer and I had gone after a tiger in the jungle. Fortunately there had been no tiger there, and on this occasion there were no Germans present either. We were in luck. Soon I found two other possible places for crossings. Both were at points where sunken farm lanes crossed the ditch. The surface of one lane was almost as sunken as the bottom of the ditch and the other not unlike it. All that was required here was a bit of excavation and some chestnut paling for surfacing. It seemed plain sailing. But there was an unnerving sequence to follow. We none of us spoke, but we heard the sound of German voices speaking in a whisper. One of the Sappers – a reinforcement, I was told – fired a shot by accident. The bullet flew into the air, but the Germans could not have been experienced troops. They must have been reinforcements too, for they started running. There was a sound as of sheep crashing through bracken. The sound seemed to continue for a long time. The Germans must have bolted.

When we got back to the *rendezvous* we had arranged, Streak told me he had also found several possible crossing places, all close to one another. One was well under way, the others not so advanced, but apparently likely to be successful. A good start had been made.

One crossing place alone looked like giving trouble. This was where the main road from Calcar crossed the ditch. At this point the retreating Germans had remembered to crater the road. The crater they made was deeper even than the ditch. There was evidence that they had burrowed from the ditch towards the road formation and detonated an aerial bomb. It had made a colossal hole. Streak Moore and his subaltern, who was dealing with this crossing, thought there was no hope of completing the job before daylight.

During the night, however, the Adjutant had managed to get a couple of bulldozers and some lorry-loads of brick rubble to a suitable place a mile or so behind us. Looking at our watches we saw that if we had to abandon silent manual methods and resort to using machinery we must make the change at once. Otherwise there was a high probability of falling between two stools. (The hitch in employing machines was that silence and stealth, which had paid such a dividend, would be forfeit. The enemy, who had remained somnolent, would be aroused and shelling was inevitable – perhaps even machine-gun fire.)

I was quite sure that we ought now to invoke the bulldozers and risk the consequences. I was prepared to order this to be done, but I felt Streak Moore ought to have a say in the matter.

"What do you think, Streak?" I asked.

Streak saw the necessity at once. We would certainly finish the work manually at the other places before dawn and in the dark it was unlikely that the enemy could shell everywhere. Moreover the ditch itself was not a bad refuge in an emergency. The sooner we started on the one difficult place, the sooner we'd finish. It was a fair risk.

"OK, Streak," I said. "Call the bulldozers and cry havoc!" (I can't think what promoted this phrase. It must have been some strange, subliminal instinct*.)

We were standing near Streak's jeep with the wireless set. He gave orders to his Company Sergeant-Major and in a few minutes the silent night which had protected us so well began to reverberate with the roar and clatter of earthmoving machinery. We had reverted from being silent dung beetles to become 20th Century public works contractors. The Sappers joyfully put down their shovels and sat on the ground, wondering what to do next. A few lit cigarettes, but not for long.

The enemy, as we had feared, were aroused and shelling began. Our own artillery replied and the Dogs of War began baying for blood. To start with the enemy fire was haphazard and had little effect, but it was now beginning to get light; mortar and machine-gun fire began to come our way. It would soon be aimed fire. I was amazed at the calmness of our bulldozer drivers. (Perhaps they could not hear the firing above their own engine noises.) Progress on the crater, however, was still being made and at a much faster rate than had been possible by hand. Our own Artillery was giving Goch "a dose of the real McCoy".

"That ought to teach the Boche not to sneeze in Church," remarked Streak.

I had seldom known anyone quite so calm. It must have been a wonderful example to his men, and as if by magic the enemy's fire became more desultory too. It eventually ceased completely; God knows why. Within half an hour the job was done. Six crossings over the ditch were complete: five alpha plus, one alpha minus, but still a pass mark, with a chesspale surface and a white tape to mark it. There were no casualties. This was by the Grace of God.

When 15 Scottish Division had made use of our six crossing places over the Goch anti-tank ditch they had some hard fighting to capture the town itself, but we had three days out of the line to get ourselves ready for the next step forward. There was much planning for this and we moved our Divisional HQ from the lunatic asylum in Cleve to another location, so as to be nearer to the scene of operations.

We moved into the ancient Schloss Moyland, south of Cleve. It had once

* See *Julius Caesar*, Act III, scene i.

been the hunting lodge of Frederick the Great, but in 1944 it was the property of a Baron who had been at the German Embassy in London. He was nowhere to be seen, but I was told that the aged Baroness, perhaps the Baron's mother, was occasionally visible, sitting erect in an armchair surrounded by out-of-date numbers of *The Tatler*. She no doubt added a tone of aristocratic distinction in contrast with the blasphemous intrusion of the British soldiery and their petrol cookers, which not infrequently erupted and spat out bacon fat on to the ballroom floor. The cold in some of the rooms of the Schloss had to be endured to be believed, which prompted Lowe to remark, "It's nice to see how the rich live, but I hope we don't have to endure it for long!" (We remained there for about ten days.)

In our new location we were transferred from under command of 30 Corps to under that of 2 Canadian Corps for an operation designed to take us to the end of our struggles for full possession of the west bank of the Rhine. In the course of this the Sappers played a prominent part in two events, of which the first seemed to come about by chance.

There was on the eastern flank of 2 Canadian Corp's operations a strip of low-lying fenland between the River Rhine and the Cleve-Xanten Road. We called it the Fens. It was fifteen miles long and varied in width from three to six miles. There were many narrow, sometimes waterlogged, roads amongst the Fens, some of which had also been cratered by the enemy. There were also stagnant water courses, some as wide as eighty feet or more, and others not unlike the dykes and rhines round Ely in Cambridgeshire. The bridges across many of these had been demolished by the German defenders, who consisted of small but determined battle groups of Parachutists. Movement in the Fens was not easy, particularly as the land on our side of the Rhine was overlooked from vantage points on the opposite bank.

The Fens certainly had to be cleared of the enemy, otherwise there was a possibility of the area becoming a natural sanctuary for enemy raiders. They might then use it as a base for disrupting our lines of communication. Sniping on the Fens was now a mere fleabite, but it might easily turn into a serious hazard if it were not promptly dealt with. When it came to crossing the Rhine, which we all foresaw as the next operation, it would add to our difficulties considerably if this flea-bite on one wrist had by then grown into a boil on the back of the left shoulder. The Fens were in 43 Division's area and it was G. I. Thomas's business to deal with them. But, except by mounting a major infantry operation, which nobody wanted, how was this to be done? I expect it was often on G. I. Thomas's mind, for without warning he told me one evening to come to his caravan after dinner to discuss it. This was the first time I had ever been consulted over anything but purely technical engineering matters. I felt I must be making progress.

He was alone, with some maps in front of him, when I arrived and he went straight to the point.

"We can't have these Boche Parachutists becoming a menace in the Fens like Hereward the Wake," he said. "But I don't want to get mixed up in such unpromising terrain with a full-blown divisional operation on my hands. What I have in mind is to leave the Fens for the Divisional Reconnaissance Regiment, with a Sapper Field Company under command, and let them get on with the job at once."

He stopped, turned his chair to face me, and frowned.

"What do you think about that?" he asked.

It so happened that, as a boy, my interest had been aroused in Hereward the Wake by a schoolmaster. He told us tales – where he got them I never inquired* – about Hereward and William I. Apparently treacherous monks in Ely informed the King about crossing the Fens. When William's men knew the pathways, it was impossible for Hereward to survive. I told G. I. Thomas that I thought it impossible to open all roads fit for tank traffic in the Fens, but that it would not be impossible to open up a slender network of roads that were enough for the lighter vehicles of the Reconnaissance Regiment. Having achieved that, it ought not to be too difficult to get to the area under surveillance by mobile armoured car patrols.

"What is required," I said, "is a combination of wits and stealth. When we have learnt how to move freely in the Fens we shall soon see how to turn the lock. It's not my business, Sir," I continued, "but for what it is worth, my view is that Kinnersley (he was CO of the Reconnaissance Regiment) has the wits you are looking for, and I have a Sapper Company Commander who will co-operate with him one hundred percent."

"Whom do you have in mind then?" he asked.

I told him I proposed Streak Moore for the Sapper side of the business. "Let Kinnersley and Streak Moore play it their own way, Sir," I said. "The Germans are only holding the Fens with a few men, using their wits. Kinnersley and Streak have more wits than a hundred Germans and the two together have far more fire-power. Darkness will be their ally. Stealth will give them surprise. This is not, I submit, a foolhardly adventure. The odds are on our side."

G. I. Thomas looked at his watch. "It's bedtime now," he said. "Warn Moore to be ready to begin tomorrow night. I'll give definite orders before noon tomorrow."

By first light next morning I was with 204 Field Company. Streak Moore had already received a signal from Kinnersley to go and see him at once. I warned him what he and his men were in for, and what equipment I had available for him. We talked for a few minutes and I was impressed by Streak's lively mind.

_____

* *Hereward the Wake* by Charles Kingsley? I have never read it, so I cannot be sure.

"Pray for cunning," was my final advice and Streak saluted politely and I departed. He was a good leader. He left the Army early and died some years ago.

That night 204 Field Company built a sizeable Bailey Bridge over the River Kalfach, which runs from Calcar to the Rhine. This gave the Reconnaissance Regiment access to the Fens by an unexpected route and Kinnersley's A Squadron occupied the village of Wissel unopposed. From there they struck southwards and surprised the enemy in Calcar. They drove them out and captured some prisoners while still asleep. This was a good start.

I went to see Streak Moore again next morning. He had been up all night and, being very young, he was too sleepy to be able to think straight. His Second-in-Command, however, had had some sleep and we arranged what should be sent to Stackpipe for the coming evening. This became a daily exercise, except that it was one of my Field Engineers who I usually sent in my place. 204 Field Company built ten or eleven bridges in the first five nights. They also picked up a lot of mines and two pigs which they ate with glee. The Reconnaissance Regiment contributed a black beret which Streak wore thereafter in the Fens with his Sapper cap badge.

The nightly routine was something like this: an Armoured Car Troop and an Assault Troop would set off after sunset. When they came to an obstacle the two troops could always surprise and overpower the enemy in the dark and call up the Sappers to bridge or clear the obstacle. This would be finished about midnight and the next obstacle also was often captured and bridged before dawn next morning. This combination of armoured cars, Infantry and Sappers made astonishing progress. But it all hinged about the rapport that existed between Kinnersley and Streak Moore, and their understanding of darkness and stealth. When it was all over, I recommended Streak for a decoration, which he got, and he, in turn, put forward two or three men from his Company.

The next call on the Sappers was for assistance of a different kind. It fell to Tony Vinycomb and 260 Field Company. After the Fens had been cleared, the going became too tough for armoured cars alone and 214 Brigade, supported by tanks, was ordered to advance along the main road towards Xanten. Their leading battalion (5th Duke of Cornwall's Light Infantry) reached a point about two miles short of the town where they were held up and dug in. Air photographs showed that between them and the town there was a man-made obstacle. It appeared to be an anti-tank ditch, dug at right-angles to the road, stretching out a long way on both sides. A combination of craters blocked the main road itself. No one had got near enough to see or measure any of these obstacles, but it was clear that the enemy intended to hold Xanten tenaciously.

G. I. Thomas thereafter decided to mount a determined attack on the town. He held his Order Group on 8 March. He ordered 214 Brigade to patrol up to the obstacles so that the Sappers could have a look at them. The attack itself was then to be led by 129 Brigade. There had been some discussion as to the best time for H-Hour. I would have liked H-Hour to be two hours before dawn, but Joe Vandeleur, who commanded 129 Brigade, preferred dawn. There were good Sapper reasons for wanting darkness for the early stages of the attack, but, because I can no longer remember Joe Vandeleur's arguments, it would be churlish in the afterlight to flaunt my own without stating his. Anyway, his Brigade was playing the leading part in the drama and the Sappers were only playing the part of the parlour-maid, using a mop, who was discovered on stage when the curtain rose! So Joe had his way and H-Hour was fixed for dawn.

I asked G. I. Thomas to use his muscle to get me all the ironmongery necessary to make this sort of dawn operation by the Sappers as effective as possible. He got me 81 Assault Squadron less one troop, under Major John Woollett whom I had known of old. He was a tower of strength and imparted to his men his own undaunted spirit and ingenuity. He and Tony Vinycomb were totally different in outlook and temperament but they always made a most effective team in any sort of rough-house.

After dark on D−1 a double-single Bailey Bridge (70′ long) was built by 553 Field Company about a mile and a half from the obstacle and mounted on improvised wooden skids. It lay in the middle of the main road, which at that point was lined by large trees then in bud. 16 Assault Squadron was to tow this on D-Day with two AVREs, escorted by the assaulting tanks and Infantry. The bridge was to be manoeuvred by the AVREs so as to bridge the craters in the main road. If anything went wrong, the bridge was to be lifted off its skids, when near the lip of the crater, and pushed across it on conventional Bailey rollers. (We hoped this would be quicker than unloading the Bailey from lorries and building in the usual manner.)

All this time no one had seen the obstacle and we were relying on the motto of the Most Exalted Order of the Star of India: "Heaven's Light our Guide". On Woollett's advice G. I. Thomas used his muscle again to borrow a Jumbo bridge layer from 34 Tank Brigade. It arrived next morning, having created havoc on the Corps main axis behind us by motoring many miles along it at a very slow speed, but it arrived just in time. It was put under command of 16 Assault Squadron for the attack. The Jumbo was to lay its bridge over the ditch to the left of the main road, having approached the site across the fields. 16 Assault Squadron was to make another crossing place over the ditch on the other side of the main road, using a fascine* mounted on the back of an AVRE.

* A fascine is a huge bundle of logs, bound in wire, to fill a ditch. Latin: *fascis*, a bundle, hence *Fascism* which, in Italy, took as its emblem a wooden bundle of sticks.

This device was operated from inside the tank, but it usually needed some luck as well as skill to get the fascine into the place intended.

If the combined circus failed to make a single suitable crossing place anywhere, the two platoons of 260 Field Company, who were to advance on foot behind it, would have to do the job by hand. For this they had picks and shovels and two armoured bulldozers as well. There were also thirty lorries full of brick rubble ready for tipping into the ditch.

This was a far cry from my pet theory of stealth and surprise, but the Infantry were dead set on attacking in daylight with masses of armour and artillery support, so a different technique, using noisy mechanical aids, was appropriate. Anyway, we were in good company with 129 Brigade!

The circus was formed up on the evening before the event, with the Jumbo in the lead, followed by an armoured bulldozer. Behind, there were two tanks harnessed to the skid Bailey. Then came the AVRE Command Tank with Woollett aboard and a fascine on its back, followed by another AVRE with another fascine, two gun tanks, another armoured bulldozer and several crocodile tanks (flame-throwers). The whole circus was commanded by a Major of the Royal Armoured Corps in one of the gun tanks. He was also in touch by wireless with the leading Infantry Commander and the two platoons of 260 Field Squadron, who joined the column before H-Hour. After some discussion, we arranged for Tony Vinycomb to remain at 129 Brigade HQ and I decided to join the circus on foot with the Sappers. Not that I expected to contribute much from there, but I could certainly contribute nothing whatever if I remained back at Divisional HQ.

During the night before the attack began, a patrol of the Duke of Cornwall's Light Infantry with a Sapper Officer crept up to the ditch to look at it. As the road was on an embankment, they advanced silently in the fields to the east of it. (They subsequently reported that the going in the fields was firm enough for a tank, but unlikely to stand up to continuous traffic.) When they got near to the obstacle, the patrol halted and the Sapper, with outstanding *sang-froid* crept silently on foot to examine it. He tried to measure the width, but found the ditch full of Germans. One of them fired at him, but missed; another threw a grenade which cut his hand, but not badly. It must have been an alarming experience, but he brought back the good news that the crater in the road did not look too wide for the skid Bailey. The patrol returned to the starting line and silence shrouded the night.

As it began to get light next morning I joined the two platoons of 260 Field Company, and we watched the attack begin behind a heavy artillery screen of our own. The enemy replied with shell fire, directed mainly at the main road. I told the Sappers to leave the main road and we descended from the embankment into the fields on the left (or west) of it. Many trees and telegraph poles had been felled by the enemy, presumably as concealment for anti-

244

personnel mines, which fortunately they had had no time to lay. The tangles of wire, tree trunks and branches made progress slow and laborious, but behind the shelter of the road embankment there was fair cover and we had no casualties. I suppose it is possible that the presence of the CRE on foot with the Sappers gave some encouragement, but I would not be too sure of that. They had their own two officers with them, one of whom, Lieutenant Bevin, the reader may remember from the Arnhem days. They both set an example worthy of such good men.

The circus moved slightly faster along the road than we did among the debris alongside it, and we could see the crocodiles belching flames at some small houses on the left of the road as they advanced ahead of us. As it got light, I could also see the tall, thin steeple of Xanten church, framed, as it were, between the much-depleted avenue of roadside trees. The road was as straight as a railroad, but the enemy fire, though noisy and menacing, was not very accurate. We stumbled and plodded on.

By the time we reached the obstacles the armoured part of the circus had arrived and work had begun. It was now broad daylight and many shells began to arrive. I kept the Sappers in the lee of the embankment while I crawled up it. I saw John Woollett directing operations from his AVRE. I was glad he was under a sheet of armour plate and I envied his coolness. There was nothing I could do except to exchange a grin occasionally when my eyes met those of a Sapper.

There was a shallow German trench system just beyond the ditch and our leading Infantry manned it. They were now well dug-in and not entirely unprotected.

John Woollett decided that his best bet was to get the Jumbo to lower its bridge over the ditch to the left of the main road, while he himself attempted to lower his fascine into the other side on the right. This was certainly a generous gesture as the left-hand billet was far less exposed to enemy fire than the right-hand one, yet this was the one he chose to tackle, leaving the less dangerous one to his comrade. Both tanks went forward under heavy fire with everything closed down. The Jumbo raised and lowered its bridge extremely accurately over the ditch. They might have been built as a pair to match one another. It then retired to let a procession of tanks cross the bridge he had made and rejoin the main road fifty yards ahead. The enemy now had something more menacing than us in the trenches to fire at, and I emerged to see what was happening.

A reasonable tank track was beginning to be in full use on the left of the road, but on the right things were not so good. The ditch there, for some recondite and Germanic reason, was both wider and deeper than elsewhere and the fascine dropped into it was nothing like large enough to fill it. The tank made several attempts to cross over it, but its tracks would not grip the spoil on the far side and there it stuck until the enemy fire slackened enough to let the Sappers of 260 Field Company do something with a bulldozer to free it.

Meanwhile the road itself was completely blocked by the skid Bailey and its towing tanks. The crater turned out to be not one crater but two. The first one was on one side of the road and the second was on the other side, overlapping the first. They must have been invisible to the officer who had taken such risks to view the site before dawn.

The skid Bailey had been faithfully towed by its tanks, but was now a useless road block: "Made in England" as one of the Sappers remarked. I told the tug-tank crews to try and pull it out of the way and I told the two platoons of 260 Field Company to set to with bulldozers and shovels and begin filling in the craters. I also spoke to Tony Vinycomb on the wireless and told him to bring down all the lorry-loads of brick rubble available and take charge of the operation. (Tony Vinycomb was a brave man and a high-grade mathematician, and I remember saying to him on this occasion, "You need not bring your slide rule too"!) He presently arrived in a jeep, followed by an RASC Corporal on a motorcycle, who was later to be the guide for the rubble lorries.

At that moment two mortar bombs burst in the grass verge of the road. Bang! Bang! and rather close. The blast whipped my beret off my head like a conjuring trick and the RASC Corporal fell off his motorbike, the hood of Tony Vinycomb's jeep flew into the air, as though by an act of God – Whom I later remembered to thank, as no one was hurt! The memory of Tony's face, suffused in astonished surprise, will ever remain in my mind. He had great difficulty in getting the skid Bailey out of the way. Enemy snipers from a clump of trees, not far distant, intervened to add to the difficulties. First the tug hauled the bridge back a few yards and one of the transoms got caught on the trunk of a felled tree and pulled the whole thing broadside across the road. The tanks hauled it to and fro, trying to free it, but in the end it could only be cleared out of the way by dismantling it. Intermittent shelling went on till about midday and four or five Sappers were wounded, though none, thank God, were killed. The lorry-loads of brick rubble soon arrived. To everyone's dismay the lorries were not tippers but ordinary 3-tonners. They required much shovelling to unload their contents where it was needed. The main road became usable by midday, which was none too soon, as the tracks in the fields on either side of the road were becoming impassable. Work continued till well after nightfall.

129 Infantry Brigade reached its objectives after heavy fighting and the town was in their hands. It was in a terrible state and holding it under our artillery and RAF bombardment must have been a ghastly experience for its German defenders. They were brave men and Brigadier Vandeleur and his Brigade Staff stood to attention in front of Brigade HQ as a mark of respect for the

defenders when they were marched off to the PoW cage in the rear.*

The capture of Xanten brought the German resistance on the west bank of the Rhine to an end at last. Now we had only to cross the river and rip the intestines of Nazi Germany to pieces as quickly as possible. The Russians also were approaching from the east.

EXTRACTS FROM LETTERS TO MY PARENTS

Written from near Nijmegen, 13 February, 1945

These are great days! I believe we really are getting to the end of the Boche. The prisoners we get come in more willingly. Even their Parachute troops don't look like what they did. I got one of them to show me the mines he himself had laid. He seemed quite happy to do so. He was a fluent French speaker. He had one wall eye, and he seemed pleased to lead me through the safe lanes. One must admire them as soldiers. He holds up a battalion with six or eight men and a machine gun. Over half of them would surrender but for one NCO with a pistol to call the tune.

Written from Cleve, 18 February, 1945

The other day one of my Officers saw a British private soldier wearing the kilt. He said to the private: "I suppose a hardy Scot like you doesn't feel the cold with bare knees?" The private replied, "Well, Sir. I come from Putney and I only put on this fancy dress for the first time yesterday and I *do* feel a bit chilly in it." My caravan is now in a lunatic asylum. It must be a special kind of asylum labelled: "For British Officers only, who camp out in February." Our mess is in a doctor's house. He has a bathroom so I shall have a bath – and catch a cold – for the first time since I arrived in France.

---

* In a book he wrote after the war Brigadier Vandeleur said that his gesture went down badly with the Press.

16

The Last Lap

When Operation Veritable started in February there had been ten first-class German Divisions against us under orders from Hitler to fight to the death to hold the west bank of the Rhine. But on 10 March the only German troops still on the west bank were in Allied PoW cages. It had been hard going, but British and Canadian troops had won the battle and the Germans had suffered a costly defeat. They were now in no fit state to hold the Rhine either, and the total defeat of Hitler was at last within our grasp. We were quite certain of this, but it did not blind us to the fact that we could not expect to win without fighting and casualties.

On 19 March G. I. Thomas held an Order Group to give out his orders for crossing the Rhine. He told us that the British Second Army was organizing a crossing between Wesel and Emmerich on a two-Corps front: 12 Corps on the right, 30 Corps on the left. The American XVIII Airborne Corps (consisting of one British and two American Airborne Divisions) would drop behind the German lines on the 12 Corps front. 43 Division was again to be in 30 Corps, but would not be used in the assault crossing. The assault crossing was to be undertaken by 51 Highland Division. We were to follow 51 Division and take up a position on its left with 3 Canadian Division on our left again.

G. I. Thomas foresaw a slogging match for four or five days, after which he expected a crack to appear in the German position. When that occurred, 30 Corps would advance on a three-Division front: 43 Division in the centre, 51 Division on our right and 3 Canadian Division on our left.

The Operation was given the codeword "Plunder". It seemed likely that the enemy's withdrawal would become less and less co-ordinated as time went on.

248

There were likely to be many pockets of fierce resistance, but with gaps between them. The aim of every formation in 30 Corps must be to get into these gaps and enlarge them. Soon the gaps would become so large that the pockets would become surrounded. The pressure must be kept up and the defence would then gradually become completely unco-ordinated. The end would come, perhaps in a month, perhaps six weeks; it was impossible to say for certain. Our essential policy must be to by-pass enemy fortified areas and leave them to rot behind us.

On 21 March General Horrocks assembled all the Senior Officers of 30 Corps in a village hall near Goch. It was a bright spring morning and the sun shone. Neither General Horrocks nor the Army Commander (Dempsey), who was also present, left us in any doubt that Operation Plunder would see the end of Hitler and all his works. I was struck by the difference in these two men – Horrocks: witty, dashing, optimistic and light-hearted; Dempsey: serious, few words, thoughtful and unassuming. He impressed on his listeners that there would be no lack of RAF and Artillery support and that plentiful ammunition of all kinds was immediately available. One breathed spirited optimism, the other calculated certainty.

That night a vast procession of "Buffaloes" (amphibious vehicles) and bridging equipment of all sorts began moving towards the river without lights. All went in pitch darkness to their correct harbouring places and a smoke-screen, generated from opposite Emmerich, drifted in the wind across the whole front concealing all that was happening. The date for the crossing could not be far away. Next evening, 23 March, 200 or more aircraft of Bomber Command flew overhead to rain their bombs on Wesel and a continuous bombardment of Artillery began at about 6 pm. The steady tapping of the pepperpot across the Rhine also began just after dark and went on all night.

In the early dawn 51 Highland Division got into their boats and set off for the east bank. The din was stupendous. It now seems an anti-climax, but in 43 Division we remained in bed! For the first time since Normandy there was a battle without us.

Saturday, 24 March was another cloudless day. About 10 am we saw an armada of 4,000 aircraft and gliders carrying the Airborne troops across the river. They released their parachutists and gliders in perfect order. This airborne landing, at last, was an unqualified success. The Infantry and Armoured Divisions were crossing the river at the same time – some had already arrived – and contact with the Airborne troops did not seem long delayed. G. I. Thomas decided he ought to go across the Rhine, "to get the feel of the other side" as he described it. He asked me to go with him and his ADC and I drove him in turns in his jeep. He told me he could not spare much time on the far bank.

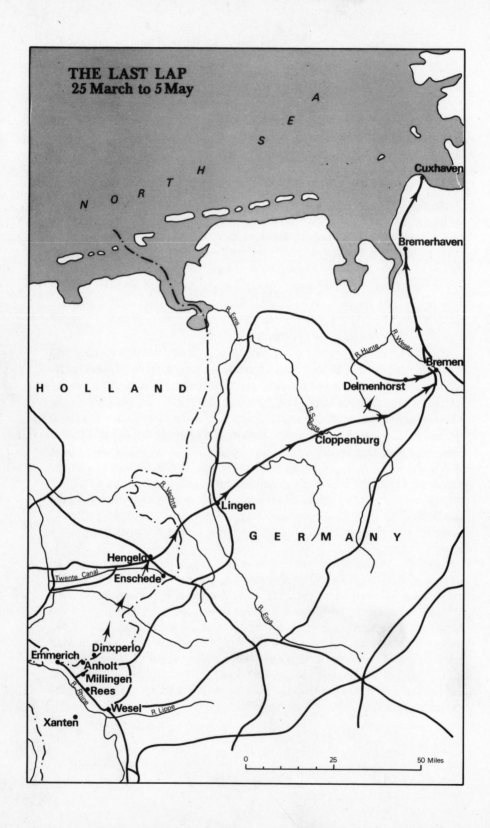

THE LAST LAP
25 March to 5 May

NORTH SEA

Cuxhaven

Bremerhaven

R. Ems

R. Weser

R. Hunte

Bremen

HOLLAND

Delmenhorst

R. Soeste

Cloppenburg

R. Vechte

Lingen

GERMANY

Hengelo

Twente Canal

Enschede

R. Ems

Dinxperlo

Emmerich

Anholt

Millingen

R. Rhine

Rees

Wesel   R. Lippe

Xanten

0   25   50 Miles

"You must drive like Jehu," he said. (Pause) "Who was Jehu's father?" he asked abruptly.

I knew that, and got more marks for Scripture than his ADC!* We crossed, jeep and all, in an amphibious vehicle. The river was as placid as the Serpentine.

We felt we had been very adventuresome, but that evening we heard that Winston Churchill had had a picnic lunch on the east bank too.

Next day, 25 March, Divisional HQ opened up on the east bank and G. I. Thomas took charge of the Corps left flank. It had been a day of hard fighting for 51 Division and Rees was not completely cleared till next day. Our 130 Brigade was the first brigade of 43 Division to cross the Rhine and their first task was to capture a small town called Millingen. Looked at from a mile away it seemed to stand on high ground, but the map revealed that it was only 35 feet above sea level. This gives an idea of how low-lying the country was. As we had expected, the Germans made Millingen a centre of resistance. It was cleared of the enemy by dawn next day with the capture of over 200 prisoners, but it had needed a ruthless pounding to achieve it. "Serve 'em right," I heard several Sappers exclaim, but most of us could only feel pity for the unfortunate people who were now driven from their shattered homes with all their worldly belongings in wheelbarrows. We did not, however, machine-gun them from the air in the manner adopted by the Luftwaffe in Belgium, Holland and France in 1940.

Slow progress continued for several days. There was nothing the enemy could do to stop us. The most they could hope for was to delay us and they set about this with their usual obstinate tenacity. Moreover, the terrain through which we were advancing lent itself to this particular form of defensive tactics. The roads were mainly narrow, with cobbled surfaces, flanked by marshy fields, and there were many culverts under the roads. By firing explosive charges under these culverts the enemy could easily create wide and deep craters that rapidly filled with water too deep for tanks to cross without a bridge first being built. The verge of every crater might be sown with mines as booby traps to add to our difficulties, and well-sited defensive positions might be manned by concealed anti-tank gunners, machine-gunners and snipers. Each position would, therefore, require a minor battle before any progress could be made.

Also, we were now about to enter the Hanseatic districts of Germany, whence came a hardy race of seamen and submariners from whom the Fatherland was wont to recruit its sailors for the German Navy. Hamburg, Bremen and Cuxhaven were Naval Bases comparable with Portsmouth or Plymouth, and it was known that vast stocks of torpedoes, mines and firing

* Jehu is wrongly called "son of Nimshi" in 1 Kings, 19, v. 16. He was actually his grandson and the son of Jehoshaphat; see 2 Kings, 9, v. 2

devices of all kinds would be readily available there.

We therefore expected to find a formidable foe ahead of us, not necessarily a very numerous one, but quite numerous enough to give us a difficult and time-consuming task to master!

To overcome the many delays inherent in this type of operation, G. I. Thomas sought to rearrange 43 Division and 8 Armoured Brigade (which worked very closely with us) into a composite force that would combine the virtues of an Infantry Division with the virtues of an Armoured Division. The lynch-pin of this new arrangement was what was called indiscriminately the Armoured Thrust *Force* or the Armoured Thrust *Group*. (Both expressions meant the same thing.)

The Armoured Thrust Group was to be built up on a nucleus of 8 Armoured Brigade, commanded by Brigadier Prior-Palmer. To this nucleus was then to be added an Infantry Battalion (4th Somerset Light Infantry from 120 Brigade) mounted in Armoured Personnel Carriers of 1 Canadian APC Regiment. For Artillery Support the Group was to include a Field Regiment of Artillery and for Engineer Support the Group was to include one of my Field Companies.

Behind the Armoured Thrust Group was to follow a Group known as the "Divisional Follow-up Group", commanded by Brigadier Vandeleur and his 129 Infantry Brigade. A third and a fourth Group were to consist of 130 Brigade and 214 Brigade, each under its own Brigadier.

Finally, there was to be a group known as the "Divisional Tail Group". This consisted of what the Army rudely refers to as the "Odds and Sods", that it is to say, a collection of very skilled and essential men who specialize in various administrative duties. These were mounted in appropriate specialized vehicles.

What G. I. Thomas hoped to achieve by this rather elaborate arrangement was a highly mobile and well-armed formation, specially suited to deal with what we all foresaw as the last stages of the war in Germany. He hoped to make rapid deployment possible, to get the enemy on the run and to chivvy them from pillar to post so that they would have no chance to dig in and build up their exasperating "strong points", each one based on a colossal road block, and requiring a pitched battle to overcome it.

Most of my brother officers in Divisional HQ tended to take a good view of this brain-child of G. I. Thomas, and I liked it in theory too, but I had an esoteric conviction that there were more drawbacks to it than advantages for the Sappers. It was thuswise:

In 43 Infantry Division there were three Infantry Brigades (129, 130 and 214) and in the Divisional Engineers there were three Field Companies (260, 553 and 204). In the course of training for war while in England before D-Day, and during operations from that day onwards, the practice had grown up of regularly employing the same Field Company with the same Infantry Brigade in every successive exercise or battle as it occurred. In consequence a regular bond of fellowship had grown up between each Field Company and what came to be regarded as its "affiliated" Infantry Brigade. These affiliations had by now taken root. It had become general practice to locate, whenever possible, the same Field Company in the territory of the same Infantry Brigade. The two usually marched in the same convoy and fought in the same actions, shoulder to shoulder, whenever necessity arose. They drew their rations daily from the same sources of supply and they collected their letters from the same Field Post Offices as a matter of course. The affiliations thus became almost "articles of faith" from which both parties drew strength. Yet in the new dispensation proposed by G. I. Thomas the principle of the Armoured Thrust Group cut across these bonds of fellowship. There was a Field Company positively nominated to operate perpetually with the Thrust Group and separated from its former affiliated Infantry Brigade. The question I had to answer therefore was: Which Field Company must I detach from its former affiliated Brigade and allot to the Armoured Thrust Group as a permanent feature? Whichever one I detailed for the Armoured Thrust Group was, by definition, separated from its affiliated Brigade, and a hallowed link was severed. Human relations were likely to be damaged and this seemed regrettable to all parties.

None of my Field Company Commanders wanted to be the one detailed for duty with 8 Armoured Thrust Group. It was not a personal affair, nor was it logical. It was simply a fact of life that both parties had become used to one particular affiliation and neither wanted to see a link broken that had come to be regarded as a source of strength.

I spoke to G. I. Thomas about it. He saw the point, but he would admit of no compromise. He insisted that the Armoured Thrust Group should have a permanently affiliated Field Company, and, as he put it, "That is that!"

I therefore arbitrarily detailed 260 Field Company to join the Armoured Thrust Group and abandon its affiliation with 129 Infantry Brigade. Tony Vinycomb (OC 260 Field Company) not unnaturally registered his regret at the severing of a valued link, but no compromise was possible and I am glad to think that we remained friends, notwithstanding.

Soon after this reorganization was promulgated in an Order Group the Armoured Thrust Group had its first assignment. I rose early in the morning to see 260 Field Company cross the startline. As I was approaching the appointed place in my scout car, the Wireless Operator with me (Lance-Corporal Ashworth) picked up on the air Brigadier Prior-Palmer, who was speaking from Tony Vinycomb's Company HQ. He wished to speak to me personally and we arranged to meet near the Start Line of his advance. But I never saw him. He was not at the rendezvous when I got there. I cannot say why we missed each other and, after this passage of forty years or so, I can only suggest that the cause of our not meeting may be accounted for by the events recorded in the History of 43 Wessex Infantry Division, page 242:

"The assembly of the Armoured Thrust Group at Anholt early next morning – it was Good Friday – produced a traffic jam of vast and fantastic proportions. The narrow streets and the only two bridges added to the complications. There was much waving and shouting before the trying process of 'marrying-up' even approached the semblance of order. As the morning wore on the traffic, as far as the eye could reach, remained jammed solid and stationary. Willpower, exhortation and force of personality exerted from the highest levels seemed equally powerless to get it on the move.

"The right column consisting of 4th Somerset Light Infantry and C Squadron 4th/7th Dragoon Guards had, in fact, struck opposition . . . five miles ahead. A tank had been lost to a bazooka and 88s were concentrating on the road."

I never met Tony Vinycomb that day either, nor did I meet him again for a very long time. He was severely wounded. He was evacuated and remained (so I was told) unconscious for twelve days having been blown up on a *shuh** mine.

His loss was a grievous one. He was an Ironside of an Officer who would "Praise the Lord and pass the ammunition", and his men in 260 Field Company followed his example. He recovered from his wounds and served on for twelve more years in the Army. We have corresponded occasionally and I rejoice that we have kept in touch.

I have often wondered whether these tiresome traffic jams that occurred so often in the last few weeks of the War in Europe were peculiar to 43 Division, or whether they were endemic throughout the British Army. The present is no place to indulge in a treatise on the subject, but I have heard it said that the American General Patton, who was famed for the speed of his moves on the battlefield, always managed to regulate his traffic without such frustrations as we seemed to endure on many occasions. A detailed study of this matter might be a useful footnote to The Military History of Mechanical Warfare, but I am in no position to supply it.

* * * * *

About this time, but I cannot remember exactly when, I heard that Gordon Lilley's only remaining brother had been killed just after the Rhine Crossing. I knew that one brother had been lost on Active Service, I believe in Normandy. Now Gordon alone remained and I could imagine the grief and anxiety of his bereaved parents. Surely it was neither necessary nor just for the last survivor to remain with the colours. He had been a marvellous Adjutant, a faithful

---

* A *shuh* mine (so called) was a German anti-personnel mine designed to blow off the foot.

friend; now he was an extremely effective Company Commander. I alone of those in authority was aware of the situation and, if I did nothing, no one else would. I resolved to speak to G. I. Thomas at once. He was leaving the Camp and might not return till the evening. Now was my chance and Fortune seldom beckons twice. I stopped him as he entered his Ark and told him what had happened. Would he support my application for Gordon Lilley to be posted out of the range of the enemy?

"Yes, certainly," he said. "Go and tell the A/Q* that your application has my approval. You are doing quite right."

It was not long before Gordon Lilley came to say farewell. He was furious! What had he done wrong, he asked, to deserve such treatment?

I said what I could, but with little avail. He left us that day and the next time we met was ten years later. It was entirely fortuitous, in the Charing Cross Road. We were still on speaking terms and I hope I have been forgiven.

For the last five weeks of the campaign 30 Corps provided the left flank guard of 21 Army Group and 43 Division was usually the left-hand Division of 30 Corps. Our main axis led us from the Rhine to Anholt, Dinxperlo, Hengelo, Enschede, Lingen, Cloppenburg, Ahlhorn, Bremen, Bremerhaven and Cuxhaven.

The nature of our advance was very much as G. I. Thomas had led us to expect. It was a continuous pursuit after stubborn and well-armed rearguards, but with less and less co-ordination between them as they withdrew. Each action was fought round what amounted to something of a fortress. The fortress was usually based on some natural obstacle such as a river or stream. Sometimes it was based on a man-made obstacle such as a culvert under a main road, but enlarged with an explosive charge fired under the road surface. The obstacle was usually riddled with personnel mines concealed in the crater.

I had managed to get 16 Assault Squadron RE attached to us from immediately after crossing the Rhine. It was command by John Woollett. At first G. I. Thomas was convinced that this unit, with its heavy tanks, would be too slow to keep up with the "Armoured Thrust Group" because its maximum speed was only 20 mph. Soon, however, it was clear to everyone that if the Division could advance twenty miles every *day* things were not too bad. John Woollett persuaded Brigadier Essame that his Squadron, far from delaying him, would help enormously. This turned out to be true and thereafter 16 Assault Squadron never looked back.

Woollett's Squadron had amongst its "funnies" a type of AVRE known as a "Petard". This was a heavy tank armed with a large-calibre mortar. The mortar fired a projectile like a domestic dustbin filled with high explosive. When the leading troops of a column came against a strongly defended area it

---

* A/Q is the abbreviation for an Officer at Divisional HQ, the Chief of the Administrative Staff.

was often found that the kernel of the area was a building of some kind strengthened with concrete and concealing an anti-tank gun. There was no better contrivance for destroying the kernel of the nut than a petard. A judicious combination of infantry with mortars, a gun tank and a petard could usually manoeuvre themselves so as to enable the AVRE to fire its petard at the kernel of the nut and crack it open. Conventional Sappers might then "delouse" the area of mines or bridge some obstacle. Each case had to be judged on its merits and Woollett or one of his officers always seemed to know the best combination to apply to the particular situation in hand. I remained much in their debt for the remainder of the campaign. I had my first practical experience of a petard in action in or near Cloppenburg.

An enemy strong-point had been overcome by a combination of all arms, including a petard AVRE, and it was essential for a Sapper to get through the streets to see whether a bridge still existed across the river. One of 16 Squadron's subalterns was very forthcoming.

"O.K. Sir," he said. "Jump aboard. I'll drive you along there and you can see for yourself."

It was a street about twenty feet wide with red brick houses on both sides. Most of the windows were broken; the street was absolutely deserted and several of the houses were on fire. We rattled along it till we came to a T-junction. Here we were about to turn to the right, where I expected to find the bridge. A German soldier then popped his head over the forecourt wall of the house ahead and fired a *panzerfaust* at us. A *panzerfaust* was a manually operated anti-tank weapon that fired an explosive projectile about the size of a flowerpot. The weapon rested on the firer's shoulder and the projectile was propelled by the exhaust gases of a rocket as they flashed to the rear over his shoulder.

There was such a din inside the AVRE that I could hear nothing, but through the visor in front of me I saw the German's head and shoulders as he fired the *panzerfaust*. (*Panzerfaust*, incidentally, means "armoured fist".) The projectile wobbled towards us and hit our tank as it were on the nose, straight between the eyes.

"God Almighty," I thought, "Heaven help us."

We had, in fact, already received the protection of our Maker, for the *panzerfaust* was defective and never exploded, but the sight that remains fixed in my mind is the rear view of the German soldier darting back into the house. I can still see in my mind's eye the heels of his jackboots.

One of the AVRE crew with great presence of mind fired his petard at the front door of the house. The house crumpled up but the German escaped. In the kitchen there was the carcass of half a pig that was about to be cooked for supper. I found the bridge was still intact. The AVRE crew and their mates ate the pig. A good time, therefore, was had by all, except, of course, the pig!

The Germans suffered a considerable mauling at Cloppenburg and, when 204 began building a Bailey Bridge over the River Lett, I hoped this would turn out to be an unopposed bridging operation. But, no. Severe shelling began during the night and work had to be stopped. Early next morning the shelling switched from the bridge site to our forward platoons nearby. About a company of German infantry and two tanks emerged from a ride through the woods and fell upon the Worcestershires' position. A battle at close quarters was fought for at least two hours. The enemy attack was halted and they withdrew, leaving many dead and over fifty prisoners.

When the advance was resumed, numerous aged Germans appeared from the woods to carry off their dead. Many corpses lay in front of the Worcestershires' position. They consisted of old men and boys, hurriedly clothed in German Army uniforms. This, I believe, was the last counterattack to be made by the enemy. From then onwards one could only hope the Germans would realize that the end was inevitable and that a formal surrender would be declared. Negotiations were, in fact, going on behind the scenes, but no local German Commanders seemed to have the authority to stop the fighting.

We had to battle on, causing untold havoc until we had subdued the resistance in Bremen and then in Bremerhaven. At every culvert on the roads an aircraft bomb would be found, pushed under the road and exploded with a time fuse. A bridge would then have to be built across the crater, or a diversion found to enable us to advance. German naval submarine technicians from the U-Boat barracks were employed on these demolitions and they certainly caused the most efficient demolitions we had ever met.

On one occasion a submarine torpedo was so well concealed under a culvert that no one saw it. It was detonated by a time switch and blew up one of our tanks. A Field Company that had already crossed the culvert had to be halted and brought back to build a replacement for the demolished culvert behind them. Thus one of our last bridge-building operations was done by a Field Company from the enemy side of the river, using bridging equipment brought to it by lorries from our side of it.

Two or three days before the end, I visited 260 Field Company building a bridge near Cuxhaven. They had established their Company HQ in a German farmhouse at the roadside. On the kitchen dresser was a framed photograph taken, according to the caption, on the Russian Front. Half a dozen Russians were being executed by hanging from a scaffold built in the form of a football goalpost. It is difficult to imagine a civilized man sending such a photograph home, nor, I think, would such a photograph have been found in a frame on the dresser of any farmhouse in Britain.

It is only fair, however, to quote also a short paragraph from the 43 Divisional History (page 244) showing another side of the coin: "Major

Beckhurst . . . relates an incident in the fighting. . . . 'During the height of the battle a captured German stretcher-bearer was brought to my HQ. All my own stretcher-bearers were fully occupied in dealing with casualties and this man at once volunteered to go and bring in two of our own wounded who were awaiting attention. Single-handed he brought both of these men back, although he was under heavy fire from his own side all the time.'"

The fighting ended quite unexpectedly on 4 May. 130 Brigade had crossed a canal near Cuxhaven over which 4th Dorsets had found a footbridge and 553 Field Company were building a Bailey Bridge to enable our tanks to follow them and secure the bridgehead. It was getting dark when I got there. The sound of enemy vehicles could be heard over the hill on the other side of the canal. What these vehicles were doing I cannot say, but it certainly sounded threatening. A few German prisoners were being disarmed. One of them, who spoke fluent English, was speaking. He was telling his British captors that the Führer still had surprises to spring. "Even at this last minute," he said, "he will win the war for Germany. Perhaps what you now hear is the arrival of the *Wehrmacht*." We had had so many surprises that the suggestion did not sound absurd. I was glad when the Bailey Bridge was finished and I saw our tanks crossing it to reinforce the Dorsets.

When I got back to Divisional HQ the Adjutant told me that the BBC had announced the "unconditional surrender of the German Forces opposing Field-Marshal Montgomery in North-West Europe."

I could hardly believe it. We had reached the end of the road.

Bibliography

The Red Beret. Hilary St George Saunders; Michael Joseph.

The 43rd (Wessex) Division at War 1944–45. Compiled by Major-General H. Essame; William Clowes and Sons Ltd.

The Royal Engineers Battlefield Tour Vol II. Prepared under the direction of the Chief Engineer, The British Army of the Rhine, 1947.

A Soldier's Story. Brigadier J. C. E. Vandeleur, DSO; printed privately for the author by Gale and Polden Ltd, 1967.

Incidents with Seventh Battalion, the Somerset Light Infantry in France and Germany 1944–45. Major W. L. Whitehead.

A number of events recalled in this book were published by the author in a different form in *Blackwood's Magazine* (now defunct), the *Royal Engineers Journal* and in *The Military Engineer* (American).

A few of the above were published while censorship was still in force and expurgation was then necessary. None of this book consists of quotations from the original censored publications. They do, however, assist memory of what happened.

Index

"A", Point, an imaginary location, 67
Aachen, 207
Abbott, Lieutenant Tony, 198
Abdiel, HMS, 153–4
Agnew, Commodore, 149
Ahlhorn, 255
Airborne Artillery Regiment, 179
Airborne Division, 1st, author posted
  to, 68–70; role of, 72–4; command
  of Divisional Engineers, 74–5;
  formation of Divisional Engineers,
  75–80; equipment for Divisional
  Engineers, 80–1; raid on Bruneval,
  84, 90; raid on Rjuken, 91–100;
  arrival at Oran, 111–3; at Tizi,
  114–22; invasion of Sicily, 123–43;
  lessons learnt following invasion of
  Sicily, 144–6; move to Taranto,
  147–9; exploits of in Taranto, 149–
  59; Christmas leave, 162; new
  Divisional Commander, role of,
  163; training, 165; plans for
  Normandy, 165; author leaves,
  166; at Arnhem, 176, 179–80,
  182–5; withdrawal from Arnhem,
  185, 188–93, 194
Airborne Division, 6th, 163
Airborne Sappers, role of, 71–2, 73–5
Airlanding Brigade, 1st, becomes
  gliderborne, 77; captures Ponte
  Grande Bridge, 125, 127, 129,
  134–8; move to Taranto, 146–7
Alanbrooke, General, 29, 66
Aldershot, 16, 62, 69
Alexander, General, 14, 81, 108, 110,
  136
Anderson, General, 108
Andrews, Captain, 127
Anholt, 255
Anti-tank Regiment, 73rd, 195–6
Antwerp, 202, 203, 207, 222
Ardennes, 1, 2, 15, 211, 221–2, 224, 229
Armitage, Major, 15–18
Armoured Division, 79th, 225
Armoured Thrust Force, 251–55
Army, 1st, 108, 122
Army, 2nd, 222, 229, 248
Army, 8th, in North Africa, 108, 122; in
  Sicily, 123, 125, 130, 139; in Italy,
  146, 157–8
Army Group, 21st, 222; author posted
  to, 165, 167–8; Bailey Bridges for,
  168; operation Market Garden,
  175; needs the port of Antwerp,
  202, 203; redeploys its Divisions,
  227; operations to expel German
  forces from West of the Rhine,
  229–30; advances from the Rhine to
  Cuxhaven, 255
Arnhem, capture of bridge at, 145, 175,
  177, 179, 202, 221
Arromanches, 166

Ashworth, Lance-Corporal, 191, 232, 253
Aspern, 230
Assault Squadron RE, 16th, 255–6
– 81st, 243
Augusta, 125, 136
Aurora, HMS, 149, 154

Bailey Bridges, 167, 168, 176, 180
Baker, Major Paul, 79
Bari, 158, 160–1
Barker, General, 19
Bastogne, 224
Battledress, 62–3
Bayeux, 166
Beasley, Captain (later Major) Basil, 116–8, 134, 136, 146
Bevin, Lieutenant, 191, 245
Binyon, Roger, 117
Bizerta, 147–8
Blackcock, Operation, 225–7
"Blank, Sapper", 64
"Blimp", 21, 67
Boise, 153
Bonham-Carter, Major, 102–8
Boylan, Brigadier Paddy, 190, 208
Bray, 55–6
Bremen, 255, 257
Bremerhaven, 257
Bridport, 66–7
Brigade, 129th, 182, 243, 244, 246
– 130th, 182, 251
– 214th, 180–83, 222, 234, 243
Briggs, Colonel, 13–15, 22, 63
Brighton Pier, 66
British Expeditionary Force, task of, 1–3; withdrawal of, 14, 18, 29–62
Bromley-Martin, Major, 87
Browning, Major-General (later Lieutenant-General) F.A.M. "Boy", commander 1st Airborne Division 70; description of, 70–1; suggests author undertakes parachute course, 72; author discusses role of Divisional Engineers with, 74–5; visits 9 Field Company, 77; attends conference regarding Bruneval, 84; discusses Rjuken with author, 86, 94; visits 1 Para Brigade in N Africa, 101; inspires troops, 102; promoted, 118; commander all airborne forces, 118
Bruneval, raid on radar station, 84–90, 146
Brunnsum, 207, 216, 222, 224, 228
Brussels, 10, 168–9, 194, 203
Bulford, 79, 84, 91, 94, 101, 103, 107

Calcar, 238, 242
Caldwell, Brigadier M.R. "Hindy", 156–7
Campbell, Chief Engineer Pat, 219–221
Canadian, 1st Army, 229
– 2nd Corps, 240
– 3rd Division, 248
Cannae, 158
Castellaneta, 155–6
Catania, 125, 138–9, 145
Cherbourg, 8–9
Chesterfield, 71–2
Chipping Sodbury, 65
Chivers, Captain (later Major) John, 78, 151
Clarke, Major G.G.S., 69
Clayton, Company Sergeant-Major, 148
Cleves, 234, 240–1
Cloppenburg, 255, 256, 257
Cochrane, Lieutenant Tom, author meets, 26; prepares bridges for demolition, 28; supports Royal Ulster Rifles, 32–3; orders to, 33; receives MC, 33; builds bridges, 37; at Dunkirk, 54
Cologne, 202, 207
Combined Operations HQ, 84, 91
Cook, Captain, 84, 87
Cooke, Brigadier Collis, 134–6, 138
Cooper, Sergeant, 114–5
Cooper, Wing Commander Bruce, 94–6, 99

Corps, 12th, 225, 227
– 30th, in Operation Market Garden,
  173–5, 179, 186; commander
  phones author at Nijmegen, 198;
  General Thomas given temporary
  command of, 225; role of in
  Operation Veritable, 229–30; in
  Operation Plunder, 248-9, 256;
  Chief Engineer of, 200-1, 206, 208
Courtice, Bob, 15
Coxwell-Rogers, Brigadier, 158
Crete, 68, 74
Cunningham, Admiral, 147–8
Cuxhaven, 251, 257–8

D-Day, 162–5
Davey, Brigadier Basil, 108–10
Davidson, Brigadier, 18, 19
Dempsey, General, 222, 249
Dendre, River, demolition of bridge
  over, 20–22
Digger, Quartermaster-Sergeant, 26, 47
Dinant, 14
Dinxperlo, 255
Division, 1st, 14
– 2nd, 1, 2, 3, 14, 16, 19, 22–3, 24,
  37, 42
– 3rd, 14, 23–24, 29, 34, 40, 42, 62–5
– 43rd, author posted to as CRE,
  168–70; author meets Field
  Engineers of, 175–6; part played by
  in Operation Market Garden, 177,
  179, 186; evacuates 1 Airborne
  Division and 4 Dorsets from
  Arnhem, 188–93; on the Island,
  194–203; moves to area between R
  Maas and German frontier, 203;
  moves to province of Limburg,
  207; Engineers undertake road
  repairs, 213–4; Engineers devise
  "Stackpipe", 214–5; plans to
  counterattack across R Meuse, 223;
  Engineers tasks along R Meuse,
  223–4; temporary change of
  commander, 225, 228; participates
  in Operation Blackcock, 225–7;

participates in Operation Veritable,
  229–39; HQ moves to Schloss
  Moyland, 239–40; clears Fens of
  German defenders, 240–1; captures
  Xanten, 241–7; participates in
  Operation Plunder, 248–58
– 51st, 251
– 78th, 9 Field Company loaned to,
  157–8
Doig, Sergeant, 96–8
Donaldson, Lieutenant, 44
Dorman, Captain Stephen, author
  meets, 71; appointed OC 1 Para
  Squadron, 75–6, 80; believed killed
  in N Africa, 101
Dorsets, 4th, 186, 187, 188, 258
– 5th, 56, 187
Dover, 60
Down, Brigadier (later General), 74, 78,
  113, 147, 156
Dragoon Guards, 4th/7th, 21, 254
Driel, 179–80, 182
Dunkirk, 34, 43–4; evacuation from, 50,
  53, 54, 55, 58–9, 62, 64
Duren, 207
Dyle, River, 14, demolition of Bridge
  over, 19; withdrawal from, 20–23
Dynamo, Operation, 30

Eagger, Colonel, gives opinion of
  General Browning, 70–1; concerned
  about water supply, 119; examines
  author's wounds, 137; attends
  wounded on Primasole Bridge,
  141–2
Eindhoven, 177
Eisenhower, General, 103, 107, 136,
  185, 222
El Kef, 108–10, 111
Elst, 182–3
Emmerich, 248–9
Enschede, 255
Escaut, River, 19
Essame, Brigadier, 222, 255
Evill, Major Tom, description of, 173;
  Engineer plans of, 173–5;
  promoted, 176, 236

Exeter, 66

Ferranti, Vincent de, 73
Field Company, 9th, becomes airborne,
76–8; volunteers participate in raid
on Rjuken, 94–100; arrives in
Oran, 113; assembly of WACO
gliders, 116–7; survivors of
detachment at Ponte Grande Bridge
and Syracuse, 134–6, 138; Second
in Command of, 146; disembarks in
Taranto, 148; operates docks and
clears roads in Taranto, 149;
Commander of, 156–7; loaned to 78
Division, 157–8
– 38th, 135
– 204th, 176, commander of, 173;
ferrying Poles across R Rhine, 183;
repairs damage to bridges at
Nijmegen, 199–200; ferry boat at
Nijmegen, 201; crossings over
anti-tank ditch, 235–6; clearing the
Fens of German defenders, 241–2;
Bailey Bridge over R Lett, 257–8
– 253rd, author takes command of,
23–5; officers and men of, 28;
looting by, 28, 29; ordered to locate
and signpost routes to static
fortifications 29, 31; assists with
infantry defensive positions, 32;
billeted in a school, 33; Monty
presents medals, 33–4, 65; bridge
demolitions, 35–6; begins
withdrawal to Dunkirk, 36; bridge
demolitions, 39–40; at Furnes, 42;
reinforces Suffolk Regiment on
Dunkirk perimeter, 45–6; rear
party formed, 51; marches to
Dunkirk beach, 52; ferrying men to
ships, 53–4; remaining men walk to
Bray, 55–6; row across Channel,
56–7; board a RN pinnace, 59;
board HMS *Locust*, 60; reassembles
on Salisbury Plain, 62;
absenteeism, 63–4; prepares piers
for demolition 66; retrains at

Wimple, 66–7; lays mines on
Bridport beaches, 66–7; author
leaves, 68
– 260th, 176; ferry airborne troops
from Arnhem, 192; crossings over
anti-tank ditches and craters, 237–
8, 242–6; builds bridge near
Cuxhaven, 257–8
– 553rd, 176; ferry 4th Dorsets and
Poles across to Arnhem, 186; builds
bridge over canal, 206–7; makes
tracks in woods, 215–7; builds
Bailey Bridge, 243
Field Park Company, 261st, becomes
gliderborne, 78; assembles
WACOs, 116–7; tradesmen from
disembark at Taranto, 148; operate
docks at Taranto, 149; sapper from
drives train for SAS, 150
Fitzjohn, Second-Lieutenant, 207
Foggia, 158
Freshman, Operation, 100
Frost, Major (later Colonel) John,
commands para forces raid on
Bruneval, 87, 89, 90, 146; returns
with author to N Africa, 143; at
Arnhem, 183

Gadsden, Colonel, 192
Gale, Richard Nelson, 71
Gammel, Lieutenant-General, 169–70
Geldern-Wesel line, 229
Geldern-Xanten line, 230
Geilen Kirchen, 221
George VI, King, 81
Gibraltar, 105–7
Gioia, 155
Gliders, types of, 80–1
Goch, 234, 235, 239, 249
Gort, Lord, Commander-in-Chief BEF,
29–30
Goschen, Lieutenant-Colonel, 88
Grave, 177–8, 179
Green, Michael, Intelligence Officer,
157
Grenade, Operation, 229–30

263

Groesbeck, 203
Guards Armoured Division, 173, 177, 178, 179–80

Hackett, Brigadier, 108, 147
Hardiman, Major, 155
Harrison, Lieutenant-Colonel Desmond, 24–5; men trained by, 40; orders from, 33–4, 37, 39, 40, 42; at bridge demolitions, 35–6; at Dunkirk, 54; visits 253 Field Company, 65
Harvey, Group Captain, 72
Heal, Captain "Tiny", 46
Heather, Sergeant, 23
Hecktel, 173, 177
Hengelo, 255
Heteren, 182–3
Hicks, Brigadier, 138
Highland Division, 51st, 248, 249
Hobart, General, 225
Holdsworth, First Lieutenant RN, 60
Home Defence, 62–9
Hopkinson, General, 145–6, 155–6
Horrocks, Lieutenant-Colonel (later General) 35–6, 64–6, 164, 173, 183, 186, 198–9, 222, 225, 228, 233, 249
Houghton, Major, 77
Hove Pier, 66
Hunter-Gordon, Subaltern "Pat", 16–18
Husky, Operation, 112
Huy, 223

Infantry, Brigade, 9th, 28–9, 32
Infantry Division, 5th, 138–9
–59th, 166
Ironside, General, 8, 30
Island, the, 180–82, 183, 186, 194–6, 201, 203, 222

Jacobs, Tony, 109
Jones, Colonel "Jonah", 127–8, 130, 132–4, 139
Jones, Lieutenant Colonel C.P., 179
Julich, 207

Kalfach, River, 241
Kinnersley, Colonel, 240, 241, 242
Knox, Colonel Fergus, 32
Krombeke, 37–8
Kyte, Major, 77–8, 116

La Panne, 52
Lathbury, Brigadier, 139–40
Lett, River, 257
Liege, 223
Lille, 1, 34, 195, 196, 199
Lilley, Captain Gordon, Adjutant 43 Division Engineers, 175, 176, 188 189; promoted to command 553 Field Company, 215, 216–7; death of brothers, 253–4
Limburg, 207
Lingen, 255
Lloyd, General, 18–9
Locust, HMS, 60–1
Looting, soldiers, 14, 28–9
Louvain, 14
Lowe, Driver (author's driver), 51, 78, 88–9, 123, 166, 168, 170, 191, 209, 224, 228, 232, 233, 240

Maas River, 175, 178, 203
Mackenzie, Lieutenant-Colonel Charles, 184
Maginot Line, 1, 2, 14
Manchester, 88–9
Market Garden, Operation, 173–93, 203
Mascara, 119, 120, 123
McNeile, Robert, promoted to command 9 Field Company, 146; organizes the docks, 148; at Taranto, 150, 156; finds ford at Cannae, 158
Meek, Sapper (author's batman), 51, 123, 126, 166, 168, 170
Messina, Straits of, 147
Meuse, River, 14, 221–2, 223
Middlesex Regiment, 8th, B Company, 196
Miles, Colonel, 46
Millingen, 251

Misa, Lieutenant-Colonel L.E., 20–1
Montgomery, General, 14, 24, 29, 33–4,
    35–6, 39, 43–4, 65, 102, 110, 135,
    136, 158–9, 186, 222, 229, 232
Moore, Major "Streak", 236–39, 241–2
Mountbatten, Admiral Lord, 84, 85, 89
Moyland Schloss, 239–40
Murray, Douglas, 25–6, 28, 33–5, 49,
    55–7, 58, 64, 76, 101
Myers, Lieutenant-Colonel Eddie, 165,
    186, 192

Neder Rhine, 183
Newman, Squadron Leader, 72
Nijmegen, 175, 177, 179, 180, 182,
    195–9, 229
Norman, Nigel, 72, 87, 90, 94, 101
Normandy, 165–6, 169, 175, 182, 185,
    194, 202, 222
North Africa, 101–22

Offanto, River, 158
Oosterhout, 3, 182
Oran, 111, 112, 114–5, 117, 120, 123
Orchies, 3
Oslo, 96, 98

Parachute Battalion, 1st, 139, 153
– 2nd, 87, 143, 179, 183
– 5th (Scottish), 154
Parachute Brigade, 1st, 71, 88, 125,
    139–40, 147
– 2nd, 113, 125, 139, 156
– 4th, 108, 147, 155
Parachute Squadron, 1st, 75–6, 123, 139
– 2nd, 78–9, 146
– 3rd, 78–80
– 4th, 108, 155
Parachute Training Centre, 72
Paris, 168
Pearl Harbor, 73
"Pepperpot", 188, 191, 212
Perrott, Colonel Dan, 56
Perry, Brigadier, 168, 170
Phibbs, Captain Otto, 25–9, 31–3, 36,
    66

Phipps, Brigadier, 23–5
Phoney War, 1, 14, 32–3, 62–3
Pickard, Wing Commander, 90, 98
Pike, Lieutenant-Colonel, 169
Plunder, Operation, 249
Ponte Grande Bridge, 125, 127–9, 133–
    4, 136, 138
Potenza, 150–1
Pound, Admiral, 103
Powell, Sergeant (later Company
    Sergeant-Major) 33, 37, 38, 39, 44,
    46, 50–1, 54–5, 57–8, 63–4
Primasole Bridge, 125, 139–43, 145
Prior-Palmer, Brigadier, 253

Rawlings, Brigadier, 225
Reconnaissance Regiment, 241–2
Redwood, Major Sir John, 78
Rees, 251
Reeves, Driver, 9, 11, 23
Reichwald Forest, 229–30
Rhine, River, 175, 179–80, 183, 186,
    195, 202, 211, 225, 229–30, 240,
    247, 248–50, 255
Ringway, 72–3
Ripon, 88
Rjuken, raid on, 91–100
Robb, Brigadier, 28–9
Robinson, Sapper, 48–9
Rommel, Field-Marshal, 167, 168, 186
Roseveare, Captain, 79
Royal Scots, 16–7
Royal Scots Fusiliers, 136–7
Royal Ulster Rifles, 32, 43

St Helens, 25, 45, 51, 64
Salerno, 147
Salisbury Plain, 62, 75, 87, 88, 91, 102
Sambre, 215, 216
Sandhurst, 71
Saunders, Hilary St George, 89–90
Schelde, River, 19
Schonlan, Colonel, 87
Scottish Division, 15th, 235, 236, 238,
    239
Sedan, 14

Shorrock, Colonel, 80–1
Sicily, 112, 116, 123–43, 144–5
Siegfried Line, 20
Signals, 126–7
Simeto, River, 125
Simpson, General, 103–4
Sousse, 123–5, 140, 144, 147, 148
South Staffords, 131–2
Special Air Service Regiment, 150–2
Special Operations Executive, 88, 100
Stackpipe, 214–5, 230–2
Stokes, Sapper "Saint Stokes", 134–6,
    137, 138, 139, 143
Suffolk Regiment, 44, 45–7, 49, 50, 59
Syracuse, 118, 125–31, 133–4, 136, 138,
    145–6, 148

Taranto, 147–61
Taylor, Willie, Adjutant, 127
Thomas, Corporal, 126–7, 138
Thomas, Major-General G.I.,
    personality of, 169–70; in
    Operation Market Garden, 177,
    179, 180, 182, 186, 188, 189, 190;
    Nijmegen Bridge Garrison, 195,
    199, 201, 205–6, 218, 223, 225,
    228, 232, 233, 235–6, 240–1; attack
    on Xanten, 243–4, 248; Operation
    Plunder, 249, 250–1; forms
    Armoured Thrust Force, 251–3,
    255
Thorburn, Subaltern, 17
Thruxton Airfield, 89
Tickell, General, 166–7, 170
Tilley, Corporal, 27
Tilley, Lieutenant-Colonel, 186–7
Tizi, 114–20,
Tomkinson, Bruce, 25–6; demolishes
    bridges, 28, 33, 34, 37; assists
    Suffolk Regiment, 44–6, 48, 49;
    withdrawal to Dunkirk, 52, 55–7,
    8; at Bridport, 67; posted to India,
    68; author meets brother of, 135

Tomkinson, Charles, 135, 147

USA Airborne Division, 82nd, 203
    – Airborne Troops, 90–91
    – Army, 9th, 229
Urquhart, Major-General R.E., 163,
    166, 186, 192

Valberg, 182–3
Vandeleur, Brigadier Joe, 243, 246
Veritable, Operation, 229–30, 234, 244,
    248
Vernon, Dennis, 86–7, 95–6, 146
Vinycomb, Major Tony, 178, 192, 242–
    3, 246, 253–4
Vise, 223

Waal, River, 175, 178
Walch, Lieutenant-Colonel Gordon, 71
Walker, Dick, 24–5, 50–1
Water Supply, at Tizi, 119–20
    – at Taranto, 154–5
Watermanship, 190–2
Watson, Mr, 70
Wavre, 14; demolition of bridge at, 14–8
Weeze-Emmerich Line, 230
Wesel, 229, 248, 249
Wharton, Rigby, 66
Wilkinson, Squadron-Leader, 142–6
Williams-Thomas, Major RS, 205
Wimple, 66
Witzig, 74
Woollett, Major John, 243, 245, 255–6
Woolwich, 104
Worthing Pier, 65

Xanten, 230, 245, 247
Xenophon, 53

Young, Major-General B.K., 69–70, 72,
    107, 108

Zuyder Zee, 175